W9-BYU-835

The relationship between everyday experience and culture – seen as a set of ideas, values, or symbolic codes – has challenged social scientists, especially anthropologists, for more than a century. In this volume, leading social scientists present and discuss recent conceptions of culture and explore their implications for understanding different aspects of subjective experience, social practice, and individual behavior.

The focus of the volume is on the role of symbols and meaning in the development of mind, self, and emotion. The contributors examine such questions as what is the content of culture and how does it interact with cognitive, social, and emotional growth; how are ideas related to attitudes, feelings, and behavior; how are concepts and meanings historically transmitted. They also explore methodological and conceptual problems involved in the definition and study of meaning, and revisit the perennial problem of "relativism" in light of recent advances in semantic analysis and in culture theory.

As a comprehensive and critical account of current knowledge and research in the field of culture theory, this book will appeal to an interdisciplinary audience of anthropologists, psychologists, philosophers, historians, and linguists, as well as those interested in hermeneutics and a science of subjectivity.

Culture theory

Social Science Research Council
Committee on Social and Affective Development During Childhood

The activities of the Social Science Research Council's Committee on Social and Affective Development During Childhood have been supported primarily by the Foundation for Child Development, a private foundation that makes grants to educational and charitable institutions. Its main interests are in research, social and economic indicators of children's lives, advocacy and public information projects, service experiments that help translate theoretical knowledge about children into policies and practices that affect their daily lives.

Culture theory

ESSAYS ON MIND, SELF, AND EMOTION

EDITED BY

Richard A. Shweder
Committee on Human Development
University of Chicago

Robert A. LeVine
School of Education
Harvard University

CAMBRIDGE
UNIVERSITY PRESS

PUBLISHED BY THE PRESS SYNDICATE OF THE UNIVERSITY OF CAMBR
The Pitt Building, Trumpington Street, Cambridge CB2 1RP, United Kingdom

CAMBRIDGE UNIVERSITY PRESS
The Edinburgh Building, Cambridge CB2 2RU, United Kingdom
40 West 20th Street, New York, NY 10011-4211, USA
10 Stamford Road, Oakleigh, Melbourne 3166, Australia

First published 1984
Reprinted 1985, 1986 (twice), 1987, 1988, 1989, 1990, 1992,
1993, 1994, 1995, 1997

Typeset in Times

A catalogue record for this book is available from the British Library

Library of Congess Cataloguing-in-Publication Data is available

ISBN 0-521-26719-6 hardback
ISBN 0-521-31831-9 paperback

Transferred to digital printing 2003

For Michelle Zimbalist Rosaldo (1944–1981)

On May 8–10, 1981, Shelly Rosaldo participated in the Social Science Research Council conference that was the inspiration for this volume. Five months later she fell into a deep ravine while hiking to a prospective field site in the Philippines. The final version of her essay, published in this volume, arrived by mail from the Philippines one week before her accident. Weeks later her husband and colleague, Renato Rosaldo, spoke to Shelly's friends and students at a memorial gathering at Stanford University: "I would never draw the moral 'don't go to the Philippines,' 'don't walk on trails,' 'never go anywhere' . . . If I had to do it over again I'd walk the same trail and I don't think the next time anyone would stumble."

The first editor of this volume was Shelly Rosaldo's classmate, both in high school and again in the Department of Social Relations at Harvard University. Inspiring and provocative, even then she was a luminary to her peers. Reading her essay in this volume, those unfamiliar with her work will realize, as we all do, how much our field has lost with her death. Those who know her work will see in her essay a powerful synthesis of her previous thinking about the creative power of symbols. We all miss her – a lot.

Contents

Preview: A colloquy of culture theorists   page 1
    RICHARD A. SHWEDER

Part I. Culture theory: an introduction

1. Anthropology's romantic rebellion against the
   enlightenment, or there's more to thinking than reason
   and evidence   27
       RICHARD A. SHWEDER
2. Properties of culture: an ethnographic view   67
       ROBERT A. LeVINE
3. Cultural meaning systems   88
       ROY G. D'ANDRADE

Part II. Culture, self, and emotion

4. "From the native's point of view": on the nature of
   anthropological understanding   123
       CLIFFORD GEERTZ
5. Toward an anthropology of self and feeling   137
       MICHELLE Z. ROSALDO
6. Does the concept of the person vary cross-culturally?   158
       RICHARD A. SHWEDER & EDMUND J. BOURNE
7. Understanding people   200
       ZENO VENDLER
8. Emotion, knowing, and culture   214
       ROBERT I. LEVY
9. Getting angry: the Jamesian theory of emotion in
   anthropology   238
       ROBERT C. SOLOMON

Part III. Culture, language, and thought

10. The development of competence in culturally defined
    domains: a preliminary framework   257
        HOWARD GARDNER
11. Language acquisition and socialization: three
    developmental stories and their implications   276
        ELINOR OCHS & BAMBI B. SCHIEFFELIN

Part IV. Commentary

12. Some reflections on cultural determinism and relativism
    with special reference to emotion and reason   323
    MELFORD E. SPIRO

List of contributors and conference participants   347
Name index   349
Subject index   355

Preview
A COLLOQUY OF CULTURE THEORISTS

Richard A. Shweder

General goals

The most general goal of this volume is to present a broad-gauged and accessible discussion of theories of culture, especially as those theories relate to current research issues in the development of mind, self, and emotion. A possible title of the book might have been "Culture: What Is It and How Do You Get It?" An alternative title might have been "The Concept of Culture: Who Needs It?" Most of the contributors to this volume think you need it.

The volume represents a stage in the development of the so-called symbols-and-meanings conception of culture. That conception of culture, expressed in an influential formulation by Geertz (1973:89), defines culture as "an historically transmitted pattern of meanings embodied in symbols, a system of inherited conceptions expressed in symbolic form by means of which men communicate, perpetuate and develop their knowledge about and attitudes towards life." One aim of the volume is to draw attention to that view of culture as shared meaning systems. A second aim is to examine conceptual and methodological problems in the definition and study of meaning. A third aim is to show how the study of meaning can help answer questions about the origins of mind, self, and emotion.

In the writings of Benjamin Lee Whorf one finds a simple yet dramatic example of the way meaning systems transform affective functioning (1956:267). Whorf points out that the sound pattern *queep* elicits a universal set of associations: *queep* is fast (vs. slow), sharp (vs. dull), narrow (vs. wide), light (vs. dark). Our affective response to *queep* is automatic and that automatic affective response is probably preprogramed, and it is the same program for !Kung Bushmen, fifteenth-century Florentines, and us. Whorf then asks us to consider the sound pattern *deep*. *Deep* is phonetically similar to *queep*, and, indeed, it elicits the same set of affective associations (fast, sharp, narrow, and light) from everyone except speakers of English. For English speakers, however, *deep* is not simply a sound pattern or non-sense sound; it is a sound with meaning. And that meaning, a subjective conventional fact, totally overrides and alters our reaction to its objective sound properties. For English speakers, and for English speakers only, *deep* is slow, dull, wide, and dark. Many essays in this volume can be viewed as elaborations of Whorf's insight into the transformative power of meaning systems. Whorf's vivid example also intimates a fourth aim of the volume: to revisit the problem of "relativism" in the light of recent advances in semantic analysis and in culture theory.

History of the volume

The volume is the product of a conference that was itself the product of a planning session. On March 14, 1980, a group of scholars met at the University of California, San Diego, to plan a conference on Conceptions of Culture and Its Acquisition. There were eight of us: Roy G. D'Andrade (University of California, San Diego), Clifford Geertz (Institute for Advanced Study, Princeton), Carroll E. Izard (University of Delaware), Robert A. LeVine (Harvard University), Theodore Schwartz (University of California, San Diego), Richard A. Shweder (University of Chicago), Michael Silverstein (University of Chicago), and Melford E. Spiro (University of California, San Diego). The planning session turned out to be a successful trial balloon for the subsequent conference: We argued for two days and the debates at the planning session anticipated many of the issues of concern at the conference itself. The conference was held one year later, May 8–10, 1981, at the offices of the Social Science Research Council in New York City. Selected edited transcripts of our debates and discussions at the planning session and conference are presented below. The conference participants are identified at the end of this volume.

Sponsored by the Social Science Research Council's Committee on Social and Affective Development During Childhood, the aim of the conference was to provide a forum for the discussion of recent developments in culture theory and to examine the potential relevance of the culture concept for the objectives of the SSRC committee under whose sponsorship we met. The planning group was motivated by two considerations. First, over the past twenty or so years, although culture theory has advanced, opportunities for scholars of various denominations to compare notes and address common theoretical issues have been rare. Those denominations can be variously defined, but, however one defines them, such sorts as symbolic or interpretive theorists, cognitive scientists, ethnoscientists, phenomenologists, psychoanalytic theorists, critical theorists, contextualists, and so on had not talked *to each other* nearly enough over the past two decades. United by a common interest in "symbols and meanings," we believed a transdenominational gathering to be not only desirable but possible.

The symbols-and-meanings conception of culture is not entirely free of conceptual and methodological difficulties, and there are several exciting and challenging areas of controversy. To study what something means is to study what it implies to those who understand it (Hirsch 1967, 1976). That much is uncontroversial. For almost every other question about meaning there are at least two answers and for every answer there is a "school of thought." How is meaning in everyday language and thought similar to, or different from, meaning in scientific language and thought? Is the concept of meaning reducible to the idea of reference? Should our concept of meaning include some of the non-referential functions of language? Is what something "implies" reducible to *logical* implication or is the idea of "necessity" (what you must conclude from what was said) broader than logic? Is there non-logical (cultural) necessity? Should the concept of meaning be broadened to include both what something means (externally and objectively) and what something means to someone (internally or subjectively)? "He's your father" does not imply "secretly he wants to mutilate or castrate you or remove you from the scene," but that's what it means to some people, even though the meaning seems to be more "in the head" than in the utterance. Such subjective unconstrained meanings are sometimes called "free" associations. Are "free associations" to be included in our concept of meaning? These are fascinating and important questions, and the answers one gives reveal presuppositions about the role of logical and scientific canons in the analysis of mind and beyond that, deeper assumptions about free will, determinism, relativism, and so on. By confronting those presuppositions and assumptions, the planning group hoped to explore the range of ways to analyze cultural forms from a symbols-and-meanings point of view. Thus, spokesmen from diverse schools of thought within the symbols-and-meanings framework were represented at the conference.

There was a second consideration for the planning group. The symbols-and-meanings approach to culture seems to be an unusually well-kept secret in the psychological sciences, most notably among developmental researchers working on such culture-saturated phenomena as personhood and self, morality and convention, social cognition and interpersonal relationships, self-regulation and emotional response. It was the bet of the planning group that this was the right time to bring recent developments in culture theory "out of the closet."

Ten years ago the bet would have been a bad one, and even now it is risky. Much research in the psychological sciences appears to be guided by five rules of thumb, or research heuristics, which, in combination, induce a feeling of resistance to the study of shared meanings, collective representations, and the social origins of mind, self, and emotion.

Heuristic 1: Be indifferent to content; process and structure are primary.

Heuristic 2: Language is epiphenomenal; it can be ignored.

Heuristic 3: What's really real is inside the skin; the individual person is the sole unit of analysis.

Heuristic 4: Search for universals and/or study automatic processes; knowledge in psychology should be modeled after knowledge in physics, chemistry, or biology.

Heuristic 5: Don't think about anything that can't be measured.

Those research heuristics have proved quite useful to experimental psychologists, especially those working on the psychophysics of perception. Unfortunately, those research heuristics, although useful for certain problems, have become too widely applied, for example, among developmental researchers working on more meaning-dependent topics such as moral judgment, interpersonal relationships, social behavior, self-regulation, inferential reasoning, and so on. Indeed, the first four research heuristics have received powerful expression in Jean Piaget's influential agenda for child development research. That agenda has dominated the field for twenty years, and during that period developmental theory has not been at all hospitable to the concept of culture.

The planning group sensed a sea change. What Ted Schwartz has aptly, even if facetiously, dubbed the "pristine processor" view of the child's mind has come to seem, in recent years, less attractive to many psychologists and developmentalists, and the field of child development is now entering what might be called a post-Piagetian stage. As Jerome Bruner commented at the conference:

> Over the last few years many social scientists have recognized the narrowness of the image of acquisition that is premised on the conception of a lone child faced with a natural physical order – with the task of the child being to somehow balance his own assimilative tendencies, to accommodate to that natural environment, and to somehow make sense of it. In this image, knowing language makes no difference. Others can't instruct the child until such a time as the child already knows. That image is an image that you get principally from Piaget, but it's also the image you get from classical behaviorism – it's the image you get from Skinnerians. Somehow, the only thing that's there is a natural order of stimulation for the lone child.

There was once a time, not so long ago, when psychology was known as the nonsocial social science. In the last decade this has changed. There has been a renewal of interest in social cognition, social relationships, and social communication (see, e.g., Flavell & Ross 1981; Higgins, Ruble & Hartup 1983), and one even finds psychologists puzzling over the question "What's social about social cognition?" There has been a growing recognition that an indifference to content denies an understanding of actual cognitive, affective, and interpersonal functioning. There has been a retreat from the excessive emphasis on generalized abstract structures (see Shweder 1979, 1982, 1983 for an overview); what psychologists have discovered is that logic is not all there is to thinking and that abstract traits are not all there is to affective and interpersonal functioning. With that discovery, what something "means," how to talk about meaning, and how to study it have become central issues. As George Miller (1981:136) puts it:

Logic was once believed to be the language of thought. That was before we understood how short the leaps are that logic can negotiate. Strictly speaking, formal logic cannot even go from "Fido is a poodle" to "Fido is a dog," because the relation between the two sentences depends on their meaning, not their form. Logic can go from "all poodles are dogs" and "Fido is a poodle" to "Fido is a dog," but it makes for dull conversation.

There are surprisingly few sources to which a psychologist can turn to find a broad-gauged and readable discussion of the "symbols and meanings" approach to cultural analysis. There may be no single source that addresses topics of traditional concern to psychologists: self, emotion, cognition. This is unfortunate, because we are entering a period when culture theorists and psychologists have much to learn from each other. Mindful that recent anthropological, linguistic, and philosophical contributions to the study of meaning and the analysis of idea systems are less widely known than is desirable, the planning group designed a conference in which culture theorists would confront hard-core psychological topics. The essays in this volume present alternative formulations of a symbols-and-meanings conception of culture. Some essays ask how meanings are transmitted in the process of cultural acquisition, and others try to show what difference cultural meanings make for the genesis of mind, self, and emotion.

Way back in 1960 the Social Science Research Council established a Committee on Socialization and Social Structure, chaired by John Clausen. That committee defined an agenda of needed research on social and emotional development and commented on the relative lack of attention that had been given to the content of what is transmitted during socialization and to processes of incidental learning. Now, after twenty years of cognitive structuralism, social scientists are finally turning to these topics.

The colloquy

In the normal course of events the most exciting part of a conference, the informal discussions and exchanges, never reaches a wider audience. All five days of the planning session and the conference were taped. Not unexpectedly, many of the exchanges were revealing, illuminating, and incisive – and the best way I know to preface this volume is to share with you some of our conversations about the problematic aspects of the field. What follows are a few edited transcripts from both the planning session and the conference. Expletives have been deleted.

PROBLEMATIC 1: DO WE HAVE A MESSAGE IF WE DON'T SPEAK IN ONE VOICE?
LeVine: The vast majority of social scientists outside anthropology are not aware of what's been going on in the area of culture theory over

the past twenty years. Even many social scientists who are sold on the idea of cross-cultural research are not convinced that there is anything in the concept of culture that's important for them to understand. Their notion of anthropological research is that it provides a travel-guide-type thumbnail sketch of areas where you might like to work – the anthropological equivalent to the PanAm guide to that area. Many social scientists are not aware of the kind of relativism that is broadly shared in anthropology. Many totally reject the notion that culture represents a complex system that structures subjective experience. Our goal should be to do something about that in the form of a scholarly communication.

Spiro: The notion that we should be a "light unto the Gentiles" is an interesting one, but then, like Saint Paul, you have to have a unified message. And I think it is obvious that we do not have a unified message; we don't have a new testament. We can't say that Christ has risen – a simple message but a very powerful one, if only because there was unanimity among the apostles who preached it. In anthropology there may be as many messages as there are apostles. I'm rather dubious about there being a consensus. For example, I would dissent from the view that we're all relativists. I'm not a relativist, not at least in the usual sense of "relativism." The conference should clarify those conceptual issues that divide us as well as those that unite us.

Shweder: I don't think our goal is to arrive at a standard version of culture theory. Indeed, I doubt it would be possible to arrive at a standard version, even over the long run. I guess I accept Gallie's [1964] notion that social concepts are "essentially contestable" – there will always be divisions between evolutionists, universalists, and relativists. What we can do at the conference is set out a range of possible positions. Fortunately there are fewer viable alternative positions than there are vocal advocates. There are not as many messages as there are apostles.

Geertz: It seems to me there is no consensus in conclusions. What has changed in the last twenty years or so is the realm of discourse as a whole. The sort of things that are discussed now were not discussed, certainly not in that way, twenty years ago. Issues that were central then, even old issues like relativism, are discussed in very different ways now. Insofar as there is any intersubjectivity, it is in this discourse realm. That could be made clear to people outside the field. I'd like to make a second point. I think it would be unwise to think that all productive thinking about culture theory goes on in anthropology. We are much more open to European social thought than before, to certain trends in philosophy and certain kinds of historical work. It's a mood change. That doesn't do away with differences because they are essentially contestable, and they'll be there long after we're all old and gone. But the frame of the discussion, the mode of discourse, that has shifted some, at least for many people. If we could invoke that, and present it as a gigantic quarrel that is going on, but a different sort of quarrel about different sorts of things said in different sorts of ways, people outside the field would stop thinking about the state of the discussion as though it were twenty or thirty years ago.

No one quarreled with Geertz's point. There is a realm of discourse shared by culture theorists. Culture theory cuts across disciplines. Disputes among culture theorists go on within a common, even if broad, framework of understandings – and I suspect most of the conferees would feel comfortable with Geertz's own definition of culture as "an historically transmitted pattern of meanings embodied in symbols, a system of inherited conceptions expressed in symbolic form by means of which men communicate, perpetuate, and develop their knowledge about and attitudes towards life" [Geertz 1973:89]. But, of course, as Geertz himself has noted, "terms such as 'meaning,' 'symbol' and 'conception' cry out for explication" [ibid.]. Indeed, it is around such questions – what kinds of meanings are there, what kinds of concepts are there, what kinds of symbols are there, how does historical transmission take place, is this or that meaning, concept or symbol historically transmitted or not, what is this or that person's or people's conception of this or that (e.g., kinship, emotions, self, etc.), how are ideas and symbols related to attitudes, feelings, and behavior – that all of the quarreling, much of it fruitful, goes on. Those are the questions addressed in this volume.

PROBLEMATIC 2: MEANINGS, CONCEPTIONS, AND SYMBOLS:
WHAT ARE IDEAS AND WHERE DO YOU FIND THEM?

D'Andrade: When I was a graduate student, one imagined people *in* a culture; ten years later culture was all in their heads. The thing went from something out there and very large to something that got placed inside. Culture became a branch of cognitive psychology; it was the content of cognitive psychology. We went from "let's try to look at behavior and describe it" to "let's try to look at ideas." Now, how you were to look at ideas was a bit of a problem – and some people said, "Well, look at language." That notion, that you look at idea systems, was extremely general in the social sciences. On, I think, the same afternoon in 1957 you have papers by Chomsky and Miller and in anthropology, Ward Goodenough. All signal an end to the era of "Let's look at people's behavior and see what they do." Before 1957 the definition of culture was primarily a behavioral one – culture was patterns of behavior, actions, and customs. The same behavioral emphasis was there in linguistics and psychology. The idea that cognition is where it's at struck all three fields at the same time – it has a slightly different trajectory in each discipline – whether you do experiments or whether you look for intuitions or whether you talk to informants. I think it was a nice replacement. But the thing is now breaking – that force set in motion in the late fifties. And I feel it's breaking in psychology, it's breaking in linguistics, and it's breaking in anthropology – and we each have different ideas about how it's breaking up.

Geertz: At the same time the revolution was going on where people were putting things inside people's heads a counterrevolution was going the other way – criticizing the whole myth of inner reality, the whole myth of private language. The one thing that anthropologists hadn't said about culture is that it is a conceptual structure. What does it mean to say that? Take, for example, the theory of infant damnation. To know what that is you have to, first of all, conceptualize it historically and with other beliefs of this type. Then you can discuss the incidence of it, and how people got it, and how they got rid of it, and what determined all these things. But, what the cultural element is, is the structure of meanings, ideas, or significances that that particular religious ideology contained. The reason I'm against putting things in people's heads is that it reduces the tension between cultural analysis and psychological analysis. By psychologizing things you don't have the kind of problematic where you can ask what is the impact of a conceptual structure or system of ideas such as the theory of infant damnation during the reformation? What psychological effect did it have on different people in different contexts? That tends to get lost because the theory is identified as a psychological phenomenon in the first place. And it's not a psychological phenomenon in the first place. It's a conceptual structure – and that's what the whole depsychologizing of the concept of sense, of meaning, was all about and still is about.

This colloquy raises the question whether meanings are internal (in the head) or external (in the theory of infant damnation). It's a hazardous question and in this case the differences between D'Andrade and Geertz may be more apparent than real. To ask whether meanings are internal or external seems as futile as to ask whether "redness" is in the color chip or in the perceptual system or whether "funniness" is in the clown or in the audience. Most culture theorists would agree that an understanding of the meaning of the theory of infant damnation is a complex psychological process. At the same time, most culture theorists would acknowledge that the content of the theory, its meaning, what it has to say about what, what it implies or suggests, can be understood "as a theory," related by similarity and contrast to other "theories," understood in terms of its consequences for institutional and individual action, and so on.

I suspect the most important feature of the D'Andrade–Geertz exchange is their *joint* emphasis on mind as meanings and ideas, with the implication that minds, just like meanings and ideas, can change and differ.

PROBLEMATIC 3: THE INTERPRETATION OF "BELIEFS" OR THE NATIVE'S MEANINGS ARE NOT TRANSPARENT, NOT EVEN TO THE NATIVE

Shweder: How should we interpret and represent the apparently false knowledge of an alien culture? The Bongo-Bongo tell you that eating the ashes of the burnt skull of the red bush monkey will cure epilepsy. What do you do with that? Do you render it as a "belief," adding that the Bongo-Bongo believe this strange false thing, that they fail to see that these things are unconnected. The same problem arises when studying children. Developmentalists are faced with many instances of apparently false knowledge. Generally, in those cases, they treat children as pre-competent – as naive scientists. The child is said to be on his way to knowledge but he hasn't gotten there yet. Now, clearly there are other possible moves you can make. You can treat apparently false knowledge as a metaphor or trope of some sort. You can try to contextualize the natives' ideas or give it a frame of reference that makes it appear rational from the point of view of the persons whose belief it is. The ground rules for making one move or the other are unclear. What seems clear is that whole "schools" have grown up over their answer to the question "Are you willing to attribute a false belief to another people?"

Geertz: It's often very hard to tell whether it's a *belief* – whether it's an assertive. It's hard to know what is really being said. Even with tropes you don't know what's being said. It's very difficult to know and it isn't that you don't think they have false beliefs. Everybody has lots of false beliefs and I'm sure that the Balinese, the Javanese, and the Moroccans have all sorts of false beliefs, as we do, but you're not always sure that you're faced with a belief, true or false. You may be faced with some other kind of statement about something. When a Javanese tells me that his son fell out of a tree because the spirit of his grandfather pushed him out, if I were to take that as a simple empirical proposition in my terms, I have no doubts about whether it is true or false. But I'm not sure that's what's being said.

To give an example of that, Susanne Langer once said, rightly or wrongly, it doesn't matter too much that the interpretation of Pueblo rain dances as causing rain is really quite wrong. People had said of the Pueblos that they waited to see if it was going to rain and then they had the rain dance as if it were a fake sort of way to keep the thing going. But Langer was saying that what the Pueblos are doing is to present to themselves a living tableaux in which the rain gods, nature, and people are all having some meaningful interaction – a drama. When it rains, the drama comes off. When it doesn't rain, it's like a failed play. Whether this is right or wrong, what she's saying is that the whole assumption that the Pueblos are thinking about this mechanistically, that they are thinking about it causally may be wrong. They may be trying to imagine for themselves the relationship between rain, people, and landscape. And they present this image to themselves to have a sense that they have an understanding of the world. But they're not thinking in the paradigm "rain dance cause, rain effect, which sometimes works and sometimes doesn't." The only point I'm trying to make is that often it's harder than it seems to understand what you're being faced with.

Schwartz: We are at a different level of sophistication now than we were thirty years ago. We realize that there is a whole range of possibilities with respect to assertive beliefs. We used to confidently describe belief systems – now we realize there are variations in the valence of beliefs.

Spiro: We don't want to fall into the other trap. In the first place we don't know, except for our own scientific *Weltanschauung*, that the Hopi rain dance doesn't have an effect causally. Even if we do accept our scientific *Weltanschauung* as valid, we don't have to go to the Hopi for examples of its rejection. Two years ago there was a drought in southern California and the mayor of San Diego declared a day of prayer, not so we could express our feelings that we were suffering but rather to influence God to bring rain. Now San Diego may not be the most sophisticated city in the world, but it's also not the least sophisticated, and if San Diegans can believe, whatever the wishful thinking involved, that prayer can affect rainfall, it is not counterintuitive for me to believe that the Hopi might have the same belief.

Shweder: An interesting question arises here – which is, whether you can know better than the native whether or not his utterances express "beliefs"? The native tells you, "This is what I believe – in fact I think it's true." And you say, "No, that's not your belief." And the native keeps on asserting something like "this dance causes rain" or "he was pushed by his grandfather's ghost." How do you make that intelligible to the readers of your ethnography?

Schwartz: Take Manus myths. Do the Manus believe they are true? This is something I've investigated. In some ways the Manus will argue that their myths are true. They'll say: "And there's the very rock he sat on" – and they'll offer this kind of evidence. At the same time, as Reo Fortune [1935] noted, in their religion the Manus never invoked these creatures of their myths. They have no other place or function other than in the narration of that myth. The Manus don't act as if those are real creatures.

Spiro: But what if they view what we call myth as history. I can say that I believe that Napoleon did such and such – and I can go to France and point to the place. But I don't invoke him in religion or believe that he has special powers – or, indeed, that he is alive and can respond to my invocation of him.

Geertz: The myth thing is the same business again. It has often been said about myths that they don't tell you what happened. They tell you what happens. This is the way it goes. This is the way things happen. Take semimythical things like *Macbeth*. Northrup Frye [1964:64] has said, you go to *Macbeth* not to find out about the history of Scotland but to find out what happens to a man when he gains the world but loses his soul. That's what it's about. You don't ask of Macbeth whether there really was a man like that. Why does the historical literalism of the nineteenth century have to be applied to myths as such? It's possible that they're like Macbeth.

Spiro: I think we have to, and precisely because both are possible. My grandfather – a person I knew fairly well – did believe that Macbeth was a fictional character. But he also believed that Adam actually existed. And that Abraham existed. And he believed that the myths regarding them recounted actual events – they were true. Whereas, if you asked him about the events in *Macbeth*, he'd say, "Well, of course, they didn't happen." He distinguished very well between narratives that he took as fictions and narratives that he took to be true.

Now one of the things that Hallowell [1967a] pointed out about the Ojibwa is that they have no concept of fiction. All traditional narratives are thought to represent actual historical happenings. That is probably not a universal among primitive peoples, let alone among sophisticated people like the Burmese, the Balinese, the Moroccans, and so on. But there are cultures that do not apply the concept of fiction to traditional narrations, so that what we are calling "myths" are from their point of view historical events.

D'Andrade: I want to say something about the rain dance. I think if you interview the Hopi, a majority of the community will tell you that the rain dance makes rain. Now the sense of the word "make" and its translation into English is very difficult indeed. There is some practical sense there about making rain. But notice how complicated the whole thing is. The anthropologist may report that "the Hopi do the dance in order to make it rain." That may be a little different from what the Hopi said. The Hopi may not say "I do this dance in order to make it rain." He may say: "I do the dance and I think the dance makes it rain." You ask: "Do you do the dance for other reasons?" and he may say "Yes" or "What are you talking about?" When we report that "the Hopi do the dance in order to make it rain" we make it sound like this making it rain is the total control over the behavior – like everything that's being done is under the control of this master intention – to make it rain. As if the decision whether or not to continue the dance is contingent on whether or not it rained. And that may be quite wrong. Now I do think people have these practical things – they say they do these practical things. But when you look at it there are so many other meanings to what they are doing – it's a lot of fun, and there *is* a vast drama there, and people *do* impersonate the Gods, and they become Gods. It's very complicated.

Spiro: But the fact that rituals, like other kinds of symbols, are polysemic does not rule out the possibility that one of the meanings of the rain dance may be "the dance causes rain." So long as we agree that that may be one of the reasons for its performance, there's no problem.

D'Andrade: Mel, people agree, in principle, that it's polysemous, but when they give explanations they stop. They have now ascertained that the Hopi think the dance makes it rain – and that is it. That is why the Hopi do it! They think it makes it rain. It's like that with folk explanations of human behavior, too. If you ask people "Why does so-and-so do that?'' – if you elicit a lot of explanations of behavior – you find that people go along and then they hit one of these explanations that allows them to stop explaining. I have a practical reason. It makes him money. I stop at this point. That's why he does it!

What seems to emerge from this spirited exchange is agreement that science or ethnoscience is not all there is to cognition. While no one denies the fact-stating functions of ordinary language and the cause-seeking inclinations of the human mind, there is a general acknowledgment that the man-as-scientist approach to language and thought can be stretched only so far. While everyone agrees that the man-as-scientist metaphor has its place, no one equates ordinary language and thought with the language and thought of the scientist, statistician, or logician. What emerges is a pluralistic view of mind, meaning, and symbolic functions. Whereas all peoples assert beliefs, true and false, ordinary language and thought aims to do more than merely report and represent the causal structure of reality, and relatively few utterances or practices serve a pure and exclusive assertive function. Indeed, what emerges here is the view that there is no general solution to the problem of interpreting utterances and practices. Myth is not history, but there are histories and there are myths and we, as culture theorists, must be sensitive to all the interpretive possibilities and know how to tell them apart. The essays is this volume present a pluralistic view of the functions of the human mind, thus, inevitably, restricting the range of application of the man-as-scientist, man-as-logician metaphor.

PROBLEMATIC 4: WHAT IS THE PROBLEM OF THE ''SELF''
ANYWAY?

Shweder: I want to raise a point about Cliff's [Clifford Geertz] fascinating essay on the "self" [Chapter 4, this volume]. It seems to me that the concept of the self Cliff refers to as a *Western* conception – that is, the notion of the person as a bounded, unique, integrated, and dynamic center of judgment and action – is precisely the concept that most developmental psychologists would say has to be there in childhood in all societies, not just in the West. That is, the force of interactional experience in infancy and early childhood with the physical and social world would quickly lead to a universal differentiation at the skin of the self from others and external events. Certainly by age 3, and perhaps much earlier, all children in all cultures would be expected by most developmentalists to have this "Western" conception – the idea of being bounded, self-motivated, of associating their observing ego and their will with their body and so on. In Bali there must be a point of transition. It seems that in Bali the adult cultural system does not build upon the child's early experience in self-definition, which may emerge out of precultural or at least "brute" interaction with the world. In fact, it seems that the adult cultural system is capable of reversing early childhood understandings of the self. But what is the process by which you can take what is presumably a very widespread sense of self in 3-year-olds and end up with adults who have these variant conceptions of the self that Cliff describes? In other words, something that fits Cliff's description of the Western adult conception of the self may also be a universal infant and early childhood conception of the self – a universal childhood conception that gets expressed among adults in the West and overridden or reversed among adults in Bali. The Balinese 3-year-old may be more like a Western adult than like a Balinese adult.

LeVine: It seems to me that Hallowell [1967b] laid out pretty well forty or so years ago a nice conceptualization of which aspects of the self are universal and which are culture-specific.

Schwartz: I think this is a very good issue for discussion. I took a yearlong course on the self with Hallowell and I remember reading Geza Roheim and things like that. Nevertheless, the course was almost entirely inferences drawn almost entirely from cultural institutions. We would make judgments about the constitution of the self from the fact that people believed that they had three souls or that they believed that the child's soul does not enter its body permanently until the age of 7. Those were the kinds of data we were working with – all ethnographic. I don't think we can say that the issue is settled. I think some analysis of the question would have some paradigmatic value.

Geertz: There's no doubt it would be useful to discuss the question of the self as a paradigmatic contrast between the way in which psychologists and anthropologists think about things.

Shweder: Let me try again. I accept Cliff's description of the Balinese, Javanese, and Moroccan adult self-concept, and I am not arguing about the facts about childhood around the world. I'm raising the possibility that you can have an intuitive early childhood system that is either built upon or reversed in later development – I think the question "How does that reversal take place?" is an interesting one. I think I could point to evidence of this type of case. Take Cal Izard's [e.g., 1980] descriptions of the emotional life of children – he would probably argue that discrete emotions like anger, sadness, and surprise are all there in the Balinese, Javanese, Moroccan, and American child. Yet we know from Cliff's descriptions of the Javanese and Balinese adult that by the time the Javanese and Balinese child is an adult he's "smoothing out" his affect, whereas American adults are still encoding and expressing the same range of discrete childhood emotions. Something very interesting has happened to those Javanese and Balinese kids.

Schwartz: There is another point I was trying to make about the Hallowell course. It's that I came to feel that even if we came to know the Balinese conception about the self in the sense of a cultural ideology about the self, we still wouldn't know all that I'd like to know about the Balinese self. I think we should make some distinction between cultural ideology and the psychological and beyond that the cultural constitution of the self.

LeVine: I agree. But one of the nice things about the self is that it can be conceptualized as both an individual mental representation and a cultural or collective representation. You can examine its status in cultural ideals and prototypes and also examine the child's or adult's individual representation of self, and then look at how that's acquired and what relationship there is between the individual's mental representation and the cultural ideal – not assuming with Hallowell that the two are fused or the same thing. There is some kind of relationship between the individual's self-representation and the culture's.

Spiro: That there is some kind of relationship I agree. But we know clinically that there is a difference between the self-representation and the ideal self-representation. And I would speculate that to the extent there is an isomorphism, it is between the individual's *ideal* self-representation and the cultural conception rather than between the self-representation and the cultural conception. I agree with Ted [Schwartz] that the inferences you would draw about the self from cultural representations would be different from whatever evidence you would get with respect to the self itself.

Schwartz: I think that Hallowell used to believe that this cultural ideology of the self not only represents but actually comes to constitute culturally different self-structures.

Spiro: I think he did believe that, but I don't agree with it.

Schwartz: I think this is the case in many other domains as well. The ideological variance is much greater than the phenomenal variance.

Izard: Mel [Spiro]. How transcultural do you think this distinction of self–ideal self is?

Spiro: I think that in all societies you would find that individuals have self-representations and ideal self-representations and that there is always a tension between them. I think, too, that it's that tension that's involved in notions of morality, notions of oughtness, as well as self-deprecation and low self-esteem. All these are functions of the tension between self-representation and the ideal self-representation. Hence, I would guess that the distinction is universal.

LeVine: I want to come back for a minute to Rick's [Shweder] formulation. What Cliff [Geertz] describes in emphasizing cultural differences – these are ideologies of selfhood that do not in themselves deny the universality of the self at some level of human experience. This is why I raised Hallowell's point. Although he was concerned with cultural differences, he nonetheless, on whatever data base – let's forget the data base – he nonetheless made a case for believing that in all cultures there was some perception of the self as a continuous entity in time and as, in some sense, the same person. There was some kind of distinction between internal experience and external things. In other words, the self was a universal and there weren't any cultures in which people simply merged into other people, however much cultures vary with respect to their emphasis on autonomy or sharing at the level of more formulated ideology. The job of cross-cultural research is to identify just what is universal and what is culturally variable. Part of it has to do with the distinction between intuitive and reflective notions that Rick has been interested in. Perhaps the kind of thing the child acquires is a primitive or intuitive distinction between self and others, the idea of itself as a continuous entity, notions of pride and shame that pertain to himself, his body, himself as a social entity that other people identify and so on. But to get at those understandings you also have to look at things like meaning systems, the cultural labels and concepts that the culture imposes on the intuitive understandings. We've only just begun to do that.

Shweder: Cliff can obviously speak to the implications of his essay better than I can. But I didn't think the essay was just a description of cultural ideology – the enshrinement of a certain notion of the self in cultural ideology. I thought you were saying that the cultural ideology became an *effective* representation for *individuals*; that individuals in fact *worked* to overcome that intuitive notion of a discrete self, which I would guess must be there in the Balinese child; that you were saying that a culture's ideology had implications for an individual's sense of individuality and separateness, his notion of continuity over time. To the extent a culture buys in to the idea that the building blocks of society are social roles, not individual persons – that there is an elaborate cast of characters and that self is tied to the roles you play – to that extent there's a sense of discontinuity that's emphasized: to change roles is to change one's identity. The theoretical question is this: Do you need an enshrinement in the cultural ideology of the self to pull that off? Do you have to have an articulated, explicit, cultural conception of the self before it's possible for individuals to alter their childhood self-conception? People work at these things – there are disciplines of self-alteration involved in South Asia and Southeast Asia.

Geertz: Actually, in the longer essay on the Balinese self I argue that. But suppose we were to turn the whole argument around. Let's imagine that the Western concept of a centered, highly continuous self really suppresses a natural fact – the fact that we're playing roles throughout our lives. That it creates a myth of continuity that has to overcome the actual experience of the fact that we behave so radically different in radically different contexts. That's where I begin to get nervous with the idea that there is one sort of pattern that is fundamental and the others are reversals of that. You can describe the Balinese pattern as a reversal of early continuity feelings. But you can just as easily describe our tremendous emphasis on continuity, sincerity, authenticity, the "true self" sort of thing, as a reversal of the fact that we are all wearing masks all the time through all the changes of social morphology. But there's nothing transcultural, as far as I can see, that would make one of those more fundamental. Suppose as a thought experiment all of psychology and anthropology had grown up in a Balinese context rather than in a Western one and then tried to interpret us. There's nothing particularly privileged about our theories of the self.

Shweder: What you're saying is that all cultural ideologies are available in all cultures, at least in an incipient form. That the Balinese or the Moroccan pattern is available in our system to both adults and children and that the question is how much we pick it up, amplify it, represent it, and enshrine it.

Geertz: Right!

Shweder: Then we return to the question: What difference do the enshrinements make?

Geertz: They make a lot of difference in my opinion, a lot of psychological difference.

Shweder: So when I sign a letter "sincerely yours," I have access to the Balinese pattern – I'm acting like one of your Balinese informants. The issue of "really feeling it" or of being sincere or authentic doesn't arise. I just write "sincerely yours" – it's a conventional form and one just follows it. Bali is "sincerely yours" amplified and made into a cultural ideology.

Spiro: Cliff, I'm not sure that if anthropology and psychology had arisen in Bali that they would have been essentially different from what they are, given their Western origins. I'm not referring to folk theories or ethno-self theories because, after all, the theories of the self in psychology or anthropology are not the Western folk theories of the self. I would think that one of the points about science is that it is about demystification – it takes these folk theories and it demystifies them. Although there might be some differences in the contours of Balinese anthropology and psychology, I would assume that they too would engage in the process of demystification. And I would like to believe that Balinese and American psychologists and anthropologists would, qua anthropologists and psychologists, arrive at some kind of common view of the nature of human beings and the nature of culture, so that the differences between them would be no greater than the differences within "Western" anthropology and psychology.

LeVine: I can tell you that the Japanese see our way of formulating things in our psychological theories as predicated on folk assumptions that are culture-specific.

Spiro: So we don't have to do this as a thought experiment. We can compare notes with Japanese and Indian psychologists and anthropologists.

D'Andrade: There are sometimes advantages to interviewing an ape [laughter]. You get to ask them about selves. Now, of course, you can only believe what they tell you [laughter]. No, I think a lot of the things Koko the gorilla is supposed to have done are interesting for people interested in the development of the self. Koko has a lot of things to say about Koko!

This is a complex discussion indicative of the complexity and richness of the problem of "the self." The self-concept is about so much that fixing the topic of the discussion proved to be a formidable task. A series of topics emerged. Distinctions were drawn between self-representations (the way the self is) and ideal self-representations (the way the self ought to be) as revealed or expressed in three quite distinguishable, and potentially independent, ways: (1) in action, (2) in individual consciousness, and (3) in cultural ideology. Several parameters of self-description were introduced: individualism, locus of control, continuity, the self as an observing ego (the "I") connected or unconnected to the organism, the self as an object classified within a social morphology (the "me"). Processes of self-formation, both cultural and noncultural, were invoked. It was even proposed that the social sciences are a folk theory in disguise, an articulate expression of our culture's ideology. Vast cross-cultural differences in reflective conceptions of the self were acknowledged as well as differences in the degree to which this or that conception of the self is elaborated, symbolized, and made consciously available to individuals in a society. Participants considered the possibility that the full spectrum of human conceptions about the self is available in tacit and/or unelaborated form in all cultures. The degree of influence of those processes promoting cultural consciousness (symbolization, labeling, elaboration) on the lived phenomenal self of individual persons remained unsettled. That unsettling topic is addressed in several essays in this volume.

PROBLEMATIC 5: CULTURAL INTEGRATION: FACT OR FICTION?

Kay: I've been wanting to say something scandalous ever since this conference started – and I think now is my chance. So I had better seize time by the forelock – and indeed "time" will be my example. The general point I want to make is this. We have heard a lot about the systematicity of culture, the organization of culture, the way it all fits together into one neat thing. I have a kind of historical theory about that view – which I admit is scandalous, but nevertheless I ask you to listen to it. First, I want to tell you why the view arose, and then I want to give a counterexample to the view. I think the view arose that cultures are integrated because anthropology arose in an institutional setting where people had to write Ph.D. theses. Ph.D. theses, if they were successful, were published as books – and books tell a consistent story. I semi-seriously propose that the exigencies of the publishing trade or literary genre have been imposed on the subject matter of cultural anthropology so as to make everyone feel that if I go out to study the "whoevers," I've got to come back and tell a consistent and entertaining story about what the "whoevers" are like – and everything they do had better fit into this one story. Let me mention one counterexample to this view.

"Time" is perhaps the favorite thing that anthropologists point to so as to exaggerate the exoticness of other peoples; they love to say things like "time" is like this for us, but it's like that for the folks that I studied. There may be other stories but I think these stories about what "time" is like come in three basic varieties. One variety is the linear view that we're supposed to have. It can be encapsulated in an image: We're walking along through a landscape and the future is ahead of us and the past is behind us. Okay. Well, it's said that the Chinese have a view of "time" that is similarly linear. In their case it's like we're standing on a railroad platform and "time" is the train, and as the train passes us the future is behind us and the past ahead of us. And then we know about all the peoples with the famous circular theory of "time," which is unlike either of these two linear images. Things go round and round and so on. Now English has all three of these images obviously present in it. We have expressions like "the future is ahead." We also have expressions that work the opposite way, like the "preceding" and the "following," which go very nicely with the image of the railroad train attributed to the Chinese. And, of course, spring comes back every year and we have a host of other usages that imply this circular or cyclical image of time. So English is full of conflicting schemata, and we pull them out and use them when they suit our needs. I want to suggest that cultures in general, and culture as carried by the English language in particular, need not be all that consistent and unified. Anthropologists who go out to study them might take that as a cautionary note.

Geertz: I think Paul's [Kay] comments are a mere parody. There are Type 1 and Type 2 errors. It's possible to overthematize, and it's possible to underthematize. That's just an explosion. The rest is a comment. This has to do with time representation. There is the kind of thing that one's grandmother says when you come home [from the field]: "You know we've got that sort of thing here, too." But I would say it's different in a culture that has a one-day calendar, a two-day calendar, a three-day calendar, and they all cycle around. The whole temple system runs this way. The days are named this way. Birthdays are celebrated this way. Sure, they have the notion that people die in a linear sort of way. We're talking about the cultural representation of time, not whatever time really is. I'd say it's a little different in Bali, and this has to do with the cultural elaboration business. The conception of time, not in a circular sense but in a combinatorial sense, is really extraordinarily elaborated. The music works that way – there's this enormous elaboration of time in music. Not everything works that way – but there's a use of time in calendrical things that we don't have. And really I think it's a bit of a dodge to say: "Yeah, we talk of things 'following' or 'coincidences.'" "Coincidence," of course, is important in our culture, but it has a different role and a different elaboration and a different power and a different scale over which it ranges in Bali than it does here – and vice versa for other kinds of things. So the question isn't really whether everybody has everything – they probably do – but rather the degree to which things are elaborated and their power and force. And that's an empirical problem that can be overthematized and overdone. It's not enough to say: "Yeah, we've got that too and everything's the same everywhere." As I've said before, the elements of a culture are not like a pile of sand and not like a spider's web. It's more like an octopus, a rather badly integrated creature – what passes for a brain keeps it together, more or less, in one ungainly whole. But we must, as anthropologists, search for as much coherency as we can find, try to find connections, and where we can't find them simply say we can't find them.

Kay: I'd like to respond to Cliff and my response is that he was exactly right. I agree absolutely with everything he said. I said what I said purposely, baldly, and offensively, and he responded with judgment and balance and put matters just right. There's nothing in his response that I disagree with. He talks about tendencies toward integration, partial separation. There's a trivial sense in which everybody's got everything, but there's a real sense in which it's quite different here from there, and anthropologists are quite interested in describing these differences and finding what system they can. And, indeed, they do find things like this pattern of repetition that goes through the calendar and so forth – and that's fascinating stuff. My point will have been made if people take exactly, literally, and seriously everything in Cliff's response about how much integration and pattern there is and how much there isn't, and the extent to which the same schemata that are integrated one way in one culture are present in another culture but are integrated into different larger patterns or not integrated at all.

Underthematization has not been a problem for culture theory. In 1934 Ruth Benedict's descriptions of "Apollonian" and "Dionysian" type cultures captured the imagination of culture theorists, and ever since then the idea of cultural integration or global thematic consistency has been assumed more then it has been tested. This is ironic, as Ruth Benedict herself [1934] emphasized that cultural integration is a *variable* and that she had *selected* for description some highly integrated cases.

The bias toward overthematization in cultural description is poorly understood. Kay facetiously attributes it to the literary standards of the publishing trade. At the conference, Robert Levy argued that if there is a bias it is not in the way we think about cultural materials but rather in the kinds of places anthropologists are willing to move into and stay at for a while. As Levy remarked, the sample of cultures studied by anthropologists "is a very strange sample that we have never adequately defined," and it may overrepresent cultures that are tightly organized. Other explanations might trace the bias to our models and metaphors for thinking about culture. Languages, games, dramas, and flow charts are rather neatly organized things – to the extent we "treat" culture as a language or a game or a script, and so on, we are theoretically predisposed to emphasize whatever is systematic at the expense of what isn't. Whatever the explanation, if the dialogue between Kay and Geertz can be taken as a common measure of things, cultural integration has become, once again, something to scrutinize, not something to presuppose, and, as Kay and Geertz acknowledge, the idea that cultures differ from one another does not require that any of them be designed like a seamless web. Perhaps Paul Kay's ecumenical reply to Clifford Geertz portends a fruitful continuation of the transdenominational dialogue initiated at the Social Science Research Council conference on Culture and Its Acquisition.

The chapters

Of the following chapters, ten are original essays prepared for this volume. The essay by Geertz (Chapter 4) and the essay by Shweder and Bourne (Chapter 6) are reprinted because of their relevance to research on the "self" and to several other chapters in the volume.

There are a number of ways to read the book. One way is to follow the table of contents.

Shweder's essay (Chapter 1) presents an overview of contemporary approaches to cultural materials. Those approaches are related to enlightenment and romantic assumptions about the place of rationality in human affairs. The chapter classifies schools of social science thought by their answer to the question "How do the canons that govern the language and thought of the ideal scientist, logician, and statistician compare with the canons that govern ordinary language and thought?" The chapter concludes with an evaluation of Piaget's enlightenment-based program of developmental research and with a proposal for a romantically based alternative in which socialization is viewed as tacit communication.

In Chapter 2, LeVine portrays a view of culture as an inherited system of ideas that structures the subjective experiences of individuals. According to that view, cultural meanings are received meanings organized into systematic codes that vary in the extent to which they enter cultural consciousness or can be verbalized by the native. LeVine examines the problem of cultural diversity (also addressed by Shweder in Chapter 1). That is, how is the existence of variations in meaning systems to be explained? The chapter examines various abstract properties of culture by reference to concrete fieldwork experiences with, for example, witchcraft beliefs and kinship avoidance practices in sub-Sahara Africa.

In Chapter 3, D'Andrade traces the contemporary shift in culture theory from a view of culture as patterns of behavior to a view of culture as knowledge, meanings, and symbols. The chapter then addresses several conceptual and methodological issues concerning the definition and ethnographic study of meaning systems. D'Andrade broadens the concept of meaning beyond the referential function of language to include the directive, emotive, and constitutive functions of language. The idea that culture is "constituted" receives detailed treatment. The chapter provides a bridge between cognitive and symbolic anthropology.

Taken together, the chapters by Shweder, LeVine, and D'Andrade introduce the reader to the conceptual underpinning of the symbols-and-meanings approach to cultural analysis. The next six chapters examine the implications of a symbols-and-meanings approach for our understanding of emotional functioning and the organization of self.

In Chapter 4, Geertz advances the provocative proposition that "the Western conception of the person as a bounded, unique, more or less integrated motivational and cognitive universe, a dynamic center of awareness, emotion, judgment and action organized into a distinctive whole . . . is, however incorrigible it may seem to us, a rather peculiar idea within the context of the world's cultures." Geertz examines Javanese, Balinese, and Moroccan conceptions of the self.

Taking Geertz's relativism a step further, Rosaldo (Chapter 5) rejects the view that culture merely provides the content that is processed by a universal mind and argues that "'contents' themselves may affect the 'form' of mental processes." She argues that several psychological processes thought to be universal inherent features of human affective and personal functioning are by-products of our Western way of symbolically constructing ourselves and our emotions. For example, focusing on the Ilongot, a headhunting people of the Philippines, Rosaldo argues that "they did not think of hidden or forgotten affects [e.g., anger] as disturbing energies repressed; nor did they see in violent actions the expression of a history of frustrations buried in a fertile but unconscious mind."

Shweder and Bourne (Chapter 6) address several conceptual and methodological issues in the comparative analysis of the self. Examined is the underlying logic of universalistic, evolutionary, and relativistic accounts of cultural diversity. Special attention is given to the claim that in some cultures the "individual" is not distinguished from the social status she or he occupies. Oriya (India) and American person descriptions are analyzed for variations in context-dependent or concrete thinking. Cross-cultural differences in abstract–concrete thinking are placed in a relativist framework. Shweder and Bourne argue that the relationship between what you think about and how you think is mediated by cultural premises and the master metaphors by which a people lives. The chapter discusses holistic and organic metaphors for the self.

The essay by Vendler (Chapter 7) is an exercise in ordinary language philosophy designed to clarify the meaning of "personhood" (vs. "thingness"). Vendler argues that sentences, theories, poems, and people are all things that are subject to "understanding," by which he means that to explain a person's actions one must appeal to unobservable "things" like reasons, motives, intentions, and other "factors of subjective consciousness." Vendler argues that understanding a person requires empathy and that empathic understanding is what divides human understanding from explanation in the natural sciences. Vendler's argument is a challenge to those of us who believe in the methodological unity of the sciences across "subject matter."

In Chapter 8, Levy introduces a rich set of distinctions for conceptualizing the relationship that exists between degrees of cultural self-consciousness (as revealed in naming systems, symbology, and ideology) and individual subjective experience. He distinguishes things in awareness from things out of awareness. Things in awareness include emotional feelings and non-emotional feelings. Things in awareness can be either expressed or not expressed, and there are cultural display rules that regulate their expression. Levy argues that for Tahitians, sadness (loss or depression) is a non-emotional feeling experienced as physical pain or sickness; sadness is somatized. This Levy relates to the fact that the idea of sadness is "hypocognized" in Tahitian culture, receiving little elaboration in local doctrine or systems of naming or classification. Levy discusses both "hypocognized" emotions (sadness, guilt) and "hypercognized" emotions (anger, shame).

Solomon (Chapter 9) presents a version of his cognitive or interpretive theory of emotions. He rejects the idea that emotions can be understood in biological or physiological terms and challenges the proposition that emotional functioning is basically the same the world over. The chapter describes the variety of ways the emotional life of different peoples can be said to be different or alike. From Solomon's cognitivist point of view, emotional functioning is a historical artifact and an emotion is *"essentially* an intepretation, a view of its cause (more accurately, its 'object') and (logically) consequent forms of behavior."

The next two chapters focus on symbols and meanings with special references to language and thought.

In Chapter 10 Gardner presents a condensed version of his "modular" conception of intellectual structure and cognitive development. Skeptical of the view that mind consists of deep, generalized operational structures that undergo broad stagelike development, Gardner partitions the mind into independent unintegrated domains. His domains are arrived at by identifying seven distinct types of competencies (visual, numerical-logical, kinesthetic, . . .) cross-cut by three realms of knowledge (the physical world, the social world, the world of artifacts) and cross-cut again by two forms of knowledge (propositional and intuitive). Gardner suggests that intellectual change in these various domains may undergo separate, independent courses of development.

Ochs and Schieffelin (Chapter 11) present a comprehensive and synthetic treatment of research on language acquisition and cultural transmission through language learning. Focusing on the context, content, and process of language learning in three cultures, white middle-class America, Kaluli (Papua New Guinea), and Western Samoa, Ochs and

Schieffelin present a communication-based alternative to current theories of socialization processes. Most contemporary theories of socialization have very little to say about talk or the content of what children and adults are saying to each other. Social learning theorists direct our attention to rewards and punishments. Piagetians direct our attention to the deepest structural features of logical thinking. Psychoanalysts direct our attention to intrapsychic conflicts and identifications. Ochs and Schieffelin take "talk" seriously.

In Chapter 12 Spiro critiques the chapters by Shweder and Rosaldo, focusing especially on the issue of relativism. The reader will find that Spiro's chapter is fun to argue with or to use as a foundation for debate with other chapters in the volume. Indeed, one way to read the volume is to start with the chapters by Shweder and Rosaldo followed by Spiro's critique.

There are, however, several other alternative pathways through the volume, depending on the reader's inclinations and interests. The chapters by Shweder, LeVine, D'Andrade, and Spiro are broad-based treatments of the problem of meaning. The chapters by D'Andrade, Rosaldo, and Solomon emphasize "culture as constituted"; their concepts of "the constituted" should be compared with each other and with Spiro's more deterministic reductionist views. The chapters by Levy and LeVine deal with the issue of tacit knowledge and cultural consciousness and are profitably read together. The chapters by Geertz, Rosaldo, and Shweder and Bourne all treat the problem of self from closely related viewpoints. Empathic understanding is addressed in the chapters by Geertz, Vendler, and Solomon, and their views should be compared. A sustained discussion of the acquisitional and developmental side of things can be found in the chapter by Ochs and Schieffelin, although also see the chapters by Gardner, Levy, and Shweder.

Whatever the reader's chosen pathway through the volume, it is hoped that this book on the symbols-and-meanings approach to culture and the social origins of mind, self, and emotion confirms the growing suspicion among anthropologists, developmental psychologists, linguists, philosophers, and historians that they have much to say to each other and that the the colloquy can be both informative and fun.

For the many ways they guided and supported this project, we would like to thank the Social Science Research Council, our fellow members of the Committee on Social and Affective Development in Childhood, and Peter B. Read, council staff to the committee. Thank you, Peter.

References

Benedict, R. 1934. *Patterns of Culture*. Boston: Houghton Mifflin.

Flavell, J. H., & Ross, L. 1981. *Social Cognitive Development*. Cambridge: Cambridge University Press.

Fortune, R. F. 1935. *Manus Religion*. Philadelphia: American Philosophical Society.

Frye, N. 1964. *The Educated Imagination*. Bloomington: Indiana University Press.

Gallie, W. B. 1964. *Philosophy and Historical Understanding*. New York: Schocken Books.

Geertz, C. 1973. *Interpretation of Cultures*. New York: Basic Books.

Hallowell, A. I. 1967a. Temporal orientation in Western civilization and in a pre-literate society. In A. I. Hallowell, ed., *Culture and Experience*. New York: Schocken Books.

1967b. The self and its behavioral environment. In A. I. Hallowell, ed., *Culture and Experience*. New York: Schocken Books.

Higgins, E. T., Ruble, D. N., & Hartup, W. W. 1983. *Social Cognition and Social Development*. Cambridge: Cambridge University Press.

Hirsch, E. D. 1967. *Validity in Interpretation*. New Haven, Conn.: Yale University Press.

1976. *The Aims of Interpretation*. Chicago: University of Chicago Press.

Izard, C. E., Huebner, R. R., Risser, D., McGinnes, G. C., & Dougherty, L. M. 1980. The young infant's ability to produce discrete emotional expressions. *Developmental Psychology* 16:132–40.

Miller, G. A. 1981. *Language and Speech*. San Francisco: Freeman.

Shweder, R. A. 1979. Rethinking culture and personality theory part 1: a critical examination of two classical postulates. *Ethos* 7:255–78.

1982. On savages and other children. *American Anthropologist* 84:354–66.

1983. In defense of surface structure. In F. Landy, S. Zedeck, & J. Cleveland, eds., *Performance Measurement and Theory*. Hillsdale, N.J.: Erlbaum.

Whorf, B. L. 1956. *Language, Thought and Reality*. Cambridge, Mass.: MIT Press.

PART I
Culture theory: an introduction

1

Anthropology's romantic rebellion against the enlightenment, or there's more to thinking than reason and evidence

Richard A. Shweder

Cognitive anthropologists draw inferences about the mind of man by studying the ideas and actions of exotic peoples. For more than one hundred years cognitive anthropologists have divided in two schools in dispute over the answer to a series of closely related questions: What inferences about the mind of man must we draw in the face of countless ethnographic and historical examples of deeply entrenched yet apparently false beliefs and deeply entrenched yet apparently irrational practices? What does the evidence from other cultures tell us about the role of reason and evidence in shaping human belief and conduct? How do the canons that govern the language and thought of the ideal scientist, logician, and statistician compare with the canons that govern ordinary (everyday, folk, mundane, or savage) language and thought? What is the place of rationality, irrationality, and nonrationality in human affairs?

The dispute is, in fact, an ancient one. On one side stand "enlightenment"[1] figures such as Voltaire, Diderot, and Condorcet; before them Socrates, Spinoza, and Hobbes; after them Frazer, Tylor, the early Wittgenstein, Chomsky, Kay, Levi-Strauss, and Piaget. The enlightenment view, provocatively summarized by Lovejoy (1974:288–314; also see Gay 1959, 1964), holds that the mind of man is intendedly rational and scientific, that the dictates of reason are equally binding for all regardless of time, place, culture, race, personal desire, or individual endowment, and that in reason can be found a universally applicable standard for judging validity and worth.

"Unity" and "uniformity" are the telltale themes of an enlightenment thinker: unity, in mankind's *respect* for the sole authority of reason and evidence (the so-called psychic unity of mankind); uniformity, in the substantive conclusions about how to live and what to believe dictated by reason and evidence (the normative uniformity of mankind).

Men, of course, may fail to understand the proper canons for correct reasoning; they may make errors in evaluating evidence, or, indeed, blinded by passion and desire, they may commit themselves to indefensible conclusions; nonetheless, man, that animal that reasons and reasons about his reasons, strives to realize his nature. Exposed to

as goal of making meaning

→ *does this always happen?*

valid norms for logical, scientific, and statistical thinking, he will bow down before them, acknowledge his errors, and seek to reform his practices.

From that enlightenment view flows a desire to discover universals: the idea of natural law, the concept of deep structure, the notion of progress or development, and the image of the history of ideas as a struggle between reason and unreason, science and superstition.

On the other side of the dispute over rationality stand the spokesmen of the "romantic"[2] rebellion against the enlightenment: Goethe, Schiller, Schleiermacher; before them, the Sophists, Hume and Leibnitz; after them, Levy-Bruhl, the later Wittgenstein, Whorf, Kuhn, Schneider, Sahlins, Feyerabend, and Geertz. A central tenet of the romanticist view holds that ideas and practices have their foundation in neither logic nor empirical science, that ideas and practices fall beyond the scope of deductive and inductive reason, that ideas and practices are neither rational nor irrational but rather *non*rational.

From that romanticist tenet flows the concept of arbitrariness and culture, the subordination of deep structure to surface content, the celebration of local context, the idea of paradigm, cultural frames, and constitutive presuppositions, the view that action is expressive, symbolic, or semiotic, and a strong anti-normative, anti-developmental presumption culminating in the view that the primitive and modern are coequal and that the history of ideas is a history of a sequence of entrenched ideational fashions.

According to the romanticist account, a social order is a self-contained "framework" for understanding experience (Lovejoy 1974), a self-sufficient "design for living" (Benedict 1946). Governed within by their own rules, different frameworks for understanding, different designs for living do not lend themselves to comparative-normative evaluation; thus, to ask which is superior, Islam or Christianity, an animistic world view or a mechanistic world view, a social order premised on individualism, equality, and monogamy or one premised on holism, hierarchy, and polygamy is like asking, "Which is the more valid mode of artistic expression, cubism or impressionism?" For the romantic, the choice between alternative self-contained worlds must be an act of faith. Wary of any attempt to make the nonrational appear rational, wary of any ploy to make a genuine and unavoidable act of faith appear as though it were dictated by reason, the romantic views science (especially social science) as 90% ideology and views tradition, religion, and ritual as indispensable components of human thought and practice.

For three thousand years the tension between enlightenment and romanticist views of mind has been a creative force in cognitive studies. Within cognitive anthropology each side has vexed the other, spawning new discoveries and inciting daring feats of reinterpretation – some of which shall be discussed in this chapter. Outside cognitive anthropology, especially in the sister discipline of cognitive developmental psychology, Piaget, an enlightenment figure, has dominated the scene. Yet even Piaget has taken his lumps; the early warning signs of a romantic rebellion are everywhere to be seen.

The ethnographic record: false belief and irrational conduct?

Across the ages, across societies, ordinary folk, apparently of sound mind, have believed the most unbelievable beliefs and engaged in the most incredible practices. For many of these ideas and practices, normative predicates such as "erroneous," "wrong," "confused," "inefficient," "impractical," "immoral," or "false" would seem to apply, at least at first blush.

The Yir-Yiront aborigines of Australia, for example, fail to acknowledge a connection between copulation and pregnancy (fertilization by animal and tree spirits is the favored theory). The Ndembu argue that quarrelsomeness increases a woman's chances of infertility, and on the Arabian Peninsula the breast milk of a pregnant women is thought to be poisonous.

The Azande go in for oracular consultation. Posed a yes or no question, administered a modest dose of strychnine, the Azande oracle, a chicken, either lives or dies – yes or no. The oracle does not lie – or so the Azande believe. Those same Azande folk have a unique way of curing epilepsy: eat the ashes of the burnt skull of the red bush monkey. It's the red bush monkey's misfortune to exhibit seizurelike stretch movements each day upon waking.

Killing people outside the clan is popular among the Gahuku-Gama – conduct worthy of commendation – unless the outsider happens to be a maternal kinsman. Scrupulous in avoiding uterine kin in battle, the moral proscriptions of the Gahuku-Gama fail to generalize: *Other* clansmen are "awarded points" for taking the head of *your* maternal relatives.

Other New Guinea groups go in for homosexuality in a big way. The "life force" of the tribe must be passed on by males from generation to generation. Contained in semen, the life force gets passed on all right, orally, fellatio between "uncles" and their young "nephews."

One could go on. Reincarnation, adolescent circumcision, kin avoidance, witchcraft, widow burning, seclusion during menstruation, men descended from gods, men descended from (red bush?) monkeys, case after case where one can imagine some enlightenment figure arguing that there are universal norms, norms that ought to have universal authority over what we think and how we act; case after case where the struggle of reason against unreason comes to mind, where one might be tempted to portray the ideas and practices of other people as superstitious, erroneous, confused, maladapted, or immoral. Indeed, the ethnographic record is so bizarre that one would not be surprised to hear that some group, convinced of a mystical bond between progeny and harvest, fertility and fecundity, ejaculated on their fields before planting the first seeds.

Rational man in (mal)adaptation: the enlightenment "point"

Shared beliefs that are false. Institutionized practices that are irrational. What do they tell us about the mind of man? Within modern anthropology, anthropology of the past one hundred years, the ancient fugue has continued – an enlightenment point, a romanticist counterpoint. The founding enlightenment figures are E. B. Tylor (1871) and J. G. Frazer (1890). The founding romantic figure is L. Levy-Bruhl (1910).

All peoples are intendedly rational and scientific. That's half of Tylor's and Frazer's enlightenment view of the mind of man. The other half is that *other* peoples (e.g., the Azande and their monkey skulls) are not very good at it. Tylor and Frazer bequeath to anthropology the image of the alien as a deficient logician, faulty statistician, and muddled empirical scientist.

By Tylor's enlightenment account, all peoples guide their lives by reason and evidence. They seek empirical knowledge of what causes what. They try to adapt their behavior to the demands of their environment. They strive for consistency in their beliefs and practices. Moreover, all peoples pursue these rational-scientific goals by engaging in such activities as gathering information, evaluating evidence, estimating likelihoods, making predictions, drawing inductive and deductive inferences, and constructing explanatory theories.

Unfortunately, other peoples don't do all this very well. Of the "primitive mind," Tylor and Frazer, promoters of the distinction between "modern" and "primitive," have the following to say: The primitive respects reason and evidence yet fails to apply the proper canons of logic, statistics, and experimental science. Thus, for example, the primitive is prone to magical thinking, confusing similarity with causation, and manipulating models (e.g., binding a replica of an infant to the back of a sterile woman) as though analogs had causal power.

The enlightenment approach, as noted earlier, is defined by the assumption that man's beliefs and practices bow down before reason and evidence and that what reason and evidence dictate is the same for all. By "reason," enlightenment figures have in mind canons of deductive logic, patterns of hypothetical reasoning, thought guided by principles of statistical inference or experimental logic, and so on. By "evidence," they have in mind sense perception and the observation of regular connections between things, (e.g., if you cut your finger deeply with a knife it bleeds).

For example, from an enlightenment point of view, the determination of contingent relationships is a rational process. If someone wants to determine whether eating the burnt skull of the red bush monkey cures epilepsy or whether quarrelsome women are prone to infertility or whether the breast milk of a pregnant woman is poisonous, there are better ways and worse ways to go about making the determination. And the proper ways do not include pointing to the seizurelike movements of red bush monkeys when they wake up or remembering a woman who was both quarrelsome and barren. Enlightenment figures are inclined to tell people who assert such connections that they are confused or wrong; and the enlightenment figure is confident that he or she could demonstrate to them the error of their ways. The assumption is that our sensory apparatus, sensory inputs, and modes of intellectual operation are (a) already sufficiently calibrated or (b) over time can become sufficiently calibrated so as to produce convergence or agreement about what the world is really like or really ought to be like.

So, the enlightenment approach assumes that the mind of man bows down before reason and evidence and that the dictates of reason and evidence are the same for all. Once this assumption is adopted there arises a crucial secondary issue: Is *valid* knowledge of what reason and evidence dictate equally possessed by all?

The answer to this question divides enlightenment figures into two camps: universalists and developmentalists. Thus, for example, for universalists such as Hobbes and Voltaire, the answer to a question like "What are the moral virtues?" (e.g., keeping promises, seeking peace, unprejudiced arbitration) not only is dictated by reason (derivable from a simple hypothetical: "If I am to preserve my own well-being I ought to do such-and-such; and I do very much want to preserve my personal well-being; Mackie 1980) but is *obvious* to reason ("intelligible even to the meanest capacity"; Hobbes 1651; or as Voltaire put it: "A day suffices to know the duties of man"). See Turiel (1979) and Nucci and Turiel (1978) for a contemporary version of universalism in the moral domain (also see Shweder, Turiel, & Much 1981; Shweder 1982a). Indeed, Turiel argues that what is moral is so obvious to reason that it is universally understood, even by young children.

Developmentalists, on the other hand, typically deny that the universally valid dictates of reason and evidence are equally *available* to all persons or peoples. Tylor, Frazer, and more recently Piaget argue that the normative standards (e.g., logic) – by reference to which a person or people judges thinking or action successful or unsuccessful – undergo development. By Tylor's, Frazer's, and Piaget's account, all people and peoples have normative standards for regulating thought, but knowledge of the proper standards (e.g., Bayes's rules for evaluating evidence, Mill's rules for experimental reasoning, Rawl's principle of justice), knowledge of those norms worthy of universal respect, is achieved by only a few cultures (the civilized ones).

Kohlberg (1981) makes a similar argument with special reference to morality. His basic claim is that what deserves to be moral is the same across cultures and history and that knowledge of that external, objective morality is possible by means of deductive and/or inductive logic. He links cross-cultural variations in moral thinking to the uneven distribution of processes of rational reasoning (e.g., formal operational thinking) from culture to culture (see Shweder 1982c for a review).

So, enlightenment figures are of two stripes, universalists and developmentalists. Each group, in its own way, has elaborated the conceptual scheme of enlightenment thinking. From the universalists we inherit a passion for discovering general laws and universals, the concept of "deep structure" (an indispensable concept if universals are to be discovered), and the idea that some things are "natural" (Man is, by nature, a creature with reason; therefore, it is "natural" to follow the dictates of right reasoning. Correct reasoning reveals what is vice and what is virtue; therefore, it is natural to be virtuous, unnatural to commit a vice – e.g., incest, biased arbitration, etc.). From the developmentalists we inherit the concept of progress (steps or stages en route to constructing the proper norms and valid understandings), an emphasis on adaptation and problem solving (earlier stages are adaptational failures; previous problems get solved by later stages), and the related view that the history of ideas is a history of more and more adequate representations of reality and that the history of man's practices is a history of better and better adaptations to the demands of the environment.

The idea of a universal is the idea of invariant content. That's not saying very much, for two crucial questions remain unanswered: "invariance under which description of the content?" and "invariance of content across what range of instances?" Imagine you know two people who have a social relationship. How is that relationship to be described? As "Ted and Alice – they love each other, live together at 10 Elm Street, and have raised two kids together" or perhaps simply as "monogamous marriage" or "pair bonding" or "attraction between two elements" or "a vector in graph theory"? Each subsequent description shifts the content, on the one hand, emptying it of something (Ted, Alice, love, Elm Street, the kids); on the other hand, enlarging the range of phenomena (from Ted and Alice to subatomic particles) across which the content is invariant. When the content gets empty enough it becomes "abstract" and we call it "structure." When the range of invariance gets large enough it becomes "general" and we call it "*deep* structure."

Enlightenment figures committed to universalism try to induce the nature of man, and the dictates of reason, from practices *common* to humanity. To do this successfully, one must search for deeper and underlying agreements hidden behind surface differences. Thus, if the peoples of the world disagree about the relative worth of monogamy versus polygamy, any preference for one over the other is not derivable from the uniform dictates of reason – not "in the nature of things." Mankind, however, may disagree about the relative virtue of polygamy versus monogamy, but at least everyone honors the institution of marriage as a "natural" expression of man's nature and/or rationality or so the argument goes.

But what if valid knowledge of the dictates of reason is a rare possession? What if the true nature of man is realized only if properly cultivated? Perhaps only a few (e.g., the monogamists) have knowledge of the proper norms for correct reasoning. The developmental approach (and most missionary efforts) are built upon that possibility.

The practices *common* to humanity are of little interest to the developmentalist. What really interests him are the canons recommended by virtuosos or experts. Developmentalists credit experts with insight into the proper norms for correct thinking, norms that the rest of humanity strives to attain. Thus, the normative schemata of the scientist, logician, and statistician (the canons of propositional calculus, Mill's principles of agreement and difference) are held out as a yardstick for comparing ideas and practices and judging their relative worth. Over time, less worthy forms (e.g., animistic magic) are held to be replaced by more and more adequate forms (e.g., mechanistic science), a progressive process ever moving in the direction of valid knowledge and correct reasoning. Tylor and Frazer, of course, held such a developmental view.

Within cognitive anthropology during the past twenty years, enlightenment research has focused not surprisingly upon the so-called ethnosciences. Folk knowledge (Agar 1973; Berlin, Breedlove, & Raven 1973; D'Andrade 1976; Frake 1961), everyday systems of classification (Levi-Strauss 1966; Tyler 1969), mundane principles of inference (Hutchins 1980), and ordinary language "representational" schemes and their influence on man's ability to observe, remember, and predict (D'Andrade 1974; Lucy & Shweder 1979; Shweder 1977a, 1977b) have all come under investigation.

One line of ethnoscience research focuses on universal processes in the lexicalization of mundane descriptive categories. Lexicalization is the process by which a distinction becomes encoded or labeled with a word or "dictionary entry." Thus in English there exists a category lexicalized as "brother," whereas the category "older brother" also exists but has yet to be lexicalized. In other languages the category "older brother" not only exists but also is lexicalized with a single term.

Berlin and Kay (1969) are responsible for most of the recent excitement about universal principles of nomenclature development. Their work focuses upon the development of a vocabulary of so-called basic color terms. Basic color terms are a subset of all available expressions for referring to color. The subset is identified by a number of criteria. Basic color terms must be single lexemes (blue is basic; sky blue is not), must not be included in the signification of any other color term (red is basic; crimson, a "kind of" red, is not), must be general terms, not restricted in their application to a special class of objects (yellow is basic; blonde is not), and must not be the name of an object having that color (yellow is basic; gold is not).

Berlin and Kay's remarkable finding is that if a language, any language (from Homeric Greek to Swahili), has N basic color terms, their referential foci – the best example of each basic color category (black, white, red, yellow, green, blue, brown, pink, orange, purple, gray) – can be predicted simply on the basis of that number. Translation of color terms between languages is greatly facilitated by the discovery.

Berlin and Kay (1969) originally portrayed the development of a basic color lexicon as a process of lexicalizing in regular order each of a series of discrete focal areas in the color spectrum. Thus, languages with two-term color systems lexicalize focal white and focal black. Three-term systems add red. Four-term systems add green or yellow. Five-term systems add both green and yellow. Six-term systems add blue and so on. The finding also can be stated in terms of so-called implicational universals (Brown 1979; Greenberg 1966): For example, if a language lexicalizes "red," it will also lexicalize white and black but not vice versa and so on. Kay and McDaniel (1978), recently reviewing cross-cultural and developmental research on color vocabularies, have replaced the image of progressive encoding of focal areas with the image of successive differentiation. Thus, evidence on the lexicalization of "basic color systems" suggests that one of the terms in any two-term system can be defined as a color category the best example of which is either focal white, focal yellow, or focal red and the other term will have as its best example either focal black, focal brown, or focal blue. Additional terms partition the focal areas in fairly regular order.

Berlin and Kay's research has spawned a series of investigations into naming behavior (see Brown 1979 for a review). Universal patterns of lexical development have been discovered for folk botanical classifications, zoological classifications, kinship classifications, and many other domains (Berlin, Breedlove, & Raven 1973; Brown 1979; Nerlove & Romney 1967). For example, Berlin, Breedlove, and Raven (1973) have discovered a universal temporal order in the way botanical classifications are lexicalized. First there develops a lexicalized set of generics (e.g., "oak," "pine"). Then there develops a binomial specification of these generics (e.g., "white oak," "yellow pine"). Finally, upper-level terms are developed to label the generics (e.g., "tree," "bush," "grass").

A second line of ethnoscience research investigates the influence of collective "representational" schemes on man's ability to act as a scientist to observe, remember, and induce. D'Andrade (1965, 1973, 1974) and Shweder (1975, 1977a, 1977b, 1982b; also Shweder & D'Andrade 1979, 1980), for example, have documented a tendency of normal, intelligent adults in all cultures to engage in something akin to "word magic." The mind of man seems disposed to confuse semantic relationships among event descriptors with empirical relationships among the events described, to confuse "propositions about language" with "propositions about the world," to confuse likeness with likelihood.

D'Andrade's and Shweder's observational and experimental research has focused on the illusory perception and memory of "behavioral syndromes," that is, "packages" of correlated behavioral characteristics. To explain their findings, they have advocated the so-called systematic distortion hypothesis, which states that under difficult memory conditions observers of behavior find it easier to retrieve semantically related memory items, confusing "what is like what" with "what correlates with what."

For example, observers view a thirty-minute videotape of interaction among four members of a family (Shweder & D'Andrade 1980). Immediately after viewing the tape, observers are asked to rate each family member on the frequency of observed occurrence of a variety of behavioral characteristics (e.g., disagrees, criticizes, jokes, praises). A second set of observers conduct on-line moment-to-moment scorings of the videotape, constructing a reliable performance criterion for assessing the validity of the memory-based observer reports. A third sample rates the behavioral descriptions (e.g., disagrees, criticizes) for pair-wise similarities of meaning. Shweder and D'Andrade discover that what correlates with what in memory-based ratings of behavior replicates the semantic intuitions of judges (e.g., criticizes and disagrees correlate + .59 in memory and are judged similar in meaning) but that neither the correlational structure of memory nor the structure of semantic intuitions parallels the actual correlational structure of behavior in the videotape (e.g., in the observed behavior, criticizes and disagrees actually correlate .00). Memory drifts in the direction of preexisting semantic intuitions, and these intuitions are far more structured and coherent than actual experience. Magical thinking seems more widespread than Tylor and Frazer led us to believe.

Sometimes our "representational schemes" interfere with observation and memory. At other times they facilitate it. Indeed, at times, language can serve as a highly effective vehicle for memory. Years ago this point was forcibly made by Lantz and Stefflre (1964:473), who urged us to view memory as a "situation in which an individual communicates to himself through time using the brain as a channel." Lantz and Stefflre argued that this process of autocommunication could be simulated "by having individuals communicate with other people. Items accurately communicated interpersonally would then be predicted to be more accurately communicated intrapersonally." The idea was to present subjects with a complex array of stimuli-to-be-remembered and then to have the subjects describe the target stimuli so that other people who had not observed the target stimuli could accurately identify them in the array. The prediction was that stimuli that are easier to encode in one's natural language are also easier to remember. The theory was that past experience can be stored in verbal descriptions and that these descriptions can later be retrieved at will and decoded to reconstruct or re-cognize experience.

In one test of the theory, Stefflre, Castillo, and Morley (1966) tested Spanish and Mayan speakers for memory of color chips. They discovered that speakers of these two languages found different colors easy to communicate about and (thus) easier to recall. Recent work by Lucy and Shweder (1979) suggests that the results of Stefflre and his associates are quite robust.

A third line of ethnoscience research has focused on broad universal dimensions of stimulus classification. Osgood, May, and Miron (1975), for example, have discovered a universal "affective reaction system" for categorizing stimulus events. For any language, contrastive adjectives (wet vs. dry, kind vs. cruel, up vs. down, smooth vs. rough, fast vs. slow, strong vs. weak, etc.) display considerable redundancy and can be reduced to three underlying dimensions of "feeling tone" or "connotative meaning" (pleasantness, strain, excitement or evaluation, potency, activity level). These three dimensions universally mediate judgments across sensory modalities (synesthesia) and conceptual domains (metaphor). Research conducted in India (Shweder 1972; Shweder & Bourne, Chapter 6, this volume) and Melanesia (White 1980) suggests that folk theories of personality trait co-occurrence (e.g., aggression and dominance go together in people; friendly and aggressive are opposed) may be universal, a reflection of the universality of Osgood's scheme.

A fourth line of ethnoscience research has revived and revised Tylor's and Frazer's image of the primitive as a "deficient scientist." Horton (1967), for example, has given a unified account of traditional African thought systems, explaining their apparent scientific shortcomings by reference to a hypothesized "closed intellectual predicament," namely, lack of information about competing alternative perspectives (theories, classifications). From the concept of a so-called closed intellectual predicament, Horton theoretically derives the traditional African's magical attitude toward words, the failure to develop abstract theories, the tendency to infuse explanations with emotional concerns, and the absence of self-conscious reflection about the canons of logic and scientific method.

Horton characterizes traditional African thought as deficient science, which he explains by reference to limited informational opportunities. For the most part, however, neo-Tylorean researchers have universalized Tylor's image of the primitive mind. Upon examination, the primitive mind studied a century ago by Tylor and Frazer turns out to be the "intuitive" or "everyday" mind of normal adults in all cultures. What contemporary cognitive scientists (in anthropology and cognitive psychology) have discovered is that most of us have a primitive mentality much of the time (see, e.g., D'Andrade 1974; Lyon & Slovic 1976; Nisbett & Ross 1980; Nisbett et al. 1976; Ross 1977; Shweder 1977b, 1980b; Tversky & Kahneman 1974; Wason & Johnson-

Laird 1972). We have deficient data-gathering strategies. We have limited deductive-reasoning skills. We have faulty inductive-inference procedures. We do not know how to calculate the likelihood of an event. We do not know what evidence is relevant for testing a generalization. We overlook base-rate information. We confuse likeness with likelihood. We are disinclined to compare conditional probabilities or to process correlation-relevant information. We are just not very good at doing applied science.

A single example of our limitations will have to suffice. Einhorn (1980) invites us to put ourselves in the shoes of a military general in a politically tense arena, worried about the possibility of an enemy invasion. Past research has shown that when enemy troops mass at the border, the likelihood of invasion is 75%. Our knowledge of enemy troop movements comes to us from our intelligence agency. Past experience has shown that if our intelligence agency reports that enemy troops are amassing on the border, they are definitely there. We have just received a report from our intelligence agency that enemy troops have amassed at the border. What is the probability of invasion? Most people answer 75%, and most people are wrong. In fact, it is possible for the probability of invasion to be zero.

Most normal adults commit the fundamental logical fallacy of affirming the consequent when solving problems of this type. They commit a conversion error of the form: if $p \rightarrow q$; therefore if $q \rightarrow p$. Thus, when told "if our intelligence agency reports that enemy troops are on the border they are there," most adults infer "if enemy troops are on the border, our intelligence agency reports it." One way to recognize the error, Einhorn notes, is to imagine a cunning enemy who lets your intelligence agents see their troops in only those 25% instances when no invasion is planned. However, when an invasion is planned, troops at the border are so well hidden that your sources do not report them. Through faulty reasoning, an invasion likelihood of zero is misperceived as 75%. Most of us have a primitive mentality much of the time!

The neo-Tylorian literature is filled with examples of this type, instance after instance of apparently faulty reasoning, false belief, and irrational practice. Recent critiques of this literature (Cohen 1979; March 1978) suggest to me that we must distinguish among three types of cases: the irrational, the rational, and the nonrational.

The irrational. There are cases of genuinely degraded performance. Either the informant has *failed to apply* a standard that he himself recognizes as authoritative and correct (see, e.g., Cole & Scribner 1974; Cole et al. 1971), or the informant has *failed to acquire* the proper standard for reasoning, judgment, or choice (see, e.g., Bruner, Olver, & Greenfield 1966). Our earlier error in calculating the likelihood of an invasion is an example of the first subtype. We recognize, upon instruction, that it is illegitimate to "affirm the consequent"; we confess our mistake and bow down before reason.

The rational. There are cases where what's apparently irrational is actually rational, that is, where the perception of irrationality is a failing on our part. A mother says to a child: "If you don't clean up your room, you can't go to the movies." The child tidies things up and is about to leave for the show as Mama shouts out: "Where are you going! It doesn't logically follow that if you do clean up your room you can go to the movies. You've committed a logical error. You're acting irrationally." This case is interesting because it's the mother not the child who has failed to understand the *tacit* rational norms governing their exchange. Mother *said*, "If you don't clean up your room, you can't go to the movies," but what was *tacitly communicated* was "*only* if you don't clean up your room, you can't go to the movies." The child, properly comprehending the logic of the biconditional, guided his action with a defensible norm. As it turns out, much that underlies rational discourse in everyday conversation "goes without saying," although what "goes without saying" to insiders may not be obvious and may *appear* irrational to outsiders.

Thus, while there are cases of genuinely degraded thinking, there are also cases where the apparent irrationality can be genuinely "rationalized." March (1978), for example, in a recent paper on human-choice behavior, provides us with a rich collection of concepts for rationalizing apparently irrational decisions, a list of goals or objectives with respect to which apparently unreasonable decisions can be made to seem sensible. Disinclined to accept the image of man living in error, ignorance, and obtuseness, March invites us to engage in interpretive charity, to imagine that people act, when making a decision, "as if" they do not in fact expect their decisions to be implemented, "as if" a person's consciously held and fully explicit goals are not his real goals, "as if" there are advantages to keeping goals ambiguous or to having no specific goals at all, "as if" some decisions are made for the sake of getting oneself to alter one's preferences, "as if" people often try to outsmart themselves, compromising between the legitimate claims of multiple internal selves. Thus, March claims, ambiguity, apparent inefficiency, and apparent inconsistency are "not necessarily a fault in human choice to be corrected but a form of intelligence."

The nonrational. There are cases where canons of rationality, validity, truth, and efficiency are simply beside the point – irrelevant! This third possibility is what the romantic rebellion against the enlightenment is all about. What is that possibility? That there's something more to thinking than reason and evidence – culture, the arbitrary, the symbolic, the expressive, the semiotic – that many of our ideas and practices are beyond logic and experience.

Man makes himself: the romanticist counterpoint

Within cognitive anthropology, the founding father of romanticism is L. Levy-Bruhl (1910). At the time Levy-Bruhl wrote, whole cultures were being characterized as "modern" or "primitive," and the prevalent view of the primitive mind was Tylor's and Frazer's image of the primitive as intendedly scientific, albeit confused. Levy-Bruhl, the romantic, recoiled at the image. Loathe to interpret other peoples' understandings and practices in a denigrating light, loathe to turn the thinking of others into a faint copy of our own thinking, Levy-Bruhl argued for the uniqueness and integrity of the so-called (and, from his point of view, mislabeled) primitive mentality. Levy-Bruhl claimed that the canons governing thinking of so-called primitives are neither deductive, inductive, nor causal. The primitive, he argued, is not a bad scientist; he is a good mystic; and the intellectual procedures of the primitive mind are not deficient applications of the rules of logic and science – they are alogical not illogical, nonrational not irrational. For example, imagine an employer saying to his factory laborers: "A boss is to his workers as a father to a son." For Levy-Bruhl, it was if Tylor and Frazer had misclassified the employer's rhetoric as science and then accused the employer of observational failure! (see Tambiah 1973).

Levy-Bruhl got himself into a lot of trouble. By trying to treat whole cultures as mystical (i.e., nonrational), he was led to say extreme things, namely, that mystical cultures could get along entirely without logic. By Levy-Bruhl's mystic light, even elementary logical principles (e.g., the law of noncontradiction or the law of the excluded middle) were irrelevant for evaluating or describing so-called primitive thought.

Obviously, there are severe difficulties with such a claim. To prohibit elementary logical rules such as "something cannot be both itself and not itself at the same time" is tantamount to denying the fact-stating function of language (Black 1963). As Black notes, it would not be possible to convey information if one could not draw inferences from empirical premises, for example, if one could not infer from the assertion "the cow is in the corn" that "the cow is not in the barn." No society could persist under such whimsical communicative conditions.

But one need not be an extremist about it! It is not necessary to deny the fact-stating, assertive, or representational function of language to recognize that science is not all there is to language and thought (see D'Andrade, Chapter 3, this volume). Forsake the view that whole societies are either mystical (nonrational) or scientific (rational vs. irrational), and Levy-Bruhl's message comes through loud and clear and in defensible form: There are many points in a cognitive structure beyond the reach of universal standards of logic and science, many points where questions of truth and falsity, error and validity, practicality and efficiency are simply beside the point. At those points there is no rule of logic and no law of nature dictating what is proper or necessary for us to believe. We enter the realm of the arbitrary. It is a realm where man is free to create his own distinctive symbolic universe, free to spend time in customary practices and ritual performances "telling" other men what his symbolic invention is all about.

Don't knock the mystical, the transcendental, or the arbitrary. In recent years cognitive scientists have advanced our understanding of the type of ideas underlying nonrational action, and it has become more and more apparent that language, thought, and society are built up out of ideas that fall beyond the sweep of logical and scientific evaluation, ideas for which there are no universally binding normative criteria.

One line of research on nonrational ideas focuses on so-called frames, paradigms, absolute presuppositions, or constitutive premises (see, e.g., Benedict 1946; Collingwood 1972; Dumont 1970; Evans-Pritchard 1937; Kuhn 1962; Mehan & Wood 1975; Schutz 1967; Wittgenstein 1969). As is well known, philosophers have traditionally classified statements (announcing ideas) along two cross-cutting dichotomous axes: *analytic* versus *synthetic* (statements about language vs. statements about the world – "a bachelor is an unmarried male" vs. "the cat is on the mat") and *a posteriori* versus *a priori* (statements whose validity can be established only by experience or evidence vs. statements whose validity can be established without reference to experience or evidence). Thus, we have four types. The two easier types are the *synthetic a posteriori* (or what empirical scientists know as "hypotheses" or "laws of nature") and the *analytic a priori* (or what logicians know as definitions, syllogisms, and tautologies), although the integrity of even these easier types has come under question (e.g., Goodman 1972b; Quine 1953). The two difficult types are the *analytic a posteriori* (a statement about language whose validity can be established only by reference to experience) and the *synthetic a priori* (a statement about the world whose validity can be established without reference to experience). Romantics deny the existence of *synthetic a priori* statements; they reclassify such statements as frames, paradigms, or constitutive presuppositions.

A frame, paradigm, or absolute presupposition is a statement about the world whose validity can be neither confirmed nor disconfirmed. A frame violates no empirical evidence, nor is it dictated by any evidence. A frame violates no principle of logic nor does it follow from logic. The litmus test of a frame is that no evidence or experience can possibly count as disproof. "People have souls and they transmigrate." "Fetuses have souls possessed of infinite value." "God blesses men in the sign of their prosperity." "Man's only motive is to maximize pleasure and minimize pain." One either supposes these particular presuppositions and comprehends the world in their terms or one doesn't – and if one person supposes and another doesn't, there is little of a rational sort for them to say to each other. Presuppositions may have been banished from the grammar of positivism but not from the mind of man.

Cultural diversity as "frame switching" is a classic idea within cognitive anthropology. Forty-seven years ago Evans-Pritchard (1937) examined the presuppositions underlying Azande oracular practices and witchcraft beliefs. A presupposition here, a presupposition there, and before he knew it, Evans-Pritchard was off poisoning chickens – and it all seemed so plausible. Ten years later, Benedict (1946) "framed" Japanese conduct in World War II in Japanese terms. The lack of respect for national sovereignty (e.g., the attack on Pearl Harbor), the suicide bombings, the "mistreatment" of American prisoners of war, all were placed in a presuppositional framework (the Japanese belief in the advantages of "taking one's proper place" in a domestic, national, and international hierarchy of individuals, groups and nations), a framework within which "militaristic expansionism" gets redescribed as the obvious remedy for international anarchy, and the "atrocities" of the prison camps are perceived instead as a valorous contempt for materialism. More recent attempts at framing have focused on Indian views of hierarchy (Dumont 1970), Balinese, Ilongot, and Oriya concepts of the person (Geertz 1973, 1975, and Chapter 4, this volume; Rosaldo, Chapter 5, this volume; Shweder & Bourne, Chapter 6, this volume), modern Western conceptualizations of "madness" (Foucault 1967), and even American ideas of kinship (Schneider 1968). For example, the Balinese, according to Geertz (Chapter 4, this volume) dramatically subordinate their individuality to their social role. "Physically men come and go – mere incidents in a happenstance history of no genuine importance, even to themselves. But the masks they wear, the stage they occupy, the parts they play, and most important the spectacle they mount remain and constitute not the facade but the substance of things, not least the self."

Society – are its building blocks individuals or social roles? Social roles – are they a facade or the substance of self? Justice – should it be to each according to his needs, to each according to his work, to each according to his effort, or perhaps to each according to his "purity" (see Dumont 1970; Perelman 1963). At certain points in a cognitive structure the dictates of logic and science give scant guidance, yet a choice between "frames" must be made (see Rosaldo, Chapter 5, and Shweder & Bourne, Chapter 6, this volume).

As far as I know no one has yet begun to compile a list of all the ideas, principles, and themes that are beyond the reach of deductive and inductive logic. Nevertheless, within the philosophical literature, one can find provocative skeptical warnings about the arbitrariness and nonrationality of such fundamental "world making" principles as similarity, causation, and utility (e.g., Goodman 1972, 1978; MacIntyre, 1981): We may well live in a world where from a logical point of view all things are equally alike and equally different, a world where all previous events are necessary and none is sufficient to cause a subsequent event, a world where the best logical advice you can give a friend is that if you don't know where you are going almost any road will take you there. Within the social-science literature one suspects that logical and evidential claims have little relevance when it comes to such society-making questions as who is entitled to protection from harm (the problem of personhood), what's me versus what's not me (the problem of personal boundaries and the territories of the self), how should life's burdens and benefits be distributed (the problem of hierarchy), which has precedence – what I want to do or what the group wants me to do (the problem of the state), and other questions – some of which I shall list later.

A second line of research on nonrational ideas focuses on the so-called illocutionary force of communicative acts (see Austin 1962; Lyons 1977:725–45; Searle 1967, 1969, 1979). The notion of illocutionary force can be ostensibly defined as the status of a communication, as, for example, a warning, a command, an apology, a criticism, a request, a promise, an exhortation (Lyons 1977:731). "Illocutionary force" is to be distinguished, on the one hand, from "perlocutionary force," the consequence or effect on a particular listener of a communication (e.g., making John angry by means of a "command") and, on the other hand, from "locutionary force," the propositional or descriptive content of the communication (e.g., that John will leave the room).

All real-world communications have an explicit or tacit illocutionary force; thus, "Go to your room" (uttered under the "right" circumstances) communicates and permits the explicit expansion "I 'order' you to go to your room."

Propositionally equivalent communications are not necessarily equivalent in "illocutionary force." Thus, "Will John leave the room?" and "John, leave the room!" share a propositional content (that John will leave the room), yet one is a "question," the other an "order."

Many varieties of "illocutionary" acts have been lexicalized as English verbs, for example, promise, state, comment, warn, apologize, define, beg, plead, exhort, congratulate, question, command (Searle 1967).

There are hundreds, possibly thousands, of illocutionary acts routinely performed in any of the languages of man. Searle (1979), having undertaken an informal factor analysis of the English corpus, has reduced illocutionary acts to five global types: assertives, directives, commissives, expressives, and declarations. Apparently, natural languages have evolved to do a lot more than merely report information about the world (the assertive function). What ordinary talk aims to do is various, but, among other things, ordinary language labels and descriptions tell you what you ought to do (the directive function) and how you ought to feel (the emotive function). Ordinary language descriptions are "conclusion-tending," which is why the predicate "mother" is sometimes inadmissible as a descriptor at a child custody hearing. The term does not simply point or refer.

Especially relevant to the present discussion is the distinction between "assertives" and "declarations." The "assertive" is the speech act of the enlightenment man of science: to "explain," to "assert," to "describe," to "hypothesize." The purpose of an "assertive" is to commit the speaker (in varying degrees) to something being the case, "to the truth of the expressed proposition" (Searle 1979:12). Assertives express beliefs. Accurate representation of the world is their aim. They invite evaluation in terms of rational criteria, the canons of logic and evidence.

"Declarations," on the other hand, are nonrational. They are the constitutive speech act of the romantic: to "define," to "appoint," to "bequeath," to "dub," to "christen." "Declarations bring about some alteration in the state or condition of the referred to object . . . solely in virtue of the fact that the declaration has been successfully performed" (Searle 1979:17). In other words "declarations" ("I dub thee Sir John"; "You're fired!") performed in conventionally appropriate ways create a reality. Representation is not their goal. They have no truth value; they are neither true nor false. They are used to make something the case rather than to report that something is (or is not) the case. The nonrational may have been banished from the grammar of positivism but not from the languages of man.

A third line of research on nonrational ideas addresses the question: "Why do we classify things the way we do?" One answer states that "if we acknowledge the empirical existence of classes of similar objects, it means that we are attaching non-uniform importance to various predicates, and that this weighting has an *extra logical* origin" (Watanabe 1969:376, my emphasis; also see Goodman 1968, 1972c). In other words, equally rational and experienced observers need not be led by their experiences or by logic to the same classification of the world. J. L. Borges, poet, quotes an ancient Chinese encyclopedia where it is written that:

> Animals are divided into: (a) belonging to the emperor, (b) embalmed, (c) tame, (d) sucking pigs, (e) sirens, (f) fabulous, (g) stray dogs, (h) included in the present classification, (i) frenzied, (j) innumerable, (k) drawn with a very fine camel hair brush, (l) *et cetera*, (m) having just broken the water pitcher, (n) that from a long way off look like flies.

This dizzying (and evocative) passage has gripped the mind of two leading cognitivists, Michael Foucault (1973) and Elinor Rosch (1978). For Rosch (at the time an enlightenment figure), the most interesting thing about the classification "is that it does not exist." For Foucault, the ancient Chinese scheme "disturbed" his mind, threatening a collapse of the distinction between the same and the different. A troubling thought – the shattering of the idea of an objectively given universal order to things – entered Foucault's Gallic mind.

> When we establish a considered classification, when we say that a cat and a dog resemble each other less than two greyhounds do, even if both [the cat and the dog] are tame or embalmed, even if both are frenzied, even if both have just broken the water pitcher, what is the ground on which we are able to establish the validity of this classification with complete certainty? On what "table,"

according to what grid of identities, similitudes, analogies, have we become accustomed to sort out so many different and similar things? What is this coherence – which, as is immediately apparent, is neither determined by an *a priori* and necessary concatenation, nor imposed on us by immediately perceptible contents? (Foucault 1973:xix)

For Foucault (1973:xvi–xvii), the Frenchman, there is a haunting, "monstrous" quality to the ancient scheme. "The animals (i) frenzied, (j) innumerable, (k) drawn with a very fine camel hair brush–where could they ever meet, except in the immaterial sound of the voice pronouncing their enumeration, or on the page transcribing it? Where else could they be juxtaposed except in the non-place of language?"

Foucault's reaction is not the reaction of the romantic. For the romantic, the opposite of the "objectively given" is not the "monstrous" but the "arbitrary" (nonrational, extralogical); and the "immaterial sound of the voice" and "non-place of language" are not alien to the real world, but rather constitutive elements in the organization of diverse realit*ies*.

Whorf's (1956:55, 214–15, 252) view is a classic romantic formulation. There is no ideal or unitary pattern of relative likeness and difference frozen into reality waiting to be discovered. The object world, as it presents itself, is "kaleidoscopic." It must be organized by our minds. To learn a language is first of all to learn which classification to impose on the object world. Logically, any classification is possible. None is better or worse except for some special purpose of man.

In recent years a neo-Whorfian-type view has been advanced by Goodman (1968, 1972a, 1972c) and Watanabe (1969:376–88; also see Shweder & Miller, in press). Goodman attacks the image of a unitary world (the world is many not one, he argues) and introduces a principle of logical equidistance among objects. The flavor of his argument is captured in the following remark.

"To make a faithful picture [representation], come as close as possible to copying the object as it is." This simple-minded injunction baffles me; for the object before me is a man, a swarm of atoms, a complex of cells, a fiddler, a friend, a fool and much more. If none of these constitute the object just as it is, then none is *the* way the object is. I cannot copy all these at once; and the more nearly I succeeded, the less would the result be a realistic picture. (1968:6)

Goodman's principle of logical equidistance among objects states that "any two things have exactly as many properties in common as any other two" (1972c:443). Indeed, Watanabe (1969:376–9) provides a formal proof that, insofar as all properties have the same weight, "there exists no such thing as a class of similar objects in the world." One implication of the proof is that, from a *logical* point of view, a dog and a cat are just as similar as two greyhounds! As Foucault dreaded, our classifications seem to be determined neither by logic nor by "immediately perceptible contents."

Where do our classifications come from? What are we left with after we reject both the "innocent eye" (i.e., "we classify things as we do because that's the way things are"; characterization borrowed from Volney Stefflre, personal communication) and the "absolute given" (i.e., we classify things the way we do because that's what reason dictates; characterization borrowed from Goodman 1968)? What we are left with is "culture," a nonrational, extralogical, arbitrary partitioning of the world that is "framed," talked about, acted upon, even labeled and is handed over from one generation to the next. An "uncle" – well, that's your parent's brother *or* your parent's sister's husband. "Food" – well, you can eat rabbits and sheep but not dogs or horses. Could logic or science have told us that? For the romantic, ideas, at their limit, are without *rational* foundation; and the way the world "really is" varies by "frame." Thus, for a romantic, it is meaningless to ask, for example, "is abortion right or wrong"; the meaningful question is "Within what frame is abortion right and within what frame is abortion wrong?" In the world of the romantic objects are not classified together because they are truly more alike than others; quite the contrary, the romantic argues: objects seem more alike because they have been classified together (Goodman 1972c). And why have these particular objects been classified together? To understand that, the romantic will retort, is to understand something quite different from logic and science. It is to understand the customary, the traditional, the symbolic, the expressive, the semiotic.

The most significant romantic development to emerge within cognitive anthropology during the past twenty years is perhaps the definition of culture as arbitrary code (see, e.g., D'Andrade & Romney 1964). Whereas enlightenment figures within cognitive anthropology certainly study the ideas of exotic peoples, their emphasis is on rational, scientific, and quasi-scientific "knowledge structures" and underlying intellectual processes. But it is the romantic within cognitive anthropology who studies "Culture" (with a capital C). "Religion *as a Cultural System*," "Ideology *as a Cultural System*," "Common-Sense as a Cultural System" (Geertz 1973); American Kinship: A Cultural Account (Schneider 1968);" Culture and Practical Reason (Sahlins 1976); The Forest of Symbols (Turner 1967); these well-known and influential studies argue for a "symbolic" anthropology, an anthropology primarily concerned with nonrational ideas (presuppositions, cultural definitions, declarations, arbitrary classifications) and their verbal and nonverbal means of expression. Indeed, the main idea of a symbolic anthropology is that much of our action "says something" about what we stand for and stands for our nonrational constructions of reality.

An expressive symbol is anything that "stands for" or says something about something else. It can be an object: a piece of cloth, the national emblem. It can be a physical disturbance: a pattern of sound, a word. It can be a movement: a gesture, bowing low. Expressive symbols are frequently subdivided, following Peirce (1955), into three main types: symbols per se, icons, and indexes. The properties of a pure symbol are said to bear no intrinsic (or causal) relationship to the properties of their referents (e.g., "microorganism," a long word, refers to a small thing), whereas "icons" are said to resemble their referents ("height" as a symbol of "authority") and "indexes" are said to be the cause, consequence, or co-occurrent of their referents (e.g., "calloused hands" as an indicator that someone is a "laborer").

It seems doubtful that categorical distinctions among expressive symbols can be sustained on these grounds, especially given Goodman's (1968, 1972a, 1972b, 1972c) analyses of the arbitrariness of judgments of resemblance and co-occurrence. What does seem clear is that expressive symbols can be arranged along a continuum: Expressive symbols differ in how easy it is to learn to "read" or interpret them. There are some expressive symbols we just seem to know how to "read" (we know what's being mentioned) and little training is necessary (e.g., any child can "read" facial expressions for "happy," "sad," and "mad," and everybody somehow "knows" that "up" stands for "authority" and that intensity of pitch does not indicate "calm"). Other expressive symbols remain inchoate except to those who, through hints, demonstrations, or instruction, are "let in" on the code (how else could we know what the sounds of a language are all "about" or that a sideways headshake means "no").

As important as the distinction between types of expressive symbols is the distinction between the "expressive" function versus the "instrumental" function of actions (Parsons 1968). As noted earlier, expressive-symbolic acts are ways of saying something about arbitrary constructions of reality, constructions of reality not dictated by logic or science. Instrumental acts, in contrast, are rationally efficient ways to accomplish practical objectives. Sleeping is an instrumental activity. Sleeping alone in a room of one's own with the door firmly shut is an expressive activity communicating a good deal about our culture's nonrational commitment to individuality, autonomy, and privacy. Eating is an instrumental activity. Inquiring of a 3-year-old "what would you like to eat for dinner tonight?" is an expressive-symbolic act communicating in yet another redundant way our culture's nonrational commitment to individuality, autonomy, and privacy.

A major contribution of a romantic (e.g., symbolic) approach is the view that the conceptual underpinnings of a social order are (ultimately) nonrational and that many of the customary practices of a society – from table manners (Elias 1978) and dress codes (Sahlins 1976) to child training practices (Shweder & Bourne, Chapter 6, this volume) and techniques of punishment (Foucault 1979) – are symbolic expressions of those nonrational choices.

As noted earlier, social life demands an answer to certain existential questions that neither logic nor science can provide. Does the group have authority over the individual? From where does that authority derive? Is the "will of the group" a mere aggregation of individual wills (hence, tally up a vote), or is it greater than the sum of the parts (hence, understood only by great leaders)? Is it "normal" to be self-sufficient or interdependent? What justifies the unequal distribution of life's pleasures? How should burdens and benefits be distributed? To each according to his work? To each according to his needs? To each equally? What's me (private) and what's not me (public)? To whom shall "rights" be granted? To male adults? To women? To children? To dogs? To the insane? To the elderly? To a fetus? To a sperm?

A social order is a design for living built up (or down) out of answers to questions such as those. Neither reason nor reality dictates a unique reply – and, indeed, men have differed in their answers to such questions. Nevertheless, the answers given by any society are written all over customary practice. How and what we eat symbolizes our differences from both animals (no "farting" at the table) and other social groups (no pork at the table). What we wear (wool vs. silk, blue collar vs. white collar) is a veritable language for expressing position (gender, occupational status, personality) in an elaborate social scheme while simultaneously announcing that social scheme and schemingly perpetuating it (Sahlins 1976). How we treat our children (early separation from bed, body, and breast of mother) communicates to our children what it is to be an (American) person (autonomous, individual, and private). Indeed, if we follow Foucault (1979:24) and rid ourselves of the instrumental "illusion that penalty is above all a means of reducing crime," we can begin to interpret modes of punishment (e.g., public beatings vs. private confinement) as expressive rituals, ways of saying things with action about our arbitrary views of responsibility, obligation, self-control, and personhood.

A good deal follows from the idea of the "arbitrary" or "nonrational." To be a romantic is to be anti-normative. It is to be suspicious of the concept of "progress." That's not to say the romantic is an anarchist – clearly there are rules to any game, and any "frame" has its own "internal" standards. If one wants to produce a pattern of sound intelligible as a sentence "in Chinese," one is up against some very stiff constraints – and certainly not any markings on a piece of canvas will count as a work of cubism, let alone a fine work of cubism. For the romantic, the idea of development is equated with the idea of skill or competence and to be skillful or competent is to be a master at functioning with the rules of the game.

The romantic's anti-normative point is that there are no standards worthy of universal respect dictating what to think or how to act. From the perspective of the romantic, to ask what is the proper way to classify the world, to ask what *the* world is like, to ask what is the proper way to design a society and so on, is like asking what is the proper food of man or what is the best language to speak! Consequently, the romantic is prone to explain ideational change by analogy to the "expressive" worlds of fashion, aesthetics, and philology, worlds in which change is rarely directional and questions of progress do not typically arise. In the world of fashion, older styles become obsolete only to be renewed. In the world of aesthetics, older modes of expression do not become obsolete. The old (realism) and the new (cubism) coexist as equally valid forms of expression (Goodman 1978). In the world of words and their meanings, older usages do disappear, but the new terms and usages that replace them are just different, not better. The concept of progress is not necessarily applicable to all instances of ideational change (see Shweder 1980b).

The whole thrust of romantic thinking is to defend the coequality of fundamentally different "frames" of understanding. The concept of nonrationality, the idea of the "arbitrary" frees some portion of man's mind from the universal dictates of logic and science, permitting diversity while leaving man free to choose among irreconcilable presuppositions, schemes of classification, and ideas of worth. Indeed, one crude but salvageable indicator of a nonrational idea is the persistence over time of diversity, the ability of each of several persistent yet incompatible frames to "handle" any and all new evidence and the fact that "facts" don't seem to alter anyone's ideas or practices. When capital punishment turns out to be "right" (or "wrong") regardless of whether (or not) it deters crime, when brother-sister incest turns out to be "wrong" regardless of whether (or not) mutant offspring are produced, when corporations continue to use interviews to select employees regardless of whether (or not) interviews help them predict job performance, in short when there seems to be more at issue than getting the facts straight, that more that is at issue is probably a matter of nonrational framing.

Yet, to raise the specter of irreconcilable disagreement is to accept the empirical challenge of documenting cultural differences and explicating their internal rules of coherence. For this reason, the romantic is interested primarily in the content of man's thought – the specific presuppositions, values, and schemes of classification communicated by specific people to other specific people on specific occasions. Members of a common culture know each other not by the deep structures or hypothesized processes underlying their thoughts but rather by the surface content of what they say and do to each other in the here and now. The more we attend to surface content, the less common is the culture of man.

Finally, romanticism tends to a view of the acquisition of ideas as communication (either tacit or explicit). That which is obvious to reason does not have to be communicated; anyone can "figure out" for himself that a whole is greater than any of its parts. That which is obvious to the senses does not have to be communicated; anyone can "see" for himself that if you cut yourself with a knife you'll bleed (see

Shweder, Turiel, & Much 1980). But the nonrational suppositions, ideas about worth, and classifications of a people (a cousin is a person not to marry; a pig is an animal not to eat; a mother's sister's husband is an "uncle"; members of a family eat together at the same time and food gets distributed equally) are not derivable from reason or direct experience with nature – one must, somehow, be "let in" on the secret, one must, somehow, receive the "frame" of understanding from others. In the study of the history of ideas this anti-developmental view leads the romantic to a concern for procedures of indoctrination and conversion into paradigms of thought (Kuhn 1962). In the study of the ontogeny of ideas in children it leads the romantic to a concern for the acquisition of ideas as tacit communication.

Socialization as tacit communication: standing Piaget on his head

For twenty years Piaget (1954, 1967; Inhelder & Piaget 1958) has been the preeminent figure among those who study children's minds – his enlightenment assumptions have dominated the cognitive "developmental" field. Basically, Piaget accepts the Tylorian-Frazerian view of man as intendedly rational and scientific, striving to figure out what causes what in the world, striving to adapt or accommodate intelligence to the demands of common reality, striving for consistency among ideas, striving to build up or "construct" a set of canons (rules of logic, principles of scientific method) for regulating one's own thought and for deciding whether a piece of one's own thinking is successful or unsuccessful.

According to Piaget, the mind of the child grows in stagelike fashion, moving from early concrete, undifferentiated context-bound thinking to later abstract, differentiated, generalized thinking. The immature mind clings to surface content; the mature mind, content-free, abstracts deep structure.

Young children are said to be concrete in that they emphasize the particularizing differences between objects (overlooking their underlying likenessess). Young children are said to be undifferentiated in that they merge categories, failing to distinguish the perspective of the self from the perspective of others (egocentrism), the necessary from the contingent (preoperational thinking), and intentions from consequences (percept-driven thought). Thus, according to Piaget, children before the age of 18 months are so bound to their own personal perspective and the particular spatiotemporal context of a stimulus that they fail to comprehend the abstract idea that an "object" has both "constancy" across changes in spatial and temporal location and "permanence" regardless of whether or not it is being perceived at any moment. For the young child, according to Piaget, out of sight means out of existence, and to move an object from one place to another is to create a new object. Similarly, according to Piaget, children under 6 or 7 years of age fail to understand the abstract ideas of "number," "mass," and "substance." Thus, for example, for six or seven years, children do not recognize that the amount of clay on a tray must of necessity remain constant despite contingent manipulations and transformations of its surface appearance and shape.

By adolescence, according to Piaget, the child abstracts invariances, freeing himself of surface content, freeing himself of the concrete spatiotemporal manifestations of objects. The apple sold by Mr. Jones in a store in the afternoon is recognized as the same apple that Mrs. Jones picked off the tree in the morning. The quantity of soup in one's short, fat bowl is not thought to change when poured into a tall, thin storage container. The dinner table viewed from Dad's seat may look to the "eye" different from the table viewed from the child's seat, but the adolescent "mind" knows it's the same table. Indeed, the adolescent mind is so abstracted from the particularizing surface texture of experience that objects and events can be abstractly represented and manipulated as p's and q's and hypothetical objects can be located in imaginary worlds.

According to Piaget, this transition from concrete, percept-driven, stimulus-bound thinking to abstract, generalized thinking is a process of *self*-construction in which the child slowly gains veridical knowledge of the world and slowly builds up more and more adequate canons for reasoning (e.g., the propositional calculus) and experimentation with the world (e.g., Mill's laws of agreement and difference). Through self-reflection, reason, and direct experience the child constructs a body of abstract knowledge and a system of logico-scientific rules adapted for his dealings with reality.

This is not the place to assess Piaget's stage theory of intellectual growth. The degree of (a) availability and (b) accessibility to children and adults of abstract ideas (e.g., "number") and proper generalized canons of reasoning (e.g., the propositional calculus) is under intense investigation by cognitive scientists (e.g., Brainerd 1978a and b; Cole et al. 1981; Gelman 1978; Gelman & Baillargeon 1983; Mehler & Bever 1967; Much & Shweder 1978; Nucci & Turiel 1978; Pool, Shweder, & Much 1981; Simon & Hayes 1976; Turiel 1979; Wason & Johnson-Laird 1972). Suffice it to say that two types of objections to Piaget have grown up in the recent cognitive developmental literature. First, the idea that children or adults are characteristically preoperational, concrete operational, or formal operational has taken a beating. If one examines the actual cognitive functioning of individuals across a series of tasks or problems one discovers that no single operational level is a general property of an individual's thought (e.g., Brainerd 1978a, 1978b; Flavell 1982; Roberge & Flexer 1979; Siegler 1981; Wason & Johnson-Laird 1972). Second, it appears that Piaget seriously underestimated the operational capacity of young children (2- to 6-year-olds). Recent evidence suggests that most mental structures are *available* to the mind of the 5-year-old child and may well be available earlier (e.g., Bullock & Gelman 1979; Goldberg, Perlmutter, & Myers 1974; Lempers, Flavell, & Flavell 1977; MacNamara, Baker, & Olson 1976; Mehler & Bever 1967; Much & Shweder 1978; Nucci & Turiel 1978; Shatz & Gelman 1973; Trabasso 1975). See Shweder (1982d) and Gelman and Baillargeon (1983) for critical reviews. The evidence suggests a strong tendency, even among adults, for human problem-solving procedures to be local and content-specific rather than abstract and general. Experimental findings show that small changes in the surface content of various cognitive tasks result in large changes in performance (see D'Andrade 1981). One disconcerting consequence of this fact is that an experimenter can demonstrate by clever manipulation of surface content either the absence of logical thinking in an adult or the presence of logical thinking in a 3-year-old! The experimental results suggest that the mind of man has difficulty learning and generalizing "deep structural" principles of deductive and inductive reasoning. Normal, intelligent adults seem less successful at constructing abstract (content-free) canons of proper reasoning than Piaget supposed, and many of the canons said by Piaget to be totally unavailable to the young child seem to surface in certain concrete contexts.

I suspect that Piaget is wrong in his view of the way logico-scientific thinking emerges in the child. However, what seems most remarkable to cognitive anthropologists observing the field of cognitive psychology is not that Piaget may be wrong but rather that Piaget's enlightenment approach has led most cognitive psychologists to overlook most of the things about children's minds of interest to the romantic. The development of rationality is not all there is to the emergence of thought. Indeed, it is quite revealing to simply invert each of Piaget's key assumptions about the ontogeny of understanding. Stand Piaget on his head and what one's got is "conversational pragmatics," or the socialization of cultural codes (see Ochs and Schieffelin, Chapter 11, this volume).

INVERSION 1: FROM SELF-CONSTRUCTED KNOWLEDGE TO
OTHER-DEPENDENT LEARNING

Piaget conceives of knowledge as an "individual invention" (1970:117). The mind of the infant confronts the practical exigencies of reality. Through a dialectical process of analogical extension (what Piaget calls "assimilation," i.e., treating the unfamiliar as if it were familiar – a rock as if it were a nipple), hypothesis revision (what Piaget calls "accommodation," i.e., a rock cannot be sucked; hence, a rock is not a nipple), and reflective abstraction, the child, over many years, constructs for himself or herself a valid body of knowledge and an adequate set of logical and scientific canons. Each boy and girl figures things out for himself or herself. It's as if each generation, indeed each individual, reconstructed the rules of thought anew. Piaget's theory is a "rediscovering the wheel" theory of cognitive development.

The inverse of Piaget's image of self-constructed knowledge is "other-dependent learning" (D'Andrade 1980). As D'Andrade notes, much that we know is learned from other people. The teaching by others can be formal, but it's usually informal. The teaching can be intended, but it's usually unintended. The teaching can be explicit step-by-step instruction, but more typically it relies on powerful hints and occasional correction. D'Andrade argues that "people are very good at discovering what they must learn under conditions of informally guided discovery, and not so good when they must learn entirely on their own."

D'Andrade describes some experiments conducted by Eisenstadt and Kareev on cognitive processing in the games of Go and Gomoku. College students were taught the rules of the game and then played a computer which could be beaten, but only if one was able to induce winning strategies or patterns (e.g., block "double-threes," set up "double-twos"). The college students played long and hard. They were highly motivated, and they were encouraged when they lost to "look-back-and-see-what-went-wrong-and-replay-from-there." Yet these motivated, bright college students performed miserably. In Gomoku they won less than 20% of their games. What was most striking to D'Andrade was that the experimenters, indeed all the people in the experimental lab, were very good at beating the computer. Somehow *they* knew the winning patterns, which the students rarely induced for themselves.

Noting that "abstracting patterns is not so easy to do by oneself," D'Andrade continues:

> But notice that most of the laboratory people did not have to learn everything by themselves. They talked to each other, had a terminology for the different kinds of winning patterns, and formed an effective social and cultural group. Thus they learned about Go and Gomoku the way most people learn most things– you try some of it by yourself, and other people – i.e., the cultural information pool – help by giving occasional procedural advice and crucial instruction in classifications when you get stuck.
>
> The point is that it is easy to overlook the way a small amount of guidance can drastically affect the success and direction of the learning process. (1980:186)

INVERSION 2: FROM RATIONAL MAN TO NONRATIONAL MAN

Piaget views the mind of man (and thus children's minds) as intendedly rational. Because the "objective" world insists that we think straight and induce correctly, rational adaptation to reality requires, according to Piaget, some knowledge of the proper dictates of reason and the regularities of nature. Thus, Piaget directs our attention to the child's emerging knowledge of canons of deductive and inductive inference, laws of motion, concepts of number, speed, mass, and so on. Undoubtedly, Piaget is correct. There are canons of reason worthy of universal respect (e.g., all A's are B's; A; therefore B), and regularities of nature are there for any rational person to see (e.g., a finger, cut deeply with a knife, bleeds). Piaget is undoubtedly correct but terribly incomplete. There's a lot more in the mind of man than logic and natural science.

What Piaget overlooks is the nonrational. Someone who only read the Piagetian literature would never guess that every child is immersed in a "framed" universe made up of distinctive constitutive presuppositions, customs, traditions, expressive rituals, and arbitrary classifications, and that somehow the expressive symbols and nonrational ideas of one generation are rapidly becoming part of the emerging sense of self of the younger generation. Just listen to American 4-year-olds talking to each other in a nursery school setting. Here are two excerpts from Much and Shweder (1978).

Excerpt 1: The inviolate body

Some nursery school children have gotten their clothes wet and are changing into extra pairs of trousers kept by the school. They are in a dressing area with a double door that opens separately above and below. Gary, Abel, and Edith stand around the open top half of the door. Edith stands on a chair looking through the door. Gary and Abel peek over the top.

Vickie: You silly dummies . . . you're all peeking. We're still getting dressed.
Teacher (approaching): What's wrong? Are you changing clothes?
Vickie: Yes.
[Teacher closes the door]
Edith (to Gary): Keep that locked. Now don't open it.
Vickie: Don't look, now, don't look!

Excerpt 2: Clothes make the man

Gary (to Sam): Why do you always dress up the same?
Sam: Uh-uh.
Gary: You always dress up in that.
Sam: No, sometimes I wear blue.

What these children know about privacy, autonomy, and self-presentation is neither natural nor logical – and it certainly was not self-constructed. These children have been "let in" on the received wisdom of their symbolic community – and the received wisdom they have been "let in" on is less wisdom and more arbitrary code. Piaget's intendedly rational child would never be caught talking the conventional nonsense offered by Vickie and Gary.

The Piagetian child is a faint copy of the abstract ideal of the logician and empirical scientist. His deep structural knowledge is content-free. He has no particular culture. He has no particular language. He has no distinctive personal identity. He has no concern for those existential questions of life (see earlier) for which there can be only arbitrary (and hence variable) answers. Dress codes, food taboos, sexuality, terms of address, hairstyle, social classifications, privacy, and personhood; – the mind of the Piagetian child is devoid of temperament, tradition, custom, or convention. To invert Piaget's passion for detached rationality into an objective romantic interest in the nonrational is to pose the content-rich question: What is it that makes the American child so American, and how is it that a very young child becomes so American so quickly?

INVERSION 3: FROM PROGRESSIVE DEVELOPMENT TO FRAME SWITCHING

It is Piaget's view that a child's earlier forms of understanding are deficient and are replaced by newer and more adequate forms of understanding. Just as pre-Copernican astronomy is replaced by post-Copernican astronomy, preoperational thinking is replaced by concrete operational thinking only to be replaced again by formal operational thinking. The image is one of progress and advance.

This image of progressive development seems best suited to rational-scientific domains. A universally valid normative model (e.g., Mill's laws of agreement and difference, rules of proper syllogistic reasoning) can be readily converted into a yardstick for comparing various forms of understanding and judging their relative worth. Logico-scientific thinking can do everything magical thinking can do plus more.

The image of progressive development begins to break down, however, as one moves from rational domains of understanding to nonrational domains. In nonrational domains of thought (e.g., kinship classification, friendship concepts, principles of justice, ideas about the meaning of dreams, concepts of personhood, animistic vs. mechanistic metaphors), there are no universally valid standards for judging the adequacy of ideas, and older forms of understanding are not necessarily deficient. For the nonrational domains of understanding there is no universal direction to change and the notion of progress is difficult to apply. It is for these nonrational domains that models for explaining "change" might well be drawn from the worlds of fashion, aesthetics, and philology (see earlier). Old forms of nonrational understanding are just different, not worse. To move from cubism to abstract expressionism is not to abandon an earlier, less adequate mode of expression. It is merely to switch "frames."

Nonrational ideas cannot be scaled in terms of comparative adequacy. Those who believe that blood is thicker than water are obviously different from those who prefer their friends to their kin. Those for whom dreams give access to the numinous realm of the soul and its wanderings are obviously different from those for whom dreams are "unreal." Those who equate "cousins" and "siblings" are obviously different from those who distinguish "brother" from "father's brother's son." Those who empathize with "starving Armenians" are obviously different from those who "take the heads" of their neighbors. Those for whom justice means "to each according to his accomplishments" are obviously different from those for whom justice means "to each according to his needs." Those for whom a fetus is a "person" are obviously different from those for whom a fetus is a fetus. Those for whom the unveiled face of a woman is a sin are obviously different from those for whom the veiled face of a woman is a shame. Those who have three gods and one wife are obviously different from those who have one god and three wives. But, is there really a criterion worthy of universal respect that ranks any of these beliefs the more rational or advanced? To the extent there is no rational way to choose, choice becomes enculturation, and to change beliefs is to have been indoctrinated into the ways of whatever new subculture one happened to encounter.

For example, many years ago Margaret Mead (1932) demonstrated that animistic thinking (e.g., attributing intentionality and responsibility to inanimate objects; treating natural forces as if they were human) could not be consistently dated to immature stages in ontogeny. There seemed to be no overall direction to ideational changes from animism to "realism" or from "realism" to animism. Among Americans, children are more animistic than adults (although one subclass of Americans, natural scientists, seem quite prone to personification). However, among the Manus of New Guinea, it is the adults who are the animists; children are dreary realists. For American adults, animistic thinking is a "frame" of understanding thought to be appropriate for children and hence tolerated, even encouraged, in the young. In Manus, animism is the adult "frame" (it apparently serves them well enough) and access to this "frame" is deliberately withheld from uninitiated youth.

More recently, Higgins and Parsons (1983) have explained social and cognitive shifts in childhood as the history of the child's sequential experiences with the demands of relatively distinct subcultures (home, classroom, peer group). Thus, for example, in the face of evidence that older American children are more skillful than younger children on certain referential communication tasks, Higgins and Parsons remind us that the subculture of the young child (home) places a premium "on social relationship goals relative to information transmission goals," whereas the opposite is true for older children. To grow up is not necessarily to become more and more rational. To grow up is just as often to enter a new "'frame' of mind."

There are other ways to invert Piaget's conception of mind. I won't have much to say about any of these inversions on this occasion, but I will, at least, mention two promising reversals.

INVERSION 4: FROM PERSONAL CONSTRAINT TO INTERPERSONAL CONSTRAINT

It is by no means apparent that the individual mind, *left to its own devices*, seeks consistency or broad integration among ideas. For any individual, the development of a consistent, integrated, and generalized world view seems to be linked to various social or *inter*personal communicative processes, for example, having to defend one's views, anticipate objections from an audience or a "public," and having to argue or lecture. Converse's (1964) study of American political culture, for example, reveals that whereas the political values of congressmen and other political *spokes*men tended to line up along a neat liberal versus conservative dimension, the political values of the general population were quite fragmented and issue-specific (e.g., favoring government aid to schools but not to housing). The less one had to present, argue, and defend one's view, the less the pressure toward global integration.

INVERSION 5: FROM PERSONAL INVENTION TO COLLECTIVE REPRESENTATIONS

As Piaget himself notes (1970:116–117), any intellectual environment is packed with "already crystallized cultural products," collective representations of the world that have undergone long-term collective development. Unfortunately, Piaget does not trace the connections between these already regulated cognitive structures and individual cognitive functioning. Others have done this. Ward and Jenkins (1965), for example, in a study of correlational reasoning, present college students with contingency information about the relationship between cloud seeding and subsequent rainfall. When information is presented unaided by any collective representation, namely, serially "on a trial by trial basis, as it usually occurs in the real world," only 17% of college students display correlational reasoning. However, when the students are presented with summary information in the form of a 2 × 2 contingency table without prior trial-by-trial experience more than 50% display correlational thinking. Notice that a 2 × 2 contingency table is one of our collective representations. It is collective in the sense that no one of us invented it – it is part of our intellectual inheritance. It is a representation in the sense that it is a way of organizing and displaying correlational relevant information. And I might add that it is a rather powerful collective representational instrument. By displaying information in a visual form that makes it obvious that one should *compare* conditional probabilities in estimating a contingent relationship, the 2 × 2 table augments the thought processes of individuals who do not typically reason in a correlational way in other situations. Collective representations are often decisive for how individuals think.

Other-dependent learning, nonrational domains of understanding, "frame" switching, interpersonal constraints, collective representations – these five inversions of Piaget's enlightenment assumptions remind us that the child's emerging ideas are, to a great extent, transmitted to him (see Schwartz 1981). There are a lot of messages implicit in social discourse: messages about what to presuppose, what to value, what to feel, how to classify; messages about what it is to be a person,

how to relate to a group; messages about what is self-evident, what
can be taken for granted, and so on. The "language games" of American parent–child discourse redundantly transmit the thematic content
of American culture. A short list of such "language games" would
include: "You're old enough now to . . . ," "Let's make a deal,"
"What if everybody did that?" "What other people want counts,"
"Play by the rules," "If you don't look after yourself, who will?"
"What did you do in school today?" "I'd rather do it myself," "You
only live once," "Can he use your toy?" "It's mine – it's yours,"
"Did you have a nice time?" "And what's your opinion about . . . ,"
and "What do you want to eat for dinner?" While social-learning theorists have focused on rewards and punishments and Piagetians have
drawn our attention to the deep structural features of logico-scientific
reasoning, parents and children have been talking to each other about
the substantive nonrational issues of social life. Until recently (Much
& Shweder 1978; Ochs & Schieffelin, Chapter 11, this volume), these
routine conversations and conversational routines have hardly been
noticed by those studying children's minds. The field is ripe for a romantic rebellion.

Epilogue

The essay you have just read is very nearly a replica of the manuscript
presented at the Social Science Research Council on May 8, 1981, and
critiqued by Spiro in this volume. I have added a few paragraphs,
expanded upon some points, and clarified some formulations, but for
the most part the essay is as it was when, at that conference, Mel Spiro,
speaking for the "right" (or was it the "left"?), viewed the essay as
a romantic advocacy of relativism. Whereas David M. Schneider,
speaking for the "left" (or was it the "right"?) viewed it as an enlightenment invocation of universal categories. Too relativistic from
Spiro's enlightenment perspective; not relativistic enough from Schneider's romantic point of view. My first reaction was to feel reconfirmed
in my thesis that the divide between enlightenment and romantic assumptions is extant and deep among contemporary culture theorists.
My second reaction was to wonder what to make of the fact that my
essay had proved difficult to reliably classify as either enlightenment
or romantic. True, I had done a lot of taxonomizing and pigeonholing,
something romantics don't usually like, and I had argued that the distinction between what's rational, what's irrational, and what's nonrational is universally available to the human mind, an ahistorical claim
of the kind that romantics typically abhor. On the other hand, I had
argued for a pluralistic (vs. monistic) view of the mind, and at the same
time provided a principled foundation for the romantic notions that
realities are of our own making, that cultural practices are not necessarily or even typically adaptations to external environmental demands, and that what's in the culture of things is not necessarily a

dictate of natural law. Much to my surprise I found myself in the middle, in between two brilliant and admired critics and antagonists. I wondered about ways to bridge the gap.

Since the time of the conference, I have benefited from Spiro's enlightenment critique of my essay (Chapter 12, this volume) and other penetrating comments by friends and colleagues (see Notes). With these critiques in mind I would like to briefly reiterate, highlight, and clarify certain points in my argument.

I have argued that each generation, each century, indeed each millennium of social theorists has divided into two opposed camps, one advancing the image of man as intendedly rational, the other advancing an image of man as inevitably nonrational. Though divided, the two camps do address a common question: How are we to explain the apparent diversity of human ideas and practices, and what warrant is there for our own ideas and practices in the light of that apparent diversity?

That question, which might be called the problem of "natural law" (or rationality), is not a question that only experts or scholars address. Sorting out the relationship between one's own ideas and practices and the ideas and practices of others, deciding what's natural or rational and what isn't, deciding what's optional, conventional, or personal and what isn't – such investigation is a widespread, perhaps universal activity of the human mind – and it is done as much by children as by adults and as much by ordinary folks as by self-reflective social theorists. The answers to those questions, of course, differ widely, both historically and across cultures. Secularized, democratized, and individualized Western social scientists are more likely than many folks to expand the realm of what's personal, conventional, or merely a matter of culture and to narrow the realm of what's natural or required of any rational person by natural law (e.g., by logic or the Koran). Nevertheless, the basic terms of the relevant issues may well have remained the same across time and culture: what's rational, what's irrational, what's nonrational, what's universal, what's relative, and what develops. People differ in what they claim to be rational (irrational or nonrational), or universal (relative or developmental), not in whether they make claims about what's rational or universal.

My essay focuses upon the theories of experts. The advantage of this focus is that the theories of experts are often more explicit, self-reflective, and systematic than the theories of laymen. Whatever else experts in the social sciences do, one thing they do fairly well is reflect upon their own lay intuitions, explicate them, evaluate them, and eliminate from them kinks and inconsistencies. The grammar of the mind is often crystallized and made available through the self-reflections of expert social theorists.

There is, however, a disadvantage to focusing upon expert social theorists. Experts in the social sciences tend to be territorial, staking out for themselves one small cell in a larger matrix of possibilities. For

Type of mental process

		Enlightenment		Romantic
		Rational	Irrational	Nonrational
Emphasize likenesses	Universalism	Levi-Strauss Chomsky Berlin & Kay Structural anthropology	Tversky & Kahneman Nisbett & Ross	Eliade
	Developmentalism	? Simon Expert versus novice	Taylor Frazer Horton Piaget	? Cultured versus uncultured
Emphasize differences	Relativism	Malinowski Cole and Scribner Ethnoscience	Gorer Whiting Culture and personality	Levy-Bruhl Whorf Symbolic anthropology

What to do when comparing ideas

Figure 1.1. Matrix of possible interpretive approaches

many social theorists, staking is followed by imperialistic expansionism – the ambitious attempt to expand one's cell to include the whole matrix: everything's rational! nothing's rational! there are no universals! all differences are merely apparent! For other social theorists, staking is followed by fortification and boundary maintenance: the inglorious attempt to wall out anything not in one's cell, to ignore or even taboo all alien phenomena. Thus, some social theorists actually tend to label and identify themselves as "relativists" or "universalists" or "developmentalists," as though there were some special virtue in only studying the way things are different (or the way things are alike, etc.).

It seems to me misleading to imagine that one must choose, *in general*, between an enlightenment and a romantic view of the human mind. Looking backward, we should be grateful to social theorists, both ancient and modern, for having staked out and developed almost every one of the cells in the matrix of logically possible interpretations of cultural diversity (Figure 1.1). But now that the matrix has been worked out, we should feel free to explore all its possibilities. The human mind is tripartite – it has rational, irrational, and nonrational aspects; and, comparing our ideas to the ideas of others, we will always be able to find some ways in which our ideas are like the ideas of others (universalism) and some ways in which our ideas are different. Sometimes those differences will suggest progress (developmentalism) and often they will not (relativism). The task for the ethnographer is to decide what's rational, what's irrational and what's nonrational and to know when it makes sense to emphasize likeness, difference, or progress.

One limitation of my essay is that I focused upon the main diagonal of a larger matrix of possibilities (Figure 1.1), emphasizing the romantic route into relativism and the enlightenment route into universalism and developmentalism (Whorf, Levi-Strauss, and Piaget are exemplary representatives of each position, respectively). It would be a mistake, however, to conclude that the distinction between what's rational versus irrational versus nonrational is equivalent to the distinction between what's universal versus developmental versus relative. Nor would it be proper to overlook the fact that some enlightenment figures (e.g., Malinowski, Cole, and Scribner) have granted the coequality of divergent cultural forms while, at the same time, arguing, in typical enlightenment fashion, that each of those divergent forms is itself a rational adaptation to the demands of its own local environment or niche. Indeed, almost every combination of the two tripartite distinctions is represented somewhere in the social-science literature. Tversky and Kahneman derive universals from irrational processes, whereas in the skillful hands of Whiting and Child irrational processes are used to explain cultural differences and so on.

The matrix of possibilities for interpreting mental events diagramed in Figure 1.1 is crude and probably incomplete, and some of my identifications of particular theorists are certainly debatable. But, at least in this context, it is not my aim to be sophisticated, complete, or indisputably correct. My aim is merely to acknowledge that each interpretive approach represented in the matrix has a legitimate, although limited, role to play in the study of mind. What we must resist is the temptation to imprison all mental events in the same cell.

Notes

Sections of this manuscript were presented at the symposium on Frontiers in the Social Sciences: New Directions in the Study of Cognition, Annual Meeting of the American Association for the Advancement of Science, January 5, 1981, Toronto, Canada. The manuscript has been read by a number of colleagues and friends and I have benefited from their comments. My thanks to Jerome Bruner, Diane D'Andrade, Roy G. D'Andrade, J. David Greenstone, Donald N. Levine, David M. Schneider, and Melford E. Spiro.
1. I use the terms "enlightenment" and "romantic" to identify patterns of thought, clusters of ideas, and sets of assumptions that I believe have been

available, both intuitively and self-reflectively, throughout the history of the mind.

It is true, of course, that the terms "enlightenment" and "romantic" are relatively recent additions to the lexicon of intellectual historians and that there are relatively recent periods in the history of the West when patterns of enlightenment thinking or romantic thinking became enshrined in cultural ideology and self-consciously canonized in philosophical treatises. It does not follow, however, that "enlightenment" or "romantic" modes of thought are merely the historical products of the eighteenth and nineteenth centuries in the West.

2. See note 1.

References

Agar, M. 1973. *Ripping and Running*. New York: Academic Press.

Austin, J. L. 1962. *How to Do Things with Words*. Oxford: Clarendon Press.

Benedict, R. 1946. *The Chrysanthemum and the Sword*. New York: New American Library.

Berlin, B., Breedlove, D. E., & Raven. P. H. 1973. General principles of classification and nomenclature in folk biology. *American Anthropologist* 75:214–42.

Berlin, B., & Kay, P. 1969. *Basic Color Terms: Their Universality and Evolution*. Berkeley: University of California Press.

Black, M. 1963. Reasoning with loose concepts. *Dialogue* 2:1–12.

Brainerd, C. L. 1978a. *Piaget's Theory of Intelligence*. Englewood Cliffs, N.J.: Prentice-Hall.

 1978b. The stage question in cognitive developmental theory. *Behavioral and Brain Sciences* 2:173–213.

Brown, C. H. 1979. Folk zoological life-forms: their universality and growth. *American Anthropologist* 81:791–817.

Bruner, J. S., Olver, R. R., & Greenfield, P. M. 1966. *Studies in Cognitive Growth*. New York: Wiley.

Bullock, M., & Gelman, R. 1979. Preschool children's assumptions about cause and effect: temporal ordering. *Child Development* 50:89–96.

Cohen, L. J. 1979. On the psychology of prediction: whose is the fallacy? *Cognition* 7:385–407.

Cole, M., Gay, G., Glick, J. A., & Sharp, D. W. 1971. *The Cultural Context of Learning and Thinking*. New York: Basic Books.

Cole, M., and the Laboratory of Comparative Human Cognition. 1981. Intelligence as cultural practice. In W. Kessen, ed., *Carmichael's Handbook of Child Psychology*, vol. 1. New York: Wiley.

Cole, M., & Scribner, S. 1974. *Culture and Thought: A Psychological Introduction*. New York: Wiley.

Collingwood, R. J. 1972. *An Essay on Metaphysics*. Chicago: Regnery.

Converse, P. E. 1964. The nature of belief systems in mass politics. In D. E. Apter, ed., *Ideology and Discontent*. New York: Free Press.

D'Andrade, R. G. 1965. Trait psychology and componential analysis. *American Anthropologist*: 67:215–28.

 1973. Cultural constructions of reality. In L. Nader and T. W. Maretzki, eds., *Cultural Illness and Health*. Washington, D.C.: American Anthropological Association.

1974. Memory and the assessment of behavior. In T. Blalock, ed., *Measurement and the Social Sciences*. Chicago: Aldine-Atherton.

1976. A propositional analysis of U.S. American beliefs about illness. In R. Basso and H. Selby, eds., *Meaning in Anthropology*. Albuquerque: University of New Mexico Press.

1981. The cultural part of cognition. *Cognitive Science* 5:179–196.

D'Andrade, R. G., & Romney, A. K. 1964. Summary of participants' discussion. Transcultural Studies in Cognition. *American Anthropologist* 66:230–42.

Dumont, L. 1970. *Homo Hierarchicus*. Chicago: University of Chicago Press.

Einhorn, H. 1980. Overconfidence in judgment. In R. A. Shweder, ed., *Fallible Judgment in Behavioral Research: New Directions for Methodology of Social and Behavioral Science*, No. 4. San Francisco: Jossey-Bass.

Elias, N. 1978. *The Civilizing Process: The History of Manners*. New York: Urizen.

Evans-Pritchard, E. E. 1937. *Witchcraft, Oracles and Magic among the Azande*. Oxford: Clarendon.

Flavell, J. H. 1982. Structures, stages and sequences in cognitive development. In W. A. Collins, ed., *The Concept of Development, Minnesota Symposium on Child Psychology*, vol. 15. Minneapolis: University of Minnesota Press.

Foucault, M. 1967. *Madness and Civilization*. New York: Random House.

1973. *The Order of Things*. New York: Random House.

1979. *Discipline and Punish*. New York: Random House.

Frake, C. O. 1961. The diagnosis of disease among the Subanun of Mindanao. *American Anthropologist* 63:113–32.

Frazer, J. G. 1890. *The Golden Bow: A Study in Magic and Religion*. London: Macmillan.

Gay, P. 1959. *Voltaire's Politics*. Princeton, N.J.: Princeton University Press.

1964. *The Party of Humanity: Essays in the French Enlightenment*. New York: Knopf.

Geertz, C. 1973. *Interpretation of Cultures*. New York: Basic Books

1975. On the nature of anthropological understanding. *American Scientist* 63:47–53.

Gelman, R. 1978. Cognitive development. *Annual Review of Psychology* 29:297–332.

Gelman, R., & Baillargeon, R. 1983. A review of some Piagetian concepts. In P. Mussen, ed., *Manual of Child Psychology*, vol. 3. New York: Wiley.

Goldberg, S., Perlmutter, M., & Myers, W. 1974. Recall of related and unrelated lists by 2-year-olds. *Journal of Experimental Child Psychology* 18:1–8.

Goodman, N. 1968. *Languages of Art*. New York: Bobbs-Merrill.

1972a. The new riddle of induction. In N. Goodman, ed., *Problems and Projects*. New York: Bobbs-Merrill.

1972b. On likeness of meaning. In N. Goodman, ed., *Problems and Projects*. New York: Bobbs-Merrill.

1972c. Seven strictures on similarity. In N. Goodman, ed., *Problems and Projects*. New York: Bobbs-Merrill.

1978. *Ways of Worldmaking*. New York: Hackett.

Greenberg, J. H. 1966. *Language Universals with Special Reference to Feature Hierarchies*. The Hague: Mouton.

Higgins, E. T., & Parsons, J. E. 1983. Stages as subcultures. In E. T. Higgins, D. N. Ruble, & W. W. Hartup, eds., *Social Cognition and Social Development: A Sociocultural Perspective.* Cambridge: Cambridge University Press.

Hobbes, T. 1651. *Leviathan.*

Horton, R. 1967. African traditional thought and Western science. *Africa* 37:50–71, 159–87.

Hutchins, E. 1980. *Culture and Inference.* Cambridge, Mass.: Harvard University Press.

Inhelder, R., & Piaget, J. 1958. *The Growth of Logical Thinking from Childhood to Adolescence.* New York: Basic Books.

Kay, P., & McDaniel, C. K. 1978. The linguistic significance of the meanings of basic color terms. *Language* 54:610–46.

Kohlberg, L. 1981. *The Philosophy of Moral Development,* vol. 1. New York: Harper & Row.

Kuhn, T. 1962. *The Structure of Scientific Revolutions.* Chicago: University of Chicago Press.

Lantz, D., & Stefflre, V. 1964. Language and cognition revisited. *Journal of Abnormal and Social Psychology* 69:472–81.

Lempers, J. D., Flavell, E. R., & Flavell, J. H. 1977. The development in very young children of tacit knowledge concerning visual perception. *Genetic Psychology Monographs* 95:3–54.

Levi-Strauss, C. 1966. *The Savage Mind.* Chicago: University of Chicago Press.

Levy-Bruhl, L. 1910. *Les Fonctions Mentales dans les Sociétés Inférieures.* Paris: Alcan.

Lovejoy, A. O. 1974. *The Great Chain of Being.* Cambridge, Mass.: Harvard University Press.

Lucy, J. A., & Shweder, R. A. 1979. Whorf and his critics: linguistic and nonlinguistic influences on color memory. *American Anthropologist* 81:581–615.

Lyon, D., & Slovic, P. 1976. Dominance of accuracy information and neglect of base rates in probability estimation. *Acta Psychologica* 40:287–98.

Lyons, J. 1977. *Semantics,* vol. 2. Cambridge: Cambridge University Press.

MacIntyre, A. 1981. *After Virtue.* Notre Dame, Ind.: University of Notre Dame Press.

Mackie, J. L. 1980. *Hume's Moral Theory.* London: Routledge & Kegan Paul.

MacNamara, J., Baker, E., & Olson, C. L. 1976. Four-year-olds' understanding of *pretend, forget* and *know*: evidence for propositional operations. *Child Development* 47:62–70.

March, J. G. 1978. Bounded rationality, ambiguity and the engineering of choice. *Bell Journal of Economics* 9:587–608.

Mead, M. 1932. An investigation of the thought of primitive children, with special reference to animism. *Journal of the Royal Anthropological Institute* 62:173–90.

Mehan, H., & Wood, H. 1975. *The Reality of Ethnomethodology.* New York: Wiley.

Mehler, J., & Bever, T. G. 1967. Cognitive capacity of very young children. *Science* 158:141–2.

Much, N. C., & Shweder, R. A. 1978. Speaking of rules: the analysis of culture in breach. In W. Damon, ed., *New Directions for Child Development: Moral Development.* San Francisco: Jossey-Bass.

Nerlove, S., & Romney, A. K. 1967. Sibling terminology and cross-sex behavior. *American Anthropologist* 69:179–87.

Nisbett, R. E., Borgida, E., Crandell, R., & Reed, H. 1976. Popular induction: information is not necessarily informative. In J. S. Carroll and J. W. Payne, eds., *Cognition and Social Behavior*. New York: Halsted Press.

Nisbett, R., & Ross, L. 1980. *Human Inference: Strategies and Shortcomings of Social Judgment*. Englewood Cliffs, N.J.: Prentice-Hall.

Nucci, L., & Turiel, E. 1978. Social interaction and the development of social concepts in pre-school children. *Child Development* 49:400–7.

Osgood, C. E., May, W. H., & Miron, M. S. 1975. *Cross-Cultural Universals of Affective Meaning*. Urbana: University of Illinois Press.

Parsons, T. 1968. *The Structure of Social Action*, vol. 1. New York: Free Press.

Peirce, C. 1955. *Philosophical Writings of Peirce*. New York: Dover.

Perelman, Ch. 1963. *The Idea of Justice and the Problem of Argument*. New York: Humanities Press.

Piaget, J. 1954. *The Construction of Reality in the Child*. New York: Basic Books.

1967. *Six Psychological Studies*. New York: Random House.

1970. *Structuralism*. New York: Basic Books.

Pool, D., Shweder, R. A., & Much, N. C. 1983. Culture as a cognitive system: differentiated rule understandings in children and other savages. In E. T. Higgins, D. N. Ruble, & W. W. Hartup, eds., *Social Cognition and Social Development: A Sociocultural Perspective*. Cambridge: Cambridge University Press.

Quine, W. V. O. 1953. Two dogmas of empiricism. In W. V. O. Quine, *From a Logical Point of View*. New York: Harper & Row.

Read, K. E. 1955. Morality and the concept of the person among the Gahuku-Gama. *Oceania* 25:233–82.

Roberge, J. J., & Flexer, B. K. 1979. Further examination of formal operational reasoning abilities. *Child Development* 50:478–84.

Rosch, E. 1978. Principles of categorization. In E. Rosch and B. B. Lloyd, eds., *Cognition and Categorization*. Hillsdale, N.J.: Erlbaum.

Ross, L. 1977. The intuitive psychologist and his shortcomings: distortions in the attribution process. In L. Berkowitz, ed., *Advances in Experimental Social Psychology*, vol. 10. New York: Academic Press.

Sahlins, M. 1976. *Culture and Practical Reason*. Chicago: University of Chicago Press.

Schneider, D. M. 1968. *American Kinship: A Cultural Account*. Englewood Cliffs, N.J.: Prentice-Hall.

Schutz, A. 1967. *Collected Papers I: The Problem of Social Reality*. The Hague: Nijhoff.

Schwartz, T. 1981. The acquisition of culture. *Ethos* 9:4–17.

Searle, J. R. 1967. What is a speech act? In M. Black, ed., *Philosophy in America*. Ithaca, N.Y.: Cornell University Press.

1969. *Speech Acts*. Cambridge: Cambridge University Press.

1979. A taxonomy of illocutionary acts. In J. R. Searle, ed., *Expression and Meaning*. Cambridge: Cambridge University Press.

Shatz, M., & Gelman, R. 1973. The development of communication skills: modification in the speech of young children as a function of listener. *Monograph of the Society for Research on Child Development* 38: No. 5.

Shweder, R. A. 1972. Semantic structures and personality assessment. (Doctoral dissertation, Harvard University). *Dissertation Abstracts International*, 1972, *33*, 2452B (University Microfilms No. 72-29, 584).

1975. How relevant is an individual difference theory of personality? *Journal of Personality* 43:455–84.

1977a. Illusory correlation and the M.M.P.I. controversy. *Journal of Consulting and Clinical Psychology* 45:917–924.

1977b. Likeness and likelihood in everyday thought: magical thinking in judgments about personality. *Current Anthropology* 18:637–58.

1979a. Rethinking culture and personality theory part I: a critical examination of two classical postulates. *Ethos* 7(3):255–78.

1979b. Rethinking culture and personality theory part II: a critical examination of two more classical postulates. *Ethos* 7(4):279–311.

1980a. Rethinking culture and personality theory part III: from genesis and typology to hermeneutics and dynamics. *Ethos* 8(1):60–94.

1980b. Scientific thought and social cognition. In W. A. Collins, ed., *Development of Cognition, Affect and Social Relations. Minnesota Symposium on Child Psychology*, vol. 13. Hillsdale, N.J.: Erlbaum.

1982a. Beyond self-constructed knowledge: the study of culture and morality. *Merrill-Palmer Quarterly* 28:41–69.

1982b. Fact and artifact in trait perception: the systematic distortion hypothesis. In B. A. Maher & W. Maher, eds., *Progress in Experimental Personality Research*, vol. 11. New York: Academic Press.

1982c. Liberalism as destiny. *Contemporary Psychology* 27:421–4.

1982d. On savages and other children. *American Anthropologist* 84:354–66.

Shweder, R. A., & Bourne, E. 1982. Does the concept of the person vary cross-culturally? In A. J. Marsella & G. White, eds., *Cultural Conceptions of Mental Health and Therapy*. Boston: Reidel.

Shweder, R. A., Bourne, E., & Miyamoto, J. 1978. *Concrete thinking and category formation: a cultural theory with implications for developmentalists* (Committee on Human Development, University of Chicago). Unpublished manuscript.

Shweder, R. A., & D'Andrade, R. A. 1979. Accurate reflection or systematic distortion? A reply to Block, Weiss and Thorne. *Journal of Personality and Social Psychology* 37:1075–84.

1980. The systematic distortion hypothesis. In R. A. Shweder, ed., *Fallible Judgment in Behavioral Research. New Directions for Methodology of Social and Behavioral Science*, No. 4. San Francisco: Jossey-Bass.

Shweder, R. A., & Miller, J. G. In press. The social construction of the person: how is it possible? In K. Gergen & K. Davis, eds., *The Social Construction of the Person*. New York: Springer-Verlag.

Shweder, R. A., Turiel, E., & Much, N. C. 1980. The moral intuitions of the child. In J. H. Flavell & L. Ross, eds., *Social Cognitive Development*. Cambridge: Cambridge University Press.

Siegler, R. S. 1981. Developmental sequences within and between concepts. *Monographs of the Society for Research on Child Development* 46: No. 2.

Simon, H. A., & Hayes, J. R. 1976. The understanding process: problem isomorphs. *Cognitive Psychology* 8:165–90.

Spiro, M. E. 1968. Virgin birth: parthenogenesis and physiological paternity: an essay in cultural interpretation. *Man* 3:242–61.

Stefflre, V., Castillo Vales, V., & Morley, L. 1966. Language and cognition in Yucatan: a cross-cultural replication. *Journal of Personality and Social Psychology* 4:112–15.

Tambiah, S. J. 1973. Form and meaning in magical acts. In R. Horton and R. Finnegan, eds., *Modes of Thought*. London: Faber & Faber.

Trabasso, T. 1975. Representation, memory, and reasoning: how do we make transitive inferences? In A. D. Pick, ed., *Minnesota Symposium on Child Psychology*, vol. 9: 135–72. Minneapolis: University of Minnesota Press.

Turiel, E. 1979. Distinct conceptual and developmental domains: social-convention and morality. In C. B. Keasy, ed., *Nebraska Symposium on Motivation* (1977), vol. 25. Lincoln: University of Nebraska Press.

Turner, V. 1967. *The Forest of Symbols*. Ithaca, N.Y.: Cornell University Press.

Tversky, A., & Kahneman, D. 1974. Judgment under uncertainty: heuristics and biases. *Science* 185:1124–31.

Tyler, S. A. 1969. *Cognitive Anthropology*. New York: Holt, Rinehart and Winston.

Tylor, E. B. 1871. *Primitive Culture*. London: Murray.

Ward, W. C., & Jenkins, H. M. 1965. The display of information and the judgment of contingency. *Canadian Journal of Psychology* 19:231–41.

Wason, P. C., & Johnson-Laird, P. N. 1972. *The Psychology of Reasoning*. London: Batsford.

Watanabe, S. 1969. *Knowing and Guessing*. New York: Wiley.

White, G. M. 1980. Conceptual universals in interpersonal language. *American Anthropologist* 82:759–81.

Whorf, B. L. 1956. *Language, Thought and Reality*. Cambridge, Mass.: MIT Press.

Wittgenstein, L. 1969. *On Certainty*. Oxford: Blackwell Publisher.

2

Properties of culture
AN ETHNOGRAPHIC VIEW

Robert A. LeVine

Anthropologists who converse with scholars in other disciplines are often asked what *culture* is, sometimes with the implication that the concept is outdated and ambiguous and that its use is an indicator of obscurantism in anthropology. Indeed, culture is often treated in quantitative social science as representing the unexplained residuum of rigorous empirical analysis, an area of darkness beyond the reach of currently available scientific searchlights. It is assumed that no progress in conceptualizing culture has been made since the publication of Ruth Benedict's popular book *Patterns of Culture* in 1934, and that progress in anthropological research is measurable by its movement away from her concept toward the specific behavioral variables of economic, demographic, and psychological research. This assumption, however, takes no account of the more sophisticated conceptions of culture that have been advanced within anthropology in recent years and found valuable in ethnographic research. For many anthropologists working with these conceptions, culture is a source of illumination, not a veil of obscurity, but their views have not been made known in other social sciences.

In this chapter I shall attempt to explain why the concept of culture has been not only useful but indispensable for me as an anthropologist interested in both social processes and the development of the individual. I shall focus on those aspects I believe are least understood, providing examples from my own fieldwork and the published literature. The conception I work with is a definition of culture as a shared organization of ideas that includes the intellectual, moral, and aesthetic standards prevalent in a community and the meanings of communicative actions. But formal definitions do little to clarify the nature of culture; clarification is only possible through ethnography.

My conversations with a wide variety of social and behavioral scientists lead me to believe that the culture concept is not understood because ethnography as a process of inquiry is not understood. Regarding ethnography as an impressionistic, hence inferior, form of scientific description or as mere background to systematic study, many nonanthropologists fail to grasp what is distinctive – and uniquely valuable – about anthropological knowledge. As a consequence, they frequently underestimate certain properties of culture that the ethnographer experiences as central. I shall discuss four of these: the collective, organized, multiplex, and variable properties of culture.

The collective nature of culture

A recurrent experience of ethnographers is that they are dealing with shared, supraindividual phenomena, that culture represents a consensus on a wide variety of meanings among members of an interacting community approximating that of the consensus on language among members of a speech-community. Speech is an individual action and each individual speaks somewhat differently from another; yet speakers of a given language can understand one another on their first meeting, though they cannot understand speech in other languages to which they have not been exposed. Their capacity for mutual understanding is accompanied by a remarkable consensus about rules of pronunciation and grammar such that linguists can discover the rules prevailing in a whole community not from an extensive survey but from a small number of informants. This redundancy of rules in a speech-community is theoretically significant in illustrating how language functions as social communication; it is methodologically significant in permitting a mode of systematic inquiry distinct from the sample survey. The same holds for culture in general (of which language is one part); namely, that there is consensus in a community (in this case about the meanings of symbols, verbal and nonverbal), that the consensus is substantively related to the importance of communication in social life, and that it produces redundancy across informants, calling for a distinctive mode of inquiry.

Doubts have often been raised about these assertions, specifically about whether culture can be validly characterized as shared or consensual in the face of individual variation and whether it can be validly investigated without a sample survey. Concerning the first of these doubts, it must be emphasized that members of a community can vary greatly in thoughts, feelings, and behavior, yet hold in common understandings of the symbols and representations through which they communicate. Indeed, without such common understandings (of symbolic forms such as gestures, dress, property, writing, visual and theatrical representations, careers, relationships), what kind of social communication, or community, would be possible? The redundancy discovered by ethnographers in cultural meanings, like that discovered by linguists in speech, suggests some minimal requisites for social life.

Controversy concerning *whether* a consensus of meanings is universal within human communities has arisen from confusion over *where* the consensus is located. When it is assumed to be universally located in institutional domains (like kinship) or in the psychological characteristics of individuals, then evidence of intracommunity variation in informants' accounts (e.g., kinship concepts) or in psychological responses is taken to contradict the universality of culture as shared meanings. But some culture theorists such as Geertz (1973) assume, however, that the consensus does not have a fixed locus in institutions or individuals but is variable in its societal and psychological organization; it is the task of the ethnographer to discover the particular forms of symbolic action in which shared meanings reside and which provide meaningful lives for members of a particular society. Thus Geertz and Geertz (1975) begin their study of Balinese kinship:

> Balinese kinship customs and practices are, on first encounter, puzzlingly irregular and contradictory. The ethnologist can find very little agreement among his informants on many basic substantive issues, such as what forms of groupings of kinsmen the Balinese recognize, or what the essential structural characteristics of these groups are thought to be. Two fully cooperative and intelligent Balinese from the same village may give completely variant accounts on matters the ethnologist believes to be crucial to his formulations. They may give strikingly different descriptions of the organization of the same concrete group of kinsmen, or they may even use completely different terms to identify that group. (1975:1)

Later, however, they report:

> Below the level of the often bewildering surface variations, the agreement among all Balinese on ideational matters, on beliefs, values, social definitions and perceptions and so on, is profound. (p. 32)

Their ethnographic account is a record of their search for the locus of order in Balinese culture. They did not interpret disagreement among informants about kinship as symptomatic of a total social dissensus or proof that the Balinese lack shared meanings but rather as indicating that the order, the consensus, the shared meanings lay elsewhere than in that institutional domain. They found it in some rather general Balinese conceptions of social order that are applied in contexts defined by, but not limited to, kinship. Geertz and Geertz conclude that in Bali kinship does not supply the idioms, prototypes, models, or master images for other social relationships, as anthropologists have reported for some other societies. All Balinese share idioms of social relationship, but such idioms were found not in any institutional locus the ethnographers could know a priori but in contexts they had to discover.

From this perspective, every human community functions with a group consensus about the meanings of the symbols used in the communications that constitute their social life, however variable their behavior and attitudes in other respects, because such a consensus is as necessary for encoding and decoding messages in social communication in general as agreement about speech rules is to encoding and decoding in the linguistic mode. The difference is that the categories of language variation among human communities (i.e., the basic categories of phonology and syntax) are known in advance of any particular investigation, whereas in the larger symbolic order of culture, the salient categories vary so widely in expressive form and contextual range from one people to another that identifying the categories becomes the primary task of the ethnographer.

The second doubt raised about this view of culture is whether it can be validly investigated without a sample survey. This question is usually asked by social scientists whose research is framed in correlational terms; that is, the question presumes that the object of study is a variable rather than a constant in the sample or population under investigation. It has long been known to social psychology that many behavioral and attitudinal characteristics exhibit the J-curve of conformity behavior, in which the overwhelming majority of individuals in a population respond identically and only a few deviate. Such characteristics are unsuitable for correlational analysis, because their distributions approximate unity too closely to permit the use of Mill's method of concomitant variations, of which correlation is a mathematical form. Thus behaviors or attitudes believed on the basis of empirical data or an investigator's intuition to have J-curve distributions are usually omitted from sociological and psychological research. It is also not considered worthwhile to conduct a national survey of 1,600 persons to find out what the investigator believes he knows as a member of the society under study, namely, that the vast majority of other members share certain of his views or practices; "common sense" suggests the futility of such research. Yet it is precisely these widely shared orientations that are the objects of study for the anthropological student of culture.

Inhabiting a world of variables with frequencies of less than 70%, social-science investigators of individual and subgroup differences sometimes view anthropological descriptions of group consensus with skepticism, as if the ethnographer's failure to conduct a survey biased his report toward the false attribution of uniformity in a population. This view overlooks the fact that the skeptics themselves regularly determine without a survey that certain characteristics are distributed in J-curve fashion and should be excluded from investigation. They thus approach ethnographic description not as students of the same phenomena with different methods but as investigators whose research attention is deliberately focused on phenomena that have been selected for their variability in the population. Survey researchers, for example, are unlikely to ask a national sample of Americans whether they believe that deaths are caused by witchcraft and sorcery performed by jealous neighbors and relatives of the deceased. Why? They consider it self-evident that no more than an insignificant proportion of Americans hold this belief; it is thus unnecessary to conduct the survey as well as useless for correlational study. Anthropologists would agree that the survey is unnecessary but might find the phemonenon itself worthy of ethnographic study in order to understand in more depth the grounds for rejecting a belief we once shared with other peoples of the world and the larger context of intellectual and value orientations that make witchcraft and sorcery implausible as causes of death. What is a mere background parameter for the survey researcher could become a topic of revealing cultural inquiry for the ethnographer.

The ethnographer's experience of culture as collective can be illustrated from my own research on witchcraft and sorcery among the Gusii of Kenya. From 1955 to 1957, I conducted fieldwork in a Gusii community. I had read the publications of Philip Mayer, who carried out fieldwork among the Gusii from 1946 to 1949 in an area about ten miles away. Guided by his descriptions of Gusii culture, I was nevertheless constantly searching for points in which my community might deviate from what he had written. I found that his account of Gusii beliefs concerning witches (Mayer, 1954) forecast my informants' descriptions down to the smallest details, not only as beliefs attributed to the community in general but also in narratives concerning personal experience. In other words, the Gusii I worked with for eighteen months told me stories of their own current encounters with witches for which Mayer's account provided the basic script, though his statements were based on interviews with other informants in a community some distance away. I discovered that Gusii accounts of personal experience with witches were in fact highly predictable in the social situations of their occurrence, the images of witches and victims, the narrative sequences of action, the emotional reactions attributed to self and others, and the outcomes of attempts to combat witchcraft (see LeVine 1963, 1973; LeVine & LeVine 1966). These were the most intense emotional experiences reported by my friends and neighbors about themselves and members of their immediate families, yet the form and contents of their reports were standardized, apparently following a conventional script with a single set of symbols and meanings. This conventional script, discovered by Mayer in one Gusii community and by me in another, is what I would call a collective phenomenon, something supraindividual even though it informs individual experience.

When I returned to my original Gusii community in 1974, seventeen years after the completion of my first field trip, I met a new generation of Gusii who had grown up under new conditions. The son of one of my old friends, whom I remembered as a toddler but who was now a secondary-school graduate, in relating to me what had happened during my absence, told me many stories about his kinsmen and neighbors that included material on witchcraft and sorcery. The narratives followed the same script I was familiar with and were as intensely believed and felt by him as they had been by his parents years before. Here was a member of another generation whose social world and emotional life were being experienced in the same terms that Mayer had discovered almost thirty years earlier in another part of Gusiiland. Here again I was confronted by the collective nature of a folk culture that had never been written down (except in technical works by Mayer and me, read only by highly educated Gusii residing outside the district) yet continued to shape personal experience. Such confrontations are common in ethnography and generate for many anthropologists the sense of culture as something shared, collective, and supraindividual.

The organized nature of culture

Nothing is more characteristic of contemporary anthropologists than the conviction that the customs they study are connected and comprehensible only as parts of a larger organization – of beliefs, norms, values, or social action. This is particularly noteworthy in light of the fact that the prevailing orthodoxy of American empirical anthropology at the turn of the century viewed customs as discrete traits varying independently across societies and coinciding only in particular historical circumstances. What happened in between was Malinowski's innovation of extended and intensive ethnographic fieldwork, (e.g., Malinowski 1924) which revealed connections among the customs of a community that had not been suspected in the days of briefer and more superficial ethnography.

No ethnographer who has followed Malinowski's (now standard) program for intensive fieldwork has failed to find increasing connectedness and coherence in customs – particularly in their ideational dimension – as he or she becomes better acquainted with their meanings in vernacular discourse and practice. There is controversy about the degree and kind of coherence – claims that cultures are deductive systems, pervasive configurations, seamless webs, have been repeatedly made and just as often disputed – but even those most skeptical of cultural coherence would not return to the earlier view of customs as discrete traits. The "shreds and patches" concept of culture has simply not survived the test of intensive field investigation, because the ethnographer, in learning to communicate with people of another culture, discovers the orderliness not only in their communicative conventions but in their version of "common sense," the framework of ideas from which they view, and act upon, the world. The framework may not be as orderly as a syllogism or a formal taxonomy, but it is far from a random assemblage of discrete elements. Most important, it is an organized set of contexts from which customary beliefs and practices derive their meaning.

Gusii witchcraft provides a case in point. Witchcraft can be considered a culture trait independent of its social and ideological contexts: The Gusii believe in witchcraft; some other peoples do not. If one attempts to understand witchcraft as the Gusii themselves understand it, however, one finds it deeply implicated in other aspects of their culture. To comprehend Gusii witchcraft in their terms, one must be able to set it in at least three contexts: (1) the interpersonal relationships, social situations, and economic distributions that generate envy and produce witchcraft accusations; (2) the representations of religious figures, living and dead, who can cause and/or eliminate afflictions, some resembling, others contrasting with, witches; (3) beliefs concerning emotions and bodily processes, including the vulnerability of the human body to the emotions attributed to witches. All Gusii adults have detailed knowledge of these three aspects of their culture and understand witchcraft not as an isolated phenomenon but in relation to its interpersonal, religious, and psychosomatic contexts. When a witchcraft accusation is made, they automatically evaluate it in terms derived from these contexts, which constitute its meaning for them, and the meaning determines how they will respond to it. Whereas this contextual understanding is automatic for a Gusii adult, it requires intensive investigation by the ethnographer seeking to attain that understanding and to describe it in a form accessible to other outsiders. Providing the background information necessary to understand why a Gusii responds as he does to an instance of witchcraft is an example of what Geertz (1973), following the philosopher Ryle, calls "thick description."

Thus, in attempting to understand a "custom" like witchcraft as the Gusii understand it, one finds that its meanings involve a knowledge of Gusii social organization, religion, and medicine. This is not because Gusii culture is more unified than any other culture. Any American who tries to explain to a foreign visitor why he finds a political cartoon in his daily newspaper funny and effective will find himself engaged in thick description and discover relationships among aspects of American culture that he takes for granted but which are not shared with other cultures. It is in meanings as they inform symbolic activities such as witchcraft accusations and political cartoons that the connections within culture and their organization are to be found.

The contemporary view of culture as an organization of ideas rather than an aggregate of independent traits sheds new light on old anthropological problems. The problem of kin-avoidance is a case in point. Anthropologists have long tried to explain why some societies have customs of avoidance between particular categories of kin (e.g., mother-in-law–son-in-law, brother–sister) and others do not. Tylor attempted to solve the problem in 1889 with a statistical cross-cultural study (the first such) showing relationships between rules of marital residence and the presence or absence of certain types of kin-avoidance. Freud (1913:19) saw the incest taboo lurking in avoidance norms, but subsequent comparative studies and theoretical formulations (notably Driver 1966; Murdock 1949; Stephens & D'Andrade 1962; Sweetser 1962) continued to focus on why particular categories of kin were or were not selected for avoidance. In the Stephens and D'Andrade study, however, it was shown that the several categories of avoidance were positively correlated in a world sample of societies and that societies could be divided into those that had avoidance norms and those that did not. This suggested what the better ethnographic accounts of recent years have documented in detail, namely, that norms of kin-avoidance form a code of interpersonal conduct in some societies, that this code is the basis for moral evaluation of self and others in such societies, and that avoidance – rather than being restricted to one or two relationships – tends to be the model for conventional moral behavior in those societies. There is always one relationship that is the prototype of avoidance and others that are paler imitations in terms of the strictness of the avoidance rules and their enforcement. Superficial ethnographic research produces reports in which only the prototypical avoidance relationship is reported or some of the milder ones omitted, so that avoidance appears to be generated by specific relationships rather than a general code of conduct and model for moral behavior.

This fallacy in the older ethnographic literature is illustrated by Murdock's (1949:277) statement, on the basis of his inventory of it, that mother–son avoidance is absent in human societies. What I found among the Gusii, for whom the father–daughter-in-law relationship serves as the prototype of avoidance, is that a milder but unmistakable avoidance norm applies to mother and son after the latter's circumcision, when he may never again enter the part of his mother's house where she cooks, sleeps, and (as informants emphasize) has sexual intercourse. Because Gusii informants tend to talk more about avoidance norms in in-law relationships and with parents' siblings, while taking mother–son avoidance for granted, it is easy to see how the latter could be overlooked in casual ethnographic interviewing. Evidence such as this suggests that earlier ethnographies tended to overlook the less salient avoidance relationships, thereby presenting avoidance customs as isolated traits rather than as parts of a moral code.

The indigenous vocabulary of kin-avoidance prevailing among those who practice it has also been largely neglected in ethnographic literature, although such information is essential to an assessment of what cultural organization they might have. In working with two culturally unrelated African peoples who practice kin-avoidance, the Hausa of northwestern Nigeria and the Gusii of southwestern Kenya thousands of miles away, I found that for both there was a word (*kunya* for the Hausa, *ensoni* for the Gusii) that referred to the avoidance norms and relationships, to the embarrassment experienced when they were breached, and to a broader concept of the shame necessary to moral behavior. In both languages the word is used in a phrase of opprobrium roughly equivalent to the (archaic) English "He has no shame," meaning a person whose moral character is defective. In both societies, then, the word for prescriptive avoidance of kin is a conceptual bridge between the private sense of embarrassment/shame when propriety is breached and public ideals of conventional morality. This suggests a conception of the ideal self in which the practice of avoidance counts as commendably upright moral behavior rather than as silly priggishness, dreary conventionalism, or immoral hypocrisy. The big gulf is between those cultures in which avoidance is unacceptable as an unsophisticated mark of morality – perhaps because it calls public attention to the very wishes that are supposedly being censored – and those in which it is acceptable as a mark of public virtue.

An investigation of kin-avoidance in its social and moral context would also show that in many societies the avoidance norms coexist with norms prescribing joking behavior that includes obscene insults and provocations between other categories of kin. A Gusii man, for example, is supposed to avoid even indirect reference to sexual matters in conversations with his father, father's brothers and their wives, but to engage in sexually explicit ribaldry with his father's mother and others of that generation. Even within his own generation, where avoidance as such does not apply, he is forbidden to act seductively toward female cousins on his father's side but is expected to do so toward his mother's brother's daughters. The kinship norms then, prescribe a dialectical drama in which the exaggerations of avoidance in one set of relationships are complemented by exaggerated expressions of incestuous and hostile intentions in another set of relationships.

Rather than analyzing the symbols of this drama in terms derived from Freud, Levi-Strauss, or Radcliffe-Brown, it is worth considering what the drama as a form of communication (and concealment) tells us about the terms of moral discourse in the community that enacts it. It tells us first of all that incestuous sexuality and aggression are not excluded from attention, disavowed, disguised, or repressed, as they might be in a thoroughly "puritanical" context; rather, they are used as the main symbolic elements in the hyperbolic representation of contrasts in kin relationships. The directness of this representation, its lack of symbolic disguise, makes a code of avoidance and joking unacceptable among peoples whose conventions of interpersonal conduct prescribe greater concealment of intentions and more subtle ways of managing the moral polarities of kinship. The drama of avoidance and joking is, from the viewpoint of the latter cultures, like melodrama or slapstick comedy viewed from the perspective of more subtle dramatic forms: ineffective because of being too vivid, too lacking in the desirable degrees of indirection, tension, distortion, multiplicity of meanings. Furthermore, the drama tells us that what matters most in relationships is the specific type of genealogical linkage, so much that in one type sex and aggression are freely expressed (in words), whereas in the other they must be avoided at all costs. But in many societies, relationships based on connections other than kinship matter as much or more than genealogy, and the drama of avoidance and joking would be experienced as giving too much weight to kin relationship. This does not mean that in more complex societies, with a greater range of relationships and more elaborately layered expressive forms, individuals do not experience anxieties about incest and intergenerational hostility or that their cultures are not addressed to these anxieties, but only that they find other ways of dealing with them. The drama that made affective and social sense for the Gusii and for many indigenous people of the Americas and Oceania as well as Africa simply does not make sense in other cultural contexts, for reasons having less to do with the nature of their underlying problems than with their cultural styles of defining, dramatizing, and dealing with them.

I have suggested, then, that kin-avoidance customs exhibit three kinds of organization: an organization of rules across kin categories into a moral code, a lexico-semantic organization linking private feelings of shame with public definitions of moral character, and a larger ideological organization in which avoidance and obscene joking complement each other as the serious and comic dramas of a community life based heavily on kin relationships. These kinds of organization represent the contexts in which members of societies with avoidance make sense of the customs among themselves. The newer ethnographic evidence indicates that avoidance customs are more accurately seen as reflecting a normative model for human relationships characteristic of certain societies than as the specific traits envisioned by Tylor.

The multiplexity of culture

Many metaphors have been used in conceptualizing culture – culture as law, drama, language, philosophical doctrine, and so on – but from an ethnographic viewpoint each has its limitations. One aspect of this problem is the issue of explicitness that led anthropologists of some years ago to distinguish overt from covert culture and explicit from implicit culture. In every culture there are rules, beliefs, and labels that are explicit in the way that legal statutes, philosophical propositions, and dictionary definitions are explicit. Informants can expound these without difficulty to an ethnographer, often supplying extensive explanations and justifications as well. As the ethnographer lives in a community, however, he discovers many other regularities of customary behavior that informants cannot easily explain and which they take for granted as self-evident responses to what is and what ought to be. Many ethnographers arrive at the conclusion that what informants find difficult to verbalize is more important, more fundamental, in the cultural organization of ideas than what they can verbalize. They argue that the more general ideas – basic assumptions – are less accessible to verbal formulation because the social consensus in a community protects them from challenge and shifts the focus of discourse to more specific points that are at issue in normal social life.

There is an analogy here with Kuhn's (1962) concept of "normal science," that is, the normal discourse and debate in a scientific community that does not challenge its basic paradigm. The ethnographer wants to know the paradigm, not only the current issues generated by it. His situation is analogous to that of the linguist investigating the grammar of a language: The informants cannot offer the rules by which they form sentences, though they use them constantly or at least speak in an orderly way that can be represented by grammatical rules. The ethnographer needs a method like that of the linguist to permit formulation of the general rules, concepts, or assumptions that generate the observed particulars to which he has ready access. The search for such a method has supplied a good deal of the intellectual excitement in social anthropology over the past twenty years.

One type of solution is illustrated by formal semantic analysis, in which informants classify words in a given cultural domain, revealing the higher order categories, named or unnamed, to which they belong. This approach is of course limited by its exclusive focus on vocabulary and may be restricted in utility to domains such as kinship and ethnobotany in which labeling and classification are important purposes of language use. It is in any event an extension of linguistic method, leaving out much of what anthropologists consider fundamental in culture and ignoring for the most part the important feature of polysemy – multiple meanings in symbols such as words – which is central to the multiplex nature of culture.

Another proposed solution, which deals directly with polysemy as formal semantic analysis does not, is Victor W. Turner's (1967) extended case-study method focused on ritual symbols. He developed this approach among the Ndembu, who could not explain to the ethnographer many of the meanings of the symbols that seemed central to the emotional and moral impact of their elaborate and frequent ceremonies. Turner's method of decoding the symbols made the ritual process itself the object of inquiry, collecting the data necessary to understand the social and ideological contexts in which the participants experienced a particular ritual event. By observing how the Ndembu use ritual objects and conduct their ceremonies with them – as well as how they talk about them – Turner was able to infer a deeper significance than the Ndembu explanation alone could provide. His theory is that ritual symbols generally derive their potency from their multivocal or polysemous nature, that is, from the fact that they combine meanings, some from the sensate level of bodily experience and body imagery, others from the more abstract level of moral, spiritual, and political ideals. Although this combination can be explicit, as in the Catholic doctrine of the Eucharist, it is probably more often hidden or disguised in symbolic forms. Thus it is expectable that much of culture is not recoverable through straightforward ethnographic interviewing but requires inferences based on observation of how symbols are used in the pragmatic contexts of social life.

To summarize: Culture cannot be reduced to its explicit or implicit dimensions. It would be fallacious to take what is given by informants at face value and assume that the rest of behavior and belief is untouched by culture. It is equally fallacious to discount explicit rules, beliefs, and labels as lacking social or psychological reality or as mere reflections of, or disguises for, implicit cultural orientations. In culture, as an organization of shared meanings, some meanings are more explicit than others, for reasons having to do with the pragmatics of social life and their history for a given society.

The multiplexity of culture can also be found in its integration of rational and nonrational elements in symbolic formulas such as ideologies. Folk cultures do not respect the fact–value distinction so dear to the hearts of Western positivists. They tend to combine, as Geertz has argued, "models of" reality – that is, descriptive statements about what is – with "models for" reality – normative statements about what ought to be. The isolated communities typically studied by anthropologists have this in common with larger religious movements and with other ideological phenomena more familiar in the West, for example, Marxism, nationalism, party politics, civic boosterism.

This combination of the normative and descriptive is conspicuous in the cultural models of child care and child rearing found among industrial and nonindustrial peoples alike. Looked at one way, such models express deep-seated preferences for virtues such as obedience and independence, though these are often formulated as beliefs describing the attributes of children and the nature of their development. Looked at differently, the same models are adaptive strategies for maximizing survival and optimizing the child's future economic adjustment, though these strategies are often formulated as moral imperatives for both parents and children. It is possible, then, to find both empirical validity and cultural values in folk conceptions of child rearing, not as independent elements but as mutually supportive dimensions of a unitary formula in which the normative component *motivates* adaptive parental behavior and the descriptive component provides parents with confidence that their fostering of virtue *makes sense* in terms of accurate environmental knowledge. The fusion of what is and ought to be in a single vision, like the many-layered meanings discussed earlier, seems to be at the heart of what gives distinctive cultural ideologies their singular psychological power, their intimate linkages with individual emotion and motivation.

It is possible, of course, to dismiss culture in this sense as mumbo jumbo, the residue of prescientific thinking needed to provide mental health for the masses, with the potential to mobilize them for good or evil but basically false in its assertions about reality. Having dismissed contemporary cultural ideologies this way, it is then but one step to assume that the cultures of nonindustrial peoples lack empirical validity, logic, and rationality, that culture without science equals error. Paradoxically, however, the same intensive ethnography that has documented such extraordinary variations in the arbitrary symbols by which humans make meaning of their lives and in the codes of conduct, piety, and aesthetic judgment that they construct of these symbols has also shown that empirical validity, logic, and rationality are not missing from these cultures – even in those at the simplest level of technology.

The lives of nonindustrial peoples are harshly disciplined by the exigencies of their climate, food supply, health, and technology. They are survivors of conditions that have eliminated other peoples, and they have remarkable survival skills, including extensive knowledge of their habitat – its plants, animals, weather; complex techniques of hunting, cultivation, food processing, construction, navigation, trade; and a pragmatic awareness of utilitarian values in anything or anybody new that comes their way. Peoples who cannot understand ends–means relationships, or who operate without calculating the costs and benefits of their survival-relevant decisions, have been sought and not found.

Whatever their religion and expressive culture, nonindustrial peoples know how to extract a living from their accustomed environment and to maintain a social organization in which such extraction remains possible; if conditions are not too suddenly disrupted, they do so in an intelligent and effective way. They do not, however, partition their culture into its instrumental and expressive components. A basic food crop like the West African yam has both spiritual and nutritious values for those who grow it, and its cultivation combines realistic agricultural techniques with ritual practices based on religious ideas. Subsistence adaptation can be, and often is, achieved in a world of conceptual discourse that takes rational techniques as given and emphasizes other symbolic meanings and significant goals.

Thus have we learned from ethnography not to impose our Western distinctions of science versus religion and natural versus supernatural on the beliefs and concepts of non-Western peoples. Cultural models can be simultaneously normative and descriptive, as argued earlier, and their descriptive aspects, when formulated in terms of religion and cosmology, can embody accurate environmental knowledge and lead to adaptive practical outcomes. How and to what extent this happens is a topic for continuing research. The theoretical opposition between culture as arbitrary symbols and culture as a means of adaption can still generate controversy, but the ethnographer – far from having to choose between these two poles – has to work with a concept of culture that encompasses both.

In my own thinking I have adopted the concept of a cultural rationale as a way of dealing with the integration of rational and nonrational elements in a single collective formula. A rationale in this sense is an explanation for a customary practice that makes logical sense – transcultural logical sense – given some arbitrary assumptions that reflect cultural values rather than contingencies in the external environment. When Monica Wilson (1952) was told by a Nyakyusa informant that it was necessary to segregate adult generations into separate villages because otherwise the intergenerational avoidance taboos would cause inconvenience in daily life, the explanation was a rational one – but only if one assumes that the avoidance taboos represent a high priority for all concerned. Given that assumption, an arrangement that maximizes conformity to the rules and minimizes the ecological probability of breaking them (by segregation), so that people can focus their attention on other priorities, is rational. But the assumption that avoidance itself is necessary is not rational in the sense of a response to environmental contingencies. My concept of rationale is thus close to Freud's concept of rationalization, wherein the individual begins with a highly motivated tendency and then seeks to justify it in terms of other considerations that are logically applicable but not primary. A cultural rationale, however, begins not with an individual wish or fear but with a collective value, arbitrary in itself, that is taken as an absolute requirement in a rational explanation of a customary practice. The ethnographer frequently finds his informants offering such rationales when asked to explain a custom; only through probing does he discover the hidden assumption. I believe that cultural models inevitably generate cultural rationales and that the operation of rational thinking (characteristic of all humans) on nonrational premises (characteristic of particular cultures) produces much of the multiplexity of culture that ethnographers uncover.

The variability of culture across human populations

Nothing divides anthropologists (and others seeking to generalize about humanity) more than issues of cultural variability. There is no serious dispute among professional anthropologists about the wide variations, documented by increasingly detailed ethnography, in the economic, organizational, and communicative patterns by which humans live. There is also a consensus regarding documented variations in cultural standards of intellectual, moral, and aesthetic judgment. Furthermore, few anthropologists consider the world a melting pot in which, as popular belief would have it, variation is disappearing so fast that ethnography has no future. On the contrary, it has become abundantly clear that, although hunter-gatherer populations are threatened and many customs have indeed disappeared, world cultures as a whole are resisting homogenization, even as they eagerly embrace Western consumer goods and bureaucratic forms. Anthropologists disagree not about these facts of cultural variation but about what to make of them in generalizing about cultural variability.

At one pole of opinion are the reductionists – Marxists, neoclassical economists, cultural materialists, orthodox Freudians, and sociobiologists – whose basic premises include uniformities of structure and content in human life, culture, and motivation at all times and places. They are inclined to minimize cultural variability and to interpret evidence of variations as surface manifestations concealing the deeper uniformities forecast by their theoretical positions. At the other pole are those cultural phenomenologists who insist on the uniqueness of each culture as the symbolism of a people who share a history and endow each aspect of human life that appears universal with a unique pattern of meanings derived from that history. They tend to reject transcultural categories and even comparative methods as based on superficial similarities in behavior that fail to take account of diversity in the meanings that define culture. For the reductionists, there was enough ethnographic evidence long ago to draw positive conclusions about humanity; for the phenomenologists, there may never be enough.

In between these hedgehogs and foxes are many anthropologists like myself who are committed to ethnography and comparison as open-ended enterprises in which new facts are constantly acquired and new theoretical formulations tried out against them; variability in this context is an unsettled question for which the answers undergo revision from time to time. One principle of this centrist position is that no a priori theoretical position could have forecast the existing findings of ethnography concerning cultural variation and that no existing theory is likely to forecast its future findings in all their significant content. In other words, the picture of cultural variability emerging from the ethnographic evidence is bigger than any of the theoretical frames currently available. Another principle, however, is that we must not give up the search for a suitable frame. Perhaps, to pursue the analogy, the frame will have to be, not a rectangle or a box, but (like environmental art) a canyon or a landscape – something with more dimensions than we can now imagine. In any event, we have the precedent of Darwin to show us that a natural history of diversity need not preclude the search for broad principles of order.

Although cultural variation as shown by modern ethnography is far greater than anyone clearly anticipated fifty years ago, variability as a property of culture raises many more theoretical issues than can be dealt with here. I shall concentrate on two aspects that illustrate current perspectives on the topic: reflective discourse, that is, indigenous cultural description and analysis within a culture, and the partitioning of culture into domains. Reflective discourse refers to conventionalized formats for commenting on cultural beliefs and norms in themselves and in their influence on social behavior. Cultures vary enormously in the development and elaboration of such formats. At one end of the spectrum are those cultures in which the formats are so few and so restricted that the ethnographer finds a lack of explicitness about norms and a lack of explanation of symbolic activities. In such societies, the ethnographer experiences ingroup cultural knowledge as a virtually secret code that he must devise special measures to break; hence Turner's observational approach. At the other end of the spectrum are those literate cultures (e.g., Hindu India) so rich in commentaries about their own symbols that the ethnographer must decide which to believe as representatives of the culture enacted by the people with whom he lives.

Intermediate in this range are those nonliterate cultures in which reflective discourse about beliefs and values is conventionalized as attributes of leaders or specialists or as a situational format for conversation among ordinary people. In such settings the ethnographer is able to find informants who give explanations of, and commentaries on, their culture and its symbolic activities. He does not have to become a cryptographer, though he may still interpret their symbols in terms that go far beyond indigenous explanations. That cultures vary in the indigenous development of reflective discourse is hardly surprising, but the recognition of that fact in contemporary anthropology is worth mentioning as a finding closely related to the task of the ethnographer and to the reading and evaluation of cultural description by anthropologists and nonanthropologists alike.

The topic of partitioning culture into domains represents an area in which significant changes in anthropological viewpoints have occurred. Up to the 1950s, there was broad agreement among anthropologists that any culture could be partitioned into institutional components – economy, kinship and marriage, political organization, religion, and so on – and that these labels supplied most of the chapter headings for descriptive monographs. The question was then raised of the extent to which this set of partitions coincided with indigenous conceptual divisions, leading anthropologists to distinguish the *emic* perspective on a culture – that which represents its folk system of classification – from the *etic* perspective – that which is constructed by an outside investigator for comparative research purposes. Many anthropologists became more sensitive to emic partitions and more critical of the institutional ones previously held to be universal. In investigating a given topic, an ethnographer was more likely than before to pursue the indigenous conceptual structure regardless of its congruence with Western categories.

This approach produced some important results. Cultures as collective organizations of ideas, symbols, and meanings do not, it turns out, come internally packaged according to the headings once conventional in monographs nor according to any other single set of partitions yet discovered. In the anthropological study of folk medicine, for example, it has been found that the Western dichotomies of mind versus body and natural versus supernatural and the corresponding divisions between psychiatry, medicine, and religion rarely hold in other cultures where diagnostic categories and therapies combine what we would call psychiatric, somatic, and religious phenomena in a variety of emic constellations.

The Gusii are a case in point. As a psychological anthropologist, I have tried to assess their psychological functioning and development not only through the categories of Western psychologies but in terms of how Gusii individuals assess themselves and each other. I have, in other words, explored Gusii ethnopsychology, their indigenous framework for understanding mental phenomena and processes. What I found is that although the Gusii language contains terms for emotional and cognitive states and for character traits, there is only a small lexicon of distinctively mental phenomena and a limited framework for conceptualizing mental processes, particularly their subjective aspects. This negative finding is related to several noteworthy facts. First, normal Gusii conversation contains very little reference to personal intentions on the part of the speaker or others; actions are described for which attributions of intention are so well established in conventional discourse that explicit reference is unnecessary – and may also be experienced as dangerous (LeVine 1979). In their social discourse, then, the Gusii avoid "psychologizing," preferring to talk about the overt behavior of adults and children. There is no conventional format for "mental" assessment of self and others, so that the ethnographer's inquiries are likely to elicit answers about the physical health, economic situation, or habitual behavior of persons rather than about their subjective experience. In other words, questions about individual well-being that might elicit descriptions of affective and cognitive phenomena among Westerners are recast by Gusii into questions of health and material welfare.

Second, the Gusii conceptual framework for explaining the situations of health and economic resources that affect individual well-being is primarily spiritual or magico-religious and is most authoritatively employed by diviners who are consulted by persons in distress. The diviners operate, along with a variety of general and specialized practitioners, by treating afflictions the symptoms of which are disease, economic failure, and severe mental disorder and which are attributed to deceased ancestors or living witches. Third, in contrast with the poverty of Gusii "psychology," their "medicine" is richly elaborated: numerous diagnostic entities, a multitude of practitioners and specialties, considerable esoteric knowledge, hundreds of curative herbs, frequent consultations, a good deal of gossip and speculation. We could say their medicine is well developed but their psychology is not. But what we are calling their medicine is concerned with disruptions of personal well-being that might well be formulated as mental phenomena in another cultural context, for example, the fear of a neighbor's jealousy, the quarreling of brothers who are business partners, psychosis in the family, sexual dysfunction. Gusii practitioners regularly deal with such problems either by the use of herbal medicines with minimal diagnosis or (more frequently) by attributing them to ancestors or witches and prescribing sacrifice or protective medicine, respectively. So in a sense, their medicine, based in part on their religion, *is* their psychology and psychiatry.

Using the categories of religion, medicine, and psychology does not help to describe or understand this cultural pattern. Gusii folk knowledge is not divided into religious, medical, and mental domains and can only be understood as applying indigenous medical and spiritual categories to the diagnoses and treatment of all afflictions of the self, including those we consider psychological. In any event, religion, medicine, and psychology are not etic categories like the phonetic features of speech or the sensory capacities for color discrimination. They are instead categories based in the history of Western institutions, during the course of which they have become more differentiated than in many other cultures. Although broadly defined in contemporary Western social science, their origins in European emic concepts such as the mind–

body dualism become obvious when they are applied to cultures such as the Gusii. As an ethnopsychologist I had to discover the categories of experience for the Gusii rather than attempt to impose those brought from my own culture.

Other examples could be given. The point is that recent ethnography has eroded the previous consensus about how to partition culture for descriptive or comparative purposes. This does not mean that universal categories of culture will not be found, but only that the task requires more effort.

This overview of properties of culture is in no way complete. I have selected four general properties I find indispensable in making sense of my own ethnographic data and in attempting to generalize from the improved ethnographic studies of the last half century. Culture as I view it is collective, organized, multiplex, and variable, not as a matter of theoretical assumption but as a result of anthropological fieldwork in many parts of the world. The intensity of their fieldwork gives many anthropologists a perspective different from other social scientists, particularly in regard to the concept of culture. I have attempted to convey through illustration the basis for the conviction that culture is uniquely useful in comprehending human variation as documented by modern social anthropology. As the other social sciences take increased account of the world at large, they will have to take the concept of culture more seriously. This will require methodological readjustment, because cultural analysis runs counter to the preference for simplification that is prevalent in social-science research. A greater tolerance for complexity, however, will reward investigators with a deeper understanding of the phemonena they are studying and a firmer basis for interpreting the data they collect. Nowhere is this more likely than in child development research, as suggested in the concluding section of this chapter.

Acquiring culture

The acquisition of culture by children has long fascinated anthropologists, but it is only recently that research has begun to illuminate the processes involved. The work by Ochs and Schieffelin (Chapter 11, this volume) represents what I consider the most promising line of research. It is focused on the meanings of communicative actions and draws upon studies of language acquisition for its methods of data collection and analysis. One lesson emerging from this work is that research into how children acquire adult patterns can only be as strong as the analysis of the adult patterns being acquired. Advances in the analysis of language during the decades preceding their work have made possible the enlightenment produced by Ochs and Schieffelin concerning the acquisition of cultural meanings by children. Thus further analysis of culture in its nonlinguistic as well as linguistic dimensions should benefit research into the child's acquisition of culture.

The multiplexity of culture, and particularly the property of multiple meanings in cultural symbols, presents a difficult question for research into the acquisition of culture: How shall we conceptualize the means by which a child acquires the combination of meanings for a cultural symbol that anthropologists have claimed gives that symbol its affective power? In considering this question I have found useful the conceptualization by Shweder (Much & Shweder 1978; Shweder, Turiel, & Much 1981) of children's thinking about moral rules and their violation, particularly the distinction between intuitive and reflective understanding of the rules. The important point for me is that moral rules, like other cultural phenomena, permit of different kinds of knowing and that just as adults of a given community may vary in their ways of knowing their shared culture, so children may change as they grow in how they know the "same" symbols, accumulating meanings encoded at different levels of cognitive development. The intuitive meanings learned earliest would come closest to the sensory pole in Turner's (1967) conception of cultural symbols, whereas the reflective understanding acquired later would approximate his ideological pole.

In contrast with Piagetian theory, this approach to cultural acquisition assumes that earlier meanings are not lost but form the intuitive basis for emotional responsiveness to symbols even after the latter have been understood at a reflective level. Thus individuals growing up in a given cultural environment from childhood onward would respond to its public symbols in a way that reflects their multiple levels of cognitive experience with them, a way distinctly different from an individual whose experience with those symbols began in adulthood.

Turner's analysis of cultural symbols has concentrated on rituals and other public events to which the dramaturgical analogy is apt. In considering the acquisition of multiple meanings by children, however, a different analogy may help. Consider culture as architecture or more specifically, a given culture as a building. There are many ways of knowing a building: The architect and building contractor know it as a deliberate design that was initially embodied in a blueprint and later realized in a structure; the people who live or work in the building know it as a fixed environment for their activities and their relationships; those who visit to look at it may classify it on the basis of its style or its place in the history of architecture. All of these kinds of knowing, varying widely in their degree of reflectiveness concerning the structural and aesthetic characteristics of the building, are valid. They are complementary rather than contradictory intellectual perspectives on the building, even though they may lead to opposite emotional reactions: An architectural masterpiece admired by professionals may be hated by those who work there; a house enjoyed by its inhabitants may be resented by the neighbors for its ugliness. As a part of collective reality for everyone who comes into contact with it, the building permits of multiple forms of apprehension according to the architectural sophistication of the person, the purposes with which the person approaches the building, the nature of the contact, and the history of contacts. Furthermore, the building lasts beyond one generation and becomes a reality for others, but they may renovate it, refurnish it, use it differently, or bring a different set of standards to the act of judging it.

If the building is a house, a child who has grown up in it and continues to live in it as an adult has an experience analogous to the acquisition of culture. The child comes to know the house from earliest awareness as a series of self-related living, sleeping, playing spaces inhabited by members of the family and other familiar creatures and objects. As the child grows older, the overall spatial and functional organization of the house becomes clearer, and a reflective conceptualization of its features transcends the intuitive knowledge of the structure as an environment for early experience. The memories of that intuitive knowledge are not lost, however, and the meaning of the house for the adult is comprised of experience at all levels of cognitive awareness. For such a person, the utilitarian perspective on the house, perfectly reasonable as an overriding standard for adult decision making, is modified by the emotionally powerful intuitive representations of the same building as remembered from childhood. The multiplicity of experience over time has produced a multiplicity of meanings.

Like all analogies, this one has limits even for conveying its central point. People have strong feelings about buildings they have not lived in as children, and buildings are both more and less permanent than cultures – depending on which building and which culture. Furthermore, it is probably more typical of human experience to know the "same" cultural symbols (with some revisions) as both child and adult than to know the same house at such different stages of life. (For peoples like the Gusii, however, an adult's house is carefully built to replicate the symbolically important features of the house he – and other Gusii – grew up in, so that the house is the embodiment of the cultural symbols known as child and adult.) The analogy is useful, however, in pointing to the enormous disparity in equally valid types of knowing permitted by both buildings and cultures (the architect vs. the night watchman; the philosophical informant vs. the inarticulate participant) and to the possibility that these types could form a developmental hierarchy during the psychological maturation of the individual so that the child's intuitive understandings of a structure, physical or symbolic, are cognitively superseded by the more reflective awareness of the adult, without the latter eradicating the former in subjective experience. Insofar as this possibility proves true, research into the child's acquisition of culture will shed important light on the problem of multiple meanings in cultural symbols.

References

Benedict, R. 1934. *Patterns of Culture*. Boston: Houghton Mifflin.
Driver, H. E. 1966. Geographical-historical *versus* psycho-functional explanations of kin avoidances. *Current Anthropology* 7:131–60.

Freud, S. 1913. *Totem and Taboo* (Standard Edition, vol. 13). London: Hogarth.

Geertz, C. 1973. *The Interpretation of Cultures*. New York: Basic Books.

Geertz, H., & Geertz, C. 1975. *Kinship in Bali*. New York: Free Press.

Kuhn, T. 1962. *The Structure of Scientific Revolutions*. Chicago: University of Chicago Press.

LeVine, R. A. 1963. Witchcraft and sorcery in a Gusii community. In J. Middleton & E. Winter, eds., *Witchcraft and Sorcery in East Africa*. London: Routledge & Kegan Paul.

    1973. *Culture, Behavior and Personality*. Chicago: Aldine.

LeVine, R. A., & LeVine, B. B. 1966. *Nyansongo: A Gusii Community in Kenya*. New York: Wiley.

LeVine, S. 1979. *Mothers and Wives: Gusii Women of East Africa*. Chicago: University of Chicago Press.

Malinowski, B. 1924. *Argonauts of the Western Pacific*. New York: Dutton.

Mayer, P. 1954. *Witches*. Inaugural lecture, Rhodes University. Grahamstown, South Africa.

Much, N., & Shweder, R. A. 1978. Speaking of rules: the analysis of culture in breach. In W. Damon, ed., *New Directions for Child Development: Moral Development*. San Francisco: Jossey-Bass.

Murdock, G. P. 1949. *Social Structure*. New York: Macmillan.

Shweder, R. A., Turiel, E., & Much, N. 1981. The moral intuitions of the child. In J. H. Flavell & L. Ross, eds., *Social cognitive development*. Cambridge: Cambridge University Press.

Stephens, W., & D'Andrade, R. 1962. Kin-avoidance. In W. Stephens, ed., *The Oedipus Complex: Cross-Cultural Evidence*. New York: Free Press.

Sweetser, D. A. 1962. Avoidance, social affiliation and the incest taboo. *Ethnology* 5:304–16.

Turner, V. W. 1967. *The Forest of Symbols*. Ithaca, N.Y.: Cornell University Press.

Tylor, E. B. 1889. On a method of investigating the development of institutions: applied to laws of marriage and descent. *Journal of the Royal Anthropological Institute of Great Britian and Ireland* 18:245–72.

Wilson, M. H. 1952. *Good Company: A Study of the Nyakyusa Age Villages*. London: Oxford University Press.

ural meaning systems

Roy G. D'Andrade

Background

Between 1955 and 1960 the human sciences changed in a radical way.
Before 1955 the dominant paradigm was behaviorism, with its assumption that most things about people – personality, culture, and
language – could be understood as complexes of stimulus and response
connections. During the late 1950s this paradigm was confronted across
a number of disciplines. In psychology, Jerome Bruner, George Miller,
and others developed cognitive and information-processing views of
action and learning. In linguistics, Chomsky showed that Bloomfield's
behavioristic concept of grammar could not in principle account for
the capacities of natural language grammars (Chomsky, 1957). And in
anthropology, Geertz, Goodenough, Hall, Schneider, Wallace, and
others presented the argument that culture consists not of behaviors,
or even patterns of behavior, but rather of shared information or knowledge encoded in systems of symbols.

While this revolution was influenced by Europeans such as Piaget,
Saussure, and later, Levi-Strauss, the main force of the revolt came,
I believe, from the intellectual wave of ideas accompanying the development of the modern computer. One might have felt convinced
when reading Skinner that the scientific study of people does not need
concepts involving unobservable mental processes, such as thinking
and feeling. Such a conviction was hard to hold, however, with the
advent of computer programs that played chess and solved logic problems. If computers could have programs, why couldn't people?

The major difference between the behaviorist and cognitive paradigms concerns the role of internal representations. In the behaviorist
tradition, what a creature does is controlled, in large part, by various
external conditions, such as the presence of conditioned and uncon-
ditioned stimuli and the number of hours of deprivation. In the cognitive
paradigm, what a creature does is, in large part, a function of the creature's internal representation of its environment. For many anthropologists, the emphasis of the cognitive paradigm on internal representations had a better fit to their intuitions about the nature of culture
than did the behaviorist notions of stimulus control.

The conception of culture as knowledge and symbol rather than habit
and behavior was rapidly assimilated into anthropology and the human

sciences. Culture came to be seen as an information-holding system with functions similar to those of cellular DNA. For individual cells, DNA provides the information needed for self-regulation and specialized growth. For humans, the instructions needed for coping with the environment and performing specialized roles are provided in learned information, which is symbolically encoded and culturally transmitted.

In considering the concept of culture from a cognitive perspective, this chapter examines several current positions and related theoretical issues. First, the characterization of culture as a body of knowledge is discussed, and the criticisms of this position are reviewed with special reference to the part of constitutive rules in culture. Related to these issues, the treatment of cultural meaning systems as purely representational in character is criticized, and the argument is advanced that meaning systems have directive and evocative as well as representational functions. Problems with the current use of the term *symbol* are discussed, along with the difficulties involved in treating meaning systems as if they existed solely in external messages. The unnoticed development of a body of experimental techniques in the investigation of meaning systems by anthropologists and other social scientists is reviewed. Finally, the relationships between culture, social structure, personality, and experience are examined, and a definition of culture presented.

Culture and culturally constructed things

The initial cognitive formulations of culture focused on *knowledge*. "A society's culture consists of whatever it is one has to know or believe in order to operate in a manner acceptable to its members" (Goodenough 1957). In Goodenough's framework, knowledge typically consists of rules – rules by which one decides where to live, how kin are to be classified, how deference is to be expressed, and so on. Thus, just as a computer operates by means of a program consisting of a set of rules that prescribe what actions are to be taken under various conditions, so the individual can be seen as operating by means of a cultural program. Although Goodenough did not adopt the information-processing terminology and flow-chart formats of computer science, such a vocabulary and set of formats were developed by others in the ethnoscience and cognitive anthropology tradition (e.g., Geoghegan 1971).

The "culture as knowledge" formulation proved to have considerable potential for ethnographic investigation and theoretical analysis. Cultural knowledge about plants, animals, land use, and navigation proved to be rich areas for ethnographic description. More theoretically, the idea that the complexity and heterogeneity of observed behavior could be accounted for by a small number of rules led to the development of formal and quasi-formal decision-making models capable of generating complex outputs from the interaction of a small number of external inputs and internal rules (Casson 1981). Descriptively adequate and psychologically plausible models were developed to account for such things as kin term systems, patterns of residence, market choices, and legal fines. (For a review and critique of these models, see Quinn 1975.)

Although the conception of culture as consisting of the shared knowledge of individual minds marked a clear advance over earlier theories of culture, problems and attendant dissatisfactions quickly arose, becoming prominent by the 1970s. Three major problems became apparent: first, many things one would want to call cultural are not completely or even generally shared; second, culture consists of more than just knowledge; and third, it is not clear whether cultural systems are to be found "inside" or "outside" the minds of individuals. The latter two issues were neatly caught in Geertz's example of a Beethoven quartet (1973:11–12).

> If . . . we take, say, a Beethoven quartet as an, admittedly rather special but for these purposes, nicely illustrative, sample of culture, no one would, I think, identify it with its score, with the skills and knowledge needed to play it, with the understanding of it possessed by its performers or auditors, nor . . . with a particular performance of it or with some mysterious entity transcending material existence. The "no one" is perhaps too strong here, for there are always incorrigibles. But that a Beethoven quartet is a temporally developed tonal structure, a coherent sequence of modeled sound – in a word, music – and not anybody's knowledge of or belief about anything, including how to play it, is a proposition to which most people are, upon reflection, likely to assent.

To continue the argument with a different example: Marriage is part of American culture, but marriage is not the same thing as knowing how to marry people or knowing how to get married or understanding what it is to be married. Most Americans have an understanding of what banishment is and how to banish someone (were they Richard II), yet these understandings do not make banishment a possibility in American culture.

If marriage is not the same thing as knowing about marriage, what is it? According to John Searle, marriage is a special kind of fact (1969:51–52):

> Any newspaper records facts of the following sorts: Mr. Smith married Miss Jones; the Dodgers beat the Giants three to two in eleven innings; Green was convicted of larceny; and Congress passed the Appropriations Bill. . . . There is no simple set of statements about physical or psychological properties of states of affairs to which the statements of facts such as these are reducible. A marriage ceremony, a baseball game, a trial, and a legislative action involve a variety of physical movements, states, and

raw feels, but . . . the physical events and raw feels only count as parts of such events given certain other conditions and against a background of certain kinds of institutions. . . . It is only given the institution of marriage that certain forms of behavior constitute Mr. Smith's marrying Miss Jones. Similarly, it is only given the institution of baseball that certain movements by certain men constitute the Dodgers' beating the Cubs 3 to 2 in eleven innings.

These "institutions" are systems of constitutive rules. Every institutional fact is underlain by a (system of) of rule(s) of the form "X counts as Y in context C."

Marriage is a part of American culture in that there is a constitutive system of rules that individuals know, which are intersubjectively shared and adhered to. Enactment of certain behaviors counts in certain contexts as "getting married," and once married, certain obligations and commitments are incurred. Marriage is a culturally created entity – *an entity created by the social agreement that something counts as that entity.* To agree that something will count as something else is more than simply knowing about it, although knowing about it is a necessary precondition. The *agreement* that something counts as something else involves the *adherence* of a group of people to a *constitutive rule* and to the entailments incurred by the application of the rule.

Probably every cultural category "creates" an entity, in the sense that what is understood to be "out there" is affected by the culturally based associations built into the category system. The English language cultural categories of stone, tree, and hand invoke a variety of shared connotations about these objects that add to whatever may be their reality as brute facts, but these cultural connotations do not manufacture the objects themselves from thin air. The cultural categories of *marriage, money,* and *theft,* on the other hand, are created solely by adherence to the constitutive rule systems that define them. Without these rule systems these objects would not exist.

Games make the most effective illustrations of constitutive rule systems, perhaps because the arbitrary nature of games makes the separation between the physical events of the game and what these events count as quite apparent. When a football player is declared "out of bounds," everyone understands that the physical fact of stepping over the line counts as being out of bounds only with respect to the game being played. However, everyday events like the theft of a sum of money are more likely to be treated as plain physical facts. To see theft as a culturally created entity, one must be able to isolate the system of rules about what constitutes theft from the fact of physical removal and realize that physical removal of an object counts as theft only if certain conditions about intentions and ownership are satisfied.

A large number of the variables of social science refer to culturally created things. Family, property, deviance, prestige, race, and nationhood, for example, are all created by social agreement about what counts as what. The point is not an obvious one: Various anthropologists have had an uphill battle in trying to convince the rest of the field that what is called kinship, for example, is created by a system of constitutive rules, not simply by facts of nature (Schneider 1968).

Not all social-science variables refer to culturally created things; some variables refer to objects and events that exist prior to, and independent of, their definition: for example, a person's age, the number of calories consumed during a meal, the number of chairs in a room, or the pain someone felt. Searle, following Anscombe (1958), calls the existence of such things "brute facts," in contrast to "institutional facts." Some social science variables, however, are not clearly either one or the other. For example, in many cases it is not clear whether the term *social class* refers to a set of cultural categories, which create the very thing they define, or to a culturally postulated entity, which exists independently of any cultural categories – or to certain aspects of both.

It is not just social scientists who are unclear about these matters. People often believe it is natural for women or fathers or Indians to act in certain ways. The problem is not whether these classes of persons have culturally learned roles – most people agree that some part of what persons in these classes do is culturally learned role behavior – but rather which parts are role-created and which parts are natural expressions of character. It seems to be the case that people have a tendency to treat culturally created things as if they were natural things, perhaps because what is culturally created is often intricately intertwined with what occurs naturally and perhaps because it gives greater moral force to the idea that one should act in some certain way if it is thought that it is natural to act in that particular way. Thus, if one thinks of constitutive rules as culturally based "verdicts" about what counts as what, one can often find these verdicts behind what seem like naturalistic observations. For example, as Schneider (1968) has pointed out, the "observation" that kinship is made of flesh and blood contains the verdict that the physical facts of biological relatedness count as shared identity, which then entails the presumption that certain kinds of rights and duties will be assumed between "kin" as a matter of course.

Although the objects created by constitutive rules are just abstractions, these abstractions can be embodied in physical tokens. For example, flags, capitals and uniforms are treated as the embodiments of a nation-state, paper bills are treated as embodiments of wealth, signatures are considered to represent personal commitment. Part of the extensive embodiment of constitutive entities seems to be a matter of practicality – it is easier to play chess with ivory pieces than to try to hold the game in one's mind, writing makes it possible to freeze talk in a timeless mode, and tokens like money and checks are a great convenience. Such embodiments as flags and uniforms also serve to create awe and respect, which, as Bentham pointed out, can be an advantage for those who rule.

Most constitutive rules are organized in a series of hierarchically linked systems. A memo, for example, involves a hierarchy of constitutive systems that link letters to sounds, sounds to words, words to sentences, and sentences to speech acts such as requests and commitments. Constitutive rules are not only linked hierarchically but are also organized into elaborate systems, creating whole complexes of cultural entities. Thus the football complex creates *touchdowns, quarterbacks, field goals, offsides, downs,* and so on. The family complex creates marriages, mothers, fathers, homes, joint property, relatives, in-laws, incest taboos, adultery, divorce, alimony, inheritance, breaking away, get-togethers, and so on. Furthermore, constitutive systems tend to interpenetrate; for example, the family complex is intertwined with the property complex, the legal complex, and the religious complex. Schneider (1976) has termed these complexes *galaxies* and discussed how the complexes that include nationality, religion, locality, ethnicity, and family interpenetrate in American culture.

It is of some interest that both Searle and Schneider have pressed the point that constitutive rules (in Schneider's terms *culture as constituted*) are to be distinguished from regulatory rules (Schneider's *norms*). According to Searle:

> Regulative rules regulate antecedently or independently existing forms of behavior; for example, many rules of etiquette regulate inter-personal relationships which exist independently of the rules. But constitutive rules do not merely regulate, they create or define new forms of behavior. . . . Regulative rules characteristically take the form of or can be paraphrased as imperatives, e.g., "When cutting food, hold the knife in the right hand," or "Officers must wear ties at dinner." Some constitutive rules take quite a different form, e.g., "A checkmate is made when the king is attacked in such a way that no move will leave it unattacked." (1969:33–4)

According to Schneider:

> Culture contrasts with norms in that norms are oriented to patterns *for action,* whereas culture constitutes a body of definitions, premises, statements, postulates, presumptions, propositions, and perceptions about the nature of the universe and man's place in it. Where norms tell the actor how to play the scene, culture tells the actor how the scene is set and what it all means. Where norms tell the actor how to behave in the presence of ghosts, gods, and human beings, culture tells the actor what ghosts, gods, and human beings are and what they are all about. (1976:202–3)

Basically, both Schneider and Searle see the distinction between the constitutive and the regulatory as a contrast between ideas that create realities and ideas that order or constrain action. The distinction is a necessary one if one wishes to analyze the relation between meanings and action, although each tends to be linked to the other, in that regulatory rules tend to be linked to the entities created by constitutive rules. For example, in a game of checkers, if a piece counts as a king, this means it can move in either direction. In the world of property, if an object is sold, this means the seller no longer has certain rights over the object. Such entailments come as part of the very definition of the entity, so that what is being constructed is not just an object, event, or relationship but is also a set of rules about what follows, given that something counts as that object, event, or relationship. Thus if war is declared in the United States, this declaration has a complex set of entailments concerning the powers of the president and the duties of citizens. It is a basic part of constitutive rule systems that the entities created have entailments to norms, and norms in turn entail action. Such entailments are not a matter of logic, but rather consist of the assumption that such linkages exist (Friedrich 1977).

Just as most, if not all, constitutive entities entail certain norms of action, so most, if not all, norms are linked to certain constitutive rules. Wearing a tie, conducting an exorcism, or holding a knife in the right hand are linked to constitutive rules by which formality is defined and created, by which the notion of a spirit that can inhabit the body of a person is defined and created, or by which the notion of politeness is defined and created. Whole systems of norms, such as a kinship system or political system, are linked to whole systems of constitutive rules. This linkage is not a matter of logical necessity – very similar constitutive rules can be linked to quite different norms. Thus, for example, exactly which norms follow from the constitutive fact that two persons are of the same flesh and blood may vary quite widely in different subcultures in the United States (Schneider 1968).

One consequence of constitutive rule systems is the enormous expansion of the behavioral repertoire of humans compared with the behavioral repertoires of other animals. For example, without the system of constitutive rules called football, the behaviors of scoring, blocking, passing, and so on would not exist. Without the constitutive systems of morality, etiquette, and efficiency, the behaviors of cheating, being rude, slacking off, and so on would not exist (Much & Shweder 1978). Even the common and basic interpersonal acts of asserting, agreeing, requesting, and promising would not exist without the system of constitutive rules for speech acts (Austin 1962; Searle 1969; 1978; Vendler 1972).

In talking about the creation of realities, it should be understood that what is being proposed is *not* the creation of realities of the type popularized by Carlos Castanada. Castanada appears to be proposing that there are alternative physical realities – as if under special conditions people can magically transform themselves into other people, fly through the air, and affect others with their thoughts. What is being proposed here is not that people can magically transform physical reality but that people can create conventions, such as nationality and marriage, which are then taken account of as facts – something that exists.

A class of culturally created entities that I have been attempting to analyze involves the domain of *success*. This domain includes a number of elements referred to by such terms as *accomplishment, recognition, prestige, self-satisfaction, goals, ability, hard work, competition*, and the like. In American culture, success is a personal characteristic of great importance to most people. Such daily events as the organization of daily effort, the evaluation of task performance, and the marking of accomplishment through self-announcement and the congratulations of others are closely attended to and much discussed.

A number of the elements of the world of success appear to be connected to each other through putative causal relations. Certain things are thought to lead to success, whereas other things are thought to result from success. Based on the initial data I have collected, it seems to be the case that Americans think that if one has ability, and if, because of competition or one's own strong drive, one works hard at achieving high goals, one will reach an outstanding level of accomplishment. And when one reaches this level one will be recognized as a success, which brings prestige and self-satisfaction.

In *success*, the boundary line that divides a high from an ordinary level of accomplishment is not precisely specified. Often people do not know if they are really a success until some special award or position has been granted. This problem – deciding exactly what fits under the constitutive rule – appears to be endemic in social life. In a personal communication on this topic, Aaron Cicourel has pointed out:

> Searle's use of the term "constitutive rule" refers more to the general ideals or beliefs we share about a marriage ceremony, a baseball game, a trial or a legislative action than to the daily organized practices that produce marriages, baseball games, trials and legislative action. . . . John Rawls' distinction (1955) between a general rule or policy and a particular case said to fall under the rule can be instructive here. The constitutive and normative rules making up institutions do not provide instructions to members of a group on how to decide which daily life activities are constructive. A policeman, for example, when making an arrest, is usually responding to a particular case as viewed under local contextual conditions and general personal conceptions of what is right and wrong. In order to justify his actions, the policeman must find a general rule or law statute to validate his actions with the particular case (Cicourel, 1968). There are many situations where this duality of knowledge about general rules and deciding that a particular case falls under one or more of them is crucially apparent. We are often confronted with situations in which our knowledge of constitutive rules becomes strained because of particular prac-

tices or cases that do not neatly fit any normal case. We tend to be comfortable with idealization in our everyday talk about institutions, but seldom examine the "normalization" required to use normative categories when we encounter discrepancies in practice. Adherence to a constitutive rule is a variable accomplishment. Interpretive procedures are needed for members to link constitutive rules with daily practices and *vice versa*.

The duality Cicourel refers to contributes to making the ongoing process of social and cultural life a matter of at least occasional dispute and negotiation. One may be quite clear that X counts as Y, but it is often difficult to decide whether one is actually in the presence of a true X. To use a constitutive rule that X counts as Y requires the dual rule that X can be identified by the presence of features f1 . . . fn. And often some of the features f1 . . . fn are missing, ambiguous, or disputable, making it problematic whether or not something is an X, thereby making it problematic whether one is in the presence of a Y.

Indeed, some of the deepest social conflicts occur over the issue of the scope of a particular constitutive rule. Current debates about abortion and the rights of the fetus, the equality of women, the determination of comparable worth for different jobs, the two-mile ocean limit to national sovereignty, and the age at which a person can appropriately engage in sexual activity attest to the importance of the determination of the scope of constitutive rules in social change. Debate about which constitutive rule is the right rule is rarely if ever resolved by means of logic or physical fact.

The functions of meaning systems

In saying that success is a personal characteristic of great importance to many Americans, I mean to say more than that some people think frequently about success. The argument I wish to make is that the meaning system involving the world of success, like most meaning systems, does more than represent facts and create entities. How one thinks of meaning depends on what one thinks meanings *do*. Meanings in general, and cultural meaning systems in particular, do at least four different things. Meanings represent the world, create cultural entities, direct one to do certain things, and evoke certain feelings. These four functions of meaning – the *representational*, the *constructive*, the *directive*, and the *evocative* – are differentially elaborated in particular cultural meaning systems but are always present to some degree in any system.

The current view, with some exceptions, treats meaning as having only representational functions. From the representational point of view, culture consists of knowledge and belief about the world, carried by true or false propositions composed of terms whose definition rests on potentially observable characteristics. This view has certain merits. First, cultural meaning systems generally have strong representational functions – with some exceptions, such as music, some of the arts, and ritual. Second, the representational function has great adaptational value – culture consists at least of knowledge about what is out there and what can be done with it, and this knowledge is carried through representation.

It seems clear, however, that most systems of meaning that are culturally acquired are not purely representational. In the earlier discussion concerning constitutive rules it was pointed out that cultural entities like marriage could not be created from representational understandings alone. Besides understanding what counts as what, the creation of cultural things logically requires that people be bound to count X as Y and accept the entailments that follow. For example, most of us are bound to use words as they are normally understood, to accept paper money for our labor, to take responsibility for our kin – otherwise words would not be words, money would not be money, kin would not be kin.

It needs to be stressed that learning a meaning system does not result in the learner's automatically and involuntarily following rules. Rather, various elements of the meaning system come to have a *directive* force, experienced by the person as needs or obligations to do something. For example, when the ordinary event of being asked a question occurs, one is not automatically impelled to answer, but the effect of normal socialization is that we experience a strong pressure to give an answer. Similarly, marriage in the United States involves a complex set of commitments that have directive force on individuals, commitments that are consciously made and experienced individually as powerful obligations (Quinn 1980).

The assertion that people feel strong obligations and pressures as a result of socialization is not an unusual claim. Often, however, such obligations and pressures are treated by social theorists as if they were generated entirely by sanctions external to the individual. Spiro (1961:95–106) has pointed out that the antipsychological position of those who believe that conformity to cultural norms is due not to individual motivation but to external social sanctions in fact contains implicitly the psychological theory that people are, as individuals, motivated by exactly these sanctions.

A related theory proposes that the directives of cultural rules are based on the individual's generalized desire to conform to whatever it is that other people are observed to do or whatever it is other people say one should do, rather than on what people really want to do. Although both external sanctions and conformity pressures certainly occur as means of social control and are probably necessary, the empirical evidence indicates that these kinds of extrinsic motivators are rarely the primary type of control in any society and are most prevalent in those historical periods marked by social anomie and mental pathology (Spiro 1961:103).

More commonly or typically, the goals stipulated in the cultural meaning system are intrinsically rewarding; that is, through the process of socialization, individuals come to find achieving culturally prescribed goals and following cultural directives to be motivationally satisfying and to find not achieving such goals or following such directives to be anxiety producing (Spiro 1961:104–5). There appear to be two major intrinsic motivational systems involved with cultural meaning systems: The first is relatively direct personal reward; the second is reward because of attachment to a particular set of values. Typically the two are mixed: For example, in the cultural meaning system involving success, accomplishment may be rewarding both because it satisfies personal needs for recognition, achievement and security, and because it represents the "good" self.

In general, the directive functions of most cultural meaning systems are highly overdetermined: Overdetermined in the sense that social sanctions, plus pressure for conformity, plus intrinsic direct reward, plus values, are all likely to act together to give a particular meaning system its directive force. For example, consider again the American meaning system of success. There are external sanctions involving money and employment, there are conformity pressures of many kinds, and there are the direct personal rewards and value satisfactions already mentioned. Perhaps what is surprising is that anyone can resist the directive force of such a system – that there are incorrigibles.

It may be objected that what I have been calling directive functions are more a part of personality and psychology than of culture and anthropology. After all, aren't things like goals and values part of an individual's personality, involving complex psychological processes like the formation of motives and the avoidance of anxiety? Doesn't the connection between symbol and motive come about only after elaborate socialization experiences, and aren't there many cultural symbols that are unrelated to motives? Isn't the inclusion of *directive* and *affective* functions in cultural systems of any sort a confusion of individual and cultural levels of analysis?

These objections are based on the assumption that for something to be truly cultural it must be acquired and performed without any significant involvement of psychological processes. There appears to be an implicit assumption in anthropology that anything that is known to involve complex psychological processes cannot also be cultural. Thus attitudes, needs, goals, and defenses, because they clearly involve complex psychological processes, are typically considered to be part of personality, not culture, no matter how shared or institutionalized a particular attitude, need, goal, or defense may be.

What is not appreciated is that *most* human behavior involves complex psychological processes. Take, for example, the formulation that culture is primarily knowledge. It is widely assumed that knowledge can be transmitted without involving psychological processes to any significant extent: Someone tells someone else something, then the other person knows it. Simple communication through the transmission of information has occurred. George Lakoff has discussed this metaphor of transmission in detail and has indicated some of the confusions it engenders (Lakoff & Johnson 1980; see also Reddy 1976).

According to the transmission metaphor of communication, the speaker puts ideas into words (like objects put into boxes) and sends them via voice or letter to a hearer, who gets the ideas from the words (more or less as the speaker packed them). The transmission of objects in boxes requires no psychological processing – all that is needed is a physical system of moving boxes. But this is not true of ideas. For ideas to be communicated there must be a set of psychological mechanisms by which meanings are mapped into and out of physical signals – a procedure that is, so far as we now understand it, psychologically complex.

There are a number of reasons why it is easy to overlook the psychological processing involved in the transmission of knowledge. First, once a person understands a language, it is easy to forget how much learning went into acquiring it. Second, it is easy to overlook the psychological processing that operates as information is transmitted, since the processes involved in understanding and producing speech are usually out of awareness and highly automatic. In general, there appears to be a sharp difference between the kind of psychological processes that are involved in cognition and perception and the kind of processes that are involved in motivation and feeling. When someone tells one something, it seems as if ideas come automatically with the words, whereas feelings and desires are experienced as aroused from some place within the mind, separate from the perceived symbol. But however these things seem, it is, I argue, the case that ideas, feelings, and intentions are all activated by symbols and are thus part of the meaning of symbols.

In general, there are a variety of lines of evidence that indicate that any human system of meaning is likely to involve affect. First, humans appear to have an affective response to almost any stimulus, no matter how decontextualized. Even a small patch of colored paint on a sheet of paper seems capable of arousing distinct and well-shared affective responses (D'Andrade & Egan 1974). Second, some symbolic forms, such as poetry and music, clearly arouse strong and well-organized affective responses. Third, in ordinary speech there is a rich variety of expressive and evocative forms, such as thanks, apologies, condemnations, regrets, condolences, curses, congratulations, exclamations, cries, and cheers. All these kinds of evidence indicate that there is an emotional side to meaning. Often the evocative function blends with the directive function into a powerful good-happy-like approach versus a bad-fright/anger-dislike-hit/flee attitude, as Osgood's work with the semantic differential, in which these terms are commonly found together, demonstrates (Osgood, May, & Miron 1975).

One objection to the postulation that meanings have an affective function is the "affective recall thesis," which says that the affective responses of people when using symbols are due just to the natural or learned emotional reactions people have to the things referred to by the symbols. Thus, for example, it could be said that the exciting quality of the symbols that involve success is due to the excitement originally instigated by the events being referred to, and recalled by, the use of symbols that refer to these events.

It seems very likely that the process of affective recall does occur. It seems unlikely, however, that this process alone can account for the kind and degree of feeling aroused by symbols. An often-mentioned counterexample to the affective recall argument illustrates that there can be different affective content to words that refer to the same physical object. For example, each of the terms *feces, shit, poo, stool, crap, excrement,* and *turd* has a distinct kind of affective charge, although all these terms refer to the same thing. Each symbol appears to be a condensation of a number of affectively linked associations within a meaning system that cannot be explained on a simple experiential basis. Furthermore, it would be very difficult to imagine how the widespread personal agreement about the affective qualities of each of these terms could be arrived at through similarities in the physical experience of individuals.

In summary, the general position presented here is that meanings involve the total human psyche, not just the part of us that knows things. Every aspect of meaning systems requires a great deal of psychological processing and often considerable experiential priming. It takes years of learning for a child to acquire the representational functions of meaning systems. Representation occurs only because symbols activate complex psychological processes. In the same way, it takes years of learning for a child to acquire the constructive, directive, and evocative functions of meaning systems, and these functions, too, require complex psychological processes. The representational, constructive, directive, and evocative functions are each a consequence of the way the human brain is organized, a biological and psychological potentiality that is highly elaborated and stimulated by cultural meaning systems.

I have presented elsewhere the thesis that part of the tendency to play down the affective aspect of culture is based on the widely shared asumption that reason and emotion are basically in conflict and that emotion comes from the more animal and less advanced part of the human psyche. I believe this thesis is wrong, that thinking and feeling are parallel processes that have evolved together because both are needed for any animal to attend to its needs in a highly intelligent way (D'Andrade 1981). Both processes tell us about how the world is. Sometimes both agree, and sometimes they disagree about what is the case and what should be done about it. The Socratic metaphor of reason and passion as two horses pulling a chariot seems much more accurate than the current metaphor of the war of reason and emotion. In any case, the assumption that reason and feeling are essentially and basically in conflict appears to be deeply ingrained in American and European culture, reinforcing the assumption that meaning is – or should be – entirely representational (Shweder 1981).

Others have expressed some of the views presented here at earlier times. Clifford Geertz, in his essay on "The Growth of Culture and the Evolution of Mind," stated:

> Not only ideas, but emotions too, are cultural artifacts in man.
> . . . The kinds of cultural symbols that serve the intellective and affective sides of human mentality tend to differ – discursive language, experimental routines, mathematics, and so on, on the one hand; myth, ritual and art on the other. But the contrast should not be drawn too sharply: mathematics has its affective uses, poetry its intellectual; and the difference in any case is only functional, not substantial. (1973:81)

When I first read this passage I did not so much disagree as believe it to be irrelevant to the kind of problems I was working on. The affective, directive aspect of symbols, I thought, was to be found in religion and art – in the kinds of symbols Levy (1981) has called "marked symbols," in contrast to the commonsense world of "embedded symbols," such as kinship terminologies or classifications of illness. What I did not see was that my model of meaning led me to select for analysis that part of any system of symbols that was most representational and least affective or directive. Thus the componential analyses of kinship terminologies I was using could account beautifully for the way in which kin types are categorized but could not account for such simple aspects of meaning as understanding what is meant by the phrase "Susan is a good mother." It was not until I came to appreciate that even (and especially) kinship terminologies were not simply representational – that kin terms had a core of culturally constructed, highly affective, and directive elements as well as a representational aspect (Schneider 1965) – that the relevance of human emotionality and intentionality to the analysis of meaning in general became apparent to me (D'Andrade 1976).

Meaning systems versus symbol systems

Throughout this chapter the term *meaning system* has been used where the more conventional term *symbol system* may have been expected. The shift in terminology is intentional, based on a particular view about where meaning is and how it is organized.

The problem of "where meaning is" has been discussed by Douglas Hofstadter in his remarkable book, *Gödel, Escher, Bach*:

> The issue we are broaching is whether meaning can be said to be inherent in a message, or whether meaning is always manufac-

tured by the interaction of a mind or a mechanism with a message. . . . In the latter case, meaning could not be said to be located in any single place, nor could it be said that a message has any universal, or objective, meaning, since each observer could bring its own meaning to each message. But in the former case, meaning would have both location and universality. (1979:158)

Hofstadter presents two different models of how messages are related to meaning, using as examples jukebox buttons versus a phonograph record. He begins by pointing out that we feel quite comfortable with the idea that a record contains the same information as a piece of music, because we know or trust that there is an isomorphism, or one-to-one correspondence, between the physical characteristics of the groove patterns in the record and the sounds we hear.

When we push buttons on a jukebox and music comes out, we do not think that the buttons themselves contain the same information as the music we hear, even though something about the buttons produced the music. Because the characteristics of the buttons do not have a one-to-one correspondence to the characteristics of the music we hear, we realize that the musical information is not "in" the buttons but rather is triggered by the buttons. We reasonably assume that inside the machine is something that already contains the information necessary to produce the music (a very small musician, perhaps).

With respect to culture, this question is usually put in the following form: Where does one look for meaning – in culturally produced messages of various sorts or in the minds of the people who interpret these messages? If variations in the physical forms that make up the manifest message have the appropriate one-to-one correspondence to the meaning carried by the message, then the cultural analyst need only have the proper intelligence to determine its meaning. But if the message is highly compacted and lacks the necessary isomorphism between variations in the physical signal and the meanings produced, then the message cannot be deciphered by the cultural analyst without recourse to the latent system already present in the mind of the decoder.

Some cultural messages appear to contain a great deal of internal structure, whereas other messages are closer to being triggers than to being records. The letters *d*, *o*, *g* are much more like jukebox buttons than a record of doggishness. On the other hand, the script of a play can have such a rich internal structure that in some ways it almost seems to be a literal record of experience.

This problem of the location of meaning has been discussed at length by Schank and Abelson (1977), who have attempted to create computer programs that can understand such standard cultural messages as newspaper stories. They define understanding as the ability to answer questions about what happened in the story and to generate a paraphrase. To create programs to accomplish this feat, Schank and Abelson have found it necessary to build into their programs knowledge about cultural roles, settings, goals, and event sequences. Say, for example, one reads the following story:

> Roger went to the restaurant. He ordered *coq au vin*. The waiter was surly and the table was right next to a cash register. Roger left a very small tip.

To answer questions such as:

What did Roger eat?
To whom did Roger give his order?
Where did Roger sit?
Did Roger like the restaurant?
Who was the tip for?

it is necessary to use cultural information (since none of the answers to these questions is explicitly contained in the story) concerning the facts that one normally gets to eat what one orders, one normally gives one's order to the waiter, one normally sits at a table, one normally indicates satisfaction with food and service by the size of the tip, one is normally not satisfied if the waiter and the surroundings are not pleasant, and normally tables right next to the cash register are not pleasant. Furthermore, readers expect, in the absence of other explicit factors, what happened was what one would normally expect to happen. Without this additional information and the normality assumption, one could not answer the questions above and the story could not be understood.

To construct a program capable of understanding stories involving restaurants, Schank and Ableson had to build into their programs a complex restaurant script containing information about physical props (table, the menu, checks, money), roles (customer, waiter, cook, cashier, owner), entry conditions (the customer must have money, is usually hungry, and is attempting to obtain food), event sequences (entering, ordering, eating, exiting), and the causal relations between these items. In general, it appears that understanding even simple messages in natural language requires considerable interaction between the information contained in the message and the information contained in the message processor. This conclusion seems reasonable for most things cultural – the meaning of rituals, games, myths, plays, texts, and other cultural forms is a complex product of what is contained in the representation and what the individual brings to the representation.

As a result of the interaction between what is contained in cultural messages and what is contained in the interpretative system of the mind, as a general rule, one cannot locate cultural meanings in the message. Thus a distinction must be made between message and meaning. It is of some interest that the term *symbol* is ambiguous on exactly this point. That is, the term *symbol* can refer to either the physical thing that carries the meaning or to the meaning carried by the physical thing. Even when the term *symbol* is used with reference to something within the mind, it typically refers to an internal image of some external form.

The ambiguity in the term *symbol* about whether the thing being referred to is something internal or external is related to the assumption that internal meanings are simply mental representations of the physical signals. Thus, if meanings are simply internal representations of external forms, then ambiguity about whether the external or internal forms are being referenced makes no great difference.

The assumption that mental processing is the internal manipulation of representations of external signs may be correct. However, current work in cognitive psychology does not treat meanings as the representation of external forms but as distinct entities having different principles of organization. Internal forms are typically called "schemata" and are considered to be composed of abstract propositionlike networks (Rumelhart 1978). Because at this point we do not know which position is more accurate, it seems better to use distinct terms for internal meanings and external signals, thereby avoiding ambiguity and smuggled assumptions. The term *meaning system* has been used here throughout for mental structures and processes, rather than the term *symbol*.

One of the obvious but nevertheless remarkable facts about meaning systems is that interpretations of past messages can change the interpretative system itself, so that new messages are understood differently than they would have been had not the previous message occurred. This makes for a very flexible system. Added to the modifiability of meaning systems is the fact that people can produce messages and meanings that then react on the producer. The result of both these potentialities – modifiability and reflexiveness – is that people can change their own meaning systems – think things through and get things straight (or get themselves into a terrible muddle). However, there seem to be limits on how much self-induced change is possible, perhaps because at some point, for reasons yet unclear, without outside stimulation no new meanings get produced.

Another notable property of meaning systems is that one can construct messages about messages and meanings about meanings. On the cultural level this phenomena is very extensive. For example, symbolic entities created by constitutive rules frequently become the topics of other constitutive rules, creating entities made of other culturally created entities. Thus theft requires the notion of property, sacrilege requires the notion of sacredness, and so on.

Related to the process in which one meaning is the topic of another meaning is the framing of symbols (Bateson 1972). In the public presentation of messages on printed signs, in books, at theaters, through ritual, on television, and in group meetings, messages are framed by context and by other messages telling what the original message is about (Goffman 1974; MacAloon 1981). To the extent that recipients of these framed messages share the same relevant meaning systems, the meanings of these messages may be shared. Even when the meanings are not entirely shared, the fact that a number of people have access to the same physical messages creates the possibility of discussion and interpersonal negotiation concerning what was really meant (Cicourel 1973; Holland 1982).

In most human groups the communication of messages, both framed and unframed, is so frequent and redundant that it suggests the hypothesis that meaning systems need messages to keep themselves alive. Without relatively constant activation perhaps meaning systems disintegrate. Although messaging, public and private, is an almost constant activity, the collecting of messages is not, I believe, the best way to start the study of a culture. The most fruitful place to start such study is with individual meaning systems. I hope that after this lengthy discussion of constitutive rules and culturally created objects I will not be taken as saying that culture is just a special sort of mentation. What I am trying to say is that the external signs, the public events, are too eliptical to serve as a good place to begin the search for organization and structure.

This is not to deny that it is helpful to have a great deal of observation of what people in a culture do and say. Field observation is often necessary in order to understand what an informant is trying to describe and always necessary in order to understand that which informants cannot describe. However, field observation has become such an unquestioned virtue in anthropology that some calling to account might be valuable. It is relevant that a presentation by Metzger and Williams (1963) that demonstrated the securing of excellent ethnographic descriptions from informants without field observation was attacked with some vigor. The basis of the attack, as I heard it, was not that Metzger and Williams had gotten their descriptions wrong but rather that such a procedure was not the way to do good ethnography. This objection presumes the very charge it seeks to prove. Objections to "white room ethnography," in which an informant is questioned in a situation removed from cultural context, may be based on misperception of what is required for effective communication between informant and investigator.

The study of culture as an experimental science

Anthropology, it is said, is an observational science. Ethnographers in particular regard themselves as observers and consider participant observation to be the principal method of field research. Certainly, with regard to things like the network of social interaction or the operation of the economic system, there is little the investigator can do but try to observe and hope that what needs to be observed can be seen. The major alternative is to find someone in the society – an informant – who has observed the event that the ethnographer cannot observe and obtain the needed information through the informant's reports.

In the study of social interaction or economic systems there is little chance for an ethnographer to use experimental techniques, because ethnographers do not usually have the power to affect such systems. There have been attempts to create partial sociocultural systems in a laboratory environment and, by varying certain conditions, to study how changes in one variable affect other variables (Rose & Fenton 1955). An interesting review of this type of work from an anthropological perspective has been presented by McFeat (1974), who also constructed in an ingenious manner a number of microsociocultural systems to observe how differences in group size and kind of task influenced the development of cultural norms. But, however interesting, these miniature worlds are highly dependent and incomplete systems, better at demonstrating that we know how to produce a particular effect than for testing a hypothesis to see if it is really true.

It is not the case, however, that anthropologists cannot affect the people they study. Just to ask someone a question is to affect that person. What kind of event is this? Does it affect something cultural? Is asking a question an experiment? What is an experiment, and do anthropologists need them?

There is a rich literature on experimentation as a scientific technique (e.g., Carlsmith, Ellsworth, & Aronson 1976). The model presented in this literature contrasts sharply with the typical folk model of an experiment, with its white-coated scientists subjecting the object of their investigation to various kinds of unusual treatment with outlandish apparatus. Actually, an experiment does not require laboratories or apparatus or unusual conditions. An experiment requires three elements: first, an idea or proposition about certain things or events; second, a way to relate these things or events to operations and observations that can be made on something; and third, the power to determine which things at which times will have the operation done to them. Of course, some experiments are better than others: The original idea can be vague or uninteresting, the experimental operations carried out and the observations made may be only ambiguously related to the original idea, and the experimenter may have only limited power to select on what and when the operations will be done and only limited power to observe the effects. Despite such problems, which are common to all the sciences, what has been done is an experiment if the three conditions can be said to be present.

There are two major reasons for doing experiments. First, it may be difficult to find an opportunity to observe what one wants to observe. For example, suppose an investigator has a hypothesis that a particular set of plants will all have the same name. It is unlikely that the investigator will have the opportunity to observe several people naming each of these plants, because naming plants is something people do infrequently. An experiment, in which the investigator presents various people with the plants and induces them to name the plants, is a reasonable way to discover what cannot be observed naturally.

A second reason for doing an experiment is that a hypothesized relationship between X and Y is confounded by the fact that, in most natural settings, when X occurs, A, B, and C also occur, so that it is difficult to know if it is really X and Y that are related or A and Y, or B and Y and so on. For example, an investigator might wonder how someone felt about his or her boss. If the person is always very respectful around the boss, it is difficult to know if this is because the person really respects the boss or because the person is afraid of the boss. By experiment, through the presentation at various times of various questions and statements, an investigator can attempt to cut through the confounding conditions of the boss's presence with the employee's expression of feeling about the boss.

A question, put to discover if somebody believes something or feels some way about something or intends to do something, makes a very simple *experimental operation*. To the extent that one tests other people for the current representative, affective, and directive state of their meaning system, one has carried out an experiment. People constantly experiment on each other, using a variety of cultural forms: for example, direct and indirect questions; apparent disagreement intended to evoke deeply held commitment; apparent untruths intended to test whether a person really knows something; withholding, acknowledging, or back-channel responses to see if someone is saying something just for effect. Lovers test lovers, believers test believers, knowers test knowers, people of purpose test the purposes of others, and ethnographers test informants. An important fact about meaning systems – idiosyncratic and cultural – is that they are accessible to this kind of experimentation.

Of course, many questions are asked not to make any specific test, but simply to try to find out something. Someone may ask "How do you get to the post office?" just to find out how to get to the post office. Strictly speaking, no experiment has been done, because no specific hypothesis has been tested. However, even in the case of a simple question there are some implicit hypotheses about a person's meaning system being tested: that the question is understandable to the person, that the person knows where the post office is, that the person can respond with an understandable answer, that the person asked is likely to respond and to be truthful, and so on. Thus a simple question does not have the goals of an experiment but does involve experimental tests of various sorts. In most cases ethnographers use a complex, mixed strategy of experiment and simple question, starting with few assumptions about what the informant knows or feels and eventually building a theoretical structure about the informant's meaning systems.

There are a variety of experimental operations to test hypotheses about meaning systems other than the use of questions. The experimenter can present an object, create an event, or present the representation of some object or event and observe the informant's reaction. The reaction observed can be something the person says, something the person chooses to do, how the person reacts emotionally, or how quickly the person responds. The common procedure, however, is the question-and-answer format of natural language.

The preponderance of the question-and-answer format in cultural experiments is partially due to the ease with which questions can be asked and answers can be recorded. Another, more compelling reason is that many of the important things in a culture, such as success or the soul, are entities that have no palpable form. To find out what an informant thinks or feels about symbolic things requires communication through a medium like natural language in which such things can be represented. In such cases discourse through natural language is almost the only means of investigation.

Given the type of question-and-answer experiment that anthropologists typically do, it is not surprising that rapport has emerged as one of the major research concerns. Unlike social psychologists, for instance, whose major difficulties in creating experiments involve the construction of conditions that have an appropriate correspondence to ordinary life, the primary experimental difficulty encountered by anthropologists is the development of appropriate interpersonal conditions for verbal expression. Ordinary life gives people many reasons to hide how they think and feel and many special conventions about when and how and to whom various kinds of things may be said, so that the establishment of a special rapport between investigator and informant becomes a major precondition for obtaining the type of communication anthropologists need. The task is to establish a relationship in which the informant understands the kinds of things the investigator wants to find out about and to trust the investigator enough to express things that might be punished in other contexts. And, since communication even under the best of circumstances tends to result in misunderstandings on both sides, the question-and-answer testing of informants' meaning systems is best done through a number of little experiments carried out over a long period of time. This kind of experimentation is typically informal, but it can also be undertaken in highly structured formats and combined with special techniques for the analysis of responses, such as multidimensional scaling (e.g., Gerber 1975; Kirk & Burton 1976; Roberts et al. 1981; Romney & D'Andrade 1964; White 1980).

From the perspective of the evolution of science, one would expect that each field would develop the experimental techniques that best fit the particular phenomena being studied. Something like this has happened in anthropology, in which there has developed in an unusually unselfconscious way a very special sort of experimentation, unrecognized as such, characterized by an emphasis on verbal interaction, subject–experimenter rapport, and successive testing. Related experimental methods have developed in linguistics, clinical psychology, psychiatry, and sociology – in all cases without the explicit recognition that what is being done involves the development of an experimental methodology.

The possibility of using experiments of certain sorts to investigate both individual and cultural systems of meaning is an important part of the development of any sort of science based on meaning, because it makes feasible the investigation of individual interpretative systems. Through informant-based experimentation it is possible to investigate what would otherwise rarely be observed and to separate otherwise confounded conditions. This kind of testing makes it feasible to try to know enough about any person's systems of meaning to understand, and even predict, why a particular message is taken to mean one thing rather than another.

To return to a previous topic: As someone who observed Metzger and Williams's field procedures, I found that one of the most salient characteristics of their method was the development of a special kind of relationship with their informants, a relationship that was long-term, task-oriented, and marked by mutual respect. Informants understood the goals of the projects in which they participated and came to understand what it was that the anthropologists did and did not know. There was a professional quality about the interaction on both sides that was remarkable. In my view, it is not the color of the walls of the room that is important in working with informants or even the particulars of interviewing technique. What is important is the character of the investigator–informant relationship. Context is usually a social relationship – that is, the meanings people have for each other.

The relationship between meaning systems and social structure

Issues about the nature of culture are intertwined with questions about the degree to which culture is shared and how culture is distinguished from social structure. In the 1940s and early 1950s, when culture was thought of primarily as the shared behavior distinctive of a social group, the problem arose that often things that seemed clearly cultural were not completely, or even generally, shared. For example, in American culture linear programing is important in engineering and business, but it is not a generally shared item of knowledge. John Roberts (1964) has pointed out that one of the functions of social organization is to create a division of labor in "who knows what." Roberts has also pointed out that societies differ in the way in which cultural information is integrated in the social process of decision making. Marc Swartz has discussed the problems of the distribution of cultural understandings across social roles in detail and has proposed that cultures contain "linking understandings," in which those who occupy certain statuses share certain understandings about what other classes of persons are likely to know (Swartz & Jordan 1976).

One of the basic things that meaning systems do for individuals is to guide their reactions and behavior. Given a systematic distribution of meaning systems across individuals – a system of systems – the reactions and behavior of groups of people can be guided in an organized and coordinated fashion. The concept of social structure appears to refer to the systems of meaning. That is, social structure is usually defined as the distribution of rights and duties across status positions in a society. Each configuration of rights and duties is a culturally created entity, based on constitutive rules learned and passed on to succeeding generations. In this sense, social structure is one aspect of the organization of culture – the achievement of systematicity across persons through meanings.

The relationship between meaning systems and systems of material flow

In suggesting that culture and social structure are really composed of the same material, it may seem that what is being assumed is that *all* important human phenomena are basically meaning systems. This is not the case. There is a major class of human phenomena that is not organized as meaning systems, which I term *material flow*. By material flow I mean the movement of goods, services, messages, people, genes, diseases, and other potentially countable entities in space and time. These materials can be grouped into various classes, such as economic transaction, demographic change, interpersonal exchange of messages, and ecosystem energy exchange, and studied scientifically as systems with certain lawful properties. In the social sciences, economics is the most developed of such disciplines, and its models have been widely extended to other kinds of systems of exchange.

It is not surprising, perhaps, that the most vehement rejection of the cognitively oriented view of culture proposed in the 1950s was voiced by those anthropologists whose major interest has been in the cross-cultural study of material flow. This group, made up primarily of cultural evolutionists and cultural ecologists, treats culture as a system of socially transmitted standing behavior patterns through which communities adapt to their ecological settings – that is, as a kind of material flow of behaviors on a par with other kinds of material flow. This approach has the virtue of staying with what is most observable and maintaining a strong connection with the methods of the natural sciences. From the point of view of this chapter, the problem with such an approach, as Roger Keesing (1981) has suggested, is that standing behavior patterns are influenced by so many variables (e.g., social crowding, climate, warfare, local geographic features, physical distribution of foodstuffs, prevalence of diseases, technological sophistication, plus meaning system characteristics) that there is little that can be said about such a phenomenon except that it seems so unstable that it is not likely to be worth studying (which in fact is what cultural materialists say about what they term *culture*). Keesing, following a long tradition, suggests that we use the term *sociocultural system* for the total system that includes behaviors, other types of material flow, and meanings, and reserve the term *culture* for meaning systems (Keesing 1981:75).

An important issue is the way in which cultural meaning systems relate to systems of material flow – that is, to systems in which material and cultural objects move across time and space. Let us consider this relationship for two systems: the social structure, defined as the distribution of rights and duties across statuses, and the social exchange network, defined as potentially observable flow of commands, services, goods, sentiments, and so on across persons. The social exchange network consists of rates by which various objects – which may be culturally constituted objects, like wealth or commands, or purely physical quantities, like bushels of wheat or pounds of iron – move from individual to individual. As defined here, the flow of such objects is not the same as the social structure, because groups with similar social structures can have very different social exchange networks and similarity in the social exchange network does not necessarily mean that two groups have similar social structures. Thus, for example, groups with very similar rules of marriage (social structure) may vary widely when one counts actual marriages (social exchange network) because many conditions – such as the size of the various marrying groups, the age composition of groups, the distribution of wealth across groups, and so on – affect marriage rates.

The meanings that make up the social structure affect the flow of the social exchange network in numerous ways. For example, the various constructions concerning rights and duties expressed in norms of inheritance, rules of land tenure, wage scales, and norms for the ascription and achievement of statuses will all affect the flow of interaction and resources. Constitutive rules create a variety of types of people, occasions, and objects, which are linked to norms concerning the rights of certain types of people over certain kinds of objects on certain occasions. These norms are major determinants of a person's actions and reactions, directly affecting the flow of things on which social life depends.

The causal relation is not a one-way street, however. As external conditions change, rates of various kinds of exchanges change, creating social opportunities and problems, which people adapt to with new norms and eventually new constitutive entities (Bailey 1960). For the last three thousand years or so, human culture and society have been undergoing extremely rapid change. Sometimes it seems to me as if trying to study human culture in the twentieth century is like trying to study the physics of moving bodies while living in the middle of an avalanche. Equilibrium conditions are rare, and what looks like stability is just the fact that most things are moving rapidly in the same direction.

The fact that there are multiple two-way causal relationships between meaning systems and conditions of material flow has some strong consequences with regard to the possible kinds of analysis one can do with even the most carefully collected data. When experimentation is impossible, determination of the size of causal effects – how much change in one variable will affect change in another variable – is sometimes possible through correlational analysis. However, when there are feedback loops among the variables (i.e., A influences B, B directly or indirectly influences A), it is mathematically impossible, no matter how many data are collected, to estimate with any accuracy the degree of influence – unless one can assume that an equilibrium condition has been reached, so that the system is stable. In the language of path analysis, models with feedback loops are called "nonhierarchical models" – because causation does not always go in just one direction. David Kenny, in a text on methods of inferring causality from correlational data, states: "My own suspicion is that the strong assumption of equilibrium is sufficiently implausible to make nonhierarchical models generally impractical for the applied social scientist" (1979:105). In general, then, if one believes that technology influences ideology and that ideology influences technology, there are no data that can be analyzed mathematically to tell us whether technology is a more powerful causal variable than ideology or the opposite – at least not until equilibrium conditions are found.

Thus causal priority debates, like the Whiting–Young debate concerning the causal priority of early experience versus factors of social organization on the severity of initiation ceremonies, are probably undecidable in principle. Rather than trying to find out which causal variables are the important ones, I believe that a more effective strategy for the human sciences, when experimentation is not possible, is to try to isolate patterns or configurations of variables that occur together frequently and have some stability over time and to try to find which sets of patterns can change into other sets of patterns. Other social scientists have come to similar conclusions for less statistically motivated reasons.

Although there may be great difficulty in determining the size of effects, there is little doubt that changes in systems of material flow do influence cultural meaning systems. Agreement, however, as to how this influence takes place has yet to be achieved. Because meaning systems are part of the human psyche, cultural meaning systems can be changed only through psychological processes. For example, changes in residence patterns appear to affect kinship terminologies – but for this to happen there must be some psychological process by which the change in people's experience leads to change in the conceptual classification of kin and the encoding of the new classification system into the language. Using one particular psychological theory of how people learn to make discriminations – a one-element stimulus-sampling theory – I developed a model that did a reasonable job of "predicting" kinship terminologies from features of social organization. Unfortunately, several years later, the particular psychological theory I had used was found to be too simplistic and is now generally considered inadequate to account for complex discrimination learning (D'Andrade 1971). Over the past years the psychological theories of the process by which experience affects concept formation have changed continually and at this point do not seem close to resolution (Cole et al. 1981). It is sometimes discouraging to work in psychological anthropology in areas in which psychological theory is not well formulated. The conclusion I have come to is that pyschological theory is most useful as a heuristic for exploring facts about the organization of culture and least useful as explanation.

The relationship between meaning systems and personality

Personality is another kind of system that is distinct from, but related to, cultural meaning systems. One formulation of the relationship between these two sets of systems is that ideas, values, and attitudes that are shared by a group are culture, but these same things, if idiosyncratic, are personality. A different formulation is that those ideas that an individual has to know to behave appropriately as a member of society are culture, whereas values and attitudes are personality.

There are problems with both these formulations. With regard to the "shared learning is culture, idiosyncratic learning is personality" formulation, most learned things are somewhat shared, but nothing is ever shared completely, so that everything people learn ends up being a little bit personality and a little bit culture. With regard to the "ideas that one has to know to behave appropriately are culture, values and attitude, are personality" fomulation, most personality theorists would want to include some of the things one has to know to behave appropriately as part of individual personality, and some cultural theorists would want to include some values and attitudes as part of culture.

The basic drawback of these content-based formulations can be illustrated by imagining that chemists and biologists had decided to divide the world into physical objects that are chemical and physical objects that are biological. One could imagine interesting arguments about whether proteins are biological or membranes are chemical.

Rather than a content-based formulation, it seems more useful to consider items of human learning as either culture or personality, depending on how they are placed within a system of relationships and processes (Kracke 1981). In the study of culture these relationships and processes involve the adaptation of groups of people to their environment and to each other through systems of meaning. In the study of personality these relationships and processes involve the organization of behavior, impulse, affect, and thought around the drives of the individual. If one considers personality and culture to be open systems that are linked together, then there must be items belonging to both systems that form the links. For example, ideas concerning success may be, for most Americans, not only part of their cultural meaning systems but also a part of their motivational system, and thus play a part in both culture and personality.

The problems concerning the relation between culture and personality raise the issue of the relation between culture and experience. Humans experience a complex universe, composed of perceptions, memories, thoughts, and fantasies about social and physical events. Only a part of any one person's experience is shaped by or represented through particular systems of cultural meaning. Modern American culture has much more to say about the experience of being young than the experience of being old, for example. There is always interplay between the world of experience and cultural meanings; in some cases cultural meanings have the potential of giving form and depth to private experience, in some cases cultural meanings may conflict with the individual's experiences, and in other cases there may be no relation established by the individual between particular experiences and cultural meanings. Just as there is a dynamic between cultural meanings and systems of materials flow that creates a potential for change, so, too, there is a dynamic between cultural meanings and private experience that also creates a potential for change.

"Culture" defined

One of the oldest terminological wrangles in anthropology is over the term *culture*. Some of the problem seems to come from the fact that the term has a sense both as a process (the "passing on" of what has been learned before to succeeding generations) and as a particular class of things (e.g., "shared knowledge"). One might think that these two aspects of the terms could coexist quite neatly if the process were used to define content. In such a definition, culture would be whatever it is that is passed on through learning to succeeding generations. The difficulty with this solution is that many things are passed on, not all of which most anthropologists would want to consider culture. For example, oedipal complexes are learned and shared widely (even in the Trobriand Islands: see Spiro 1982) but would not usually be considered to be culture by most anthropologists, as such complexes are an indirect, unintended, and unrecognized consequence of the learning of other things. A second strategy is to define culture as having a particular content. The problem with this solution is that there are different kinds of content – which should get to be called culture?

Such terminological quarreling might seem to be academic foolishness. However, most of the battles about the nature of culture have been generally enlightening, perhaps because they make explicit our assumptions about what is out there, and perhaps because as our assumptions about what is out there become explicit, we find that there are more kinds of things out there than we had thought.

Technically, anthropological "definitions" of culture are not definitions at all: According to Suppes, for example, a definition should not introduce a new axiom or premise in a theory or strengthen the theory in any substantive way (1957:153). Technically, a definition should be a paraphrase that maintains the truth or falsity of statements in the theory when substituted for the word defined. But to produce substitutable paraphrases for already existing propositions has not been the goal of those who have attempted to define culture. Rather, their attempts have been to describe what is out there – that is, to formulate substantive propositions about one aspect of the human world.

There are, at present, at least three major views about the nature of culture. One is a notion of culture as knowledge, as the accumulation of information. According to this view, culture can and does accumulate and does not need to be shared if the distribution of knowledge is such that the proper "linking understandings" are maintained. The amount of information in the total cultural pool of knowledge is very large – even for simple societies my estimate is that there are between several hundred thousand and several million "chunks" of information in the total pool (D'Andrade 1981). Furthermore, in this view culture is not highly integrated; the knowledge concerning what to do about illness has no particular connection or relation to the knowledge needed to build houses, for example.

A second view is that culture consists of "conceptual structures" that create the central reality of a people, so that they "inhabit the world they imagine" (Geertz 1983); or, according to Schneider, culture consists of "elements which are defined and differentiated in a particular society as representing reality – not simply social reality, but the total reality of life within which human beings live and die" (1976:206). According to this view, culture is not just shared, it is intersubjectively shared, so that everyone assumes that others see the same things they see. In this view culture does not particularly accumulate, any more than the grammar of a language accumulates, and the total size of a culture with respect to information chunks is relatively small. The entire system appears to be tightly interrelated but not necessarily without contradictions.

A third view of the nature of culture falls between the "culture as knowledge" and the "culture as constructed reality" positions. It treats culture and society as almost the same thing – something made up of institutions, such as the family, the market, the farm, the church, the village, and so on, that is, systems or clusters of norms defining the roles attached to various sets of statuses. For Nadel, for example, these clusters of norms, if analyzed from the "who does what to whom" perspective constitute social structure; if analyzed from the "how one activity relates to another activity" perspective, they constitute culture (Nadel 1951). These clusters of norms fall between the "knowledge" position and the "constructed reality" position with respect to accumulation, size, and integration. Accumulation occurs, but relatively slowly; the size of the body of information that must be learned is very large, but not thousands of thousands of chunks; and the degree of integration is important, but problematic.

Given the position taken in this chapter, all three are views of cultural meaning systems. The difference between the views is in the prominence given to the various functions of meaning: to the directive function for the "norms and institutions" view, to the representative function for the "knowledge" view, and to the potential of systems of meaning to create entities for the "constructed reality" view. Although there is a certain amount of differentiation among symbols and meanings – some seem primarily representational, some seem primarily directive, and some seem primarily reality-constructing – this differentiation is not sharp, and much of the apparent difference is in the conceptual framework of the analyst, not in what things mean to the individuals involved.

In summary, the position taken in this chapter treats culture as consisting of learned systems of meaning, communicated by means of natural language and other symbol systems, having representational, directive, and affective functions, and capable of creating cultural entities and particular senses of reality. Through these systems of meaning, groups of people adapt to their environment and structure interpersonal activities. Cultural meaning systems affect and are affected by the various systems of material flow, such as the flow of goods and services, and an interpersonal network of commands and requests. Cultural meaning systems are linked to personality systems through the sharing of specific items that function in both systems for particular individuals. Various aspects of cultural meaning systems are differentially distributed across persons and statuses, creating institutions such as family, market, nation, and so on, which constitute social structure. Analytically, cultural meaning systems can be treated as a very large diversified pool of knowledge, or partially shared clusters of norms, or as intersubjectively shared, symbolically created realities. On the individual level, however, the actual meanings and messages that people learn, encounter, and produce are typically not divided into separate classes of items that can be labeled knowledge, norm, or reality, but rather form multifunctional complexes of constructs, organized in interlocking hierarchical structures, which are simultaneously constructive, representive, evocative, and directive.

Note

I wish to thank Clifford Geertz, David Jordan, Robert I. Levy, David M. Schneider, Richard A. Shweder, Melford E. Spiro, Marc Swartz, and Elliot Turiel for their comments on an earlier draft of this chapter.

References

Anscombe, G. E. M. 1958. On brute facts. *Analysis* 18:3.
Austin, J. L. 1962. *How to Do Things with Words.* Oxford, England: Oxford University Press.

Bailey, F. G. 1960. *Tribe, Caste, and Nation.* Manchester, England: Manchester University Press.

Bateson, Gregory. 1972. A theory of play and fantasy. In G. Bateson, *Steps to an Ecology of Mind.* New York: Ballantine.

Carlsmith, J. M., Ellsworth, P. C., & Aronson, E. 1976. *Methods of Research in Social Psychology.* Reading, Mass.: Addison-Wesley.

Casson, Ronald W. 1981. *Language, Culture, and Cognition.* New York: Macmillan.

Chomsky, Noam. 1957. *Syntactic Structures.* The Hague: Mouton.

Cicourel, Aaron. 1968. *The Social Organization of Juvenile Justice.* New York: Wiley.

 1973. *Cognitive Sociology: Language and Meaning in Social Interaction.* London: Penguin.

Cole, Michael, & the Laboratory of Comparative Human Cognition. 1981. Intelligence as culture practice. In W. Kessen, ed., *Carmichael's Handbook of Child Psychology.* New York: Wiley.

D'Andrade, Roy. 1971. Procedures for predicting kinship terminologies from features of social organization. In Paul Kay, ed., *Explorations in Mathematical Anthropology.* Cambridge, Mass.: MIT Press.

 1976. A propositional analysis of U. S. American beliefs about illness. In Keith Basso & Henry Selby, eds., *Meaning in Anthropology.* Albuquerque: University of New Mexico Press.

 1981. The cultural part of cognition. *Cognitive Science* 5:179–95.

D'Andrade, Roy & Egan, Micheal. 1974. The colors of emotion. *American Ethnologist* 1:49–63.

Friedrich, Paul. 1977. Sanity and the myth of honor: the problem of Achilles. *Ethos* 5(3):281–305.

Geertz, Clifford. 1973. Thick description: Towards an interpretive theory of culture. In C. Geertz, *The Interpretation of Cultures.* New York: Basic Books.

 1983. The way we think now: towards an ethnography of modern thought. In C. Geertz *Local Knowledge.* New York: Basic Books.

Geoghegan, William. 1971. Information processing systems in culture. In Paul Kay, ed., *Explorations in Mathematical Anthropology.* Cambridge, Mass.: MIT Press.

Gerber, Eleanor. 1975. *The cultural patterning of emotion in Samoa.* Unpublished doctoral dissertation, University of California, San Diego.

Goffman, Erving. 1974. *Frame Analysis.* New York: Harper.

Goodenough, Ward H. 1957. Cultural anthropology and linguistics. In Paul Garvin, ed., *Report of the Seventh Annual Round Table Meeting on Linguistics and Language Study.* Georgetown University Monograph Series, *Language and Linguistics* 9. Washington, D.C.: Georgetown University.

Hofstadter, Douglas R. 1979. *Gödel, Escher, Bach: An Eternal Golden Braid.* New York: Random House.

Holland, D. 1982. Samoan folk knowledge of mental disorders. In A. Marsella & Geoff White, eds., *Cultural conception of mental health and therapy.* Boston: Reidel.

Keesing, Roger M. 1981. Theories of culture. In R. Casson, ed., *Language, Culture and Cognition.* New York: Macmillan. Originally published 1974.

Kenny, David. 1979. *Correlations and Causality*. New York: Wiley.

Kirk, Lorraine, & Burton, Michael. 1976. Physical versus semantic classification of non-verbal forms: a cross-cultural experiment. *Semiotica* 17(4):315–31.

Kracke, Waud H. 1981. The complementarity of social and psychological regularities: leadership as a mediating phenomenon. *Ethos* 8(4):273–85.

Lakoff, George, & Johnson, Mark. 1980. *Metaphors We Live By*. Chicago: University of Chicago Press.

Levy, Robert I. 1981. *Embedded and marked symbolism*. Unpublished manuscript, University of California at San Diego.

MacAloon, John J. 1981. *Olympic games and theory of spectacle in modern society*. Unpublished manuscript, University of Chicago.

McFeat, Tom. 1974. *Small Group Cultures*. Toronto: Pergamon Press.

Metzger, Duane, & Williams, G. 1963. A formal ethnographic analysis of Tenejapa Ladino weddings. *American Anthropologist* 65(5):1076–1101.

Much, Nancy C., & Shweder, Richard A. 1978. Speaking of rules: the analysis of culture in breach. In William Damon, ed., *New Directions for Child Development*. San Francisco: Jossey-Bass.

Nadel, S. F. 1951. *The Foundation of Social Anthropology*. London: Cohen and West.

Osgood, Charles E., May, W. H., & Miron, M. S. 1975. *Cross Cultural Universals of Affective Meaning*. Urbana: University of Illinois Press.

Quinn, Naomi. 1975. Decision model of social structure. *American Ethologist* 2:19–45.

    1980. *"Commitment" in American marriage: analysis of a key word*. Paper presented at the meeting of the American Anthropological Association, Washington, D.C.

Rawls, John. 1955. Two concepts of rules. *Philosophical Review* 64:3–22.

Reddy, Michael. 1976. The conduit metaphor. In A. Ortony, ed., *Metaphor and Thought*. Cambridge: Cambridge University Press.

Roberts, John M. 1964. The self management of cultures. In W. Goodenough, ed., *Explorations in Cultural Anthropology: Essays in Honor of George Peter Murdock*. New York: McGraw-Hill.

Roberts, John M., Chick, Garry E., Stephenson, Marian, & Hyde, Laurel Lee. 1981. Inferred categories for tennis play: a limited semantic analysis. In Alyee B. Cheska, ed., *Play as Context*. West Point, N.Y.: Leisure Press.

Romney, A. K., & D'Andrade, Roy. 1964. Cognitive aspects of English kin terms. *American Anthropologist* 66:146–70.

Rose, Edward, & Fenton, William. 1955. Experimental histories of culture. *American Sociological Review* 20(4):383–92.

Rumelhart, David E. 1978. Schemata: the building blocks of cognition. In R. Spiro, B. Bruce, & W. Brewer, eds., *Theoretical Issues in Reading Comprehension*. Hillsdale, N. J.: Erlbaum.

Schank, Roger, & Abelson, Robert. 1977. *Scripts, Plans, Goals, and Understanding*. Hillsdale, N.J.: Erlbaum.

Schneider, David. 1965. American kin terms and terms for kinsmen: a critique of Goodenough's componential analysis of Yankee terminology. *American Anthropologist* 67:part 2.

    1968. *American Kinship: A Cultural Account*. Englewood Cliffs, N.J.: Prentice-Hall.

1976. Notes toward a theory of culture. In Keith Basso & Henry Selby, eds., *Meaning in Anthropology*. Albuquerque: University of New Mexico Press.

Searle, John R. 1969. *Speech Acts: An Essay in the Philosophy of Language*. Cambridge: Cambridge University Press.

1978. A classification of illocutionary acts. *Language and Society* 5:1–23.

Shweder, Richard A. 1981. *Anthropology's romantic rebellion against the enlightenment; or, there's more to thinking than reason and evidence*. Paper presented at meeting of the American Association for the Advancement of Science, Toronto, January.

Spiro, Melford E. 1961. Social systems, personality, and functional analysis. In Bert Kaplan, ed., *Studying Personality Cross-Culturally*. Evanston, Ill.: Row, Peterson.

1982. *Oedipus in the Trobriands: The Making of a Scientific Myth*. Chicago: University of Chicago Press.

Suppes, Patrick. 1957. *Introduction to Logic*. Princeton, N.J.: Van Nostrand.

Swartz, Marc J., & Jordan, David K. 1976. *Anthropology: Perspectives on Humanity*. New York: Wiley.

Vendler, Zeno. 1972. *Res Cognitans: An Essay in Rational Psychology*. Ithaca, N.Y.: Cornell University Press.

White, Geoffrey M. 1980. Conceptual universals in interpersonal language. *American Anthropologist* 82(4):759–81.

PART II
Culture, self, and emotion

4

"From the native's point of view"
ON THE NATURE OF ANTHROPOLOGICAL
UNDERSTANDING

Clifford Geertz

Several years ago a minor scandal erupted in anthropology: one of its ancestral figures told the truth in a public place. As befits an ancestor, he did it posthumously, and through his widow's decision rather than his own, with the result that a number of the sort of right-thinking types who are with us always immediately rose to cry that she, an in-marrier anyway, had betrayed clan secrets, profaned an idol, and let down the side. What will the children think, to say nothing of the layman? But the disturbance was not much lessened by such ceremonial wringing of the hands; the damn thing was, after all, already printed. In much the same fashion as James Watson's *The Double Helix* (1968) exposed the way in which biophysics in fact gets done, Bronislaw Malinowski's *A Diary in the Strict Sense of the Term* (1967) rendered established accounts of how anthropologists work fairly well implausible. The myth of the chameleon fieldworker, perfectly self-tuned to his exotic surroundings, a walking miracle of empathy, tact, patiences, and cosmopolitanism, was demolished by the man who had perhaps done most to create it.

The squabble that arose around the publication of the *Diary* concentrated, naturally, on inessentials and missed, as was only to be expected, the point. Most of the shock seems to have arisen from the mere discovery that Malinowski was not, to put it delicately, an unmitigated nice guy. He had rude things to say about the natives he was living with, and rude words to say it in. He spent a great deal of his time wishing he were elsewhere. And he projected an image of a man about as little complaisant as the world has seen. (He also projected an image of a man consecrated to a strange vocation to the point of self-immolation, but that was less noted.) The discussion was made to come down to Malinowski's moral character or lack of it, and the genuinely profound question his book raised was ignored; namely, if it isn't, as we had been taught to believe, through some sort of extraordinary sensibility, an almost preternatural capacity to think, feel, and perceive like a native (a word, I should hurry to say, I use here "in the strict sense of the term"), how is anthropological knowledge of the way natives think, feel, and perceive possible? The issue the *Diary* presents, with a force perhaps only a working ethnographer can fully appreciate, is not moral. (The moral idealization of fieldworkers is a mere sentimentality in the first place, when it isn't self-congratulation or a guild pretense.) The issue is epistemological. If we are going to cling – as, in my opinion, we must – to the injunction to see things from the native's point of view, where are we when we can no longer claim some unique form of psychological closeness, a sort of transcultural identification, with our subjects? What happens to *verstehen* when *einfühlen* disappears?

As a matter of fact, this general problem has been exercising methodological discussion in anthropology for the last ten or fifteen years; Malinowski's voice from the grave merely dramatizes it as a human dilemma over and above a professional one. The formulations have been various: "inside" versus "outside," or "first person" versus "third person" descriptions; "phenomenological" versus "objectivist," or "cognitive" versus "behavioral" theories; or, perhaps most commonly, "emic" versus "etic" analysis, this last deriving from the distinction in linguistics between phonemics and phonetics, phonemics classifying sounds according to their internal function in language, phonetics classifying them according to their acoustic properties as such. But perhaps the simplest and most directly appreciable way to put the matter is in terms of a distinction formulated, for his own purposes, by the psychoanalyst Heinz Kohut (1971), between what he calls "experience-near" and "experience-distant" concepts.

An experience-near concept is, roughly, one which someone – a patient, a subject, in our case an informant – might himself naturally and effortlessly use to define what he or his fellows see, feel, think, imagine, and so on, and which he would readily understand when similarly applied by others. An experience-distant concept is one which specialists of one sort or another – an analyst, an experimenter, an ethnographer, even a priest or an ideologist – employ to forward their scientific, philosophical, or practical aims. "Love" is an experience-near concept, "object cathexis" is an experience-distant one. "Social stratification," or perhaps for most peoples in the world even "religion" (and certainly "religious system"), are experience-distant; "caste" or "nirvana" are experience-near, at least for Hindus and Buddhists.

Clearly, the matter is one of degree, not polar opposition – "fear" is experience-nearer than "phobia," and "phobia" experience-nearer than "ego dyssyntonic." And the difference is not, at least so far as anthropology is concerned (the matter is otherwise in poetry and physics), a normative one, in the sense that one sort of concept is to be preferred as such over the other. Confinement to experience-near concepts leaves an ethnographer awash in immediacies, as well as entangled in vernacular. Confinement to experience-distant ones leaves him stranded in abstractions and smothered in jargon. The real question, and the one Malinowski raised by demonstrating that, in the case of "natives," you don't have to be one to know one, is what roles the two sorts of concepts play in anthropological analysis. Or, more exactly, how, in each case, ought one to deploy them so as to produce an interpretation of the way a people lives which is neither imprisoned within their mental horizons, an ethnography of witchcraft as written by a witch, nor systematically deaf to the distinctive tonalities of their existence, an ethnography of witchcraft as written by a geometer.

Putting the matter this way – in terms of how anthropological analysis is to be conducted and its results framed, rather than what psychic constitution anthropologists need to have – reduces the mystery of what "seeing things from the native's point of view" means. But it does not make it any easier, nor does it lessen the demand for perceptiveness on the part of the fieldworker. To grasp concepts which, for another people, are experience-near, and to do so well enough to place them in illuminating connection with experience-distant concepts theorists have fashioned to capture the general features of social life, is clearly a task at least as delicate, if a bit less magical, as putting oneself into someone else's skin. The trick is not to get yourself into some inner correspondence of spirit with your informants. Preferring, like the rest of us, to call their souls their own, they are not going to be altogether keen about such an effort anyhow. The trick is to figure out what the devil they think they are up to.

In one sense, of course, no one knows this better than they do themselves; hence the passion to swim in the stream of their experience, and the illusion afterward that one somehow has. But in another sense, that simple truism is simply not true. People use experience-near concepts spontaneously, unselfconsciously, as it were colloquially; they do not, except fleetingly and on occasion, recognize that there are any "concepts" involved at all. That is what experience-near means – that ideas and the realities they inform are naturally and indissolubly bound up together. What else could you call a hippopotamus? Of course the gods are powerful, why else would we fear them? The ethnographer does not, and, in my opinion, largely cannot, perceive what his informants perceive. What he perceives, and that uncertainly enough, is what they perceive "with" – or "by means of," or "through" . . . or whatever the word should be. In the country of the blind, who are not as unobservant as they look, the one-eyed is not king, he is spectator.

Now, to make all this a bit more concrete, I want to turn for a moment to my own work, which, whatever its other faults, has at least the virtue of being mine – in discussions of this sort a distinct advantage. In all three of the societies I have studied intensively, Javanese, Balinese, and Moroccan, I have been concerned, among other things, with attempting to determine how the people who live there define themselves as persons, what goes into the idea they have (but, as I say, only half-realize they have) of what a self, Javanese, Balinese, or Moroccan style, is. And in each case, I have tried to get at this most intimate of notions not by imagining myself someone else, a rice peasant or a tribal sheikh, and then seeing what I thought, but by searching out and analyzing the symbolic forms – words, images, institutions, behaviors – in terms of which, in each place, people actually represented themselves to themselves and to one another.

The concept of person is, in fact, an excellent vehicle by means of which to examine this whole question of how to go about poking into another people's turn of mind. In the first place, some sort of concept of this kind, one feels reasonably safe in saying, exists in recognizable form among all social groups. The notions of what persons are may be, from our point of view, sometimes more than a little odd. They may be conceived to dart about nervously at night shaped like fireflies. Essential elements of their psyche, like hatred, may be thought to be lodged in granular black bodies within their livers, discoverable upon autopsy. They may share their fates with *Doppelgänger* beasts, so that when the beast sickens or dies they sicken or die too. But at least some conception of what a human individual is, as opposed to a rock, an animal, a rainstorm, or a god, is, so far as I can see, universal. Yet, at the same time, as these offhand examples suggest, the actual conceptions involved vary from one group to the next, and often quite sharply. The Western conception of the person as a bounded, unique, more or less integrated motivational and cognitive universe, a dynamic center of awareness, emotion, judgment, and action organized into a distinctive whole and set contrastively both against other such wholes and against its social and natural background, is, however incorrigible it may seem to us, a rather peculiar idea within the context of the world's cultures. Rather than attempting to place the experience of others within the framework of such a conception, which is what the extolled "empathy" in fact usually comes down to, understanding them demands setting that conception aside and seeing their experiences within the framework of their own idea of what selfhood is. And for Java, Bali, and Morocco, at least, that idea differs markedly not only from our own but, no less dramatically and no less instructively, from one to the other.

In Java, where I worked in the fifties, I studied a small, shabby inland county-seat sort of place; two shadeless streets of whitewashed wooden shops and offices, and even less substantial bamboo shacks crammed in helter-skelter behind them, the whole surrounded by a great half-circle of densely packed rice-bowl villages.[1] Land was short, jobs were scarce, politics was unstable, health was poor, prices were rising, and life was altogether far from promising, a kind of agitated stagnancy in which, as I once put it, thinking of the curious mixture of borrowed fragments of modernity and exhausted relics of tradition that characterized the place, the future seemed about as remote as the past. Yet in the midst of this depressing scene there was an absolutely astonishing intellectual vitality, a philosophical passion really, and a popular one besides, to track the riddles of existence right down to the ground. Destitute peasants would discuss questions of freedom of the will, illiterate tradesmen discoursed on the properties of God, common laborers had theories about the relations between reason and passion, the nature of time, or the reliability of the senses. And, perhaps most importantly, the problem of the self – its nature, function, and mode of operation – was pursued with the sort of reflective intensity one could find among ourselves in only the most recherché settings indeed.

The central ideas in terms of which this reflection proceeded, and which thus defined its boundaries and the Javanese sense of what a person is, were arranged into two sets of contrasts, at base religious, one between "inside" and "outside," and one between "refined" and "vulgar."[2] These glosses are, of course, crude and imprecise; determining exactly what the terms involved signified, sorting out their shades of meaning, was what all the discussion was about. But together they formed a distinctive conception of the self which, far from being merely theoretical, was the one in terms of which Javanese in fact perceived one another and, of course, themselves.

The "inside"/"outside" words, *lair* and *batin* (terms borrowed, as a matter of fact, from the Sufi tradition of Muslim mysticism, but locally reworked), refer on the one hand to the felt realm of human experience and on the other to the observed realm of human behavior. These have, one hastens to say, nothing to do with "soul" and "body" in our sense, for which there are in fact quite other words with quite other implications. *Batin*, the "inside" word, does not refer to a separate seat of encapsulated spirituality detached or detachable from the body, or indeed to a bounded unit at all, but to the emotional life of human beings taken generally. It consists of the fuzzy, shifting flow of subjective feeling perceived directly in all its phenomenological immediacy but considered to be, at its roots at least, identical across all individuals, whose individuality it thus effaces. And similarly, *lair*, the "outside" world, has nothing to do with the body as an object, even an experienced object. Rather, it refers to that part of human life which, in our culture, strict behaviorists limit themselves to studying – external actions, movements, postures, speech – again conceived as in its essence invariant from one individual to the next. These two sets of phenomena – inward feelings and outward actions – are then regarded not as functions of one another but as independent realms of being to be put in proper order independently.

It is in connection with this "proper ordering" that the contrast between *alus*, the word meaning "pure," "refined," "polished," "exquisite," "ethereal," "subtle," "civilized," "smooth," and *kasar*, the word meaning "impolite," "rough," "uncivilized," "coarse," "insensitive," "vulgar," comes into play. The goal is to be *alus* in both the separated realms of the self. In the inner realm this is to be achieved through religious discipline, much but not all of it mystical. In the outer realm, it is to be achieved through etiquette, the rules of which here are not only extraordinarily elaborate but have something of the force of law. Through meditation, the civilized man thins out his emotional life to a kind of constant hum; through etiquette, he both shields that life from external disruptions and regularizes his outer behavior in such a way that it appears to others as a predictable, undisturbing, elegant, and rather vacant set of choreographed motions and settled forms of speech.

There is much more to all this, because it connects up to both an ontology and an aesthetic. But so far as our problem is concerned, the result is a bifurcate conception of the self, half ungestured feeling and half unfelt gesture. An inner world of stilled emotion and an outer world of shaped behavior confront one another as sharply distinguished realms unto themselves, any particular person being but the momentary locus, so to speak, of that confrontation, a passing expression of their permanent existence, their permanent separation, and their permanent need to be kept in their own order. Only when you have seen, as I have, a young man whose wife – a woman he had in fact raised from childhood and who had been the center of his life – has suddenly and inexplicably died, greeting everyone with a set smile and formal apologies for his wife's absence and trying, by mystical techniques, to flatten out, as he himself put it, the hills and valleys of his emotion into an even, level plain ("That is what you have to do," he said to me, "be smooth inside and out") can you come, in the face of our own notions of the intrinsic honesty of deep feeling and the moral importance of personal sincerity, to take the possibility of such a conception of selfhood seriously and appreciate, however inaccessible it is to you, its own sort of force.

Bali, where I worked both in another small provincial town, though one rather less drifting and dispirited, and, later, in an upland village of highly skilled musical instruments makers, is of course in many ways similar to Java, with which it shared a common culture to the fifteenth century.[3] But at a deeper level, having continued Hindu while Java was, nominally at least, Islamized, it is quite different. The intricate, obsessive ritual life, Hindu, Buddhist, and Polynesian in about equal proportions, whose development was more or less cut off in Java, leaving its Indic spirit to turn reflective and phenomenological, even quietistic, in the way I have just described, flourished in Bali to reach levels of scale and flamboyance that have startled the world and made the Balinese a much more dramaturgical people with a self to match. What is philosophy in Java is theater in Bali.

As a result, there is in Bali a persistent and systematic attempt to stylize all aspects of personal expression to the point where anything idiosyncratic, anything characteristic of the individual merely because he is who he is physically, psychologically, or biographically, is muted in favor of his assigned place in the continuing and, so it is thought, never-changing pageant that is Balinese life. It is dramatis personae, not actors, that endure; indeed, it is dramatis personae, not actors, that in the proper sense really exist. Physically men come and go, mere incidents in a happenstance history, of no genuine importance even to themselves. But the masks they wear, the stage they occupy, the parts they play, and, most important, the spectacle they mount remain and comprise not the facade but the substance of things, not least the self. Shakespeare's old-trouper view of the vanity of action in the face of mortality – all the world's a stage and we but poor players, content to strut our hour, and so on – makes no sense here. There is no make-believe; of course players perish, but the play doesn't, and it is the latter, the performed rather than the performer, that really matters.

Again, all this is realized not in terms of some general mood the anthropologist in his spiritual versatility somehow captures but through a set of readily observable symbolic forms: an elaborate repertoire of designations and titles.[4] The Balinese have at least a half-dozen major sorts of labels, ascriptive, fixed, and absolute, which one person can apply to another (or, of course, to himself) to place him among his fellows. There are birth-order markers, kinship terms, caste titles, sex indicators, teknonyms, and so on and so forth, each of which consists not of a mere collection of useful tags but a distinct and bounded, internally very complex, terminological system. When one applies one of these designations or titles (or, as is more common, several at once) to someone, one therefore defines him as a determinate point in a fixed pattern, as the temporary occupant of a particular, quite untemporary, cultural locus. To identify someone, yourself or somebody else, in Bali is thus to locate him within the familiar cast of characters – "king," "grandmother," "thirdborn," "Brahman" – of which the social drama is, like some stock company roadshow piece – *Charley's Aunt* or *Springtime for Henry* – inevitably composed.

The drama is of course not farce, and especially not transvestite farce, though there are such elements in it. It is an enactment of hierarchy, a theater of status. But that, though critical, is unpursuable here. The immediate point is that, in both their structure and their mode of operation, the terminological systems conduce to a view of the human person as an appropriate representative of a generic type, not a unique creature with a private fate. To see how they do this, how they tend to obscure the mere materialities – biological, psychological, historical – of individual existence in favor of standardized status qualities would involve an extended analysis. But perhaps a single example, the simplest further simplified, will suffice to suggest the pattern.

All Balinese receive what might be called birth-order names. There are four of these, "firstborn," "secondborn," "thirdborn," "fourthborn," after which they recycle, so that fifthborn child is called again "firstborn," the sixth "secondborn," and so on. Further, these names are bestowed independently of the fates of the children. Dead children, even stillborn ones, count, so that in fact, in this still high-birthrate, high-mortality society, the names don't really tell you anything very reliable about the birth-order relations of concrete individuals. Within a set of living siblings, someone called "firstborn" may actually be first, fifth, or ninth born, or, if somebody is missing, almost anything in between, and someone called "secondborn" may in fact be older. The birth-order naming system does not identify individuals as individuals, nor is it intended to; what it does is to suggest that, for all procreating couples, births form a circular succession of "firsts," "seconds," "thirds," and "fourths," an endless four-stage replication of an imperishable form. Physically men appear and disappear as the ephemerae they are, but socially the acting figures remain eternally the same as new "firsts," "seconds," and so on emerge from the timeless world of the gods to replace those who, dying, dissolve once more into it. All the designation and title systems, so I would argue, function in the same way: They represent the most time-saturated aspects of the human condition as but ingredients in an eternal, footlight present.

Nor is this sense the Balinese have of always being on stage a vague and ineffable one either. It is, in fact, exactly summed up in what is surely one of their experience-nearest concepts: *lek*. Lek has been variously translated or mistranslated ("shame" is the most common attempt); but what it really means is close to what we call stage fright. Stage fright consists, of course, in the fear that, for want of skill or self-control, or perhaps by mere accident, an aesthetic illusion will not be maintained, that the actor will show through his part. Aesthetic distance collapses, the audience (and the actor) lose sight of Hamlet and gain it, uncomfortable for all concerned, of bumbling John Smith painfully miscast as the Prince of Denmark. In Bali, the case is the same: what is feared is that the public performance to which one's cultural location commits one will be botched and that the personality – as we would call it but the Balinese, of course, not believing in such a thing, would not – of the individual will break through to dissolve his standardized public identity. When this occurs, as it sometimes does, the immediacy of the moment is felt with excruciating intensity and men become suddenly and unwillingly creatural, locked in mutual embarrassment, as though they had happened upon each other's nakedness. It is the fear of faux pas, rendered only that much more probable by the extraordinary ritualization of daily life, that keeps social intercourse on its deliberately narrowed rails and protects the dramatistical sense of self against the disruptive threat implicit in the immediacy and spontaneity even the most passionate ceremoniousness cannot fully eradicate from face-to-face encounters.

Morocco, Middle Eastern and dry rather than East Asian and wet, extrovert, fluid, activist, masculine, informal to a fault, a Wild West sort of place without the barrooms and the cattle drives, is another kettle of selves altogether.[5] My work there, which began in the mid-sixties, has been centered around a moderately large town or small city in the foothills of the Middle Atlas, about twenty miles south of Fez. It's an old place, probably founded in the tenth century, conceivably even earlier. It has the walls, the gates, the narrow minarets rising to prayer-call platforms of a classical Muslim town, and, from a distance anyway, it is a rather pretty place, an irregular oval of blinding white set in the deep-sea-green of an olive grove oasis, the mountains, bronze and stony here, slanting up immediately behind it. Close up, it is less prepossessing, though more exciting: a labyrinth of passages and alleyways, three-quarters of them blind, pressed in by wall-like buildings and curbside shops and filled with a simply astounding variety of very emphatic human beings. Arabs, Berbers, and Jews; tailors, herdsmen, and soldiers; people out of offices, people out of markets, people out of tribes; rich, superrich, poor, superpoor, locals, immigrants, mimic Frenchmen, unbending medievalists, and somewhere, according to the official government census for 1960, an unemployed Jewish airplane pilot – the town houses one of the finest collections of rugged individuals I, at least, have ever come up against. Next to Sefrou (the name of the place), Manhattan seems almost monotonous.

Yet no society consists of anonymous eccentrics bouncing off one another like billiard balls, and Moroccans, too, have symbolic means by which to sort people out from one another and form an idea of what it is to be a person. The main such means – not the only one, but I think the most important and the one I want to talk about particularly here – is a peculiar linguistic form called in Arabic the *nisba*. The word derives from the triliteral root *n-s-b*, for "ascription," "attribution," "imputation," "relationship," "affinity," "correlation," "connection," "kinship." *Nsīb* means "in-law"; *nsab* means "to attribute or impute to"; *munāsaba* means "a relation," "an analogy," "a correspondence"; *mansūb* means "belonging to," "pertaining to"; and so on to at least a dozen derivatives, from *nassāb* ("genealogist") to *nīsbīya* ("[physical] relativity").

Nisba itself, then, refers to a combination morphological, grammatical, and semantic process which consists in transforming a noun into what we call a relative adjective but what for Arabs is just another sort of noun by adding *ī* (f. *īya*): *Sefrū*/Sefrou – *Sefrūwī*/native son of Sefrou; *Sūs*/region of southwestern Morocco – *Sūsī*/man coming from that region: *Beni Yazġa*/a tribe near Sefrou – *Yazġī*/a member of that tribe; *Yahūd*/the Jews as a people, Jewry – *Yahūdī*/a Jew; 'Adlun/surname of a prominent Sefrou family – *'Adlūnī*/a member of that family. Nor is the procedure confined to this more or less straightforward "ethnicizing" use, but is employed in a wide range of domains to attribute relational properties to persons. For example, occupation (*hrār*/silk–*hrārī*/silk merchant); religious sect (*Darqāwā*/a mystical brotherhood – *Darqāwī*/an adept of that brotherhood or spiritual status) (Ali/The Prophet's son-in-law – *'Alawī*/descendent of the Prophet's son-in-law, and thus of The Prophet).

Now, as once formed, nisbas tend to be incorporated into personal names – Umar Al-Buhadiwi/Umar of the Buhadu Tribe; Muhammed Al-Sussi/Muhammed from the Sus Region – this sort of adjectival attributive classification is quite publicly stamped onto an individual's identity. I was unable to find a single case where an individual was generally known, or known about, but his or her nisba was not. Indeed, Sefrouis are far more likely to be ignorant of how well-off a man is, how long he has been around, what his personal character is, or where exactly he lives, than they are of what his nisba is – Sussi or Sefroui, Bhuadiwi or Adluni, Harari or Darqawi. (Of women to whom he is not related that is very likely to be all that he knows – or, more exactly, is permitted to know.) The selves that bump and jostle each other in the alleys of Sefrou gain their definition from associative relations they are imputed to have with the society that surrounds them. They are contextualized persons.

But the situation is even more radical than this; nisbas render men relative to their contexts, but as contexts themselves are relative, so too are nisbas, and the whole thing rises, so to speak, to the second power: relativism squared. Thus, at one level, everyone in Sefrou has the same nisba, or at least the potential of it – namely, Sefroui. However, within Sefrou such a nisba, precisely because it does not discriminate, will never be heard as part of an individual designation. It is only outside of Sefrou that the relationship to that particular context becomes identifying. Inside it, he is an Adluni, Alawi, Meghrawi, Ngadi, or whatever. And similarly within these categories: There are, for example, twelve different nisbas (Shakibis, Zuinis, etc.) by means of which, among themselves, Sefrou Alawis distinguish one another.

The whole matter is far from regular: What level or sort of nisba is used and seems relevant and appropriate (to the users, that is) depends heavily on the situation. A man I knew who lived in Sefrou and worked in Fez but came from the Beni Yazgha tribe settled nearby – and from the Hima lineage of the Taghut subfraction of the Wulad Ben Ydir fraction within it – was known as a Sefroui to his work fellows in Fez, a Yazghi to all of us non-Yazghis in Sefrou, an Ydiri to other Beni Yazghas around, except for those who were themselves of the Wulad Ben Ydir fraction, who called him a Taghuti. As for the few other Taghutis, they called him a Himiwi. That's as far as things went here, but not as far as they can go, in either direction. Should, by chance, our friend journey to Egypt, he would become a Maghrebi, the nisba formed from the Arabic word for North Africa. The social contextualization of persons is pervasive and, in its curiously unmethodical way, systematic. Men do not float as bounded psychic entities, detached from their backgrounds and singularly named. As individualistic, even willful, as the Moroccans in fact are, their identity is an attribute they borrow from their setting.

Now as with the Javanese inside/outside, smooth/rough phenomenological sort of reality dividing, and the absolutizing Balinese title systems, the nisba way of looking at persons – as though they were outlines waiting to be filled in – is not an isolated custom but part of a total pattern of social life. This pattern is, like the others, difficult to characterize succinctly, but surely one of its outstanding features is a promiscuous tumbling in public settings of varieties of men kept carefully segregated in private ones – all-out cosmopolitanism in the streets, strict communalism (of which the famous secluded woman is only the most striking index) in the home. This is, indeed, the so-called mosaic system of social organization so often held to be characteristic of the Middle East generally: differently shaped and colored chips jammed in irregularly together to generate an intricate overall design within which their individual distinctiveness remains nonetheless intact. Nothing if not diverse, Moroccan society does not cope with its diversity by sealing it into castes, isolating it into tribes, dividing it into ethnic groups, or covering it over with some common-denominator concept of nationality, though, fitfully, all have now and then been tried. It copes with it by distinguishing, with elaborate precision, the contexts – marriage, worship, and to an extent diet, law, and education – within which men are separated by their dissimilitudes, and those – work, friendship, politics, trade – where, however warily and however conditionally, they are connected by them.

To such a social pattern, a concept of selfhood which marks public identity contextually and relativistically, but yet does so in terms – tribal, territorial, linguistic, religious, familial – which grow out of the more private and settled arenas of life and have a deep and permanent resonance there, would seem particularly appropriate. Indeed, the social pattern would seem virtually to create this concept of selfhood, for it produces a situation where people interact with one another in terms of categories whose meaning is almost purely positional, location in the general mosaic, leaving the substantive content of the categories, what they mean subjectively as experienced forms of life, aside as something properly concealed in apartments, temples, and tents. Nisba discriminations can be more specific or less, indicate location within the mosaic roughly or finely, and they can be adapted to almost any changes in circumstance. But they cannot carry with them more than the most sketchy, outline implications concerning what men so named as a rule are like. Calling a man a Sefroui is like calling him a San Franciscan: It classifies him, but it doesn't type him; it places him without portraying him.

It is the nisba system's capacity to do this – to create a framework within which persons can be identified in terms of supposedly immanent characteristics (speech, blood, faith, provenance, and the rest) – and yet to minimize the impact of those characteristics in determining the practical relations among such persons in markets, shops, bureaus, fields, cafés, baths, and roadways that makes it so central to the Moroccan idea of the self. Nisba-type categorization leads, paradoxically, to a hyperindividualism in public relationships, because by providing only a vacant sketch, and that shifting, of who the actors are – Yazghis, Adlunis, Buhadiwis, or whatever – it leaves the rest, that is, almost everything, to be filled in by the process of interaction itself. What makes the mosaic work is the confidence that one can be as totally pragmatic, adaptive, opportunistic, and generally *ad hoc* in one's relations with others – a fox among foxes, a crocodile among crocodiles – as one wants without any risk of losing one's sense of who one is. Selfhood is never in danger because, outside the immediacies of procreation and prayer, only its coordinates are asserted.

Now, without trying to tie up the dozens of loose ends I have not only left dangling in these rather breathless accounts of the senses of selfhood of nearly ninety million people but have doubtless frazzled even more, let us return to the question of what all this can tell us, or could if it were done adequately, about "the native point of view" in Java, Bali, and Morocco. Are we, in describing symbol uses, describing perceptions, sentiments, outlooks, experiences? And in what sense? What do we claim when we claim that we understand the semiotic means by which, in this case, persons are defined to one another? That we know words or that we know minds?

In answering this question, it is necessary, I think, first to notice the characteristic intellectual movement, the inward conceptual rhythm, in each of these analyses, and indeed in all similar analyses, including those of Malinowski – namely, a continuous dialectical tacking between the most local of local detail and the most global of global structure in such a way as to bring them into simultaneous view. In seeking to uncover the Javanese, Balinese, or Moroccan sense of self, one oscillates restlessly between the sort of exotic minutiae (lexical antitheses, categorical schemes, morphophonemic transformations) that make even the best ethnographies a trial to read and the sort of sweeping characterizations ("quietism," "dramatism," "contextualism") that make all but the most pedestrian of them somewhat implausible. Hopping back and forth between the whole conceived through the parts that actualize it and the parts conceived through the whole that motivates them, we seek to turn them, by a sort of intellectual perpetual motion, into explications of one another.

All this is, of course, but the now familiar trajectory of what Dilthey called the hermeneutic circle, and my argument here is merely that it is as central to ethnographic interpretation, and thus to the penetration of other people's modes of thought, as it is to literary, historical, philological, psychoanalytic, biblical, or for that matter to the informal annotation of everyday experience we call common sense. In order to follow a baseball game one must understand what a bat, a hit, an inning, a left fielder, a squeeze play, a hanging curve, or a tightened infield are, and what the game in which these "things" are elements is all about. When an *explication de texte* critic like Leo Spitzer (1962) attempts to interpret Keats's "Ode on a Grecian Urn," he does so by repetitively asking himself the alternating question "What is the whole poem about?" and "What exactly has Keats seen (or chosen to show us) depicted on the urn he is describing?" emerging at the end of an advancing spiral of general observations and specific remarks with a reading of the poem as an assertion of the triumph of the aesthetic mode of perception over the historical. In the same way, when a meanings-and-symbols ethnographer like myself attempts to find out what some pack of natives conceive a person to be, he moves back and forth between asking himself "What is the general form of their life?" and "What exactly are the vehicles in which that form is embodied?" emerging in the end of a similar sort of spiral with the notion that they see the self as a composite, a persona, or a point in a pattern. You can no more know what *lek* is if you don't know what Balinese dramatism is than you can know what a catcher's mitt is if you don't know what baseball is. And you can no more know what mosaic social organization is if you don't know what a nisba is than you can know what Keats's Platonism is if you are unable to grasp, to use Spitzer's own formulation, the "intellectual thread of thought" captured in such fragment phrases as "Attic shape," "silent form," "bride of quietness," "cold pastoral," "silence and slow time," "peaceful citadel," or "ditties of no tone."

In short, accounts of other peoples' subjectivities can be built up without recourse to pretensions to more-than-normal capacities for ego effacement and fellow feeling. Normal capacities in these respects are, of course, essential, as is their cultivation, if we expect people to tolerate our intrusions into their life at all and accept us as persons worth talking to. I am certainly not arguing for insensitivity here, and hope I have not demonstrated it. But whatever accurate or half-accurate sense one gets of what one's informants are, as the phrase goes, really like does not come from the experience of that acceptance as such, which is part of one's own biography, not of theirs. It comes from the ability to construe their modes of expression, what I would call their symbol systems, that such an acceptance allows one to work toward developing. Understanding the form and pressure of, to use the dangerous word one more time, natives' inner lives is more like grasping a proverb, catching an illusion, seeing a joke – or, as I have suggested, reading a poem – than it is like achieving communion.

Notes

Reprinted by permission of the American Academy of Arts and Sciences, Boston, Massachusetts. *Bulletin of the American Academy of Arts and Sciences* 28, no. 1 (1974).
1. For a full description of the town, see Geertz (1965).
2. For a fuller discussion of these concepts, see Geertz (1960).
3. For the town, see Geertz (1963); for the village, Geertz (1966).
4. For these see Geertz (1973). A few sentences in following paragraphs have been taken verbatim from that essay.
5. The Moroccan work is in process of completion. For a general characterization of the country, see Geertz (1968).

References

Geertz, Clifford. 1960. *The Religion of Java*. Glencoe, Ill.: Free Press.
  1963. *Peddlers and Princes*. Chicago: University of Chicago Press.
  1965. *The Social History of an Indonesian Town*. Cambridge, Mass.: MIT Press.
  1966. Tihingan: A Balinese village. In Koentjarahingrat, ed., *Village Communities in Indonesia*. Ithaca, N.Y.: Cornell University Press.
  1968. *Islam Observed*. New Haven, Conn.: Yale University Press.
  1973. Person, time and conduct in Bali. In Clifford Geertz, *The Interpretation of Cultures*. New York: Basic Books.
Kohut, Heinz. 1971. *The Analysis of the Self*. New York: International Universities Press.
Malinowski, Bronislaw. 1967. *A Diary in the Strict Sense of the Term*. New York: Harcourt, Brace and World.
Spitzer, Leo. 1962. *Essays on English and American Literature*. Princeton, N.J.: Princeton University Press.
Watson, James. 1968. *The Double Helix*. New York: Atheneum.

5
Toward an anthropology of self and feeling

Michelle Z. Rosaldo

For purposes of argument, my past is mythic. Once upon a time (it sometimes helps to think), the world was simple. People knew that thought was not the same as feeling. Cognition could be readily opposed to affect, explicit to implicit, "discursive" to "presentational" forms of symbols, outer "mask" to inner "essence," mere facts of "custom" to less malleable dispositions and personalities.

For comparatists, these oppositions merged with the contrast between the variable and the universal, the relatively cultural and the relatively biological. For sociologists, the opposition between the social and the individual was evoked. And for psychologists, these contrasts paired with processes that were conventionally assigned to either "shallow" or "deep" aspects of the mind. Finally, to anthropologists, such oppositions made good sense because we recognized that, however strange the customs of the people that we studied in the field, we all could speak of individuals who, in personality, recalled our enemies, friends, or mothers: There was, it would appear, a gap between the personality and its culture. Moreover – although in an almost contradictory vein – we knew that learning any culture's rules (like how to bow or to ask for a drink) was not the same as feeling that *their* ways of doing things could satisfy *our* impulses and needs: Affective habits, even when culturally shaped, appeared autonomous from the sorts of facts that cluttered our ethnographies.[1]

Has there been progress? Although it strikes me that in some ways the dichotomies mentioned here are inevitable, as they appear unduly wedded to a bifurcating and Western cast of mind, I want to argue that the development, in recent years, of an "interpretive" concept of culture provides for changes in the way we think about such things as selves, affects, and personalities. The unconscious remains with us. Bursts of feeling will continue to be opposed to careful thought. But recognition of the fact that thought is always culturally patterned and infused with feelings, which themselves reflect a culturally ordered past, suggests that just as thought does not exist in isolation from affective life, so affect is culturally ordered and does not exist apart from thought. Instead of seeing culture as an "arbitrary" source of "contents" that are processed by our universal minds, it becomes necessary to ask how "contents" may themselves affect the "form" of mental process. And then, instead of seeing feeling as a private (often animal, presocial) realm that is – ironically enough – most universal and at the same time most particular to the self, it will make sense to see emotions not as things opposed to thought but as cognitions implicating the immediate, carnal "me" – as thoughts embodied.

In what follows, I will begin by speaking first about the power and limitations of the contrasts just evoked, discussing a set of intellectual developments that suggest a need for revised models. I then sketch some sorts of evidence likely to support a different, and more culturalist, account of how our feelings work – one that insists upon the sociocultural bases for experiences once assigned to a subjective and unknowable preserve of psychic privacy.

Signs of the times

To begin, it is quite clear that a discomfort with "our" opposed terms is not original to myself. One can trace something of the movement with which I am concerned in developments in the last twenty or so years in psychology, anthropology, and philosophy.

Thus, years ago structuralists abolished affect, posited an identity between "mind" and the world, and then recovered "energy" through notions like "anomaly" and "liminality."[2] "Cognitive dissonance" placed feeling *inside* cognitive discourse.[3] Social psychologists and anthropologists argued that "personalities" are the illusory product of reflections that abstract from social life.[4] And psychoanalysts, in a different but related vein, retreated from instinctual, unreflective, and mechanical conceptions of the self in elaborating such terms as "ego" and "object."[5] More recently, Foucault (1978) has argued that "repression" is itself the product of a world where we "confess." A stress on "narcissism" has made concern with "face" (rather than with tabooed drives) a central motive for the psyche,[6] and "action language" has attempted to displace "unconscious structures" in psychoanalytic accounts of mental process.[7] That all of this has happened at a time when terms like *action* and *intention* have become the problematic foci of much philosophical discourse,[8] when literary theorists have attempted to "deconstruct" our views of selves and actors,[9] and, finally, when anthropologists, like myself (Rosaldo 1980),[10] have shown renewed concern for how selves, affects, and persons are constructed in a particular cultural milieu – all this suggests that something deeper is at stake than hackneyed cultural relativism or youthful distrust of received categories.

An advocate may not be the best person to name the substance of a trend. Nor is the "trend" of which I speak sufficiently delimited or well formed for me to claim that an enriched concept of culture is the key to recent arguments in fields as different as anthropology and psychoanalysis. What I would argue, however, is that central to the developments evoked here is an attempt to understand how human beings understand themselves and to see their actions and behaviors as in some ways the creations of those understandings. Ultimately, the trend suggests, we must appreciate the ways in which such understandings grow, not from an "inner" essence relatively independent of the social world, but from experience in a world of meanings, images, and social bonds, in which all persons are inevitably involved.

Perhaps one of the deepest and most probing instances of this contemporary turn of thought is P. Ricoeur's masterful *Freud and Philosophy* (1970). In it, Ricoeur contrasts two interdependent and yet – he suggests – irreconcilable perspectives in the writings of the founder of psychoanalysis. First and most critically, Freud's texts make use of what Ricoeur sees as an hermeneutic, or interpretivist, approach, wherein our symptoms and the images in our dreams reflect experiences, things heard and seen, as these are linked to one another through associative chains and established in the course of living in the world. But, at the same time, Ricoeur makes clear that in the Freudian account our psychic images have force, our symptoms depth, because they interact with biologically based energies and histories of repressed desires. Surely, the subsequent history of psychoanalysis can be traced through theorists concerned with universally given instincts and those who stress the ego – or the patient, whose development is shaped by understanding, intelligence, social relationships, and self-knowledge. The "energetics" and "hermeneutics" that Ricoeur discerns in Freud have thus, in fact, become mutually dependent yet uneasy bedfellows in most academic psychoanalysis. Ricoeur's contribution was, at once, to emphasize the central place of meaning, language, and interpretation in psychoanalytic discourse and then to show the tensions that accompany a seemingly insoluble split between the poles of meaning and desire.

Desire and meaning are not, of course, identical to such opposed terms as affect and cognition, feeling and thought, or, for that matter, personality and culture/society. And yet, much of the interest of the formulations developed by Ricoeur is that one apprehends a commonality between his terms and more pervasive analytic themes. In anthropology, as in psychology, the cultural/ideational and individual/affective have been construed as theoretically, and empirically, at odds. And, furthermore, in both one finds the second set of terms described as basic, brute, precultural fact – and therefore granted analytical primacy. Thus, among most early writers in the culture and personality school, the organization of culture was that of the culturally typical personality writ large; just as, for later thinkers, culture answered to the typical actor's typical problems.[11] Subsequently, such theories of "reflection' were abjured, but psychological anthropologists tended continually to see in culture a set of symbols answering to (or perhaps channeling) unconscious needs,[12] whereas social anthropologists like Victor Turner (1967) readily proclaimed that symbols work at opposed poles, serving as tokens of society's rules while making an immediate appeal to semen, feces, blood, and the desires fixed within our universal bodies. Durkheim's (1915) insistence on the dual nature of "mankind" (and his assumption that our social worlds are made to organize, or transcend, a selfish, biologically given individuality) was thus reiterated in a tradition that construed the individual's inner world in terms of processes that could be channeled by, but were in essence separate from, the culturally variable facts of social life.

Although the "dual" nature Durkheim saw may prove a legacy – or truth – impossible to avoid, it seems to me that cultural analysis in recent years has (much like the "hermeneutics" highlighted by Ricoeur) led to a reordering of priorities. Loathe to deny desire or the inner life, the recent trend has been to stress the ways that innerness is shaped by culturally laden sociality. Instead of emphasizing the psychological cast of cultural forms, this recent turn – elaborated perhaps most tellingly in the works of Clifford Geertz (1973a)[13] – insists that meaning is a public fact, that personal life takes shape in cultural terms, or better yet, perhaps, that individuals are necessarily and continually involved in the interpretive apprehension (and transformation) of received symbolic models.

For present purposes, what is important here is, first, the claim that meaning is a fact of public life and, second, the view that cultural patterns – social facts – provide a template for all human action, growth, and understanding. Cultural models thus derive from, as they describe, the world in which we live, and at the same time provide a basis for the organization of activities, responses, perceptions, and experiences by the conscious self. Culture so construed is, furthermore, a matter less of artifacts and propositions, rules, schematic programs, or beliefs than of associative chains and images that suggest what can reasonably be linked up with what: We come to know it through collective stories that suggest the nature of coherence, probability, and sense within the actor's world. Culture is, then, always richer than the traits recorded in ethnographers' accounts because its truth resides not in explicit formulations of the rituals of daily life but in the practices of persons who in acting take for granted an account of who they are and how to understand their fellows' moves. Thus, for ethnographers in the field, a set of rules that tells them what the natives do can never show them how and why a people's deeds make psychological sense because the sense of action ultimately depends upon one's embeddedness within a particular sociocultural milieu.

What then of affect? One implication of this recent "culturalist" style of thought is that our feeling that something much deeper than "mere" cultural fact informs the choices actors make may itself be the product of a too narrow view of culture. If culturally organized views of possibility and sense must figure centrally in the acquisition of a sense of self – providing images in terms of which we unselfconsciously connect ideas and actions – then culture makes a difference that concerns not simply *what* we think but how we feel about and live our lives. Affects, then, are no less cultural and no more private than beliefs. They are instead, cognitions – or more aptly, perhaps, interpretations – always culturally informed, in which the actor finds that body, self, and identity are immediately involved.[14]

It thus becomes, in principle, no more difficult to say of people that they "feel" than that they "think." Nor is it necessary to assume that affect is inherently more individual than belief or that individuality is itself something other than the apprehension, by a person over time, of public symbols and ideas. One recognizes that it makes no sense to see in culture personality writ large. But neither, from the "interpretivist" point of view, does it make sense to claim that individuals – with their different histories, different bodies, and different ways of being more or less emotionally involved – are cultural systems cast in miniature. Through "interpretation," cultural meanings are transformed. And through "embodiment," collective symbols acquire the power, tension, relevance, and sense emerging from our individuated histories. It may well be that we require psychologies – or physiologies – or "energy" to fully grasp the ways in which symbolic forms are shaped, and given sense, through application to "embodied" lives. But then (as Ricoeur saw) it seems that insofar as they are culture-bound, psychologies lose their energetic force; whereas, when culture-free, accounts of psychic energies are, at best, provisional.

"Hot" mindless passion and its opposite, "cold" de-contexted thought, may have their use as ideal types. But danger lies in blindness, on the one hand, to the fact that histories of experience, and so of affect, are essential to all thought, and, on the other, that we could perhaps respond with fear but not with love or hate, desire, shame, resentment, or joy were not emotion schooled by public cultural discourse. A grasp of individuality requires a grasp of cultural form; analyses of thought must figure centrally in analyses of feeling. Or stated otherwise, I would insist that we will never learn why people feel or act the way they do until, suspending everyday assumptions about the human psyche, we fix our analytic gaze upon the symbols actors use in understanding human life – symbols that make our minds the minds of social beings.

Toward ethnographies

To some of you, these claims may seem ridiculous; to others, careless; to others, common sense. In what follows I want to ground my somewhat sweeping stance with reference to a set of concrete observations. The ethnographic materials to follow are presented with a goal of showing how my abstract claims may have empirical implications: They make a difference for the things we look at and the ways we understand. The first example argues that emotions are not things but processes that are best understood with reference to the cultural scenarios and associations they evoke. The second seeks to challenge a prevailing view that tells us to distinguish private "selves" and social "persons." And in my third example I discuss comparative findings, which suggest that selves and feelings, shaped by culture, may be understood in turn as the creation of particular sorts of polities.

WHAT ARE EMOTIONS?

I gather that among psychologists in recent years it has become fashionable to note that affect enters into thought and to suggest that "selves" and "personalities" are not enduring inner things but congeries of ways of acting and understanding that derive from social life. But at the same time most recent writers appear to be impressed by evidence claiming that "hot" cognitions, "preferences," and our "basic" and apparently "unthinking" styles of emotional response are relatively independent of the stuff of culture, thought, and reason. Experimental data – some have argued – are thus challenging unduly cognitive and rational conceptions of the self. Emotions are, it seems, neither as conscious nor as controllable as certain Philistines might like. Thus Freud is vindicated.[15]

The difficulty with such formulations, I suggest, is that they make things sound too simple. Freud's unconscious, Ricoeur makes clear, is far from lacking in such things as cultural experience, knowledge, or thought. Nor does the fact that some emotions (and, of course, some thoughts!) appear to have no reasoned cause mean that our lives are ordinarily split into "hot" feelings somehow wired in and "cold" and variable styles of reason.[16] Surely, experience argues forcefully that thoughts and feelings are not the same. And it seems easier to insist that people elsewhere think differently about their agriculture or gods than to insist (as it was at one time fashionable to say) that primitives are unrepressed or then again (to parody myself) that there is nothing universal about such things as happiness and anger. But that the Balinese no more feel "guilt" than we feel *lek*, the Balinese emotion closest to our "shame" – and that these difference relate to how we think about the world – is, to me, equally clear.[17]

My point is not to argue that contemporary academic psychology, located, as it is, within our oppositional terms, is but "our" folk belief disguised in weighty tomes[18] – by observing, for example, that the Ilongots (the Philippine people I studied in the field) do not conceptualize an autonomous inner life in opposition to life-in-the-world. I could, for instance, demonstrate that most Ilongots tend to see in feelings hidden facts no more disturbing or long-lasting than feelings expressed and that they speak of hearts that think and feel without distinguishing thought and affect. But, then again, I would remark that Ilongot concepts, even though they do not match our own, make implicit contrasts closely parallel to ours in that they speak at times of *nemnem* (thought, to think, reflect), at times of *ramak* (want, to want, desire), at times of *rinawa* (heart, desire, to will, feel, think of moving/doing). Thought and feeling are not distinguished, but Ilongot discourse comprehends a gap between passive reflection and thought fueled with affect, or acts of desiring, in a way that parallels our dichotomies. Ilongots are, in short, both like and unlike us. What is at stake is not so simple as the abandonment of "our" constructs in confrontation with a people who appear to challenge our discourse but rather a reflection on the limits of the ways in which the problem has hitherto been posed.

Or stated otherwise, rather than argue that the stuff of feeling is – in some essential and "brute" sense – either "the same" or "different" from the stuff of thought, it seems to me that what an anthropologist should do is point to ways in which, where psychological issues are concerned, the public and symbolic stuff of culture makes a difference. Thus, for me, the crucial point – and one much more profound than it initially appears – is recognition of the fact that feeling is forever given shape through thought and that thought is laden with emotional meaning. I can then argue – much as proposed earlier – that what distinguishes thought and affect, differentiating a "cold" cognition from a "hot," is fundamentally a sense of the engagement of the actor's self. Emotions are thoughts somehow "felt" in flushes, pulses, "movements" of our livers, minds, hearts, stomachs, skin. They are *embodied* thoughts, thoughts seeped with the apprehension that "I am involved." Thought/affect thus bespeaks the difference between a mere hearing of a child's cry and a hearing *felt* – as when one realizes that danger is involved or that the child is one's own.[19]

What processes account for such involvement of the self – what sorts of histories, capacities, desires, frustrations, plans – may well belong to the psychologist's domain. Among other things, they will include propensities for physical response and the awareness that enduring images of who one is are intimately at stake: Emotions are about the ways in which the social world is one in which *we* are involved. But this aside, the stakes, solutions, threats, and possibilities for response are apt, in every case, to take their shape from what one's world and one's conceptions of such things as body, affect, and self are like. Feelings are not substances to be discovered in our blood but social practices organized by stories that we both enact and tell. They are structured by our forms of understanding.[20]

Thus stated, a view that feelings can be classified into a set of universal kinds becomes no more acceptable than the view that one can speak of a generality of personalities. One *can*, of course. And partial clarity is obtained – but only because our words for kinds of people, kinds of feelings, and so on evoke a background of assumptions that then guide the way to see and thus may keep us from attending to what in fact is going on. Somebody slights me. I respond with tension, anger, rage. But what I feel depends on how I understand what happened and construe my options in response.

For example, it is common knowledge within our world that events like slights make people angry. Anger felt can be expressed, but if denied or – even worse – repressed, it is "turned inward" in a manner that can lead to everything from melancholy to explosion. We can "vent" anger, arbitrarily, on unfortunate innocents within our view. We can "deny" true feelings and, in consequence, be damned to inner turmoil. But what we cannot do are two things common among the Philippine Ilongots I knew: We cannot be "paid" for "anger," which, so satisfied, then dissolves, and we cannot "forget" an "anger" whose expression would prove undesirable. The Ilongots understood that feelings could be hidden. But they did not think of hidden or forgotten affects as disturbing energies repressed; nor did they see in violent actions the expression of a history of frustrations buried in a fertile but unconscious mind.

I recall an incident in which a man who I had thought to have been frustrated by his "brother's" carelessness in making plans, got drunk and fought with the offender. To me, the deed stood as a clear expression of disruptive feelings hitherto repressed. To the Ilongots, however, the fight was seen as nothing more than an unfortunate consequence of drink, which "dissolved" consciousness and in so doing led the fighter to forget bonds with his brother. By my account, one would expect to see in subsequent actions further symptoms of a conflict that to me seemed real and deep. If seething anger *was* in inner truth revealed in drink, I should have found its symptoms lingering in sobriety. But what in fact ensued were simply signs of "shame" – an affect dictated by the brawler's restored knowledge of significant, though forgotten, kinship ties. Ilongots who – to my observer's eye – had failed to recognize the psychological bases for the brawl proved right in that their understanding was the one that guided both men in the days that followed.

It would be possible, of course, to translate this event into the terms of Western psychological discourse and argue that a need for solidarity in this case had led the relevant actors to deny their true emotions. But what is difficult to understand, as long as Ilongot "anger" is construed within our analytic frame, is how and why the Illongots concerned could be content with what to me appeared the sort of outcome that could only lead to renewed conflict. Certainly, the event bore some relation to a history of tensions that my friends saw no cause to address. But the failure of my vision – of how "anger" grows and is resolved – to comprehend their very real success in keeping "anger" from disrupting bonds of kin suggests that in important ways their feelings and the ways their feelings work must differ from our own.

Further probing into how Ilongots think that "anger" works – the fact that Christianity was seen as an alternative to killing in response to death of kin because "God does away with grief and anger"; their reasons for surprise in learning that American soliders had not received compensatory payments from their former enemy, the Japanese; their sense that I was wrong when I desired to talk a feeling through instead of treating a prestation as an "answer" to my "anger" at a friend; their claim that since "I couldn't kill my wife, I just decided to forget my anger" – would of course be necessary to a satisfying understanding of the Ilongot account. How and why *we* think of "anger" as a thing to be expressed, whereas Ilongots tend to think of "anger" less in terms of volatility repressed and more in terms of how and if it can be answered, cannot be explicated here.

And yet I hope this anecdote suggests the viability of what strikes me as its theoretical counterpart: That affects, whatever their similarities, are no more similar than the societies in which we live; that ways of life and images of the self (the absence, in the Ilongot case, of an interior space in which the self might nurture an unconscious rage) decide what our emotions can be like in shaping stories of their likely cause and consequence. Ilongot discourse about "anger" overlaps with, yet is different from, our own. The same thing can be said about the things Ilongots feel. Or stated otherwise, the life of feeling is an aspect of the social world in which its terms are found.

PERSON AND SELF

People everywhere – as Irving Hallowell[21] proposed – are apt to have some notion of personal identity over time and of the boundaries between themselves and others. Whatever the connections we may feel with fellow men, we recognize (and grant significance to) some of our differences as well – and in this limited sense a concept of the self is apt to be a cultural universal.

Less certain are the questions of what self-constructs may be like, how vulnerable they are to facts of context and of sociocultural milieu, and how and if they contrast with ideas concerning other aspects of what people are about.

Anthropologists, following such diverse thinkers as the Frenchman Marcel Mauss and the American G. H. Mead,[22] have held to a distinction between the "me" and "I" – between the social person characterized by ideas about the body, soul, or role and a more intimate and private self. Thus, Meyer Fortes[23] has taken pains to show that African peoples typically enjoy vocabularies for talking first about "the person" as described for kinsmen, courts, or cures and, then again, about the "individual" who enjoys a "destiny" that is hers or his alone. Similarly, Ilongots have ways of talking about kinds of kin, of workers and the like, and ways to speak of what is *talagatu* (really hers or his) – those actions that can only be explained with reference to an individual's way of being in the world. Thus, Ilongots see the *rinawa* or (heart) as something that responds and acts within the world, but also claim that actions of the "heart" are often hidden, inexplicable, opaque, autonomous. The Ilongot notion of the "heart" would then – to Fortes – be a token of the individuated self that is but masked, presented, staged in public life.

In challenging this standard view, I would not claim that Ilongot individuals do not exist. Rather, I want to argue that an analytic framework that equates "self/individual" with such things as spontaneity, genuine feeling, privacy, uniqueness, constancy, the "inner" life, and then opposes these to the "persons" or "personae" shaped by mask, role, rule, or context, is a reflection of dichotomies that constitute the modern Western self. And in this case "our" distinctions prove misleading as a frame on which to hang Ilongot constructs.

A number of points seem relevant. First, Ilongot hearts are not fixed entities that stand behind or underneath a public world where personhood is both affirmed and challenged. As numerous ethnographies suggest, our notions of a constant "I" – alluded to by the experiences that make a lengthy dossier[24] – are not found in tribal cultures in which kinship *and* identity are forever things to be negotiated in diverse contexts. The Ilongot who today confronts me as an affine may well tomorrow be my son, a difference that describes not only how we speak but how we act and feel in daily life. Personal names may change when one contracts disease, moves to a new locale, makes friends, or marries. And character is seen less as a product of one's nature or experience in life than of the situations in which the actor currently is found. Success in headhunting, Christian conversion, birth of children, illness, age, the loss of kin or confrontation with a slight – are all things that can "go to" the heart and make *it* "different." Yesterday's "energy" and "anger" can – through marriage or conversion – turn to utter calm.

Correspondingly, among Ilongots, personality descriptions are extremely rare, as are strategic reckonings of motivation. Accounts of why particular persons acted as they did refer almost exclusively to public and political concerns – surprising actions giving rise to the despairing claim that "one can never know the hidden reaches of another's heart." In general, Ilongots do not discern intentions, trace responsibility, or reckon blame by asking if offenders "knew" that they wronged others through their actions. Nor do they promise or hold fellows to account for failure to fulfill the expectations of their kin and friends. People can, of course, be duplicitous – "hide the wishes of their hearts" and "lend their tongues" to parties whom they only formally support in public meetings. But what they do not do is receive gifts in "payment" for the "anger in their hearts" and then insist that a mere ritual is inadequate to resolve emotions that continue to be strong. Most of the time there is no gap between the inner heart and what one does or says: Hearts move and in so doing make for human life and talk.

For Ilongots, in short, there is no necessary gap between "the presentation" and "the self."[25] What is most true of individuals, their deepest sense of who they are, is located in a set of actions – hunting, headhunting, growing rice – that displays the "energy" or "anger" that gives shape and focus to all healthy human hearts. What is more, these deeds do not achieve the separation of the individual from the group. Lack of focus makes one "different," but the Ilongot ideal is best described as one of "sameness," parity, or equality. Deviance, illness, madness, and failure to perform are typically attributed to things outside the self: Spiritual forces may cause crops to fail or make a person wild or weak by taking the heart out of one's body. But no one sees in deviant acts the telling symptoms of a person's character or worth. Nor do Ilongots in their self-reflections speak of personal histories or distinctive psychic drives to account for the peculiarities of deeds or dreams. For Ilongot men, the act of taking heads is probably the occasion for their most intense, most magical, and most focused sense of self. And yet the irony, from our point of view, is that self-realization in this form is what makes adult men "the same" as equal fellows. The act of killing does not prove the individual's inner volatility or worth; it is a social fact, permitting equal adult men to engage in the cooperation appropriate to adults. In short, it seems misleading to identify individuality with the Ilongot sense of self, first, because Ilongots do not assume a gap between the private self and public person and, second, because the very terms they use in their accounts of how and why they act place emphasis not on the individual who remains outside a social whole but rather on the ways in which all adults are simultaneously autonomous and equal members of a group.

A last point follows from those just discussed. In thinking about personhood and selves, the analyst distinguishes between a public discourse and a less accessible inner life, the first described by role and rule, the second by a less articulate discourse of gesture, tone, and hidden truth. I proposed earlier that what individuals *can* think and feel is overwhelmingly a product of socially organized modes of action and of talk, and that society itself, as in the Ilongot case, provides its actors images that combine such things as action, thought, emotion, and health, connecting "anger" in the self to public life in which one wants to be "the same" as equal fellows. It would seem to follow that what we call "real feelings" or the inner self are simply silences discerned, given *our* analytical discourse, silences that do not necessarily help us to grasp the ways that culture shapes and is shaped by human experience.

For us, the attributes of individuals describe the core of what we really are. Ritual actions, things we do "because of" roles and norms, become mere artifice and play; the "masks" that mundane rules provide do not describe subjective life. But our concern with the individuals and with their hidden inner selves may well be features of *our* world of action and belief – itself to be explained and not assumed as the foundation for cross-cultural study.

COMPARISONS

Self and person, I have argued, need not be conceptually opposed, although it strikes me as perfectly reasonable to insist that, given variations in experience-in-the-world, all individuals will differ. The distinction can be challenged first of all with reference to ethnographic materials like those just sketched. But second, it can be questioned on the basis of comparative accounts that show how notions of the person, affective processes, and forms of society itself are interlinked. My hunch, in very general terms, is that there is a good deal of cross-cultural variability in the ways that people think about the opposition between private and public, inner life, and outer deed, and that these differences prove related, on the one hand, to conceptions of such things as bodies, souls, relationships, and roles and, on the other, to the life of feeling.

Perhaps the area in which anthropologists have come closest to exploring linkages of this sort is that described by the classic opposition between the affects "guilt" and "shame."[26] Assuming people everywhere to have destructive impulses requiring their society's control, several theorists have suggested that affective sanctions – "shame" or "guilt," the eye of social expectation, or the voice of inner principle and rule – will operate (either together or apart) in checking the asocial strivings of the self. Thus, "guilt" and "shame" have been proposed as guardians of social norms and the foundations of a moral order in a world where individuals would not readily pursue unselfish goals. "Guilt" as a sanction is then associated with our individualistic and rapidly changing social form, and "shame" with those societies that subordinate the person to a hierarchical whole, displaying more concern for continuity than for change.

The contrast has been criticized, of course, and I would not defend it here. The "shameful" Japanese have "guilt," and we, it seems, have "shame." And yet the contrast speaks to something many of us find true: That there are correspondences between emotions, social forms, and culturally shaped beliefs. The difficulty with "guilt and shame" is that it sorts just "us" from "them," asking how "they" achieve adherence to their norms and rules in lieu of mechanisms we use to an equivalent sort of end. What is not recognized is the possibility that the very problem – how society controls an inner self – may well be limited to those social forms in which a hierarchy of unequal power, privilege, and control in fact creates a world in which the individual *experiences* constraint.

For Ilongots – and, I suggest, for many of the relatively egalitarian peoples in the world – there is no social basis for a problematic that assumes need for controls, nor do individuals experience themselves as having boundaries to protect or as holding drives and lusts that must be held in check if they are to maintain their status or engage in everyday cooperation. In reading recently about the hierarchical Javanese,[27] I was impressed that "shame" for them is something of a constant sentinel, protecting the (male) self from a distressing mundane sphere; whereas, for Ilongots – and people like them, I would think – "shame" operates only with reference to occasional sorts of contexts and relationships. Rather than (as seems the case, e.g., with Mediterranean peasants or with Benedict's Japanese)[28] needing to guard a public presence and restrain such forces as might undermine the status of their families and homes, Ilongots are concerned primarily not to protect but rather to assert the potency of equal, "angry" hearts in everyday affairs. Thus, Ilongot "shame" is not a constant socializer of inherently asocial souls, but an emotion felt when "sameness" and sociality are undermined by confrontations that involve such things as inequality and strangeness. For Ilongots, such inequalities breed feelings of "anger" and the shows of force through which imbalances are overcome. But "shame" emerges when – because of weakness, age, or the relationships involved – inferiors accept their place and then withdraw in "shamed" acceptance of subordination.[29]

My point, in short, is that the error of the classic "guilt and shame" account is that it tends to universalize our culture's view of a desiring inner self without realizing that such selves – and so, the things they feel – are, in important ways, social creations. "Shames" differ as much cross-culturally as our notions of "shame" and "guilt." Further investigation would, I am convinced, make clear that "shame" in the Ilongot world differs from that experienced by participants in somewhat more inegalitarian African tribal groups and that these differ in turn from that experienced in societies organized as states. Symbolic bonds of "shame" and sex; the question as to whether "shame" requires that men or women be restrained; the sense of boundaries to defend; issues of who feels "shame" and when, and of relationships between the sense of "having shame" and "being shamed" by fellows – all are, I would imagine, cultural variables dependent on the nature of encompassing social formations. Thus, whereas the affect "shame" may everywhere concern investments of the individual in a particular image of the self, the ways that this emotion works depends on socially dictated ways of reckoning the claims of selves and the demands of situations.

Once it is recognized that affects and conceptions of the self assume a shape that corresponds – at least in part – with the societies and polities within which actors live their lives, the kinds of claims that they defend, the conflicts they are apt to know, and their experiences of social relations, it becomes possible furthermore to suggest that the ethnocentric error of exporting "our" view is closely linked to the distinctions criticized in this chapter. In brief: Because we think of a subjective self whose operations are distinct from those of persons-in-the-world, we tend to think of human selves and their emotions as everywhere the same. Taking a somewhat opposed view, I am led – as it should now be clear – to note significant ways that people vary. Not only does "shame" appear to differ, given differences in socio-political milieu, but tentative observations argue that much the same thing can be said of the emotions called by names like "envy," "happiness," "love," and "rage."

Thus, for instance, in my recent work, I have been struck by what appears a constancy in the ways that "anger" works in what I call "brideservice" – loosely, hunter-gatherer – groups, in which people appear to think of "anger" as a thing, that, if expressed, will necessarily destroy social relations.[30] The Ilongots – whose social relationships are of this sort – respond to conflict with immediate fear of violent death; they say they must forget things lest expression make men kill; and, as suggested in the anecdote described earlier, they seem quite capable of "forgetting anger" in those contexts where a show of violence has no place. The notion, common in more complex, tribal – in my terms, "bridewealth" – groups, that "anger" can and should be publicly revealed in words and, correspondingly, that "anger" held within may work to other people's harm in hidden, witchlike ways[31] appears as foreign to them as it does to foraging brideservice groups around the world for whom disputing persons either separate or fight – and the expression of violent feelings is seen as always dangerous.

More detail than is possible here would be necessary to clarify and explain the forms of "anger" in these groups. The shapes of witchcraft, the contrast between the use of ordeals in bridewealth groups and duels in the brideservice case, the fact that peoples like Ilongots "pay" for "anger" rather than loss suffered in the case of marriage or the murder of one's kin – all would figure in such an explanation. But what I hope is clear is that my earlier claims – that Ilongot "anger" differs from our own and that Ilongots do not generally differentiate self and person – are not the simple arguments of a relativist who fears that use of our terms will blind us to the subtle ways that Ilongots construe their situation. So much is obvious. More significant is the theoretical point that relates lives of feeling to conceptions of the self, as both of these are aspects of particular forms of polities and social relations. Cultural idioms provide the images in terms of which our subjectivities are formed, and, furthermore, these idioms themselves are socially ordered and constrained.

Conclusion

Society – I have argued – shapes the self through the medium of cultural terms, which shape the understandings of reflective actors. It follows that insofar as our psychology is wedded to our culture's terms in its accounts of people elsewhere in the world, it is unlikely to appreciate their deeds. Previous attempts to show the cultural specificity of such things as personality and affective life have suffered from failure to comprehend that culture, far more than a mere catalogue of rituals and beliefs, is instead the very stuff of which our subjectivities are created. To say this is, of course, to raise more questions than I can pretend to solve – old questions about the nature of both mind and culture. But it strikes me that considerations like the ones evoked here are valuable as correctives to those classically employed in helping us to go beyond a set of classic answers that repeatedly blind our sight to the deep ways in which we are not individuals first but social persons.

Notes

This chapter has grown out of reflections following completion of my monograph *Knowledge and Passion* (1980); in particular, I have been reading and thinking about the sense in which cultural analyses may also be accounts of affect. Much of the relevant reading was completed while I was a fellow at the Center for Advanced Study in the Behavioral Sciences, partially supported by a grant from the National Endowment for the Humanities. The paper was first presented at the SSRC conference on Concepts of Culture and Its Acquisition organized by Richard A. Shweder and Robert A. LeVine. I am particularly grateful to Clifford Geertz, Sherry Ortner, Renato Rosaldo, David Schneider, Mari Slack, and Mark Snyder for their comments.

1. The notion that experiences such as these might testify to a divide between affect and cognition, psychology and culture were occasioned by a reading of the early chapters of Robert A. LeVine's useful book, *Culture, Behavior and Personality* (1973). My conclusions, however, differ from LeVine's, as the chapter should make clear.
2. Here I have in mind, first of all, Claude Levi-Strauss, who, of course, abolishes "affect" as something other than a consequence of cognitive processes in, e.g., *Totemism* (1963b) and "The Effectiveness of Symbols" (1963a). Furthermore, it seems to me that "mediation" in Levi-Strauss, like "anomaly" in Douglas (1966) or "liminality" in Turner (1967, 1969), can be seen as a concept designed to "recover" energy and affect within the context of a structuralist perspective.
3. For classic sources on cognitive dissonance, see Festinger (1964).
4. D'Andrade's (1965) classic study in this regard has been followed by the research and theoretical writings of Shweder (1979a, 1979b, 1980). Among psychologists, the works of Daryl Bem (1974) and Walter Mischel (1973) are relevant.
5. Here I am pointing to a commonality (noted also, I believe, by Roy Shaefer) in impulse shared by ego psychologists like Erikson (e.g., 1963) and object relations theorists like Winnicott (1953) and Fairbairn (1954). See Chodorow (1978) for an extremely useful discussion of the significance of object relations theory.
6. In reading Kohut (1971), I was struck by the sense in which his work seemed a psychodynamic counterpart to the masterful sociology of "face" developed by Erving Goffman (1959). Hochschild's (1979) suggestion that we see "emotion work" and "emotion rules" as the "deep" counterpart to Goffman's "face work" (1967) provides the missing link. Interestingly, in all of these writers, there is an ambiguity as to whether their analytic constructs are intended to be universal (and thus the product of strictly analytical concerns) or more local reflections of self-constructs and problems peculiar to the modern West. My hunch is that both factors are operative; this is a piece of intellectual history that remains to be told.
7. Shaefer (1976) is quite explicit as to the continuities between his efforts and those of "self," "ego," and "object" psychologists, although he claims that they sought to accomplish through "structure" and "mecha-

nism" analytical ends that require an emphasis, instead, on agency, consciousness, or intention.

8. I have in mind here the work of linguistically oriented philosophers like Searle (1969), and Grice (1975), on the one hand, and of philosophers interested in conceptions of self, person, and affect (e.g., Perry 1975; 1976, 1980; Williams 1973), on the other. For many of these people, one important context for their reflections is the rise of the notion of a "cognitive science" and a desire to clarify the kind of analysis appropriate to "thought" itself.

9. The key name here, of course, is Derrida (1976), but his continuity with structuralism's attack on "the subject" (see, e.g., Donato 1977) and the challenge to conventional "humanism" posed by other "post-structuralists" such as Foucault (1972) also deserve to be noted.

10. The concern has a history, but key recent texts include: Crapanzano (1973), Dieterlen (1973), C. Geertz (1973b), H. Geertz (1959), Levy (1973), Myers (1979), Paul (1976), and Turner (1970). One could, in addition, list a host of dissertations and unpublished papers and several symposia at recent anthropology meetings.

11. Among those who see cultural organization as essentially that of personality, I would cite (whatever their differences), Benedict (1959), Kardiner (1939), Kardiner et al. (1945), and Mead (1935). Whiting (e.g., 1964) and his collaborators tend more to the view that culture-formation processes resemble those of symbol-formation in Freud; in this view, personality (or, more narrowly, child development) is seen as something that *explains* (rather than paralleling, or being reflected in) culture.

12. Key exemplars are Spiro (1967) and Obeyesekere (1974).

13. To his name should be added, minimally, those of David Schneider (1968) and Dell Hymes and J. Gumperz (1972), who have stressed the need for a properly cultural understanding of the apparently "natural" or "functional" domains of kinship and language, respectively. The culturalist turn also is reflected, of course, in a host of monographs by younger scholars: e.g., Ortner (1978), M. Rosaldo (1980), R. Rosaldo (1980), and Schieffelin (1976). See also the work of such historians as N. Davis (1975) and W. Sewell (1980).

14. Although I would reject his formulation of emotions as "judgments," R. Solomon's somewhat uneven attempts to reconceptualize *The Passions* (1976) have influenced my own. One contribution of his that deserves particular note is his attempt to describe differences among emotions in terms of differences in situations and inclinations toward action rather than differences in internal feeling states; (Solomon, Chapter 9, this volume) on this, contrast Davitz (1969).

15. I cannot begin to cite the relevant psychological literature, which ranges from Schachter and Singer's classic study (1962) of the impact of thought on affect to Ekman's materials (e.g., 1974) on universals in the expression of emotion to more recent formulations of the relation between "hot," or "energized," emotional states and "cooler" modes of thought (e.g., Mandler 1975). For a provocative – though ultimately, I think, unsatisfactory – overview, see Zajonc (1980). For a dissident – although, to me, more promising – view, see Smith (1981).

16. Of course, one can find *both* variability and relative universality in *both* domains. A complement, perhaps, to Ekman's work on universals in emo-

tional experience/expression is that of Berlin (1972) and Berlin and Kay (1969) on universals in the categorization of plants and colors. But my argument in this chapter (in particular, my discussion here of "anger") is that in neither case do universals begin to tell the whole story. The observation that some kinds of feelings or perceptions may be relatively "given" in the nature of the world, of human society, or of the human "processing" apparatus will prove misleading if taken as "bedrock" for an account of the ways that thought and feeling work in human minds. What is most deeply felt or known, what is felt first, perceived most clearly, or experienced as a standard base or core need not be the "common denominator" Western analysts perceive among such diverse things as Ilongot and American styles of anger. And I would argue that we are most likely to understand the force of "anger, passion" in Ilongot hearts by starting not with isolated experiences we share, but with those Ilongot lives and stories in which *their* "anger" is described.

17. See Geertz 1973b.

18. These remarks owe a good deal to an unpublished paper by Catherine Lutz, "Talking About 'Our Insides': Ifaluk Conceptions of the Self."

19. To cast the matter in linguistic terms, it is the difference between a statement cast in universal terms – "John's rug is green" – and deixis, a statement anchored in the speaking self – "I know John"; "I see the rug"; "I hate the color green." Deixis, of course, has proved problematic for propositionally oriented linguistics (see, e.g., Silverstein 1976), and, from conversations with John Perry, I gather that the "I" in sentences like those just presented gives metaphysical headaches to philosophers. My suggestion is that the "problem" of emotions is in some ways *the same* as the problem of deixis – a parallel suggesting that reflections in one domain might prove illuminating to the other.

20. Hochchild's (1979) work on "emotion rules" is probably the most explicit formulation in this regard. Given my problems with the notion of culture-as-rule, I find more useful a comparable but more flexible formulation by Schieffelin in which he talks about "cultural scenarios" (1976).

21. See Hallowell 1955.

22. Mauss's distinctions (1938) are between "person," "self," and "individual" and are understood in terms of a developmental cultural sequence, with "the individual" a modern construct. But the opposition between "person" and "self/individual" parallels Mead's (1934) analytical formulation of a split between the interdependent constructs "me" and "I."

23. See Fortes 1959. Unfortunately, Fortes is more concerned to document the presence in African thought of notions of individual uniqueness than to develop the Meadian concern with an interaction between social typifications ascribed to persons and their sense of individual identity.

24. I owe the point about the dossier to a paper by Jean Jackson, "Bara Concepts of Self and Other" (1980).

25. There *is* in Ilongot a gap between the things I say, reveal, and those I hide, but the latter are not associated with such things as self and essence. As indicated in note 6, it is not clear to me if Goffman's classic formulation is intended to describe universal or more local processes of self-definition.

26. In fact, I would suggest that of all themes in the literature on culture and personality, the opposition between guilt and shame has proven most resilient (e.g., Benedict 1946; Dodds 1951; Doi 1973; Levy 1973; Lynd 1958;

Piers & Singer 1953), at least in part because guilt and shame are affects concerned at once with psychological state and social context (thus providing a significant terrain for culturally oriented social scientists) and in part because the opposition is consistent with numerous others in our psychological and sociological vocabularies (inner/outer, Oedipal/pre-Oedipal, male/female, The West/The Rest, modern/primitive, egalitarian/hierarchical, change-oriented/traditional, and so on).

27. The reference is to Ward Keeler's doctoral dissertation on Javanese *wayong wang* theater "Father Puppeteer," and his article, "Shame and Stage Fright in Java" (1983).

28. For classic cases in which shame seems to operate as a "fence," protecting, in particular, such things as personal or family honor, see Benedict 1946 for Japan; Campbell 1964 for Greek shepherds; Pitt-Rivers 1954 for Spanish peasants. In reading about shame in hierarchical Southeast Asia (e.g., Java, Bali), one senses that something slightly different is going on (see C. Geertz 1973b; H. Geertz 1959; Keeler 1982, 1983).

29. See my paper "The Shame of Headhunters and the Autonomy of the Self" (1983) for a fuller formulation.

30. The birdeservice/bridewealth division is developed in Collier and Rosaldo (1981). This typological cut – like its predecessors band/tribe, hunting/agriculture – is, needless to say, vulnerable to challenge. It is proposed here primarily as an illustration of the *kinds* of ways in which differences in social formation might interact with differences in self/affect constructs. One needs some notion of the kinds of differences that make a difference if interactions of any kind are to be grasped.

31. Examples abound. See, e.g., Harris 1978 and Strathern 1975 for the dangers of hidden anger. See, e.g., Briggs 1970, Robarchek 1977, and Rosaldo 1980 for the danger of anger expressed.

References

Bem, D., & Allen, A. 1974. On predicting some of the people some of the time: the search for cross-situational consistencies in behavior. *Psychological Review* 81(6):506–20.

Benedict, R. 1946. *The Chrysanthemum and the Sword*. Boston: Houghton Mifflin.

1959. *Patterns of Culture*. Boston: Houghton Mifflin.

Berlin, B. 1972. Speculations on the growth of ethnobotanical nomenclature. *Language in Society* 1:51–86.

Berlin, B., & Kay, P. 1969. *Basic Color Terms: Their Universality and Evolution*. Berkeley: University of California Press.

Briggs, J. 1970. *Never in Anger*. Cambridge, Mass.: Harvard University Press.

Campbell, J. 1964. *Honour, Family and Patronage*. Oxford: Clarendon Press.

Chodorow, N. 1978. *The Reproduction of Mothering*. Berkeley: University of California Press.

Collier, J., & Rosaldo, M. 1981. Sex and politics in simple societies. In S. Ortner & H. Whitehead, eds., *Sexual Meanings*. Cambridge: Cambridge University Press.

Crapanzano, V. 1973. *The Hamadsha*. Berkeley: University of California Press.

D'Andrade, R. 1965. Trait psychology and componential analysis. *American Anthropologist* 67:215–28.

Davis, N. 1975. *Society and Culture in Early Modern France*. Stanford, Calif.: Stanford University Press.

Davitz, J. 1969. *The Language of Emotion*. New York: Academic Press.

Derrida, J. 1976. *Of Grammatology*. Gayatri C. Spivak, trans. Baltimore: Johns Hopkins University Press.

Dieterlen, G. 1973. *La Notion de la Personne en Afrique Noire*. Paris: CNRS.

Dodds, E. 1951. *The Greeks and the Irrational*. Berkeley: University of California Press.

Doi, T. 1973. *The Anatomy of Dependence*. Tokyo: Kodansha International.

Donato, E. 1977. *The Structuralist Controversy: The Languages of Criticism and the Sciences of Man*. Baltimore: Johns Hopkins University Press.

Douglas, M. 1966. *Purity and Danger*. New York: Praeger.

Durkheim, E. 1915. *The Elementary Forms of the Religious Life*. New York: Macmillan.

Ekman, P. 1974. Universal facial expressions of emotion. In R. LeVine, ed., *Culture and Personality*. Chicago: Aldine.

Erikson, E. 1963. *Childhood and Society*. New York: Norton.

Fairbairn, W. 1954. *An Object-Relations Theory of the Personality*. New York: Basic Books.

Festinger, L. 1964. *Conflict, Decision and Dissonance*. Stanford, Calif.: Stanford University Press.

Fortes, M. 1959. *Oedipus and Job in West African Religion*. Cambridge: Cambridge University Press.

Foucault, M. 1972. *The Archeology of Knowledge*. A. M. Sheridan Smith, trans. London: Tavistock.

   1978. *The History of Sexuality*. Robert Hurley, trans. New York: Pantheon Books.

Geertz, C. 1973a. *The Interpretation of Cultures*. New York: Basic Books.

   1973b. Person, time and conduct in Bali. In C. Geertz, *The Interpretation of Cultures*. New York: Basic Books.

Geertz, H. 1959. The vocabulary of emotions: a study of Javanese socialization process. *Psychiatry* 22:225–37.

Goffman, E. 1959. *The Presentation of Self in Everyday Life*. Garden City, N.Y.: Doubleday.

   1967. On face work. In E. Goffman, ed., *Interaction Ritual*. New York: Pantheon Books.

Grice, P. 1975. Logic and conversation. In P. Cole & J. C. Morgan, eds., *Syntax and Semantics*, vol. 3: *Speech Acts*. New York: Academic Press.

Hallowell, A. I. 1955. The self and its behavioral environment. In A. I. Hallowell, ed., *Culture and Experience*. Philadelphia: University of Pennsylvania Press.

Harris, G. 1978. *Casting Out Anger*. Cambridge: Cambridge University Press.

Hochschild, A. 1979. Emotion work, feeling rules, and social structure. *American Journal of Sociology* 85:551–75.

Hymes, D. & Gumperz, J. eds. 1972. *Directions in Sociolinguistics*. New York: Holt, Rinehart, and Winston.

Jackson, J. 1980. *Bara concepts of self and other*. Paper presented at the 1980 Meetings of the American Anthropological Association. December.

Kardiner, A. 1939. *The Individual and His Society*. New York: Columbia University Press.

Kardiner, A., Linton, R., DuBois, C., and West, J. 1945. *The Psychological Frontiers of Society*. New York: Columbia University Press.

Keeler, W. 1982. *Father puppeteer*. Unpublished doctoral dissertation, University of Chicago. *Comprehensive Dissertation Index*. 1982 Supplement 5:227.

  1983. Shame and stage fright in Java. *Ethos* 11:152–65.

Kohut, H. 1971. *The Analysis of the Self*. New York: International Universities Press.

LeVine, R. 1973. *Culture, Behavior and Personality*. Chicago: Aldine.

Levi-Strauss, C. 1963a. The effectiveness of symbols. In C. Levi-Strauss, ed., *Structural Anthropology*. New York: Basic Books.

  1963b. *Totemism*. Boston: Beacon Press.

Levy, R. 1973. *The Tahitians*. Chicago: University of Chicago Press.

Lutz, C. N.d. *Talking about "our insides": Ifaluk conceptions of the self*. Unpublished manuscript, State University of New York (Binghamton).

Lynd, H. 1958. *On Shame and the Search for Identity*. New York: Harcourt, Brace.

Mandler, G. 1975. *Mind and Emotion*. New York: Wiley.

Mauss, M. 1938. Une Catégorie de l'Espirit Humaine: La Notion de Personne Celle de "Moi." *Journal of the Royal Anthropological Institute* 68:263–82.

Mead, G. H. 1934. *Mind, Self and Society*. Chicago: University of Chicago Press.

Mead, M. 1935. *Sex and Temperament in Three Primitive Societies*. New York: Morrow.

Mischel, W. 1973. Toward a cognitive social learning reconceptualization of personality. *Psychological Review* 80(4):252–83.

Myers, G. 1979. Emotions and the self: a theory of personhood and political order among Pintupi aborigines. *Ethos* 7(4):343–70.

Obeyesekere, G. 1974. Pregnancy cravings (dola-duka) in relation to social structure and personality in a Sinhalese village. In R. LeVine, ed., *Culture and Personality*, pp. 202–21. Chicago: Aldine.

Ortner, S. 1978. *Sherpas Through Their Rituals*. Cambridge: Cambridge University Press.

Paul, R. 1976. The Sherpa temple as a model of the psyche. *American Ethnologist* 3(1):131–46.

Perry, J., ed. 1975. *Personal Identity*. Berkeley: University of California Press.

Piers, G., & Singer, M. 1971. *Shame and Guilt*. New York: Norton.

Pitt-Rivers, J. 1954. *The People of the Sierra*. New York: Criterion Books.

Ricoeur, P. 1970. *Freud and Philosophy*. New Haven, Conn.: Yale University Press.

Robarchek, C. 1977. Frustration, aggression, and the nonviolent Semai. *American Ethnologist* 4(4):762–79.

Rorty, A. 1976. *The Identities of Persons*. Berkeley: University of California Press.

  1980. *Explaining Emotions*. Berkeley: University of California Press.

Rosaldo, M. 1980. *Knowledge and Passion: Ilongot Notions of Self and Social Life*. Cambridge: Cambridge University Press.

  1983. The shame of headhunters and the autonomy of the self. *Ethos* 11:135–51.

Rosaldo, R. 1980. *Ilongot Headhunting 1883–1974*. Stanford, Calif.: Stanford University Press.

Schachter, S., & Singer, J. 1962. Cognitive, social and psychological determinants of emotional state. *Psychological Review* 65:379–99.

Schieffelin, E. 1976. *The Sorrow of the Lonely and the Burning of the Dancers*. New York: St. Martin's Press.

Schneider, D. 1968. *American Kinship: A Cultural Account*. Englewood Cliffs, N.J.: Prentice-Hall.

Searle, J. 1969. *Speech Acts*. Cambridge: Cambridge University Press.

Sewell, W. 1980. *Work and Revolution in France: The Language of Labor from the Old Regime to 1848*. Cambridge: Cambridge University Press.

Shaefer, R. 1976. *A New Language for Psychoanalysis*. New Haven, Conn.: Yale University Press.

Shweder, R. 1979a. Rethinking culture and personality theory part I: a critical examination of two classical postulates. *Ethos* 7:255–78.

1979b. Rethinking culture and personality theory part II: a critical examination of two more classical postulates. *Ethos* 7:279–311.

1980. Rethinking culture and personality theory part III: from genesis and typology to hermeneutics and dynamics. *Ethos* 8:60–95.

Silverstein, M. 1976. Shifters, linguistic categories, and cultural description. In K. Basso & H. Selby, eds., *Meaning in Anthropology*, pp. 11–55. Albuquerque: University of New Mexico Press.

Smith, M. Brewster, 1981. *The metaphorical basis of selfhood*. Paper presented to a symposium on Culture and Self, University of Hawaii.

Solomon, R. 1976. *The Passions: The Myth and Nature of Human Emotion*. New York: Anchor/Doubleday.

Spiro, M. 1967. *Burmese Supernaturalism*. Englewood Cliffs, N.J.: Prentice-Hall.

Strathern, A. 1975. Why is shame on the skin? *Ethnology* 14(4):347–56.

Turner, T. 1970. Oedipus: time and structure in narrative form. In R. Spencer, ed., *Forms of Symbolic Action*, pp. 26–68. Seattle: University of Washington Press.

Turner, V. 1967. *The Forest of Symbols*. Ithaca, N.Y.: Cornell University Press.

1969. *The Ritual Process: Structure and Anti-Structure*. Chicago: Aldine.

Whiting, J. 1964. Effects of climate on certain cultural practices. In Ward Goodenough, ed., *Explorations in Cultural Anthropology*, pp. 511–44. New York: McGraw-Hill.

Williams, B. 1973. *Problems of the Self*. Cambridge: Cambridge University Press.

Winnicott, D. W. 1953. Transitional objects and transitional phenomena. *International Journal of Psycho-Analysis* 34:89–97.

Zajonc, R. B. 1980. Feeling and thinking: preferences need no inferences. *American Psychologist* 35(2):151–75.

6

Does the concept of the person vary cross-culturally?

Richard A. Shweder & Edmund J. Bourne

Our concern in this essay is with other people's conceptions of the person and ideas about the self. Our aim is to interpret a widespread mode of social thought often referred to as concrete, undifferentiated, context-specific, or occasion-bound thinking, a mode of social thought culminating in the view that specific situations determine the moral character of a particular action, that the individual person *per se* is neither an object of importance nor inherently worthy of respect, that the individual as moral agent ought not be distinguished from the social status s(he) occupies; a view that, indeed, the individual as an abstract *ethical* and *normative* category is not to be acknowledged.

Our aim, we wish to emphasize, is to interpret an alien mode of social thought. Thus, before we look at the person concepts of such peoples as the Oriya, Gahuku-Gama, and Balinese we feel obliged to consider a more fundamental question: In what terms should we understand the understandings of other peoples and compare those understandings with our own?

For over 100 years anthropologists have tried to make sense of alien idea systems. For over 100 years anthropologists have been confronted with all sorts of incredible and often unbelievable beliefs, as well as all sorts of incredible and often unbelievable accounts of other people's beliefs. A review of the history of the anthropological attempt to translate the meaning of oracles and witchcraft, wandering and reincarnated souls, magical "therapies," unusual ideas about procreation, and all the other exotic ideational formations that have come their way would reveal, we believe, a tendency to rely on one of three interpretive models for rendering intelligible the apparent diversity of human understandings. These three interpretive models can be referred to as *universalism*, *evolutionism*, and *relativism*.

There is a fourth model; perhaps it should be named *confusion(ism)*. Confusion(ism) calls for the honest confession that one fails to comprehend the ideas of another. We will not have much to say about confusion(ism) in this essay. We would, however, like to confess, right here, that not infrequently we are left in a muddled condition, especially when we are told, without exegesis, such incredible things as, e.g., the Bongo-Bongo believe that their sorcerers are bushcats, their minds are located in their knees, and their father is a tree, or when we read, e.g., that the Guki-Gama cannot distinguish between the products of their imagination and the objects of their perceptions.

Many anthropological accounts lack intelligibility. One does not know what to make of them; whether to treat them as accurate reports about the confused and/or erroneous beliefs of others or dismiss them as bad translations; whether to search for common understandings hidden behind superficial idiomatic differences; or whether, alternatively, to generously assume that the ideas of the other form a coherent system derived from premises, or related to purposes, that the anthropologist has failed to appreciate. Although we will not have much to say about confusion(ism) we would like to discuss, however briefly, the three other deeply entrenched models of anthropological interpretation: *universalism*, *evolutionism*, and *relativism*.

Universalists are committed to the view that intellectual diversity is more apparent than real, that exotic idea systems, alien at first blush, are really more like our own than they initially appear.

Evolutionists are committed to the view that alien idea systems not only are truly different from our own, but are different in a special way; viz., other people's systems of ideas are really incipient and less adequate stages in the development of our own understandings.

Relativists, in contrast, are committed to the view that alien idea systems, while fundamentally different from our own, display an internal coherency which, on the one hand, can be understood but, on the other hand, cannot be judged.

The universalist opts for homogeneity. "Apparently different but really the same" is his slogan. Diversity is sacrificed to equality; equal because not different! The evolutionist, however, opts for hierarchy. Diversity is not only tolerated, it is expected, *and it is ranked*. "Different but unequal" is the slogan of the evolutionist. The relativist, in contrast, is a pluralist. "Different but equal" is his slogan; equality *and* diversity his "democratic" aspiration.

Universalism, evolutionism, and relativism: interpretive rules of thumb

Universalists, evolutionists, and relativists all try to process information about alien idea systems following rules of thumb peculiar to their interpretive model of choice. Indeed, the universalist, evolutionist, and relativist each has his way of processing data to help him arrive at his desired interpretation.

UNIVERSALISM

Confronted with the apparent diversity of human understandings, there are two powerful ways to discover universals in one's data: (a) emphasize general likenesses and overlook specific difference ("the higher-order generality rule"); and/or (b) examine only a subset of the evidence ("the data attenuation rule").

1. *The higher-order generality rule.* Osgood's (1964) investigations of universals in connotative meaning illustrate the application of the "higher-order generality rule". Emphasizing the way things are alike, and ignoring the ways they are different, Osgood discovers that all peoples appraise objects and events in terms of three universal dimensions, viz. good vs. bad (evaluation), strong vs. weak (potency), and fast vs. slow (activity). The universals are discovered, in part, by moving to a level of discourse so general that "God" and "Ice Cream" are descriptively equivalent; both are perceived as good, strong, and active.

The tendency to overlook specific difference and emphasize general likeness is ubiquitous among universalists. In Levi-Strauss' mind (1963, 1966, 1969a, 1969b), for example, the distinction between, e.g., voiced/unvoiced (in phonetics), raw/cooked (in the culinary arts), sexual reproduction/asexual reproduction (in the Oedipus Myth), and exogamy/endogamy (in marriage systems) are all rendered equivalent, each an example of a purported human tendency to think in terms of binary oppositions [Is this a trivially true logical claim, or a false empirical claim?]. For ethologists and sociobiologists it is "conversation" (in human primates) and "barking" (e.g., in canine folk) that are voiced in the same breath, each an example of a universal "signaling" function of communication systems [What does a cow say? Moo! What does a sheep say? Baa! What does a person say?], while for others it is "marriage" and "pair-bonding" whose general affinities are made much of at the expense of potentially significant grounds for divorce [whatever happened to the "sanctity" of marriage?].

2. *The data attenuation rule.* Not infrequently, the discovery of a universal is the product of a sophisticated process of data restriction and data attenuation. Berlin and Kay (1969), for example, discover universal prototypes for the definition of color categories, and a universal sequence for the emergence of a color lexicon. Their study begins with two applications of the data attenuation rule. First, "color" classification is equated with the task of partitioning a perceptual space, pre-defined in terms of hue, saturation, and intensity (thus, attenuating the referential range of the "color" concept as understood by, at least, some cultures (Conklin 1955). Secondly, all color categories whose linguistic expression fails to meet certain formal criteria (e.g., superordination, monolexemic unity) are eliminated from consideration. The consequence of the application of these two data attenuation rules is that 95% of the world's expressions for color and most of the world's color categories are dropped from the investigation.

A second illustration of the data attenuation rule can be found in Nerlove and Romney's (1967) work on universal cognitive processes underlying the formation of "sibling" terminological systems. A major finding of their study is the universal disinclination of the human mind to process disjunctive categories (e.g., it is rare to have the same "sibling" term apply distinctively to both a younger sister and an older brother). Yet Nerlove and Romney consider only one portion of the referential range of "sibling terms" (nuclear family referents). Secure in the conviction that nuclear family referents are expandable proto-types, they decide not to examine the application in many cultures of "sibling" terms to such (disjunctive?) kin types as "cousins," etc.

3. *Universalism's benefits and costs.* There are benefits and costs to the adoption of a universalist stance. A major benefit is the thrill of recognition [My God! They're just like me after all!] that comes with the identification of a significant point of resemblance. An Azande consults the chicken oracle (see Evans-Pritchard 1937). "Will I be killed on my journey to Z?" The chicken is administered a magical "poison". If the chicken dies it means "Yes"; if it lives, "No". The chicken lives. A second chicken is consulted. This time the chicken's survival is taken as a caution to stay at home. But, the chicken dies. Reassured, our Azande goes on the journey to Z. He is murdered en route! Do the Azande doubt the veracity of their oracle? No! Instead they explain away the event in one of two ways. Counter-witchcraft was being practiced at the time of consultation, or perhaps women, standing too close, had polluted the consultation grounds. Should one fail to notice within these practices some of the methodological concepts of the Western applied scientist (?), viz., reliability checks (double consultations), interfering background variables (counter-witch-craft), and measurement error (pollution). The idioms differ, but they are easily overlooked in the light of the recognition that the Azande's search for truth relies on principles not unlike our own.

Universalism, however, has its difficulties. All too often the pursuit after a "higher-order generality" is like searching for the "real" artichoke by divesting it of its leaves (Wittgenstein 1968, paragraph 164). The "higher-order" sphere is all too often a higher-order of vacuity, the air gets very thin.

Consider, for example, the concept of "justice" ("fairness" or "equity"). Stated as a higher-order generality ("treat like cases alike and different cases differently"), "justice" is a universal concept. Appreciate, however, the laundered emptiness of this higher-order formulation. As Hart (1961:155) remarks: the abstract concept of justice

cannot afford any determinate guide to conduct . . . This is so because any set of human beings will resemble each other in some respects and differ from each other in others and, until it is established what resemblances and differences are relevant, "treat like cases alike" must remain an empty form.

For example, Americans deny 10-year-olds the right to vote, enter into contracts, etc. This exclusion, however, does not violate our abstract concept of justice. Quite the contrary, it indicates that we subscribe to the belief that in certain crucial respects, children are different from adults (e.g., they lack the information and judgment to make informed decisions, etc.). From a cross-cultural and historical perspective there have been many places in the world where, given received wisdom and without relinquishing the "higher-order" concept of justice, the difference between male and female, Jew and Christian, Brahman and untouchable, Black and White, has seemed as obvious to others as the difference between an adult and a child seems to us. Unfortunately, all these concrete, culture-rich ("thick" if you will; see Geertz 1973) variations in the way people treat each other get bleached out of focus in the "higher-order" description of "justice" as an abstract universal. Universality of agreement wanes as we move from higher-order abstract principles to substantive cases.

Application of the "data attenuation rule" has its costs, as well. These costs are clearly understood by Berlin and Kay (1969:160) who note:

> . . . it has been argued, to our minds convincingly, that to appreciate the full cultural significance of color words it is necessary to appreciate the full range of meanings, both referential and connotative, and not restrict oneself arbitrarily to hue, saturation, and brightness. We thus make no claim – in fact we specifically deny – that our treatment of the various color terminologies presented here is an ethnographically revealing one.

The path traveled by the universalist is rarely the one that leads to ethnographic illumination; only occasionally does it lead to a powerful, context-rich universal generalization. However, when it does it should not be scorned.

EVOLUTIONISM

Confronted with the apparent diversity of human understandings, evolutionists rely on a powerful three-stage rule of thumb for ordering that variety into a sequence of lower to higher (primitive to advanced, incipient to elaborated) forms; viz., (a) locate a normative model (e.g., the canons of propositional calculus, Bayes' rules of statistical inference, Newton's laws of motion, Rawl's theory of justice, Mill's rules for experimental reasoning, etc.); (b) treat the normative model as the endpoint of development; (c) describe diverse beliefs and understandings as steps on an ideational Jacob's ladder progressively moving in the direction of the normative endpoint (see, e.g., Piaget 1966; Kohlberg 1969, 1971).

The normative model *defines* what it is to have an adequate understanding (e.g., given that $P \rightarrow Q$, it is more adequate to conclude $\sim Q \rightarrow \sim P$ than to conclude $\sim P \rightarrow \sim Q$). Variations in thought are ranked in terms of their degree of approximation to the endpoint. The image is one of subsumption, progress, and hierarchical inclusion. Some forms of understanding are described as though they were incipient forms of other understandings, and those other forms of understanding are described as though they can do everything the incipient forms can

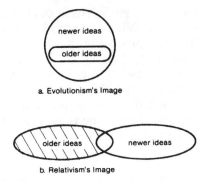

a. Evolutionism's Image

b. Relativism's Image

Figure 6.1. Evolutionism's and relativism's image of relationship between historically sequenced ideas (adapted from Feyerabend 1975:177–8)

do plus more (see Figure 6.1a); post-Copernican astronomy replaces pre-Copernican astronomy – experimental logic (Mill's laws of agreement and difference) replaces magical thinking (Frazer's laws of contagion and similarity). If the subsumed, less adequate form of understanding can also be time-dated, i.e., linked to early periods in history and/or childhood, so much the better.

Evolutionism has its appeal. For one thing, it permits the existence of variety. Instead of searching for "higher-order" equivalences it takes variety and difference at its face value (and tries to assign it a rank). Secondly, it does provide a yardstick (the normative model) for talking about *progress*. The vocabulary of the primitive vs. modern, adequate vs. inept, better vs. worse, adaptive vs. maladaptive, is highly "developed" in the evolutionist literature.

Evolutionism, however, has its pitfalls. There is no normative model for many domains of social thought – no way of saying whether one form of understanding is better or worse than another. Which is better? A kinship system where older and younger brothers are terminologically distinguished, or one where the distinction is not encoded? The mind boggles at the evolutionary presumption of the question. Which is better? A policy for allocating resources based on the principle "to each equal amounts" or one based on the principle "to each according to his work" (or "to each according to his needs"). There seems to be no *general* answer (see Perelman 1963).

There is a second difficulty with the evolutionary model, viz., the problem of "presentism." "Presentism" is the tendency to perceive the ideas of others through the filter of one's own current concerns. This pattern of perception is diagrammed in Figure 6.1b (see Feyerabend 1975). It is all too easy to unwittingly rewrite (and distort) the historical and ontogenetic record on others' ideas, dropping out or overlooking those problems, ideas, and principles which are no longer of contemporary concern. This is especially true when one's search through the ideas of others is guided by a contemporary normative model. But, consider the possibility that our ideas have succeeded the ideas of others, not through a process of subsumption, betterment, and advance, but rather, merely by "giving up" on the problems, principles, and concepts of our ancestors (see the hatched-in area of Figure 6.1b). "Presentism" obscures the historical record, making it appear our ideas can do everything the ideas of our predecessors could do, plus more, when all we may have done is shifted our field of interest and *altered the questions* to be answered.

RELATIVISM

Confronted with the apparent diversity of human understandings, relativists seek to preserve the integrity of the differences and establish the co-equality of the variegated "forms of life." Relativists typically process evidence according to two rules of thumb: (a) the "contextualization rule" and (b) the "principle of arbitrariness".

1. *The contextualization rule.* A primary goal of the relativist is to seek, and display, more and more information about the details of other peoples' objectives, premises, presuppositions, standards, knowledge, meanings, etc. [the famous "native's point of view"]; so much detail that the ideas and conduct of others come to make sense *given* the "context" (premises, standards, etc.). Thus, for example, Benedict (1946), in her classic analysis of Japanese culture, takes bits and pieces of Japanese conduct in World War II, their lack of respect for national sovereignty (e.g., the invasion of China and attack on Pearl Harbor), the suicide bombings, the "mistreatment" of American prisoners of war, etc., and places them in a conceptual framework (the Japanese understanding of the advantages and necessity of "taking one's proper place" in a domestic, national, and international hierarchy of individuals, groups, and nations), a conceptual framework *within which* "militaristic expansionism" is redescribed as an obvious remedy for international anarchy and the "atrocities" of the camps are redescribed as a valorous contempt for materialism and scorn of "damaged goods".

2. *The principle of arbitrariness.* A closely related goal of the relativist is to show that equally rational folk can look out on the "same" world and yet arrive at different understandings; the relativist must find a way for reason to leave us a free choice. To the extent that no rule of logic and no law of nature dictates what is proper or necessary for us to believe or value, that is, to the extent there is an element of "arbitrariness" or "free-choice" in our understandings, to that extent reason is consistent with relativism. Socrates may be right that the concept of "truth" implies "one" not many, but there are many points in a cognitive structure where questions of truth and falsity, validity, error, etc., are simply beside the point.

Hence, the passionate interest among relativists in the types of ideas underlying *non*-rational action, ideas that fall beyond the scope of scientific evaluation, for example, *constitutive presuppositions* (Collingwood 1972) (e.g., "all behavior is motivated by a desire to maximize pleasure and minimize pain"; what could possibly count as a disproof?), *performative utterances* (Austin 1962) (e.g., "You're fired", "I dub thee . . ."; in such cases the problem of getting one's words to correspond to, or match, reality does not seem to arise) and other *declarative speech acts* (Searle 1979) (e.g., various acts of "definition"), *categorical judgments of value* (e.g., Hempel 1965) (e.g., "Killing is evil" and other avowals or expressions of a commitment to a norm of conduct) and, of course, Pareto's *"sentiments"* (1935).

Hence, the rejection among relativists of both the "innocent eye" (i.e., "we classify things as we do because that's the way things are") and the "absolute given" (i.e., "we classify things the way we do because that's the way people are") (Goodman 1968; quoted phrases from Volney Stefflre: personal communication). For the relativist, knowledge, at its limits, is without foundation; what is of value and importance is a matter of consensus; social "facts" are created not discovered. The world of the relativists is a world where objects and events are not classified together because they are more alike than other things; quite the contrary, the relativist argues, objects and events seem to be alike because they have been classified together (Goodman 1972). And why have those folk classified things together in that way? That, the relativist will retort, "depends on their purposes". And, why do those folk pursue the purposes they pursue? That, the relativist will say, is a question for the historian.

3. *Relativism's benefits and costs*. Relativism, like universalism and evolutionism, has its distinctive benefits and costs. Relativism is consistent with a kind of pluralism or cognitive egalitarianism, a definite benefit, at least for some observers. Relativists provide us with a charitable rendition of the ideas of others, placing those ideas in a framework that makes it easier to credit others, not with confusion, error, or ignorance, but rather with an alternative vision of the possibilities of social life.

Relativism, however, has its problems. Despite its egalitarian intentions, relativism ironically lends support to a world based on intellectual domination and power assertion. The relativist views the understandings of others as self-contained, incommensurate, ideational universes (i.e., "paradigms"): *across* these universes there is no comparability, no common standard for rational criticism (see, e.g., Rorty 1979). Consequently, if people change ideational worlds (as they do), it can only be explained, by the relativist, in terms of domination, force, or non-rational conversion. And, if two or more peoples should disagree, as they often do, the only means of adjudication is "force of arms" – there is nothing to discuss. When "consensus" is the final arbiter of what's real, numbers count, and the powerful and/or the masses have their way.

Kurt Vonnegut, in his novel *Slaughterhouse Five*, points to relativism's second bane. Says Vonnegut:

> I think of my education sometimes. I went to the University of Chicago for a while after the Second World War. I was a student in the department of anthropology. They taught me that nobody was ridiculous or bad or disgusting. Shortly before my father died he said to me – "You know you never wrote a story with a villain in it." I told him that was one of the things I learned in school after the war.

An alternative concept of the person: the phenomenon

Any observer of an apparently alien concept, belief, or value must address the question: in what terms shall this understanding be understood? How shall this idea be translated? In this section we describe an apparently alien concept of the person – we introduce the phenomenon of interest. In the next section we discuss universalist, evolutionary, and relativist interpretations of the phenomenon.

Many Western observers of *some* non-Western peoples have made note of a distinctive apperceptive style or mode of social thought; it goes under a variety of cognate descriptions – concrete, non-abstractive, non-generalizing, occasion-bound, context-specific, undifferentiated, situational.

Levy (1973:24) illustrates this "concrete style" of social thinking by reference to one of his Tahitian informants, Poria. Poria is asked to define the word *hoa* which Levy glosses abstractly as "friend". Poria, however, responds by enumerating a list of restricted, context-dependent conditions:

> A hoa – we love each other – I come and get you to go to my house so that we may eat together. Sometimes we go and stroll together on the path. Sometimes I go to your house to eat. Sometimes I want you to help me with my work. Sometimes I go to help you. Sometimes we joke with the girls.

Levy notes that "much of village behavior having to do with personal and social description" is marked by an emphasis on "contexts and cases" (262), and is "oriented to richness of detail . . ." (268). He believes that Poria's thinking and the thinking of most Tahitian villagers involves "a calculus in which terms are understood on the basis of a large number of contextual factors" (262). Numerous other observers in Africa, Central America, New Guinea, and Central Asia (e.g., Werner and Kaplan 1956; Bruner et al. 1966; Piaget 1966; Horton 1967; Greenfield 1972; Luria 1976) concur in the observation that certain cultures perceive things (e.g., "an apple found in a store" and "an apple found on the ground") in terms of unique contextual features (e.g., time, place, coterminous objects, co-occurrent events, etc.) while failing to generalize across cases or equate things in terms of cross-contextual invariances (e.g., they're both "apples"; see Price-Williams [1975:28] for an illuminating discussion of concrete thinking). Informants either respond to questions about how things are alike by enumerating the ways in which things are different, or else emphasize the way objects and events fit together in functional complexes or action sequences, without abstracting a common likeness.

This same style of concrete, contextualized, non-abstractive, apparently undifferentiated thinking is found in various cross-cultural reports about the concept of the "person." What is noted is a tendency to *not* abstract out a concept of the inviolate personality free of social role and social relationship – a tendency to not separate out, or distinguish, the individual from the social context.

Geertz (1975:48), for example, asserts that

the Western conception of the person as a bounded, unique, more or less integrated motivational and cognitive universe, a dynamic center of awareness, emotion, judgment, and action organized into a distinctive whole and set contrastively both against other such wholes and against a social and natural background is, however incorrigible it may seem to us, a rather peculiar idea within the context of the world's cultures.

There is, he notes, in Bali

. . . a persistent and systematic attempt to stylize all aspects of personal expression to the point where anything idiosyncratic, anything characteristic of the individual merely because he is who he is physically, psychologically or biographically, is muted in favor of his assigned place in the continuing, and, so it is thought, never-changing pageant that is Balinese life. It is dramatis personae, not actors, that endure; indeed it is dramatis personae, not actors, that in the proper sense really exist. Physically men come and go – mere incidents in a happen-stance history of no genuine importance, even to themselves. But the masks they wear, the stage they occupy, the parts they play, and most important, the spectacle they mount remain and constitute not the facade but the substance of things, not least the self (Geertz 1975:50).

Twenty years earlier, in a brilliant discussion of morality and personhood, Read (1955) spoke in similar terms about the Gahuku-Gama of New Guinea. The Gahuku-Gama conception of man "does not allow for any clearly recognized distinction between the individual and the status which he occupies" (255). The Gahuku-Gama do not distinguish an *ethical* category of the person. They fail

. . . to separate the individual from the social context and, ethically speaking, to grant him an intrinsic moral value apart from that which attaches to him as the occupant of a particular status (257).

The Gahuku-Gama recognize "no common measure of ethical content which would serve as a guide for the moral agent in whatever situation he finds himself" (260). For the Gahuku-Gama, people

> are not conceived to be equals in a moral sense; their value does not reside in themselves as individuals or persons; it is dependent on the position they occupy within a system of inter-personal and inter-group relationships (250).

What this means is that for the Gahuku-Gama being human *per se* "does not necessarily establish a moral bond between individuals, nor does it provide an abstract standard against which all action can be judged . . ." (261). Rather, the "specific context", the particular occasion, "determines the moral character of a particular action" (260). For example, the Gahuku-Gama believe it is wrong to kill members of their own tribe

> but it is commendable to kill members of opposed tribes, always provided they are not related to him. Thus, a man is expected to avoid his maternal kinsmen in battle though other members of his own clan have no such moral obligation to these individuals (262).

Dumont's (1970:1, 9) observations on India almost sound redundant. He warns us against "inadvertently attributing the presence of the individual to societies in which he is not recognized", and he points to a relational, contextualized "logic" in which justice consists primarily in "ensuring that the proportions between social functions [and social roles] are adapted to the whole [i.e., society as a primary, not derivative, object]".

Geertz, Read, and Dumont contrast Bali, New Guinea, and India with a Western mode of social thought in which the "individual" is abstracted from the social role, and the moral responsibilities of this abstracted, inviolate individual are distinguished from his/her social responsibilities and duties. Read (1955:280) puts it this way: In the West

> the moral duties of the person are greater than any of the duties which the individual possesses as a member of society. His moral responsibilities, both to himself and others, transcend the given social context, are conceived to be independent of the social ties which link him to his fellows.

In the West, as Trilling (1972:24) so aptly remarks, the person, inviolate in his self-image, supposes that he is

> an object of interest to his fellow man [and worthy of respect?] not for the reason that he had achieved something notable or been witness to great events but simply because as an individual he is of consequence.

How are we to interpret this widespread mode of social thought in which the individual is not differentiated from the role, and where the person achieves no abstract, context-independent recognition?

The person in context: evolutionary, universalistic, and relativistic interpretations

THE EVOLUTIONARY ACCOUNT

In keeping with their respect for intellectual variety and their desire to rank diverse forms along a scale of progress, evolutionary theorists argue that concrete, occasion-bound thinking (in both the social and non-social domain) is unequally distributed across cultures and can be explained by reference to one of four types of cognitive "deficits," viz., the absence of (a) cognitive skills; (b) intellectual motivation; (c) pertinent information; or (d) linguistic tools.

1. *Deficit 1: Cognitive skills.* Luria's (1976) work illustrates the evolutionary emphasis on the absence of cognitive skills. He argues that "for some people abstract classification is a wholly alien procedure" (60), and he suggests that illiterate, unschooled peasants in the Uzbekistan and Kirghizan regions of Central Asia lack the *skill* to "isolate (abstract) a common feature" of things "as a basis for comparison" (80–81). Luria credits schools with fostering the ability to abstract, to generalize and to think scientifically (also see Bruner et al. [1966] on schooling effects and Greenfield [1972] and Goody [1977] on literacy effects).

Kohlberg (1969, 1971) adopts a similar approach. His evolutionary scheme for the ethical category of the person would account for the occasion-bound, socially contextualized person concept of the Balinese, Gahuku-Gama, and Hindu by locating it as a stage in the evolution of an adequate moral orientation in which respect for the abstract person transcends social roles. Thus, for example, the Gahuku-Gama view that the moral value of life cannot be separated from the social status of a person, and the cognate view that in a "catastrophe" important people, people of status should be saved first, would be interpreted by Kohlberg as an early childlike form of understanding, an initial step on the ladder ascending to the more mature recognition of universal respect for the value of life *per se*. For Kohlberg, movement through the stages of his evolutionary scheme is ultimately explained by reference to the development of certain cognitive processing skills, e.g., the ability to differentiate, take the perspective of another, and generalize.

2. *Deficit 2: Intellectual motivation.* Levy's (1973:269–270) work illustrates the evolutionary emphasis on intellectual motivation instead of cognitive skill. Levy interprets concrete thinking as an adaptation to life in a "cultural cocoon." Tahitian villagers, he argues, are deeply "*embedded*" in their own mundane daily contexts. They are not *motivated* to reflect upon the alternative cultural practices that surround them (e.g., the Chinese) nor do they have any *need* to conceptually locate their own customs in a more general comparative framework. Consequently, much of Tahitian village behavior "having to do with

personal and social description'' is marked by an emphasis on ''contexts and cases'' (262) and is ''oriented to richness of detail . . .'' (268). Levy speculates that such contextual embeddedness is ''not conducive to science [and abstraction]'' (269–270).

3. *Deficit 3: Pertinent information.* Horton's (1967) evolutionary interpretation explains concrete thinking by reference to informational limitations. Contextual-embeddedness, he argues, is primarily a cognitive concomitant of living in a ''closed intellectual predicament'', one too limited in opportunities to become aware of alternative visions of reality. Informational opportunities wax with the development of external trade, literacy, and urbanization, and thus these three conditions, Horton argues, are conducive to the development of abstract modes of thought. Also see Super et al. (1977) for a discussion of the informational conditions favoring abstract thought. They conclude that cultures that are ''materially simple will rarely require [abstract] categorical organization . . .''

4. *Deficit 4: Linguistic tools.* It is occasionally suggested that concrete thinkers are speakers of impoverished languages, viz. languages lacking *general terms* as a symbolic resource (e.g., Jesperson 1934). Thus, e.g., in Tasmanian each variety of gum-tree and wattle-tree has a name but there is no equivalent for the expression ''a tree'', while in Bororo (the classic illustration) each parrot has its special name but the general lexical entry ''parrot'' is absent. Deficient in their symbolic resources, lacking general terms, speakers of such languages are said to be prone to overlook the likenesses between things; hence the failure to abstract.

THE UNIVERSALIST ACCOUNT

Evolutionary theorists, as we have just seen, argue that some peoples are distinctively concrete in their thinking; this distinctive mode of thought is explained by reference to deficits in cognitive processing skills, intellectual motivation, pertinent information, or requisite tools. Universalists, in contrast, are skeptical of the claim that some peoples are concrete thinkers, others abstract thinkers. From the perspective of the universalist, *attributions* of *differential* concreteness (or abstractness) by one people about another are illusory and amount to little more than an indication that the category system of the observers fails to align with the category system of the people observed.

There are three claims implicit in the universalist interpretation of concrete and/or abstract thinking. First, it is argued that apparent evidence of concrete and abstract thinking is *equally* present in all cultures (concrete vs. abstract thinking is not a *variable* that can be used to distinguish one culture from another). Secondly, it is argued, the attribution of concreteness or abstractness to other people's thinking is the inevitable result of the confrontation between uncalibrated conceptual systems. More specifically, the universalist argues, we describe other people's thinking as concrete when they overlook likenesses or truths that we emphasize; we describe their thinking as abstract where they emphasize likenesses or truths that we overlook. Finally, it is argued, since no one conceptual system can take note of, or encode, all possible likenesses, or record all possible truths, where conceptual systems clash there will always be areas of *both* apparent concreteness and apparent abstractness. The works of Kroeber (1909) and Frake (1962) illustrate the universalist interpretation.

Frake's (1962) universalist argument is advanced against the evolutionary view of Jesperson (1934) that the mind of the "primitive" is concrete (overlooks likenesses) in its classification of flora and fauna [remember those "parrots"]. Ironically, Kroeber's (1909) universalist argument is advanced against the opposite evolutionary view (Morgan 1871) that the mind of the "primitive" is excessively abstract (overlooks differences) in its classification of kinsmen (e.g., a "father-in-law" and a "grandfather" are similarly labeled in the Dakota language).

It would be a mistake to conclude from this irony that primitive terminological systems are concrete when it comes to plants and animals yet abstract for kinsmen. Rather, the main point of the universalist interpretation is that the contrast between concrete and abstract systems of classification is an *illusion* that:

> . . . has its origin in the point of view of investigators, who, on approaching foreign languages, have been impressed with their failure to discriminate certain relationships [e.g., father-in-law and grandfather] between which the languages of civilized Europe distinguish, and who, in the enthusiasm of formulating general [evolutionary] theories from such facts, have forgotten that their own languages are filled with entirely analogous groupings or classifications which custom has made so familiar and natural that they are not felt as such [e.g., overlooking the difference between cousins older and younger than oneself and denoting them both with the same term]. (Kroeber 1909:77)

Frake (1962:75) makes a similar point. He remarks that there is "no necessary reason" that other people should heed those particular attributes which, for the English-speaker, make equivalent all the diverse individual organisms he labels "parrots" [see Findley 1979 for an example of the way attribute selection can radically influence which organisms get categorized together]. As Frake notes, any comparison of unaligned category systems will reveal cases where the others' thought seems quite concrete (they overlook likenesses that we emphasize) *as well as* cases where their thought seems quite abstract (they emphasize likenesses that we overlook).

To this point we have described the "logic" of universalist, evolutionary and relativist understandings of other people's understandings, and we have characterized the evolutionary and universalist interpretations of concrete, context-dependent, occasion-bound thinking. We now focus our attention on one specific example of concrete thinking, that is, occasion-bound *social* thinking, more particularly, the concept of the context-dependent person. In presenting the results of a cross-cultural study of person description in India and the United States, we display our reasons for rejecting the evolutionary and universalist interpretations of the Hindu, Balinese, and Gahuku-Gama context-dependent person concept. Finally, we construct an alternative, relativist interpretation which argues that the context-dependent concept of the person is one aspect of a broader sociocentric "organic" (or holistic) conception of the relationship of the individual to society. It is a feature of holistic thinking that "units" (organs, body parts, groups, individuals, etc.) are believed to be necessarily altered by the *relations* into which they enter (Phillips 1976). We argue that concrete thinking (as a general phenomenon) is a by-product of the commitment to a holistic world view, and we discuss the implications of the sociocentric organic conception of the individual-social relationship for the developing ego's view of its-"self".

Contexts and cases: a study of person description in India and the United States

It is by reference to "contexts and cases" that Oriyas in the old town of Bhubaneswar (Orissa, India) describe the personalities of their friends, neighbors, and workmates. These personal accounts of Oriyas are concrete and relational. They tell you what someone has done; behavioral instances are often mentioned. They tell you where it was done. They tell you to whom or with whom it was done. The descriptive attention of Oriyas is directed towards the behavioral context in which particular behavioral instances occurred, e.g., "whoever becomes his friend, he remembers him forever, and will always help him out of his troubles" (Jaha sange thɔre sangɔ hoichɔnti, tanku sɔbudinɔ pain mɔne rɔkhithanti o tankɔrɔ jɔdi kichi subidha hue, taku dɔbaku cesta kɔrɔnti), "has no cultivable land, but likes to cultivate the land of others" (Casɔ jɔmi nahi, ɔthɔcɔ pɔrɔ jɔmi casɔ kɔribaku bhɔlɔ paanti), "when a quarrel arises, cannot resist the temptation of saying a word" (GɔndɔgoLɔtae hele pɔde nɔkɔhi rɔhi parɔnti nahi), "will talk right in the face of even a British Governor" (laat saheb hele mɔdhɔyɔ muhe muhe jɔbab diyɔnti), "comes forward whenever there is an occasion to address a public meeting" (Sɔbha sɔmitire kɔhibaku agua), "behaves properly with guests but feels sorry if money is spent on them" (Bɔndhu bandhɔbɔ asile bhɔlɔ byɔbɔharɔ dekhanti, kintu tɔnka pɔisa khɔrcɔ hele dukhɔ kɔrɔnti).

This concrete-relational way of thinking about other persons differs from the abstract style of our American informants. Americans tell you what is true of a person's behavior (e.g., he's friendly, arrogant, and intelligent) while tending to overlook behavioral context. Below we discuss the results of a comparison of Oriya and American personality descriptions. As we shall see, the striking tendency of Oriyas to be more concrete and relational than Americans does not readily lend itself to evolutionary interpretation in terms of either (a) relative amounts of formal schooling; (b) relative degrees of literacy; (c) relative socio-economic status; (d) the presence or absence of abstract terms in one's language; (e) the absence of skills of abstraction among Oriyas; or (f) relative awareness of alternative behavioral contexts or variations in behavior.

The concrete-relational style of Oriya social thought seems unrelated to variations in cognitive skill, intellectual motivation, available information, and linguistic resources. By elimination, we are led to consider the way a culture's world view and master metaphors *per se* influence the relationship between what one thinks about and how one thinks. We consider differences in Indian and American conceptualizations of the relationship of the individual and society with special reference to the sociocentric organic vs. egocentric reductionist view of "man-in-society".

METHODOLOGY

1. *Informants.* The 17 informants in the American sample came from three separate groups: (1) counseling psychologists (3 women, 2 men); (2) a college fraternity (6 men), and (3) nursery school teachers (6 women). In each group they had known each other for at least one year. Their ages ranged from 19 to 47, and they all had received or were about to complete a college education. They all lived in or around Chicago, Illinois. Socio-economically they were predominantly middle-class.

The 70 Indian informants resided in the old town of Bhubaneswar, Orissa. They were selected on the basis of caste criteria as part of a general enquiry into household composition and caste interaction patterns. Thus, the full range of the local caste hierarchy was represented. With two exceptions the Oriyas were all males and spanned a wider age range (18–70) than the Americans. Educational variability among them was also greater, ranging from no formal education to the attainment of the M.A. degree. Seventeen informants had no education at all. Eighteen informants were illiterate.

Caste, formal schooling, and literacy are not orthogonal in the Indian sample. Informants from the lower castes tend to be less educated and illiterate, although there are a number of informants from the upper castes who are literate but relatively unschooled. The confounding of caste, literacy, and schooling in the sample is less worrisome than it might at first appear. The cultural differences in concrete-relational thinking, to be reported below, are stable across the entire Indian sample and do not vary by caste, education, or literacy. Unschooled, illiterate untouchables and highly educated, literate Brahmans differ from Americans in the same way and do not significantly differ from each other.

2. *The task*. Informants in both populations responded to the task of describing a close acquaintance. However, in the Indian group each informant described up to three friends, neighbors, or workmates, whereas in the American group each described the other four or five members of his/her group. There were also slight differences in the instructions and format of the descriptive task between the two cultures, an inevitable consequence of the fact that they had originally been associated with independent studies. Indian informants were presented with the instructions: "Tankɔrɔ cɔritrɔ, prɔkruti, o byɔbɔharɔ bisɔyɔre mɔte bhalɔbhabɔre kuhɔntu" (Tell me in depth about so-and-so's character, nature [personality] and behavior), whereas Americans were asked: "How would you characterize so-and-so's personality?" Indians could respond in as many or few ways as they chose (they averaged between seven and eight descriptive phrases), whereas Americans were asked to provide 20 descriptive sentences or phrases. Finally, Indians responded orally while Americans wrote out their description.

Because these procedural differences could have interacted with the cultural difference observed on the various dependent variables (see results section), the following "ex-post-facto" study was done with a sample of 10 Americans. Informants were divided into two groups and given one or the other of the two instructions mentioned above. In each of these groups some informants were permitted to make as many responses as they wished, the others told to give 20 responses. All responses were given orally. While the different instructions had a slight, statistically nonsignificant effect on the tendency of informants to give concrete or abstract descriptions, this effect was nominal in comparison with that associated with cultural differences, as reported in the results section.

3. *The coding of descriptions*. To facilitate coding, all descriptions were broken down into constituent sentences. Where a sentence was compound or complex, it was further broken down into units, each of which contained no more than one subject-predicate-object sequence. These units were subsequently referred to as "descriptive phrases". Each descriptive phrase was typed on a 3 × 5 card. In this fashion a total of 3,451 descriptive phrases for both cultures was obtained.

A coding system was developed to enable judges to decide on the presence or absence of a number of features related to concrete thinking, in particular (a) descriptive reference to abstract traits; (b) descriptive reference to concrete action; (c) descriptive incorporation of contextual qualifications.

An abstract trait reference (abbreviated "*T*") was operationally defined as any attribute that answered the question "What kind of person *is* the ratee?" The judgment was made independently of the presence or absence of contextual qualifications in the descriptive phrase. Thus "she is stubborn" and "she is stubborn about family matters" would both be coded "*T*", although the final coding for the two phrases would differ in the specification of additional contextual qualifiers.

An action reference ("*A*") answered the question "Is this something the ratee does?" This judgment also was made independently of the presence or absence of contextual qualifiers. Thus, "she uses dirty language" and "she uses dirty language when her friends give her advice about family matters" would both be coded "*A*," though they differ in the specification of additional contextual qualifiers.

Pure emotive-evaluative terms ("*TE*") such as "he is a good man" were not considered traits ("*T*") in our final analysis. One reason for drawing the distinction was the reference to (moral) "character" (*cɔritrɔ*) in the Oriya instructions. This tended to elicit a ritualized initial response from most informants. They would first say "he is a good man" or "he is not a good man" and then go on with their description. "*TE*" phrases in both the American and Oriya descriptions were dropped from the analysis discussed below. The total number of descriptive phrases actually analyzed numbered 3,209 (1,524 Oriya, 1,685 American).

Contextual qualifications were coded under the following categories:

Personal Reference: (a) reference to a specific individual, often denoted by a proper or common noun (e.g., "he gets angry with his father"), coded "*P1*", (b) reference to a specific group of others (e.g., "he makes fun of his family") coded "*P2*", (c) reference to people or others in general (e.g., "he is honest with others") coded "*P3*", (d) reference to the person described himself (e.g., he gets angry with himself") coded "*SR*", (e) reference to the rater (e.g., "he gets angry with me") coded "*RR*".

Qualification: (a) temporal: statement of when or how frequently the attribute occurs (e.g., "last year he did favors frequently") coded "time", (b) locale: statement of where or in what location the attribute occurs (e.g., "At school she puts on a front") coded "place", (c) general qualification: any statement of the conditions under which an attribute occurs or obtains (e.g., "He gets irritable if provoked") coded "qual", (d) inferential qualification: statement of the conditions under which the *rater* makes the attribution (e.g., "judging from what others say, he is reserved") coded "inf", (e) any phrase which states an action, trait, etc. *without* qualification is coded "No qualification" (Noqual).

A coding category called *Miscellaneous Types* allowed us to make more refined judgments about the presence or absence of references to traits or actions:

Miscellaneous Types: (a) a reference to what the ratee *likes* (*L* or *LA*), (b) *wants, seeks,* or *desires* (*D* or *DA*), (c) *experiences* (*E* or *EA*), (d) *feels* (*F* or *FA*), (e) is *interested* in (*I* or *IA*), (f) is *capable* of or *able* to do (*C* or *CA*), (g) *values* (*V* or *VA*), (h) a reference to what *type* of person the ratee is (e.g., "he's a joker, a friend," etc.) (*R*), (i) a reference to the *social role* the ratee fills (e.g., "he's a leader," "he's a teacher," etc.) (*R* social), or (j) a reference to the *physical characteristics* of the ratee (Phys).

The coding system provided explicit criteria, with positive examples, for the identification of all the preceding categories. Phrases which were refractory to any of the categories were coded "questionable" (?). Two illustrations of a descriptive "phrase" and its coding according to the above system follow:

(a) "He jokes with his friends" (Coding: *A*, *P2*).
(b) "She is stubborn" (Coding: *T*, Noqual).

Several composite categories consisting of combinations of those listed above were also defined. These categories can be arranged along two dimensions of abstractness – concreteness, which, following Levy (1973), we shall label "Cases" and "Contexts". They are defined as follows:

> *Cases:* The contrast between trait-type references ("*T*" or "*R*" or "*R*Social") (e.g., "he is a leader"), on the one hand, and action references ("*A*" or "*LA*" or "*DA*") (e.g., "he lends people money"), on the other hand.

> *Contexts:* The contrast between context-free references ("Noqual") (e.g., "he is verbally abusive"), on the one hand, and context-dependent references ("P_1" or "P_2" or "P_3" or "time" or "place") (e.g., "he is verbally abusive to his father-in-law whenever they meet at his home"), on the other hand.

4. *Reliability and the determination of consensual codings.* Four judges, all graduate students, were trained to use the coding system. At least two judges independently coded all 3,451 phrases comprising the basic data. In a majority of cases three or all four of the judges coded the phrase.

Judges were originally asked to provide their first, second, third, etc. alternative codings of a phrase in cases where there was some ambiguity about the correct coding. Only the first coding of each judge was used in our study. If anything, this reduced intercoder agreement (reliability) from what it would have been if the "closest" codings of a phrase among all of the two, three, or four judges' several alternatives had been used.

For the final data analysis it was necessary to arrive at a single, common coding for each phrase. Two alternative procedures suggested themselves at this point: (1) judges might have discussed the discrepancies among their independent codings for each phrase and achieved a consensus or (2) a mechanical procedure could be used to derive a "consensual coding" from among the two to four alternatives for each phrase. The latter procedure was chosen for two reasons. First, time considerations advised against the laborious process of having judges reconcile their differences for each of the 3,451 phrases. Secondly, a

mechanical procedure ensured that exactly the same impartial procedure would be applied to each set of alternative codings for a phrase.
Otherwise, consensual codings would have been based upon the subjective decisions of different combinations of judges.

A computer program was devised to consider the alternative codings
for a particular phrase and include in the final, consensual coding any
category (i.e., trait, action, personal reference, etc.) which occurred
in 2 out of 2 independent codings, 2 out of 3, 3 out of 3, 3 out of 4, 4
out of 4 (thus, e.g., excluding cases where the category occurred in
only 2 out of 4 codings). To illustrate, suppose four judges' codings of
a particular item were as follows: (1) T, $P3$, time, qual; (2) T, $P1$, qual;
(3) R, $P3$, qual; and (4) T, qual. The consensual coding here, on the
basis of the above criterion, would be "T, qual".

Out of a total of 3,451 phrases, this procedure achieved a consensual
coding for 3,290 phrases or 95% of the corpus. This in itself suggests
a relatively high level of interjudge agreement. Interjudge reliability
was operationalized more precisely, however, by determining the percentage out of the total number of instances of all categories among
the alternative codings of a phrase which were represented in the consensual coding. To illustrate, in the above example the two categories
comprising the consensual coding – "T" and "qual" – occur seven
times among the various alternative codings. Since the total number
of instances of all categories among the alternatives is 12, it follows
that 7/12, or approximately 58%, of the alternative codings are represented in the consensual coding. In brief, this particular reliability
index estimated the proportion of variance among the alternative codings which was "common" or consensual.

Averaging over the interjudge reliability estimates for the total of
3,290 phrases for which consensual codings were obtained, the mean
estimate was found to be 77%. This level of agreement seems both
satisfactory and surprising, given the difficulty the judges reported in
applying the coding system.

5. *Data analysis.* With the consensual codings of phrases available,
it was possible to compare the frequency and proportion of occurrence
of any category between the two cultures or among caste, literacy, or
educational groups within India. This constituted the first step of the
data analysis.

Chi-square tests were performed to test the significance of the difference in frequencies observed for each comparison from the expected
frequency. The major results are reported in the following section.

The second step of the data analysis examined the relationship between the two composite categories representing the "cases" and
"contexts" dimensions of abstraction discussed above. Each dimension was dichotomized. The "cases" dimension was scored 1 or 0
depending upon whether a particular phrase contained a trait, type, or
social role attribution (T, R, Rsocial) or any of the action attributions

included under the composite category (*A, LA, DA*) (see the section on the coding system above). The "contexts" dimension was scored 1 if the phrase contained any instance of the category P_1, P_2, P_3, time, place, and 0 if it contained no qualification (i.e., was coded NoQual).

RESULTS

1. *Contexts*. Oriyas are more likely to say "she brings cakes to my family on festival days". Americans are more likely to say "she is friendly". Contextual qualifications having to do with personal reference ("P_1", "P_2", "P_3"), "time" and "place" each occur significantly more often in Oriya descriptions of personality ($p = <.001$ for all five variables). American descriptions are noteworthy for the frequency of descriptions that are entirely unqualified by context ("Noqual") ($p = <.001$). There are two exceptions. Americans use more self-referential qualifiers ("SR") (e.g., "she is beginning to accept herself"; "he is hard on himself") than Oriyas ($p = <.001$). Americans also use more inferential qualifiers ("inf") (e.g., "judging from what others say, he is very reserved") ($p = <.001$). Earlier we discussed a composite variable entitled "Contexts" (P_1, P_2, P_3, time, place, vs. Noqual). The ratio of context-free to context-dependent phrases is 3 to 1 in the American descriptions and 1 to 1 in the Oriya descriptions.

2. *Cases*. Oriyas tell you what someone has done, e.g., he shouts curses at his neighbors. The emphasis is upon behavioral occurrences or "cases". Americans tell you what is true of what someone has done, e.g., he is aggressive and hostile. Americans describe personality by means of trait ("T") (e.g., "friendly") and type ("R") (e.g., "a friend") concepts ($p = <.001$). Oriyas describe personality by reference to actions ("A", "LA", "DA") ($p = <.01$ for all three variables). The only time Americans are more likely than Oriyas to mention what someone does is when they describe a person's capabilities ("CA"; $p = <.05$) or interests ("LA"; $p = <.01$).

Earlier we discussed a composite variable entitled "Cases" (*A, LA, DA*, vs. *T, R, R*Social). The ratio of abstractions to actions is 3 to 1 in the American descriptions but only 1 to 1.8 in the Oriya descriptions.

3. *Contexts and cases*. Case reference and context reference are not entirely independent descriptive acts, although their associational relationship, while statistically significant ($p = <.001$), is only weak to modest (Phi $= .30$ for the Oriyas and .18 for the Americans). The relationship can be summarized as follows: There is a greater tendency to contextualize descriptions that make reference to a behavioral case. One is more likely to contextualize "he curses" [his mother-in-law] than "he is aggressive" [to his mother-in-law]. "He is aggressive" is more likely to stand alone. We emphasize again that the positive association between cases and contexts is weak to modest.

DISCUSSION

Oriyas are more concrete than Americans in their descriptions of personality. 80% of Oriya descriptions are either contextually qualified (P_1, P_2, P_3, time, place) or make reference to a behavioral instance (A, LA, DA) (in contrast to 56% for the Americans). 46% of American descriptions are *both* context-free (Noqual) and abstract (T, R, RSocial) (in contrast to 20% for the Oriyas). This result compares favorably with the findings of Fiske and Cox (n.d.). When American informants were asked to describe someone "so that someone else would know what it's like to be around this person," 40% of the items were abstract traits. Trait attributions were twice as frequent as references to behavioral patterns.

How is this cross-cultural difference in the thinking of Americans and Oriyas to be explained? We believe that each of the following plausible evolutionary hypotheses is *not* supported by the evidence.

1. *Hypothesis 1:* The Oriyas have less formal schooling than the Americans. Therefore, they are more concrete.

Formal schooling is often viewed by evolutionary theorists as a condition for the development of skills of abstraction (e.g., Bruner et al. 1966; Luria 1976). Considered as an aggregate, the Oriyas are less educated than the Americans. 24% of the Oriya descriptive phrases came from informants who had never been to school. 65% came from informants with less than three years of schooling. Nevertheless, the relative concreteness of the Oriya personality descriptions is not related to this difference in education. Table 6.1 shows that the descriptive phrases elicited from Oriyas with an educational level comparable to the Americans (beyond high school) are more concrete than the American descriptive phrases. In the Oriyan sample, concreteness does not significantly vary across educational levels for either "cases" (p = n.s.) or "contexts" (p = n.s.). Concrete thinking in the personality domain transcends variations in formal schooling experience. See Table 6.2.

2. *Hypothesis 2:* The literacy level of the Oriyas is less than the Americans'. Therefore, they are more concrete.

Literacy is often cited by evolutionary theorists as a condition for the development of skills of abstraction (e.g., Greenfield 1972; Luria 1976; Goody 1977). The overall literacy level of the Oriyas is certainly less than the Americans. 25% of the Oriya descriptive phrases were elicited from entirely illiterate informant. Nevertheless, this relative difference in literacy levels does not explain the relative concreteness of Oriya descriptions of personality. Literate and illiterate Oriyas do not significantly differ in the relative concreteness of their personality descriptions for either "cases" (p = n.s.) or "contexts" (p = n.s.). Concrete thinking in the personality domain transcends variations in literacy in Orissa. Moreover, if the illiterate Oriya informants are eliminated from the sample, the difference in concrete thinking between Americans and literate Oriyas continues to be significant. See Table 6.1

3. *Hypothesis 3:* The Oriyas are of lower socio-economic status than the Americans. Therefore, they are more concrete.

Social and economic impoverishment is sometimes cited by evolutionary theorists as a condition retarding the development of skills of abstraction (e.g., Luria 1976). Considered as an aggregate, the Oriya sample is probably of lower socio-economic status than the American. We say "probably" because the notion of relative socio-economic status is difficult to apply in a comparison of India and the United States. A high status Brahman can be relatively impoverished without serious threat to his/her caste position. Wealthy and powerful informants can come from middle-level or even relatively low-status castes. However, since 16% of the descriptive phrases came from Bauris, an untouchable or so-called "scheduled" caste, and since these informants were uniformly impoverished, it seems safe to conclude that by most standards the Oriyas, as an aggregate, are not as high status as the Americans.

Socio-economic status, an elusive cross-cultural yardstick, does not seem to explain the relative difference in concrete thinking in the personality domain between the two cultures. Within Orissa, concrete thinking does not vary by caste status for either "cases" (p = n.s.) or "contexts" (p = n.s.). A comparison of Brahman informants to American informants continues to reveal a cultural difference in concrete thinking. Brahman informants differ little from the overall Oriyan sample (see Table 6.1). In fact, the truly remarkable feature of Tables 6.1 and 6.2 is the stability of the evidence of concrete thinking across all the Oriyan sub-samples. In Orissa the concrete style of personality description transcends variations in education, literacy, and caste.

4. *Hypothesis 4:* Concrete-abstract thinking is a global cognitive process variable that distinguishes Oriyas from Americans. Oriyas lack the skill to abstract or generalize across cases.

5. *Hypothesis 5:* The Oriya language lacks general terms with which to refer to individual differences in behavior. Therefore Oriyas are deficient in linguistic resources for generating abstract descriptions of personality.

An investigation carried out by Shweder (1972: see Chapters 2 and 4 for a detailed discussion) makes it apparent that hypotheses 4 and 5 are not very helpful. The study concerned the influence of pre-existing conceptual schemes and taxonomic structures on judgment. A sub-set of the descriptive phrases elicited from our Oriya informants played a part in the study. The study revealed the ability of our Oriya informants to generate and intellectually manipulate abstract behavioral descriptions, and to recognize and utilize conceptual likenesses among them.

Table 6.1. *Comparison of the relative emphasis on contexts and cases in the descriptive phrases of all Americans, all Oriyas, and various sub-groups of Oriyas*

	All Americans	Oriyas						
		All Oriyas	Beyond high school	No school	Literate	Illiterate	Brahmans	Bauris
Context-dependent (P_1, P_2, P_3, time, place)	28.3%	49.6%	48.3%	51.8%	48.4%	53.2%	50.6%	50.4%
Context-free (Noqual)	71.7%	50.4%	51.7%	48.2%	51.4%	46.8%	49.4%	49.6%
$n =$	1685	1505	215	357	1135	370	494	244
Actions (A, DA, LA)	25.4%	64.8%	58.8%	66.7%	64.6%	65.5%	66.1%	70.1%
Abstractions (T, R, RSocial)	74.6%	35.2%	41.2%	33.3%	35.4%	34.5%	33.9%	29.9%
$n =$	1333	1194	117	282	901	293	392	201

Table 6.2. *Comparison of the relative emphasis on contexts and cases across educational levels within the Oriya sample*

			Formal schooling			
		None	1–3 years	4–7 years	8–11 years	Beyond high school
Contexts						
Context-dependent (P_1, P_2, P_3, time, place)		51.8%	50.0%	48.2%	49.6%	48.4%
Context-free (Noqual)		48.2%	50.0%	51.8%	50.4%	51.6%
	$n =$	357	328	455	125	215
Cases						
Actions (*A, LA, DA*)		66.7%	62.5%	68.2%	64.4%	58.8%
Abstractions (*T, R, R*Social)		33.3%	37.5%	31.8%	35.6%	41.2%
	$n =$	282	259	349	104	177

Figure 6.2. Two-dimensional scaling solution for Oriya personality terms

Ninety-nine representative descriptive phrases were written on cards and presented to 43 Brahman informants from the community whose concrete style of personality description we have been discussing. Most of these 99 phrases were concrete, i.e., they were either case-specific or contextually qualified or both. A full list appears in Shweder (1972:56–60).

Each of the 43 informants was asked to sort the descriptive phrases into piles, placing together in the same pile items that might "go together" in the same person. Each informant was then asked to name or label the piles he had created. Informants were free to make as many piles as they liked and to place as many descriptive phrases in each pile as they wished. After making an initial sorting and labeling their piles, informants were asked to collapse their piles into fewer, more general piles. They were asked to name or label these new piles. This process of collapsing their groupings of phrases and naming their new groupings went on as long as the informant was willing to produce fewer and fewer piles, with more and more descriptive phrases in each.

The crucial point for our present discussion is that the sorting task successfully generated abstract and general terms (trait and type concepts) for describing personality from every one of the 43 informants. Using 43 informants, 420 different abstract trait and type terms were generated by means of the sorting task. English translations of 81 of these terms are shown in Figure 6.2 (see Shweder 1972:65–66 for the original Oriya terms). (A casual perusal of G. C. Praharaj's seven-volume lexicon of the Oriya language, 1931–1940, should dissuade anyone who believes our Oriya informants speak a language that is lacking in abstract personality trait and type concepts.)

Oriya informants have no difficulty recognizing and arranging things in terms of overarching conceptual likenesses. This was most clearly revealed by a second sorting task study. 81 personality trait and type concepts (see Figure 6.2) were selected to represent the 420 terms that had been generated in the first sorting task. They were written on cards and presented to 25 Brahman informants from the community whose concrete style of person description we have been discussing. Except for one additional feature, the sorting task was identical to the one previously discussed. Informants were asked to place items together that "went together" in people. They were asked to label (or describe) the piles. They were *also* asked to indicate which items in each pile were exemplary instances of the concept suggested by the pile. After an initial sorting they were asked to construct abstract hierarchies or taxonomies by collapsing the initial piles into a small number of general categories. Again they were asked to label (or describe) the categories, etc. The hierarchies of all 25 informants can be found in Shweder (1972:Appendix 1).

A measure of association between all possible pairs of 81 terms was calculated on the basis of the sorting task data. The particular measure has been described by Burton (1968:81–84). It is a normal variate score which is sensitive to three indices of "proximity" between a pair of terms. The primary index of "proximity" is the number of times two terms are placed together in the same pile over a sample of informants. This simple frequency count is adjusted to the number of terms in the pile in question (the larger the pile, the less proximate the two terms) and the total number of piles made by the particular informant (the fewer the piles, the less proximate the two terms). The final measure of association is a Z score. It was calculated using each level in the hierarchy of each informant as if it were the sorting task of a different informant. The measure was thus based on 73 partitionings of the 81 terms into piles. Subsequent analysis revealed that a simple frequency count of the number of times two items appear together in a pile over each of the hierarchical levels of each of the informants correlates .98 (Pearson r) with the Z score used in our analysis.

The matrix of association among all possible pairs of 81 terms generated from the second sorting task was scaled in two-dimensional space using the multidimensional scaling program (MDSCALE) devised by Donald C. Olivier. A two-dimensional spatial representation of the associational relationships among the 81 terms is shown in Figure 6.2.

The most relevant feature of the scaling solution for our present discussion is that it demonstrates that our Oriya informants have consistently classified the terms on the basis of two independent underlying conceptual likenesses that they have abstracted from the 81 terms. The vertical axis in Figure 6.2 is interpretable as a "dominance vs. submission" (or "power") dimension. The horizontal axis is interpretable as a "social desirability" dimension. In its abstractness, generality, and dimensional content the Oriya scaling solution in Figure 6.2 is comparable to the conceptual organization of the personality domain discovered in America (see, e.g., Leary and Coffey 1955; Lorr and McNair 1963, 1965; also see White 1980 on the possible universality of the scaling solution in Figure 6.2). Figure 6.2 suggests that the concreteness displayed by our Oriya informants when they freely describe personality or answer a request for information about someone's character, personality (nature), and behavior is *not* an indication of a deficit in the cognitive skills of abstraction and generalization. Hypothesis 4 and Hypothesis 5 must be rejected.

6. *Hypothesis 6:* Oriyas live in a "closed" intellectual environment in which they never have to confront alternative customs, behavioral styles, or viewpoints. However, abstract thinking (the search for likenesses between diverse phenomena) presupposes that one has access to information about variant phenomenon and different perspectives. Oriyas, lacking such information, are disinclined to abstract or generalize across cases.

Hypothesis 6 can be construed at a global level or at a level that is specific to the way Oriyas freely describe personality. At a global level it might be argued that Oriyas are so culturally insulated that they ought to display concrete thinking in all domains. We have already discussed the evidence that has led us to reject the notion that Oriyas lack the ability to abstract (see Hypothesis 4). There are also a number of features of life in the old town of Bhubaneswar and India in general that make it difficult to even seriously entertain the hypothesis that Oriyas live in a "closed" informational environment.

There are 24 Oriya castes (including five major Brahman sub-castes) represented in the residential wards and quarters of the old town of Bhubaneswar. There is considerable consensus concerning the relative status position of these castes, a judgment that takes into account the relative "purity" of the customs and behavior of a caste community. The concept of a caste hierarchy itself pre-supposes (a) an awareness of the diverse life styles of interdependent communities (e.g., do they eat meat, do they let their widows remarry, do they cut their own hair, wash their own clothes, etc.); (b) the ability to evaluate and rank caste communities in terms of the common yardstick of "purity" (see, e.g., Dumont 1970). India is a land where diversity has always been accommodated by means of the sophisticated device of explicit hierarchical interdependence. Oriyas, evolutionists to the core, encourage diversity and rank it.

Caste disputes over relative status are a frequent occurrence in Orissa. Whenever they occur, one has the opportunity to observe social cognition in action over matters of importance to the participants. What one sees is a keen sensitivity to behavioral variations and to the way those behavioral variations will be judged from a third person perspective, e.g., in the eyes of a particular outside community or in the eyes of the general community.

A characteristic pattern of Oriyan social thought surfaces in disputes over the relative status of caste communities. Consider a typical instance. Three untouchable castes are involved in a dispute over the relative status of the two lowest. The issue at stake is simply, "who is the lowest of the low?" In order of relative "purity" the cast of castes includes community A (they are washerman), community B (they are agricultural laborers), and community C (they are scavengers, basketmakers, and drummers). A's wash other people's dirty linen. The "unclean" nature of this work guarantees their untouchable status. Nevertheless, A's are unquestionably higher in rank than either of the other two communities; their relative superiority is asserted and in part constituted by their refusal to wash B or C clothing. B's and C's are too impure even for the A's. The A's are the highest of the untouchable castes. Their superiority was never assailed in the dispute that arose between the B's and C's. In fact, the competitive status claims of the B's and C's could only be resolved because both communities accepted unquestionably the A's perspective on matters of "purity". At the time the dispute surfaced, the C's were generally thought to be the most "polluted" of all the castes. Their caste position was asserted and in part constituted by their traditional activity of cleaning the latrines (and thus handling excrement) in the wards of other castes. But then events got underway.

(a) The status ploy by the C's. They refuse to clean the latrines in the B ward, thus, symbolically asserting their superiority. The move is effective. The B's have a serious dilemma. Either the B's must let their ward latrines accumulate excrement, etc., thereby polluting their neighborhoods, associating themselves with filth, confirming their untouchable status, and aggravating an already unpleasant living condition, or else they must clean their own latrines, thereby sacrificing the one taboo or restraint they have to their credit that distinguishes them from the C's in the eyes of outside communities. What to do?

(b) B–A status negotiations. B representatives approach representatives of the A community. They seek a trump card to use against the C's. In fact, they seek no less than to convince the A's to wash their clothes. "Impossible", assert the A's. "Your linen would pollute us and disgrace our community." The B's persist. They remind the A's that without the B's, A weddings could not take place. B's blow the conch shell at A weddings; they threaten to withdraw. The ploy is effective. Either the A's must cease marrying their children (that's no option) or else they must blow the conch shell themselves or find someone else to do it (Would it really be a wedding?).

(c) B–A compromise. A compromise is struck. The A's will wash B clothing. Not all B clothing. Not even most B clothing. They will

wash the ritual clothing that B performers wear in one particular religious ceremony on one particular day. It is reasoned that ritual cloth
is not polluted even if worn by a B. The B's are pleased. At least the
A's wash their clothing on some occasion. They never wash the C's
clothes (as the C's are soon to be informed, and redundantly reminded).
The A's are pleased. They can continue marrying their daughters at
no cost to their community's status. And the C's? They go back to
cleaning the latrines in the B ward. The absence of diversity and the
nonrecognition of alternative perspectives is just not an Indian problem.

However, hypothesis 6 might be construed narrowly. It might be
argued that Americans are more likely to experience their intimates in
diverse behavioral settings, and thus are more likely to abstract out a
common feature of their behavior for personality diagnosis. We can
only suggest that the situation with our Oriya and American informants
may be the reverse of that supposed by hypothesis 6. Ethnographic
observation suggests that our Oriya informants experience their intimates in a relatively small and standard set of contexts, e.g., at work,
in family affairs, in ritual contexts, at public meetings, etc. They also
have much second-hand knowledge via gossip and rumor. However,
the number of settings in which teachers in a nursery school, college
students in a fraternity and psychologists in a counseling center experience one another may be even less. Hypothesis 6 does not seem
relevant to the cultural differences we have discovered in the concrete
vs. abstract way Oriyas vs. Americans describe individual differences.

We seem to be left in an explanatory void. In their free descriptions
of personality Oriyas are more concrete than Americans. They describe
their intimates by reference to behavioral instances (cases) and they
qualify their descriptions by reference to contexts. These differences
hold up even when one is comparing Americans to literate Oriyas,
educated Oriyas, and high caste Oriyas. Within the Oriya community,
the concrete style of describing individual differences is stable across
castes and across educational and literacy levels. The difference cannot
be explained in terms of the "intellectual predicament" of the Oriyas.
They are aware of alternative behavioral styles. It is not a reflection
of a deficiency in skills of abstraction. In sorting tasks, Oriyas display
a facile ability to think abstractly. The difference has little to do with
education, literacy, socio-economic status or language. It seems to be
a cultural phenomenon, and it is perhaps as a cultural phenomenon
that we should try to understand it.

A relativist theory of the context-dependent self: holism and its cognitive consequences

As we have seen, Oriyas are less prone than Americans to describe
people they know in abstract, context-free terms. Instead of saying so-
and-so is "principled" they tend to say "he does not disclose secrets".

Instead of saying so-and-so is "selfish" they tend to say "he is hesitant to give away money to his family". While this difference in person perception is only a "tendency" (e.g., 46% abstract, context-free descriptions from Americans, 20% from Oriyas), it is a pervasive tendency, stable across Oriya sub-samples, a tendency significant enough to reject a universalist interpretation of context-dependent thinking.

Our results also lend little support to an evolutionary interpretation. As noted earlier, Oriya informants do not lack skills of generalization and abstraction. They are aware that the behavior of someone who "does not become partial while imparting justice" and "does not disclose secrets" can be described as "principled" (*nitibadi*); they recognize that there are likenesses that link together such very different behavioral occurrences as imparting justice and keeping secrets. If asked to select from a corpus of concrete behaviors those that generally "go together" in people, Oriyas, like Americans, will utilize conceptual likenesses to assist them in the task ("all those are principled behaviors"; see hypothesis 5 above; also Shweder 1972, 1975, 1977a, 1977b, 1980a, 1980b; D'Andrade 1965, 1973, 1974; Shweder & D'Andrade 1979, 1980). Similarly, our results suggest that the concrete mode of person perception of our Oriya informants cannot be explained by reference to deficient information, motivation, or linguistic resources (see hypotheses 1–6 above). Why then are Oriyas more prone that Americans to describe their intimates by reference to "cases and contexts".

HOW TO CONSTRUCT A RELATIVIST INTERPRETATION OF CONCRETE THINKING

Relativists acknowledge that concrete, contextualized, occasion-bound thinking is unequally distributed across human cultures. However, it is the position of the relativist that the prevalence of context-dependent thinking in some cultures tells us little about underlying deficits in cognitive processing skills, intellectual motivation, available information, or linguistic tools. The trick for the relativist is to acknowledge diversity while shunning the evolutionary notion of "cultural deficits". How can this be done?

1. *Distinguish ideational products from intellectual processes.* Why are Oriyas more prone that Americans to describe their intimates by reference to "cases and contexts"? Relativists answer this question by drawing a sharp distinction between intellectual *process* and ideational *product*. The relativist hypothesizes that cultures differ less in their *basic* cognitive skills (e.g., generalization, abstraction, reversibility) than in the metaphors by which they live (Lakoff & Johnson 1980), the world hypotheses (Pepper 1972) to which they subscribe, and the ideas underlying their social action. Thus, according to a relativist account, the Oriyas, Balinese, and Gahuku-Gama are perfectly competent information processors, not unskilled at differentiating, generalizing, and taking the perspective of others, etc. What really distin-

guishes them from us is that they place so little *value* on differentiating (e.g., person from role), generalizing (e.g., "treat outsiders like insiders"), or abstracting (e.g., the concept of "humanity"); and, the relativist is quick to point out, they show so little interest in such intellectual moves because Oriyas, Balinese, and other such folk live by a metaphor and subscribe to a world-premise that directs their attention and passions to particular systems, relationally conceived and contextually appraised, Indeed, a central tenet of a relativist interpretation of context-dependent person perception is that *the metaphors by which people live and the world views to which they subscribe mediate the relationship between what one thinks about and how one thinks.*

2. *Holism: A mediating world premise.* Holism is a mode of thought elaborating the implications of the "part-whole" relationship: viz., (a) what's true of, or right for, the whole is not necessarily true of, or right for, any or all of the parts of the whole [e.g., "an arm can throw a football", and "an elbow is part of the arm" does not imply that "an elbow can throw a football"]; (b) diverse parts of the whole are not necessarily alike in any crucial respects [e.g., while different "kinds of" canines, say terriers and spaniels, are alike in some characteristic ways, different "parts of" a body, say finger nails and red blood cells, or different "parts of" an automobile, say the axle and the fan belt, need not commune in any way whatsoever]; (c) each part is defined by the particular relationships into which it enters within the specific whole of which it is a part [e.g., try defining a "tongue" or "brake" without functional, relational, or contextual references]. For a holist, "unit" parts are necessarily altered by the relations into which they enter (Phillips 1976).

From a holistic perspective unit-parts (e.g., an elbow) change their essential properties when isolated from the unit-wholes (e.g., an arm) of which they are a part. Thus, the holist concludes, it is not possible to understand or appraise an entity in isolation, in the abstract. The holist is prone to seek contextual clarification before making a judgment; the holist is disinclined to examine or judge things in vacuo.

3. *The body: "A metaphor people live by".* All societies are confronted by the same small set of existential questions, and some societies even try to answer them. A minimal set includes: (a) the problem of "haves" vs. "have-nots". It is a fact of life that the things all people want are unequally distributed within any society. Have-nots must be told in convincing terms why they have not. "Haves" must have confidence that their privileges are justifiable and legitimate; (b) the problem of *our* way of life vs. *their* way of life. Diversity of custom, value, belief, and practice is also a fact of life. Why should I live this way and not some other way? "There but for fortune goes you or goes I" is not a satisfying answer; (c) the problem of the relationship of nature to culture. Are we merely "naked apes", or better yet "rational feath-

erless bipeds'', or still yet better ''the children of god''; (d) the problem of the relationship of the individual to the group, to society, to the collectivity. There seem to be relatively few ''solutions'' to this last problem; the ''sociocentric'' solution subordinates individual interests to the good of the collectivity while in the ''egocentric'' solution society becomes the servant of the individual, i.e., society is imagined to have been created to serve the interests of some idealized autonomous, abstract individual existing free of society yet living in society.

Holistic cultures seem to embrace a sociocentric conception of the relationship of individual to society, a sociocentric conception with an organic twist. Some Indologists (see Dumont 1960, 1970:184–186; Marriott 1976), for example, have noted that the concept of an autonomous, bounded, abstract individual existing free of society yet living in society is uncharacteristic of Indian social thought. ''Man-in-society'', for Indians, is not an ''autonomous, indivisible, bounded unit'' (see Marriott 1976). Like most peoples, Indians do have a concept of ''man-in-society'' but ''man-in-society'' is not an autonomous individual. He is regulated by strict rules of interpendence that are context-specific and particularistic, rules governing exchanges of services, rules governing behavior to kinsmen, rules governing marriage, etc. (See our earlier discussion of negotiations over caste status; hypothesis 6 above.)

The idea that man-in-society is not an autonomous individual is not unique to India. Selby's (1974, 1975) discussion of Zapotec culture in Oaxaca, Mexico makes this apparent. Selby (1974:62–66, 1975) argues that the ''folk explanatory model that puts responsibility for morality and cure on the individual'' is ''deeply rooted in Western thought''. It is ''as old as Thucydides, who wrote 2,400 years ago and was rediscovered and glorified in the Renaissance and Reformation''. [Indeed, in the West, the fact that good works (e.g., scientific discoveries) are often the products of base motives (e.g., envy) is treated as a disturbing anathema, a glaring insult to our faith in the individual as the ultimate measure of all things.] It is otherwise among the Zapotecs. Selby explicates the Zapotec expression ''we see the face, but do not know what is in the heart'' as follows: It is

> not an expression of despair. They [Zapotecs] do not have to know what is in the heart, because it isn't defined as being very interesting and it shouldn't have anything to do with human relations.

With regard to perceptions of deviant behavior, Selby notes

> [Zapotecs] do not, therefore, have to overcome their own prejudices about the *character* of people who go wrong. They know their own society and how it works, and they are aware of the sociological nature of deviance. They have no need to peer into people's hearts and minds . . . [my emphasis].

Selby presents case material indicating that even blatantly deviant acts (e.g., murder) do not elicit characterological attributions.

Oriyan culture is not Zapotec. Indians do peer into one another's hearts and minds; Indians, unlike the Zapotecs, do have a concept of "autonomous individualism". But, and this is the main point, for an Indian to be an autonomous individual one must leave society. The autonomous individual is the holy man, the renouncer, the sadhu, the "drop out" (Dumont 1960, 1970). Yet even here the goal is not to find one's distinctive identity but rather to merge one's soul with the soul of others. When Indians peer into one another's hearts and minds they are more likely than most peoples to look for the ultimate universal, the ground of all things, God.

What makes Western culture special, then, is the concept "autonomous distinctive individual living-in-society". What makes Indian culture special is the concept "autonomous non-distinctive individual living-outside-society". When it comes to "man-in-society," Indian views are not unique (indeed, their views are prototypical and lucid expressions of a widespread mode of social thought), but they do diverge considerably from the "natural man" tradition of Western social thought. In America, men-in-society conceive of themselves free of the relationships of hierarchy and exchange that govern all social ties and are so central to theories of the self in Orissa.

The sociocentric conception of the individual-social relationship lends itself to an organic metaphor. Indeed in holistic sociocentric cultures like India the human body, conceived as an interdependent system, is frequently taken as a metaphor for society (and society, conceived as an organic whole, is sometimes taken as a metaphor for nature).

The human body is a pregnant metaphor. It has its ruler (the brain), its servants (the limbs), etc. Political affairs, interpersonal dyads, family organization are all easily conceived after a model of differentiated parts arranged in a hierarchy of functions in the service of the whole.

What we think follows from a holistic world view and sociocentric organic solution to the problem of the individual-social relationship are some of the features of the context-dependent, occasion-bound concept of the person: (a) no attempt to distinguish the individual from the status s(he) occupies; (b) the view that obligations and rights are differentially apportioned by role, group etc.; (c) a disinclination to ascribe intrinsic moral worth to persons merely because they are persons. [To ask of a holist: "Is killing wrong?" is like asking a morphologist or physiologist to assess the value of a body part or organ without knowledge of, or reference to, its function in the interdependent organic structure of this or that particular species.] Indeed, with their explicit cultural recognition and even deification of obligatory, particularistic interdependence, Oriyas would seem to be culturally primed to see context and social relationships as a necessary condition for behavior.

By contrast, in the West, as Dumont (1970) notes, each person is conceived of as "a particular incarnation of abstract humanity", a monadic replica of general humanity. A kind of sacred personalized self is developed and the individual qua individual is seen as inviolate, a supreme value in and of itself. The "self" becomes an object of interest *per se*. Free to undertake projects of personal expression, personal narratives, autobiographies, diaries, mirrors, separate rooms, early separation from bed, body, and breast of mother, personal space – the autonomous individual imagines the incredible, that he lives within an inviolate protected region (the extended boundaries of the self) where he is "free to choose" (see Friedman & Friedman 1980 for the purest articulation of this incredible belief), where what he does "is his own business".

More than that, the inviolate self views social relationships as a derivative matter, arising out of consent and contract between autonomous individuals. Society is viewed as mere "association" (see Dumont 1970). It, thus, hardly seems surprising that despite much evidence to the contrary (Hartshorne & May 1928; Newcomb 1929; Mischel 1968; D'Andrade 1974; Shweder 1975, 1979a; Nisbett 1980), our culture continues to promote the fiction that within the person one can find a stable core "character". Nor is it surprising that this abstract individual, "man-as-voluntary-agent", is protected by deeply enshrined moral and legal principles prescribing privacy and proscribing unwanted invasions of person, property, and other extensions of the self. Americans are culturally primed to search for abstract summaries of the autonomous individual behind the social role and social appearance.

4. *From concrete thinking in particular to concrete thinking in general.* We have argued that concrete, "cases and contexts" person perception is an expression of a holistic world premise and sociocentric organic conception of the relationship of the individual to society. But, what of concrete thinking in other domains? For example, what about the evidence on "functional complexes", i.e., the tendency for informants in some cultures to respond to requests about how things are alike by linking the things together in an action sequence or activity structure? Consider one of Luria's (1976:56) informants. The informant is presented with four objects (hammer-saw-log-hatchet). He is asked: "which of these things could you call by one word". He is told: ". . . one fellow picked three things – the hammer, saw, and hatchet – and said they were alike". The informant responds: "a saw, a hammer, and a hatchet all have to work together. But the log has to be there too . . . if you have to split something you need a hatchet".

To interpret this type of finding within a relativist framework one might speculate that from the point of view of a holistic thinker it makes no sense to ignore the functional interdependencies among objects and events. Indeed, Luria's illiterate, unschooled peasants repeatedly try, in vain, to explain to him that it is "stupid" to ignore the way objects and events fit together in action sequences (e.g., 1976:54, 77). One is reminded of Glick's (1968) Kpelle informant who insisted on grouping objects into functional complexes while commenting "a wiseman can do no other". Only when asked, "How would a fool group the objects" did he give the Westerner what he wanted, a linguistically-defined equivalence structure!

Is it farfetched to imagine that holism, the sociocentric conception of the individual-social relationship, and the organic metaphor have a generalized influence on cognition. Perhaps! But, one should not overlook the following fact about the cultural organization of knowledge. Although in our culture it is the "natural" sciences that have an elevated position, in many non-Western cultures (see Fortes 1959; Smith 1961; Durkheim & Mauss 1963; Horton 1968) much of the intellectual action is in the arena of *social* thought. For us it is the organization of knowledge in physics and chemistry that is adopted wholesale as the ideal for social understanding. More than a few social scientists are busy at work searching for a "periodic table" of social elements. Many more have been enamored of physical metaphors (forces, energy, mechanisms, etc.). In the West, the physical world has become the model of the social world. Why should not a reverse extension take place in other cultures, the social order as the model of nature. Metaphors, deliberately selected to guide our thinking, often have generalized effects on how we think.

PRIVACY AND THE SOCIALIZATION OF THE INVIOLATE SELF
We have sketched the outline of a relativist interpretation of both "cases and contexts" person perception, in particular, and concrete thinking in general. The concept of the context-dependent person, we have argued, is one expression of a broader sociocentric organic view of the relationship of the individual to society which in turn is an aspect of the holistic world view adopted by many cultures. The holistic model, the sociocentric premise, and the organic metaphor focus one's attention on the context-dependent relationship of part to part and part to whole; the holist, convinced that objects and events are necessarily altered by the relations into which they enter, is theoretically primed to contextualize objects and events, and theoretically disinclined to appraise things in vacuo, in the abstract.

To the question "Does the Concept of the Person Vary Cross-Culturally?" our answer is obviously "yes"; we have tried to identify two major alternative conceptualizations of the individual-social relationship, viz., the "egocentric contractual" and the "sociocentric organic". It is crucial to recognize that neither of these conceptualizations of the relationship of the individual to society has the epistemological status of a scientific category. They are not inductive generalizations. They are not the discoveries of individual perception. Quite the contrary, the egocentric and sociocentric views of man are creations of the collective imagination. They are ideas, *premises* by which people guide their lives, and only to the extent a people lives by them do they have force. How do people live by their world views?

It is instructive to reflect, for example, on the socialization of autonomy in the West.

We find it tempting to argue that Western individualism has its origins in the institution of privacy – that privacy promotes a passion or need for autonomy, which, for the sake of our sense of personal integrity, requires privacy (see Trilling 1972:24). Socialization is terroristic. The young are subject to all sorts of invasions, intrusions, and manipulations of their personhood, autonomy, and privacy. Where they go, when they sleep, what they eat, how they look, all the intimacies of the self are managed for them, typically without consent. Heteronomy is the universal starting point for socialization; it may or may not be the end point.

It is sobering to acknowledge that our sense of personal inviolatability is a violatable social gift, the product of what *others* are willing to respect and protect us from, the product of the way we are handled and reacted to, the product of the rights and privileges we are granted by others in numerous "territories of the self" (Goffman 1971) (e.g., vis-à-vis eating, grooming, hair length, clothing style, when and where we sleep, who we associate with, personal possessions, etc.). Simmel (1968:482) notes that "the right to privacy asserts the sacredness of the person". And, where are these "assertions" redundantly (even if tacitly) reiterated? Well, the assertion is there in the respect shown by a parent for a child's "security blanket". It's there as well when an adult asks of a three-year-old "What do you want to eat for dinner?" and again in the knock on the door before entering the child's personal space, his private bedroom, another replica of the assertion.

The ego's view of its-"self" is the product of the collective imagination. In the West, the messages implicit in many of our child handling *practices* may well socialize deep *intuitions* about the "indecency" of outside (external) intrusions, regulations, or invasions of our imagined inviolatable self. Practices cultivate intuitions, intuitions about what's decent, which then support such Western notions as "free to choose" (Friedman & Friedman 1980), "autonomy in decision-making", "sanctuary" and "my own business" (see the literature on privacy law, e.g., Bostwick 1976; Gerety 1977).

Of course not all cultures socialize autonomy or redundantly confirm the right of the individual to projects of personal expression, to a body, mind, and room of his own. To members of sociocentric organic cultures the concept of the autonomous individual, free to choose and mind his own business, must feel alien, a bizarre idea cutting the self off from the interdependent whole, dooming it to a life of isolation and loneliness (Kakar 1978:86). Linked to each other in an interdependent system, members of organic cultures take an active interest in one another's affairs, and feel at ease in regulating and being regulated. Indeed, others are the means to one's functioning and vice versa.

It is also sobering to reflect on the psychic costs, the existential penalties of our egocentrism, our autonomous individualism. There are costs to having no larger framework within which to locate the self. Many in our culture lack a meaningful orientation to the past. We come from nowhere, the product of a random genetic accident. Many lack a meaningful orientation to the future. We are going nowhere – at best we view ourselves as "machines" that will one day run down. The social order we view as the product of our making – an "association" based on contract and individual consent. In our view, society is dependent on us. And what are our gods? Personal success and wealth; "the tangible evidences of financial success have come to symbolize . . . the whole expectancy of ego satisfaction" (Smith 1952:398). Cut adrift from any larger whole, the self has become the measure of all things, clutching to a faith that some "invisible hand" will by sleight of hand right things in the end.

Of course what we've just said about egocentrism and autonomy in the West could easily be rewritten in terms of psychic benefits and one should not forget that sociocentrism has severe costs as well. Perhaps the real point is that the costs and benefits of egocentrism and sociocentrism are not the same (*pace* universalism), nor are the benefits mostly on one side and the costs mostly on the other (*pace* evolutionism).

Conclusion

In 1929 Edward Sapir remarked that "the worlds in which different societies live are distinct worlds, not merely the same world with different labels attached". In this essay we have tried to show that different peoples not only adopt distinct world views, but that these world views have a decisive influence on cognitive functioning.

People around the world do not all think alike. Nor are the differences in thought that do exist necessarily to be explained by reference to differences or "deficits" in cognitive processing skills, intellectual motivation, available information, or linguistic resources. It is well known in cognitive science that what one thinks about can be decisive for how one thinks (e.g., Wason & Johnson-Laird 1972). What's not yet fully appreciated is that the relationship between what one thinks about (e.g., other people) and how one thinks (e.g., "contexts and cases") may be *mediated* by the world premise to which one is committed (e.g., holism) and by the metaphors by which one lives (Lakoff & Johnson 1980).

Note

Recipient of the 1982 American Association for the Advancement of Science (AAAS) Socio-Psychological Prize. Reprinted with the permission of Reidel Publishing Co. from A. J. Marsella and G. M. White, eds., *Cultural Conceptions of Mental Health and Therapy*, pp. 97–137. Copyright © 1982 by D. Reidel Publishing Company, Dordrecht, Holland.

References

Austin, J. L. 1962. How to Do Things with Words. Oxford: Clarendon Press.

Benedict, R. 1946. The Chrysanthemum and the Sword. New York: New American Library.

Berlin, B., and P. Kay. 1969. Basic Color Terms: Their Universality and Evolution. Berkeley: University of California Press.

Bostwick, G. L. 1976. A Taxonomy of Privacy: Repose, Sanctuary, and Intimate Decision. California Law Review 64:1447–1483.

Bruner, J. S., R. R. Olver, and P. M. Greenfield. 1966. Studies in Cognitive Growth. New York: John Wiley and Sons.

Burton, M. L. 1968. Multidimensional Scaling of Role Terms. Unpublished Ph.D. dissertation. Stanford University.

Collingwood, R. G. 1972. An Essay on Metaphysics. Chicago: Henry Regnery Co.

Conklin, H. 1955. Hanunoo Color Categories. Southwestern Journal of Anthropology 11:339–344.

D'Andrade, R. G. 1965. Trait Psychology and Componential Analysis. American Anthropologist 67:215–228.

1973. Cultural Constructions of Reality. In Cultural Illness and Health. L. Nader and T. W. Maretzki (eds.). Washington: American Anthropological Association.

1974. Memory and the Assessment of Behavior. In Measurement in the Social Sciences. T. Blalock (ed.). Chicago: Aldine-Atherton.

Dumont, L. 1960. World Renunciation in Indian Religions. Contributions to Indian Sociology 4:3–62.

1970. Homo Hierarchicus. Chicago: University of Chicago Press.

Durkheim, E. and M. Mauss. 1963. Primitive Classification. Chicago: University of Chicago Press.

Evans-Pritchard, E. E. 1937. Witchcraft, Oracles and Magic Among the Azande. Oxford: Clarendon.

Feyerabend, P. 1975. Against Method. Atlantic Highlands, N.J.: Humanities Press.

Findley, J. D. 1979. Comparisons of Frogs, Humans and Chimpanzees. Science 204:434–435.

Fiske, S. T., and M. G. Cox. n.d. Describing Others: There's More to Person Perception Than Trait Lists. Unpublished manuscript, Department of Psychology and Social Relations, Harvard University.

Fortes, M. 1959. Oedipus and Job in West African Religion. Cambridge: Cambridge University Press.

Frake, C. O. 1962. The Ethnographic Study of Cognitive Systems. In Anthropology and Human Behavior. T. Gladwin and W. C. Sturtevant (eds.). Washington: Anthropological Society of Washington.

Friedman, M., and R. Friedman. 1980. Free to Choose. New York: Harcourt Brace Jovanovich.

Geertz, C. 1973. Interpretation of Cultures. New York: Basic Books.

1975. On the Nature of Anthropological Understanding. American Scientist 63:47–53. Chapter 4, this volume.

Gerety, T. 1977. Redefining Privacy. Harvard Civil Rights-Civil Liberties Law Review 12:233–296.

Glick, J. 1968. Cognitive Style Among the Kpelle. Symposium on Cross-Cultural Cognitive Studies. Unpublished manuscript, American Education Research Association, Chicago.

Goffman, E. 1971. Relations in Public. New York: Harper and Row.

Goodman, N. 1968. Languages of Art. New York: Bobbs-Merrill.

1972. Seven Strictures on Similarity. In Problems and Projects. N. Goodman (ed.). New York: Bobbs-Merrill.

Goody, J. 1977. The Domestication of the Savage Mind. New York: Cambridge University Press.

Greenfield, P. M. 1972. Oral or Written Language: The Consequences for Cognitive Development in Africa, the United States, and England. Language and Speech 15:169–178.

Hart, H. L. A. 1961. The Concept of Law. London: Oxford University Press.

Hartshorne, H., and M. A. May. 1928. Studies in the Nature of Character, Volume 1. Studies in Deceit. New York: Macmillan.

Hempel, C. G. 1965. Science and Human Values. In Aspects of Scientific Explanation. C. G. Hempel (ed.). New York: Free Press.

Horton, R. 1967. African Traditional Thought and Western Science, Part 2. Africa 37:159–187.

1968. Neo-Tylorianism: Sound Sense or Sinister Prejudice? Man 3:625–634.

Jespersen, O. 1934. Language: Its Nature, Development, and Origin. London: Allen and Unwin.

Kakar, S. 1978. The Inner World: A Psychoanalytic Study of Childhood and Society in India. Oxford: Oxford University Press.

Kohlberg, L. 1969. Stage and Sequence: The Cognitive-Developmental Approach to Socialization. In Handbook of Socialization Theory and Research. D. A. Goslin (ed.). New York: Rand McNally.

1971. From Is To Ought: How to Commit the Naturalistic Fallacy and Get Away With It in the Study of Moral Development. In Cognitive Development and Epistemology. T. Mischel (ed.). New York: Academic Press.

Kroeber, A. L. 1909. Classificatory Systems of Relationship. Journal of the Royal Anthropological Institute 39:77–84.

Kruskal, J. B., and R. Ling. 1967. How to Use the Yale Version of MDSCALE, A Multidimensional Scaling Program. Unpublished manuscript.

Lakoff, G., and M. Johnson. 1980. Metaphors We Live By. Chicago: University of Chicago Press.

Leary, T., and H. S. Coffey. 1955. Interpersonal Diagnosis: Some Problems of Methodology and Validation. Journal of Abnormal and Social Psychology 50:110–124.

LeVine, R. A. 1976. Patterns of Personality in Africa. In Responses to Change. G. A. DeVos (ed.). New York: Van Nostrand-Reinhold.

Levi-Strauss, C. 1963. Structural Anthropology. New York: Doubleday.

1966. The Savage Mind. Chicago: University of Chicago Press.

1969a. The Elementary Structures of Kinship. Boston: Beacon Press.

1969b. The Raw and the Cooked. New York: Harper and Row.

Levy, R. I. 1973. Tahitians: Mind and Experience in the Society Islands. Chicago: University of Chicago Press.

Lorr, M., and D. M. McNair. 1963. An Interpersonal Behavior Circle. Journal of Abnormal and Social Psychology 2:823–830.

1965. Expansion of the Interpersonal Behavior Circle. Journal of Personality and Social Psychology 2:823–880.

Luria, A. 1976. Cognitive Development: Its Cultural and Social Foundations. Cambridge, Mass.: Harvard University Press.

Marriott, M. 1976. Hindu Transactions: Diversity Without Dualism. *In* Transactions and Meaning. B. Kapferer (ed.) Philadelphia: Institute for the Study of Human Issues.

Mischel, W. 1968. Personality and Assessment. Stanford: Stanford University Press.

Morgan, L. H. 1871. Systems of Consanguinity and Affinity of the Human Family. Smithsonian Contributions to Knowledge. No. 218. Washington, D.C.: Smithsonian Institution.

Nerlove, S., and A. K. Romney. 1967. Sibling Terminology and Cross-Sex Behavior. American Anthropologist 69:179–187.

Newcomb, T. M. 1929. The Consistency of Certain Extrovert-Introvert Behavior Patterns in 51 Problem Boys. Contributions to Education 382. New York: Teachers College, Columbia University.

Nisbett, R. E. 1980. The Trait Concept in Lay and Professional Psychology. *In* Forty Years of Social Psychology. L. Festinger (ed.). New York: Oxford University Press.

Osgood, C. E. 1964. Semantic Differential Technique in the Comparative Study of Cultures. American Anthropologist 66:171–200.

Pareto, V. 1935. The Mind and Society. New York: Harcourt Brace.

Pepper, S. C. 1972. World Hypotheses: A Study in Evidence. Berkeley: University of California Press.

Perelman, C. 1963. Idea of Justice and the Problem of Argument. Atlantic Highlands, N.J.: Humanities Press.

Phillips, D. C. 1976. Holistic Thought in Social Science. Stanford, California: Stanford University Press.

Piaget, J. 1966. Need and Significance of Cross-Cultural Studies in Genetic Psychology. International Journal of Psychology 1:3–13.

Praharaj, G. C. 1931–1940. Purnnachandra Ordia Bhashokosha (A Lexicon of the Orya Language), Vol. 1–7. Cuttack: Utkal Sahitya Press.

Price-Williams, D. R. 1975. Explorations in Cross-Cultural Psychology. San Francisco: Chandler and Sharp.

Read, K. E. 1955. Morality and the Concept of the Person Among the Gahuku-Gama. Oceania 25:233–282.

Rorty, R. 1979. Philosophy and the Mirror of Nature. Princeton, N.J.: Princeton University Press.

Sapir, E. 1929. The Status of Linguistics as a Science. Language 5:207–214.

Searle, J. R. 1979. A Taxonomy of Illocutionary Acts. *In* Expression and Meaning. J. R. Searle (ed.). New York: Cambridge University Press.

Selby, H. A. 1974. Zapotec Deviance. Austin: University of Texas Press.

    1975. Semantics and Causality in the Study of Deviance. *In* Sociocultural Dimensions of Language Use. M. Sanches and B. G. Blount (eds.). New York: Academic Press.

Shepard, R. 1962a. The Analysis of Proximities: Multidimensional Scaling with an Unknown Distance Function I. Psychometrics 27:125–140.

    1962b. The Analysis of Proximities: Multidimensional Scaling with an Unknown Distance Function II. Psychometrics 27:219–246.

    1963. Analysis of Proximities as a Technique for the Study of Information Processing in Man. Human Factors 5:33–48.

Shweder, R. A. 1972. Semantic Structures and Personality Assessment. Unpublished Ph.D. dissertation. Cambridge: Harvard University. University Microfilms, Ann Arbor, Michigan, Order #72–79, 584.

1975. How Relevant is an Individual Difference Theory of Personality? Journal of Personality 43:455–484.

1977a. Likeness and Likelihood in Everyday Thought: Magical Thinking in Judgments About Personality. Current Anthropology 18:637–658. Reprinted in Thinking: Readings in Cognitive Science. P. N. Johnson-Laird and P. C. Wason (eds.). Cambridge: Cambridge University Press (1978).

1977b. Illusory Correlation and the MMPI Controversy. Journal of Consulting and Clinical Psychology 45:917–924.

1979a. Rethinking Culture and Personality Theory Part I: A Critical Examination of Two Classical Postulates. Ethos 7:255–278.

1979b. Rethinking Culture and Personality Theory Part II: A Critical Examination of Two More Classical Postulates. Ethos 7:279–311.

1980a. Factors and Fictions in Person Perception: A Reply To Lamiell, Foss and Cavenee. Journal of Personality 48:74–81.

1980b. Rethinking Culture and Personality Theory Part III: From Genesis and Typology to Hermeneutics and Dynamics. Ethos 8:60–94.

Shweder, R. A., and R. G. D'Andrade. 1979. Accurate Reflection or Systematic Distortion? A Reply to Block, Weiss and Thorne. Journal of Personality and Social Psychology 37:1075–1084.

1980. The Systematic Distortion Hypothesis. In Fallible Judgment in Behavioral Research: New Directions for Methodology of Social and Behavioral Science, No. 4. R. A. Shweder (ed.). San Francisco: Jossey-Bass, Inc.

Simmel, A. 1968. Privacy. International Encyclopedia of the Social Sciences 12:480–487.

Smith, H. 1961. Accents of the World's Philosophies. Publications in the Humanities No. 50. Department of Humanities, Massachusetts Institute of Technology. Cambridge, Massachusetts.

Smith, M. W. 1952. Different Cultural Concepts of Past, Present and Future. Psychiatry 15:395–400.

Super, C. M., S. Harkness, and L. M. Baldwin. 1977. Category Behavior in Natural Ecologies and in Cognitive Tests. The Quarterly Newsletter of the Institute for Comparative Human Development 1(4). Rockefeller University.

Trilling, L. 1972. Sincerity and Authenticity. Cambridge, Mass.: Harvard University Press.

Wason, P. C., and P. W. Johnson-Laird. 1972. The Psychology of Reasoning. London: Batsford.

Werner, H., and B. Kaplan. 1956. The Developmental Approach to Cognition: Its Relevance to the Psychological Interpretation of Anthropological and Ethnolinguistic Data. American Anthropologist 58:866–880.

White, G. M. 1980. Conceptual Universals in Interpersonal Language. American Anthropologist 82:759–781.

Wittgenstein, L. 1968. Philosophical Investigations. New York: Macmillan.

7
Understanding people

Zeno Vendler

What is so special about people that some of us are inclined to put them, at least in some aspects of their being, beyond the reach of unified science? Why is it that we feel that no scientific model can fully represent, and no covering law adequately explain, man in his inner life and free activity?

The aim of science is to provide a representation of reality, in terms of which its processes can be explained and predicted. The reality science is concerned with is empirical, publicly observable reality; scientific theories are supposed to fit the appearances, even if – to use Quine's happy phrase – only at the "periphery" of their network (1953:42).

Now, obviously, human beings too belong to the physical world, are observable entities, and thus are open to scientific representation as much as anything else. Yet, *we* claim, this is not the entire story: Persons (and animals to some extent) are not merely objects but also subjects of experience – of sensation, feeling, thought and action. When viewed as such, the resulting representation, though based upon the observable data of structure, situation, and behavior, is not continuous with the system of unified science and cannot be fitted into the scientific world view.

Let me illustrate, by means of a quite simple comparison, the need for such a double representation.

Suppose we see a motorcar being "tortured" by an incompetent or impatient driver. The "behavior" of the car, the bucking and shaking, the shrieks and explosions, can all be explained in terms of its structure and the mistreatment it undergoes. If one knows cars, one can imagine the movement of the parts, the strain on the rods, the friction of surfaces, and so forth. Except for further details of the same kind, the representation of the process is complete and can be brought under the laws of physics and chemistry without a remainder.

But now imagine a person being tortured. No doubt, if one knows physiology, an analogous representation explaining the behavior of the victim is forthcoming, in terms of contracting muscles, excited nerves, processes in the central nervous system, and the like. These things, again, are entirely subsumable under the laws of natural science.

In this case, however, the representation of the *person* is by no means complete. For one can imagine not only the condition of that organism and its parts under stress from the outside, as it were, that is, what they would *look* like when exposed or examined under a microscope, but one can also imagine what it must *be* like, for the subject himself, to undergo the process: his pain, agony, fear, and so on. In other words, one can represent him, in imagination, as a subject of experience. After all, it is this way of thinking of him that provokes our sympathy, pity, and moral outrage – all absent in the case of the car.

What is thus represented, however, is not something empirical, that is, publicly observable. Not even the subject can be said to "observe" his pain and other afflictions – he simply *is* in pain and *has* those afflictions. Thus science has no foothold on subjective states. The physiologist may explain how, for instance, a certain neural state causes pain behavior, because both terms of the connection are observable states. But no scientist can establish a connection between a neural state and a certain experience, simply because the second element is not something that can be found and observed in an organism. Subjective states – sensations, feelings, and emotions – cannot be found, recognized, or discovered in bodies but are attributed to them on the basis of certain observable manifestations that warrant such attribution.

How do they? Not because there is a scientifically established causal nexus between experience and behavior, but because we have learned the applicability of such predicates as *being in pain, being angry*, and so on in terms of observable marks in others and in ourselves. We realize, however, that what is meant by such an attribution cannot be just the observable state, because in that case I would have to look into the mirror to see if I am in pain. . . . These terms are self-applied without observable criteria, yet by no means at whim or caprice either. Because furthermore, I use these terms for myself and for others in the same sense, to say for instance that somebody else is in pain must mean that he is in a state in which I would be inclined to say that I am in pain. And that state I can represent by imagining being in those conditions, for example, stretched out on the rack. But what if somebody complains of a slight headache without observable manifestations? Even in this case, I can imagine what condition would prompt me to make a similar complaint.

Thus the connection between subjective states and overt manifestation is to be found in one's own experience alone: And this is not a scientific datum. Yet it enables one to represent, in imagination, the state of another mind. Without the power of the imagination we all would be solipsists.

Yet these unobservable features of inner life are invoked in the explanation of overt human action. The agent's mental state – his sensations, feelings, beliefs, and desires – provides the motives and the reasons in terms of which his intentional activities are to be understood. Without these factors one would not view him as an agent, as a person at all but merely as an automaton determined to move in certain ways.

The special position persons enjoy in our world view is enshrined in language. It is people, not machines or other contraptions of industry or nature, that we hold responsible for their deeds, that we praise or blame, that we pity, envy – and try to understand.

But what does it matter what we say? What do the "archaic relics of past superstitions" enshrined in language have to do with the nature of reality? Simply this: There is no "ready-made world," a realm of virginal noumena, immaculately perceived and untainted by the perceptual patterns and conceptual network imposed upon it by the human observer. And this conceptual network manifests itself in the way we talk, in the "logical geography" of the natural language. Of course, there is nothing sacrosanct and incorrigible about these "a priori" elements: They can and should be progressively reviewed and improved upon. But they should not be excluded or ignored *ab ovo* without the absurdity of literally not knowing what one is talking about, what the questions mean, and what the problems are. "Ordinary language is *not* the last word: In principle it can everywhere be supplemented and improved upon and superseded. Only remember it *is* the *first* word" (Austin 1961:133).

Thus there are these peculiar beings, people, *given* in the world. And, until shown otherwise, there is no reason to fit them to the Procrustean bed of "unified science" from the outset.

It makes perfect sense to say that we do, or do not, understand certain people. Parents may fail to understand their children, wives often complain that their husbands do not understand them, some Western tourists claim that they cannot understand Orientals, and anthropologists may accuse one another of not really understanding the Bungo-Bungo man.

This fact, namely, that people belong to the class of things that are subject to understanding, is somewhat peculiar. For what are the other members of that class? By and large they form a rather abstract lot. We understand sentences, what one said, theories, explanations, novels, and poetry. On the other hand, we do not say that we understand, or fail to understand, things like stones, houses, planets, locomotives, palm trees, or porcupines. Yet, one would like to ask, are people not more like machines and porcupines rather than sentences and theories?

Admittedly, there is some leakage into the domain of understanding, letting in some machines and higher animals – at least on a limited basis. A good trainer understands his horses, and, perhaps, a good mechanic his racing cars. With respect to individual beasts and contraptions, the negative form applies almost exclusively. "I don't understand this dog: He barks his head off when the mailman comes, yet not a whimper when the burglar climbs in"; "I don't understand this car: Yesterday it started just fine, and now it would not even turn over." But it requires some imagination to make sense of such positive contexts as "Now I understand this jaguar" or "Try to understand my washing machine." No such effort is needed to appreciate similar contexts about people: It is possible to understand Castro or Khadaffi if one tries. There is nothing surprising about this leakage: We are apt to anthropomorphize animals and machines in other respects, too. Think of "nasty" animals, "capricious" engines, and so on.

To find out what it is to understand something in general, and to understand people in particular, I shall first compare the verb *to understand* with the kindred verb *to know*. Indeed, in many contexts mentioned thus far the latter verb could replace the former without much change in meaning. The trainer knows his horses, the anthropologist his favorite tribesman, and so forth. And, of course, saying that one knows a theory, a poem, or a play comes close to saying that one understands these things. There are, on the other hand, spectacular divergences too. One can know, but hardly understand, mountains, trees, and beetles; and one can understand, but hardly know, the first sentence of the latest best seller. Again, think of the remarks we just quoted about the dog that barked inappropriately and the car that failed to start. *Know*, in the place of *understand*, just would not do.

There is, furthermore, a formal difference, which is more illuminating than the intuitive examples given thus far. *Know* takes all kinds of *wh*- clauses as complements. The detective may know who killed the grocer, when and where (Vendler 1972:94). He may also come to know why the woman killed that man and how she did it. Now *understand* can take only *why* and *how* but not *who, what, (whom), when*, and *where*. Let us try:

*I understand what he ate.
*I don't understand where Joe lives.
*I can't understand when he arrived.

On the other hand:

I don't understand how he did it.
Now I understand why he took that job.

What is behind this difference? The answer is obvious. *Who, what, when*, and *where* stand for something simple: an ordinary noun phrase (*Joe, an apple*) or a simple adverbial (*in New York, at 5 P.M.*). *Why* and *how*, on the other hand, stand for a reason or explanation, that is, something more complex, something like a story: "She did it by putting a few grains of arsenic into the full saltshaker and . . ."; "He took the job, because his wife was nagging him about the cold climate in Saskatoon, and . . ."

It seems to be the case, therefore, that whereas *know* takes both simple and complex objects, *understand* is restricted to more involved objects. A nice illustration: One knows words but understands sentences.

Even with respect to objects that fall into the common domain of *know* and *understand*, the latter verb is more demanding that the former. To say that one knows a poem is a far less ambitious claim than to say that one understands it. To know a poem, basically, is to be able to tell how it runs. For understanding more is required: to be able to interpret and explain. Similarly, if a student is able to handle problems of calculus, he knows calculus (he knows "how it works"). For all that, he may not "really" understand calculus. His teacher, we hope, does understand it: He is able to give reasons, offer explanations, show coherence, and so forth.

This difference holds with respect to people, too. Parents who merely know their children are familiar with their behavior, can anticipate their reactions, and are thus able to deal with them. These facts, however, do not entail that they understand them. The difference, in this case, goes much deeper than in the case of a poem or calculus, and we shall return to it later on.

That there is a difference in all these domains can be shown in another way too. One can *try* (and, accordingly, succeed or fail) to understand poems, theories, and people. But there is no such thing as trying to know. One may try to learn or find out, but even if these attempts are crowned with success, the task of understanding might still remain. Learning a poem by heart does not entail understanding, and the man who does not understand his wife is by no means assured of improvement by observing her with greater scientific precision. These attempts, even if helpful, are mere preliminaries to the proper task of understanding. A poem can be easy to learn but difficult to understand, and a person who is difficult to understand may be in plain view of the observer. To put it bluntly: To understand, it may not be enough to know.

Let us return to our original problem: What do people share with sentences, theories, and poems to warrant their inclusion into the domain of understanding? "They are complex and difficult, that is what" – you say. Indeed, we remarked a while ago that some degree of complexity characterizes all things that are subject to understanding. But this cannot be the whole story.

What is more complex, a simple sentence or a locomotive? what Joe just said about his dinner or a cow? I know that this is like comparing apples and oranges and that the notion of complexity is very complex indeed. Yet intuition tells us that the latter things are more complex, but it is the former that can be understood.

To see for instance, what it is in a simple sentence, that calls for understanding, I shall proceed in a roundabout way. We mentioned earlier that sometimes we say that we do not understand a machine, for example, a motorcar that would not start. What is a typical situation?

Not one in which the car is unfamiliar or has just been returned to us by the neighbor's adolescent offspring. For in that case there may be an obvious trouble that we do not know but may find out. If it is our own familiar car, however, that refuses to start, in spite of the fact that it did start yesterday and nothing has happened to it since, and the battery and the starter and the plugs and so on are all right, then we might say, in desperation, that we do not understand the car. But now suppose instead, that we find the trouble: The forgotten domelight has been turned on all night and drained the battery. Would we say, then, that we understand the car? Not at all. What we might say is that we understand *why* it did not start or *how* the battery got low, but that is not the same thing. For in this case we *see* the reason, we *know* what went wrong.

What is the moral of the story? There is a malfunction to be explained. If the known facts are sufficient to account for it, all is well. If the facts are not known, we can still hope that they will do so. Understanding, or the lack of it, does not enter the picture in either case. If, however, the facts are known, or at least *appear* to be known, and they still fail to provide an explanation, then we say that we don't understand. The dimension of understanding opens up after the facts are known.

Now let us return to simple sentences: spoken, written, or remembered – it does not matter. You listen carefully to the sound, peer intently at the marks on paper: There is nothing hidden, everything is out in the open, all the "facts" are perceived. Yet none of these facts will contain the meaning of the sentence. What you cannot see, or hear, you have to understand. In this case, moreover, unlike the case of the car, this is inherently so. The car's malfunction, after all, *can* be explained by some physical fact. It was just "hidden" from us, creating the illusion of mystery, which drove us to despair and a profession of lack of understanding. There are, however, no "hidden" facts about a sentence we do not understand; it may be as clearly perceived as the ones we do understand. The point is that understanding is not continuous with what can be perceived; it is a new dimension.

"But," you object, "words don't wear their meanings on their sleeves either, yet we don't say we understand words." True, I answer, but their meaning is not something that one has to construe, compose, or arrive at: You either know what the word means or you don't; you have learned that word, or not. But we do not learn what sentences mean: We have to construe their meaning on the basis of our knowledge of words, grammer, and so on – we have to understand. Understanding requires a constructive effort of the mind to supplement features that are not observable to the senses.[1]

The whole conceptual environment of *understand* betokens the fact that understanding, unlike knowledge, is no mere passive state but a result of the mind's constructive labor. We *try* to understand, we speak of "flashes" of understanding, and, in difficult cases, our understanding may be only partial or incomplete.

Our remarks concerning the understanding of sentences can easily be extended to cover the understanding of what one said, of poems, plays, theories, and other more or less "verbal" things. In all these cases "what is perceived" (i.e., heard, read, or otherwise observed) falls short of what these things "mean," yet, obviously, it is the latter that interests us the most.

To understand, say, calculus, or the theory of relativity, it is not sufficient to learn the theorems and master the routine of applications. The person who understands these theories is the one who has an "account" of the theorems, who could derive them himself, and so forth, in short, who has made these theories his own by reconstructing them in his own mind.

Similarly, one way at least of trying to understand a poem or a play may consist of an attempt at duplicating the poet's mind in one's own. One tries to think and to feel as the poet did, so that those lines may appear a natural expression of those sentiments and thoughts.

With respect to all these things, the approach of the understanding is "from the inside." To understand such a product of the human mind – from simple sentences to the loftiest creations of science and art – one has to reproduce the vital principle, which accounts for its visible appearance, in one's own mind. This need is answered, for instance, by the "generative" approach to the understanding of sentences (e.g., in the works of Noam Chomsky).

The etymology of the very word *understanding*, no less than of its Latin equivalent *intelligere*, is unusually revealing. The metaphor behind the English word suggests the idea of support or foundation, whereas the Latin verb, a combination of *inter* and *legere*, literally means "reading between the lines." Just to play with words: To understand is to "read" what does not appear in the lines yet gives sense to what does.

Now we are ready to answer the question originally raised: How come that people, too, no matter how unlike the "verbal" entities thus far discussed, are objects of understanding?

Once more I shall begin with examples that mention objects we only marginally can be said to understand, or rather fail to understand: machines and animals. We did not understand that car and that dog because their behavior appeared capricious, unpredictable, and thus unaccountable in terms of the regularities we normally employ to explain their conduct. It is as if they had "free will" enabling them to defy the set patterns. Of course, as we explained previously, in these cases freedom is but an illusion (I am not sure about animals in this respect): If we did know more about that car, its functioning, or malfunctioning, would be fully explained, and, accordingly, there would be no room left for understanding.

But with humans, freedom is by no means an illusion. Without committing myself to any metaphysical theory in this matter, I simply insist upon the perfectly obvious and uncontroversial conceptual truth that peoples' actions are not "caused" by any physical conditions but are performed for reasons. Accordingly, they are not determined by the given situation but embody free choice. "Why did his arm go up?" "Because the neurons fired, and the muscles contracted, and so on." Here we are talking about not a human action but a physical event determined by causes. "Why did he raise his arm?" "Because he wanted to signal the engineer to start the train." This is an action, and in the sequel I shall restrict my discussion to free human acts and actions of this kind, whether they be overt performances (like the raising of one's arm) or internal moves (like imagining the Eiffel Tower or concentrating on a problem). The distinction just sketched is widely recognized in philosophical literature (e.g., Melden 1961).

If so, then human conduct, by definition, cannot be explained on the basis of what we perceive and know about the observable world. Accordingly, people, at least inasmuch as they are agents, call for understanding, no less than sentences, poems, and theories, at least insofar as these are meaningful entities.

Indeed, when talking about understanding people, we *never* mean human bodies at rest or performing biological functions. To say things like "I don't understand Joe, he does not decompose proteins" would be silly. But, of course, what is supposed to decompose proteins is Joe's stomach and digestive system, that is, an organ or a system of organs. And organs are not agents. It is Joe, not his brain, nerves, and muscles, who signals the engineer. People act; organs only do things. Therefore, it is people who need to be understood, not things like stomachs. In much the same way, sentences, spoken and written, and the like are subject to understanding, not noises or marks on paper.

Thus we see what connects people with those abstract and mainly "verbal" entities in the domain of understanding. Agency in the one case, meaning in the other, no matter how unlike, have a thing in common: They are not accountable for in terms of the observable, physical features of the world.

We have demonstrated *that* people are of the kind that can be understood. The question still remains: *What* does this understanding consist of? With respect to sentences, theories, and poems, we concluded that the understanding of them consists in the reconstruction of a "principle" accounting for the observable structure (think of generative grammar). Now what do we have to "generate," or rather "regenerate," in our minds in understanding a person?

The answer to this question is bound to be rather ambitious: nothing less than the mind of a free agent, that is, his thoughts, feelings, desires, and intentions in the unity of one consciousness. For it is the person who acts, *in indivisibili*, not his organs or their sum, not his thoughts and feelings or their sum.

As we just mentioned, a person's actions are explained in terms of reasons, motives, intentions, and the like, that is to say, in terms of factors belonging to his subjective consciousness rather than to the objective and observable features of his body, behavior, or physical surroundings. Accordingly, just as the meaning of a sentence proved to be something belonging to a dimension other than its mere physical shape, so the mind of an agent is something distinct from, and not continuous with, his physical appearance. For this reason, in either case, the knowledge of the observable facts is not enough, and understanding has a role to play.

But, remember, mere words do not call for understanding, in spite of the fact that their meaning, too, lies beyond the physical realm. And, as we have pointed out, the reason is that the meaning of words can simply be learned and does not need the constructive labor characteristic of understanding. Now, in a similar way, we learn to attribute *simple* elements of human (and animal) consciousness on the basis of typical stimuli and behavior, without the need for understanding. It is not a matter of understanding to realize that the man on the rack is in pain or that the bull charging the matador is angry.

But now consider more "complex" sentiments, emotions, and feelings. Are there any "typical" manifestations of envy, jealousy, nostalgia, or disappointment, as there are of pain, anger, and fear? There are not, but this is only half the story. The other half is that not even the circumstances evoking such emotions can be given a general and objective description. For what matters is not the actual situation in which the subject finds himself but rather his perception of that situation. As there are no "paradigms" of envy behavior, there are no "paradigms" of envy-producing setups. Nevertheless, we are able to learn these terms and ascribe them to people in a reasonable manner. There must be, therefore, certain observable situations that license or allow for such attributions, even if they do not justify them conclusively.[2] But then it is up to us to reconstruct the pattern by connecting the situation of the person with his reactions via his perception of the situation and the appropriate emotion: Did he do what he did out of envy, jealousy, disappointment, or just plain ill humor? In other words, we have to try to understand the subject.

How do we do it? Owing to the complexity of the circumstances, not to speak of the uniqueness of individual persons, it cannot be a matter of simply following rules or applying paradigms. There is a way, however, which is available in every case, no matter how exotic. We always can project, or at least try to project, ourselves into the situation in which the agent finds himself by imagining what it must be like for him to be in that situation.[3] What would *I* feel, how would *I* react, if I were he?

We have to watch out, though, concerning the sense of the "I" in this context. For it is one thing to imagine what I, that is, Z.V., would feel and do, given my temperament, background, beliefs and values, and so forth, and quite another thing to perform total transference and try to assume in addition our subject's beliefs, values, prejudices, hang-ups, and the rest.[4] Obviously, to understand people, the latter move is called for.

Suppose you are reading a history of Hitler's last days in the bunker. Before the bitter end, Dr. Goebbels kills his wife, his five children, and himself. Can you understand him? Certainly not if you just imagine what *you* would do in those circumstances. No, the question is what you would do *if you were Goebbels*, that is, had the mind of a fanatical Nazi, fearing, but at the same time relishing, the unfolding *Götterdämmerung*. This is the state of mind you have to assume in your fancy. Then and only then can you say that you at least tried to understand him.

Did Dr. Goebbels kill his children out of despair, fear, spite, or what? It is impossible to give an answer in these general terms. The situation is unique – none of the standard labels seems to fit, not even in a combination with others. Yet he surely did have emotions and feelings in performing his abysmal deed. The point is that names, in such cases, do not really matter: We can understand him, if we do, even without being able to categorize the sentiments involved.

In some less outrageous situations the understanding of the person may yield a label or a choice of labels. Take the following case. The slow-witted and homely husband is rude to his pretty and vivacious wife while driving home from a party in which she was the center of attention. Does he treat her so badly out of a feeling of envy, jealousy, resentment, or inferiority? These are all likely candidates, and if we knew more about that couple, about what exactly happened at the party, the choice could narrow down. But, even then, the attribution of such a motive would be the result of our understanding of the husband in that setup, rather than a conclusion based on the satisfaction of some fixed set of behavioral criteria. By the way, even if we had a complete record (say, film, tapes, etc.) of Goebbels's conduct in the bunker, our understanding of his act would remain a formidable task.[5]

To conclude: The understanding of an agent requires empathy, that is, the reproduction, by means of imaginary transference, of the agent's consciousness in one's own mind so that his conduct may appear as a result of free, but rational, choice. Because, of course, "mad" acts cannot be understood. Freedom does not exclude, but requires, rationality: assessment of the situation, deliberation, and choice.

"I just don't understand him – he had everything going for him: good looks, intelligence, wealth, success, everything! And then he goes and shoots himself!" What do we mean by saying things like that? Well, simply put, what we mean is this: No matter how hard I try to put myself into his place, I do not succeed in assuming a frame of mind that would be compatible with what I know about his circumstances, on the one hand, and that would allow for suicide as a reasonable option, on the other. But now suppose you discover that our subject has recently learned that he suffers from an incurable and disfiguring disease. In that case it is not that difficult to understand him. You have to add a good dose of vanity to his mental makeup, and the fatal choice becomes understandable. Short of such a discovery, you either attribute his deed to a momentary aberration (i.e., renounce understanding) or attribute it to some perception or emotion you cannot capture but assume to have been there (he might have despaired of the state of the world) to save rationality.

But, in any case, that his action is understandable does not make it into a necessary one. The discovery of the incurable disease explains his choice, but it remains a choice. In reconstructing his mind in your own, you assume the mental state of a free agent. Compulsive acts need no understanding.

We see, then, that the failure to understand a person can be due to two reasons: ignorance of some relevant circumstances and failure to capture some features of the subject's mind (passions, beliefs, perceptions, etc.). It is important to note that, unlike in the car case, the correction of ignorance does not preempt understanding but makes it possible: It is a *removens prohibens*, not a substitute. Remember, no amount of detailed knowledge about Dr. Goebbels's behavior in the bunker would "explain" what he did.

The same point can be argued by considering fictional characters: Hamlet, Raskolnikov, and so on. In these cases no "fact" is hidden to the beholder: What can be "known" about them is all contained in the text. Yet, obviously, some of us understand these characters better than others. Consequently, understanding them is an act distinct from mere acquaintance.

Now what about the other factor: the failure to "capture" some features of the subject's mind? Needless to say, this is the main source of trouble: The most exasperating cases of lack of understanding obtain between people who know each other quite well. As far as I can see, such failures can be attributed to three factors: insensitivity, lack of experience, and differences in background.

There could be, of course, a fourth reason, namely, that some people are just "created" different from us. This would be a reasonable assumption with respect to Martians (if they existed) or dolphins (if they were really rational). Concerning humans, however, we assume the native element to be basically the same. This assumption, in our context, is something like a "regulative idea," the denial of which would amount to giving up the hope of understanding some rational creatures.

Notice, I said about the native element that it is assumed to be "basically" the same. For we do allow for some variations in individual makeup, which are not due to upbringing: temperament, degrees of intelligence, age, state of health, and, of course, gender.

Returning now to the three factors mentioned previously, I have little to say about insensitivity. Common experience teaches us that as some people are more or less apt to see another person's point of view, so also there is a difference among people in being able to empathize with their fellow men. That this is an independent factor can be shown by considering, say children of the same family and of comparable intelligence. It is quite possible that one child is far more "sensitive" in this respect than another, in spite of the common background and upbringing. Such sensitivity can be developed by appropriate training but not beyond the potential of the person's native endowment, which in some cases seems to be quite limited.

Lack of experience is another independent factor. Not even the most sensitive and bright child will understand Karamazov *père*'s lust for Grushenka for this reason. And, of course, most of us are hampered by this factor in trying to understand mystics, drug addicts, and the like, who, presumably, enjoy experiences not shared by the majority of people.

Last, but not least, difference of background. This presents the crucial difficulty in understanding people belonging to another culture, from either the past or the present. The difficulties thus created range from the ones we all experience in understanding our own "rock bound" adolescents to the ones historians or anthropologists have to overcome in trying to understand medieval monks or New Guinea tribesmen. Moreover, this is the inhibiting factor that demands the hardest work to overcome. Insensitivity can hardly be removed, and lack of experience is usually remedied in time (except the "exotic" cases, which are not that important). Cultural differences, however, need to be overcome by study and effort.

What does one have to do to achieve this aim? The answer to this question will consist in an extension of the principle we applied in explaining the understanding of people in general. At that time we said that to understand a person is to imagine being in his situation, where the term *situation* is interpreted in the broadest possible sense, that is, including not only his "external" circumstances but also his state of mind: what it must be like to be that person in those conditions.

But a person is not a momentary being: His life extends in time, and the past is "present" in his mind in the form of "traces" left behind: acquired dispositions, beliefs, and memories. Unfortunately, however, these traces are not discernible to the beholder: He has to reconstrue them. And, of course, this reconstruction cannot be the result of merely observing the present conduct of the subject. For that is but the result of his perception and assessment of his situation, and these elements are heavily dependent upon those "traces" from the past.

What the observer has to do, therefore, is to apply the principle of transference extended over time. He has to try to imagine what it must be like being born and brought up in that society, that culture, and in those individual circumstances. How would *I* look at the world if I had grown up in that total environment? Naturally, knowledge of the external circumstances is a necessary condition for achieving this: circumstances of life, customs, traditions, rituals, legends, and so forth. Yet the knowledge of these things is by no means sufficient. The effort of the imagination must follow till the subject's conduct is understood, till one can say: Yes, in fancying being he, what he does appears to me as the thing to do – or at least one of the things it is reasonable to do.

The understanding of a person I am talking about here is not an act that lies in the public domain. It is as private, subjective, and unobservable as the state of mind itself, which is evoked in the process. Thus, by itself, it is not a scientific datum, theory, or projection. Yet, if I am right, the feat of understanding people is intimately tied to the *practice* of the social sciences.

For, in the first place, we have seen that the understanding of humans remote in time or cultural background would be impossible without the data and interpretations offered by such sciences as history and anthropology. On the other hand, the attempt to understand his subjects, that is, to reproduce their minds in his own, is likely to guide the scientist in his search for those features in their environment and cultural background that might have been instrumental in shaping those minds.

This "mutual causality" is by no means a vicious circle. Traveling is no part of geography; but geography could not have developed without traveling, and one main use of geography is to facilitate traveling. In a similar way, understanding some people would hardly be possible without the help of history and anthropology; but these sciences themselves could not have developed without the stimulus provided by our desire to understand other people.

Notes

1. Certain compound words form an exception. We understand what a milkman or a snowman is but not what a starman might be. But, if one thinks about it, such exceptions confirm the rule: They require "construction," thus understanding.
2. This much at least is required because of the impossibility of a "private language" demonstrated by Wittgenstein (1960:part I, nos. 243 ff.).
3. The importance of this notion was first brought out by Thomas Nagel (1974).
4. I tried to resolve some of the logical difficulties with the notion of transference in "A Note to the Paralogisms" (1977). The idea of transference

of consciousness is of Kantian origin; one typical quote: "It is obvious that if I represent to myself a thinking being, I must put myself in his place, and thus substitute, as it were, my own subject for the object I am seeking to consider (which does not occur in any other kind of investigation)" (Kant 1953:A. 353–4).

5. Some writers, particularly Jane Austen, succeed admirably in conveying their characters' minds, without the crutch of using labels to name their feelings directly, by simply describing what they say and do. By understanding them, *we* can supply the names, if possible.

References

Austin, J. L. 1961. A plea for excuses. In J. L. Austin, *Philosophical Papers*. Oxford: Clarendon Press.

Kant, E. 1953. *Critique of Pure Reason*. Norman Kemp Smith, trans. London: Macmillan.

Melden, A. I. 1961. *Free Action*. London: Routledge & Kegan Paul.

Nagel, Thomas. 1974. What is it like to be a bat? *Philosophical Review* 83:435–50.

Quine, W. V. O. 1953. *From a Logical Point of View*. Cambridge, Mass.: Harvard University Press.

Vendler, Zeno. 1972. *Res Cogitans: An Essay in Rational Psychology*. Ithaca, N.Y.: Cornell University Press.

1977. A note to the paralogisms. In Gilbert Ryle, ed., *Contemporary Aspects of Philosophy*. London: Oriel Press.

Wittgenstein, L. 1960. *Philosophical Investigations*. New York: Macmillan.

notion, knowing, and culture

Robert I. Levy

The study of "emotion" in radically non-Western communities – the kind of places in which anthropologists have traditionally worked – throws light both on the nature and functions of emotion (and of the individual emotions) and on the relations of individuals in those places to the historically transmitted ambient forms that constitute their "culture." As the temptation to put the two key terms ("emotion" and "culture") within quotation marks suggests, both terms are problematic, and we will encounter some of the confusions of Alice's croquet game, with both mallets and balls, not to mention the wickets, in eccentric motion.

I

If "emotion" is taken to mean "an emotion," a bounded sequence of anger, sadness, fear, and so forth (which are the sorts of events I will for the most part be considering here), rather than some more abstract or derivative usage, than it has not been of central concern in anthropology until recently. Clyde Kluckhohn, for example, in a forty-seven–page review of "Culture and Behavior" (1954), gave only one and one-half rather thin pages to "affect." His emphasis was on the relativistic aspects, noting that although "there may well be a sense in which emotions, as biological events, are the same the world over . . . the expression of emotions and the circumstances arousing particular emotions vary culturally."[1] In the second edition of the same handbook the new review of psychologically relevant anthropological studies by George DeVos and Arthur Hippler (1969) dealt with emotion primarily as an element in "expressive affective symbolic behavior," that is, as expressed in such forms as folklore and art in various cultures.

"Emotion" was always taken note of in "culture and personality" studies, but in keeping with the psychoanalytic emphasis of most of these studies it was usually of interest as a clue for the understanding of a psychodynamically conceived "personality organization." As Robert LeVine put it:

The commonly observable bodily symptoms (such as weeping, blushing, trembling) of intense affective reactions can provide a series of anchor points from which to begin the comparative study of affective experience. . . . Discovering the diverse cultural and psychological contexts in which these symptoms occur (or are narrowly avoided) should yield comparable informations relevant to the understanding of personality and development. (1973:229)

Within the same tradition, emotion in its relation to motivation has been of central concern, as in the work of Melford Spiro, notably in his attempts to understand the nature of individuals' commitments to cultural systems of belief and action (see, e.g., Spiro 1967:76).

The concern with a narrowly conceived cognition of the last twenty years, with an accompanying emphasis on culture as "a system of knowledge," pushed both "culture and personality" in general, and emotion in particular, to one side. As a recent British polemic against French structuralism put it with dialectic scorn in relation to one wing of the intellectualist movement:

It is Levi-Strauss' stated view that because human emotions and impulses are difficult to explain they can have no part in any theory of human nature; they belong to the world of the body and as such have no interest for anthropology, whose exclusive concern, in Levi-Strauss' view, is with the mind. It is to a condition of passionless mental purity that he seeks to reduce human nature. (Webster 1981)

A similar mood of rebellion is expressed in some recent comments by psychologists involved in the study of emotion. Silvan Tomkins, for example, has noted the general neglect of emotion as a thing in itself, which he felt limited understanding.

Behaviorism, psychoanalysis, and cognitive theory each subjected affect to the status of a dependent variable. The cognitive revolution was required to emancipate the study of cognition from its co-option and distortion by behaviorism and by psychoanalytic theory. An affect revolution is now required to emancipate this radical new development from an overly imperialistic cognitive theory. (1981:306)

In the typical oscillation generated in the social sciences by the neglected, interest in emotion is coming back in anthropology, particularly in the work of some younger anthropologists. One example is a reconsideration of the relations of symbolic action and emotion, a reexamination of assumptions such as those entailed in Durkheim's dictum about mourning rites that "mourning is not a natural movement of private feelings wounded by a cruel loss; it is a duty imposed by the group. . . . It is a ritual attitude, which [a person] is forced to adopt out of a respect for custom, but which is, in a large measure, independent of his affective state" (1915:397, quoted in Kapferer 1979). Bruce Kapferer, in an analysis of Sinhalese healing rites, argues that the relation between felt and displayed emotion, although problematic, cannot be so easily dismissed and that it is a relationship that is essential for understanding the form and function of the rite itself. Focusing on ritual as performance, he analyzes how, "in the actions of participants ideas, feelings and emotions are organized, oriented and structured," so that a connection is formed between "the conventional display of emotion in performance and the real internal and privately felt emotional and mental condition of participants" (ibid., p. 153). Such approaches try to go beyond the limits suggested by Turner for the analysis of ritual symbols.

> [The anthropologist] cannot, however, with his present skills, discriminate between the precise sources of unconscious feeling and wishing, which shape much of the outward form of the symbol; select some natural objects rather than others to serve as symbols; and account for certain aspects of the behavior associated with symbols. For him, it is enough that the symbol should evoke emotion. He is interested in the fact that emotion is evoked and not in the specific qualities of its constituents. . . . In other words, the anthropologist treats the sensory pole of meaning as a constant, and the social and ideological aspects as variables whose interdependencies he seeks to explain. (1967:36)

Another reanimated emphasis, on the "person" and the "self" as important foci for the understanding of the effect of symbol systems and other aspects of culture on social action, also emphasized emotion as a central issue. "An anthropological theory of the person in culture must take account of the fundamental and organizing role of the emotions in behavior, thought, and meaning systems" (Lutz 1980). I have tried – for Tahiti (1969, 1973, 1978) and for the Newars of the Kathmandu Valley (in preparation) – as part of a general person-centered ethnography, to describe "emotion" and various emotions as systematically related to a variety of sociocultural, historical, and psychological phenomena in each community. Also of recent interest has been the "ethnopsychology" of the emotions, the ways in which the members of the domain are conceived, named, and structured (e.g., White 1981; Lutz 1982, among others).

Claims that emotion is in one way or another of relevance to anthropological analysis has generated opposition. A polemic reaction by Edmund Leach provides a useful example. Clifford Geertz in his recent book, *Negara: The Theater State in Nineteenth-Century Bali* (1980), had argued that the imagery of Balinese kingship provides in itself part of the power of the state. "The state drew its force . . . from its imaginative energies, its semiotic capacity to make inequality enchant." But, he adds:

> The notion that politics is *an unchanging play of natural passions*, which particular institutions of domination are but so many devices for exploiting, is wrong everywhere; in Bali, its absurdity is patent. The passions are as cultural as the devices; and the turn

of mind – hierarchical, sensory, symbolistic, and theatrical – that informs the one informs the other. (p. 124; italics mine)

In a review of *Negara*, Edmund Leach attacked Geertz's assertion about the specifically Balinese cultural shaping of the passions with (culturally shaped?) passion and intemperance. He wrote of the statement I have quoted that it is,

> . . . in my view, complete rubbish. I can make no sense of a line of thought which claims that "passions" are culturally defined. From my prejudiced position as a social anthropologist this passage reveals with startling clarity the ultimately radical weakness of the basic assumption of cultural anthropology, namely, that not only are cultural systems infinitely variable, but that human individuals are products of their culture rather than of their genetic predisposition. (1981:32)

Leach's credo marks one extreme position. The other exteme, not quite as absolute but present as a limit toward which the position strives, is a tendency to maximize claims for the effect of "culture" in the production and shaping of emotion (as well as other forms of private experience and response). This is implied, for example, in Geertz's claim that the passions are *as cultural* as the institutions and in Michelle Rosaldo's statement:

> If culturally organized views of possibility and sense must figure centrally in the acquisition of a sense of self – providing images in terms of which we unselfconsciously connect ideas and actions – then culture makes a difference that concerns not simply *what* we think but how we feel about and live our lives. Affects, then, are no less cultural and no more private than beliefs. (Chapter 5, this volume)

The status of emotion in relation to local cultural forms is, I believe, rather more complex and more interesting for a theory of culture than either of these simplified opposed positions.

II

Carroll Izard (1980) has recently noted with approval a "psychologically radical" thought of Susanne Langer's to the effect that "the human being's departure from the normal pattern of animal mentality is a vast and special evolution of *feeling* in the hominid stock" (1967:xvi).

The thought is radical in the face of the traditional conception of emotions as passions, as *distempers* of the mind and thus of rationality, which has served (at least for what Richard Shweder – Chapter 1, this volume – has called the enlightenment position in the human sciences) to obscure the relationship between emotion and knowing.

Roy D'Andrade (1981) has similarly remarked, in criticism of the assumption commonly found in Western culture – that reason and emotion are in opposition, and that feelings and emotions interfere with efficient problem solving – that there is a "strong positive correlation phylogenetically between intelligence and emotionality" (p. 190). Whereas Langer's emphasis on "feeling" was its basis for, and representation in, certain aspects of meaningful symbolic form, D'Andrade speculates on feelings as an aspect of cognition. "Feelings and emotions tell us how the world is, in a very vivid way, typically increase the activation of various schemas for action and evaluation, while still permitting delay so that planning, goal sequencing, reappraisal, and other complex procedures can occur" (p. 191). The feeling of hunger, for example, is a constant reminder to an individual, telling him something about his "needs" and "how the world is" while he decides "cognitively" what he must do. As D'Andrade notes:

> The more [the] complex procedures which we consider the mark of intelligence, are used to cope with the environment, the more the creature needs an information holding system such as feelings to permit the required delay. Feelings and emotions, in my view, are like reverberating loops. They hold information in an active form, so that it doesn't go away, and yet does not preempt everything else.

The idea that feeling has something essential to do with the encounter with the world as represented cognitively has recently been articulated in psychodynamic theory by George Devereux, who argues that only the emotional-laden symbolic processing of percepts gives the infinite number of pieces of the perceived world some kind of integrated unity. "Symbolization helps to hold man's segmental capacities together and fosters a broader direct involvement with the situation" (Devereux 1979:28). A similar idea was suggested in 1930 by the psychoanalyst Melanie Kline, who "saw in symbolization the process by means of which the infant apprehends reality and endows it with value. Failure of symbolic substitution leads to a state of autism in which the external world is lacking in interest" (Hook 1979:272).[2]

III

I will consider emotion here in its relation to knowing, particularly to the cultural structuring of knowing. I will deal with *emotion* as a subcategory of *feeling* and touch on the question of *awareness*, which both emotion and feeling entail. I will distinguish "emotional feeling" (an awkward but necessary term for my present purposes) from the events that precede it and follow it in the "emotional response." Let us begin with some Tahitian data that illuminate something of the nature of the relations at issue.

In comparing Tahitian terminology, conception, and action in regard to what are in Western conception various emotions, it is striking that there is a great difference in their cultural visibility. Various forms of anger, for example, are named; there are separate words for irritability, for rage, for the "ordinary" feeling of anger. There is much doctrine about what stirs anger up in personal relations, how it works in the individual, what to do about it, and how to evaluate it. Anger is, relative to some other emotions, "hypercognized"[3] – that is, there are a large number of culturally provided schemata for interpreting and dealing with it.

There are other emotions for which such cultural "amplifiers of human ratiocinative capacities" (as Jerome Bruner [Bruner, Olver & Greenfield 1966:56] has called them) are minimal; sadness is an example.

> There are words for severe grief and for lamentation. There are, however, no unambiguous terms which represent the concepts of sadness, longing, or loneliness . . . People would name their condition, where I supposed that [the body signs and] the context called for "sadness" or "depression," as "feeling troubled" (pe'ape'a, the generic term for disturbances, either internal or external); as "not feeling a sense of inner push" ('ana'anatae); as "feeling heavy" (toiaha); as "feeling fatigued" (haumani); and a variety of other terms all referring to a generally troubled or subdued bodily state. *These are all nonspecific terms, which had no implications of any external [social] relational cause about them, in the sense that being "angry" implies an offense or a frustration.* (Levy 1973:305; italics for the purposes of the present chapter)

I have called such underschematized emotional domains "hypocognized." Another Tahitian example of a hypocognized domain of feeling is "guilt," which contrasts to the elaborated hypercognized system of naming, classification, and doctrine having to do with "shame" or more properly "shame/embarrassment."

One of the consequences of hypocognition is that the felt disturbance, the "troubled feelings," can be interpreted both by the one who experiences them and by others around him as something other than "emotion." Thus, the troubled feelings that persist too long after the death of a loved one or those that occur after some loss that Tahitian ideology holds to be trivial and easily replaceable are in the village often interpreted as illness or as the harmful effects of a spirit. In many cases connections between the feeling of disturbance with what the sequence suggested (in my "etic" analysis) to be the eliciting event are not in any way recognized. A young man whose transient woman has just left him, taking their baby with her to a distant island, may look sluggish and despondent and, diagnosing himself as physically ill owing to some extraneous cause, seek some herbal medicine. If the bad feelings persist, he may go to a spirit doctor who will help him identify and treat the spirit that is possessing him. There will often be much collaboration by the community in reinforcing the dissociation of certain kinds of causes from the man's feeling.[4] (One can trace the emphasis on disguising the clear understanding of precursors of feelings of loss to the ideological emphases of the traditional Tahitian exchange system.) Note that for the young Tahitian man there are two kinds of knowing involved: that covert knowing, which recognized certain events as a loss and which produced a felt organismic response, and a later overt knowing, which is associated with a culturally patterned evaluation of, and response to, the feeling.

Most emotional sequences in Tahiti are not characterized by such a clear disjunction. Where the covert and overt processes have some or many symmetrical features, as in "anger," the transformations and relations of the two phases are more subtle, but the disjunctive cases make certain important issues particularly clear.

IV

In dealing with what I took to be "sadness" as, say, "fatigue," the Tahitians were accepting the "feeling" but denying that it was an "emotion." "Emotion" can be thought of as a subset of the larger category of "feeling." All this requires further definition and discussion, but before turning to emotion itself, I would like to propose that "feeling" in general is a significant issue for a discussion of the ways in which "culture" enters into thought and action. Neither awareness, feeling, nor emotion is necessary for internally adjustive or externally adaptive action. All kinds of bodily processes involving the central nervous system (and nonneurological physiological processes also) respond to problems and initiate corrections without any awareness being involved. A minor lack of oxygen is "automatically" adjusted by unconscious changes in respiration. But if this response is not sufficient, then an *awareness* associated with a pressure for action, a *feeling*, arises and mobilizes a conscious program. One decides to open a window or to stop running and sit down.

That one is aware of only certain kinds of central nervous system processes is an intriguing matter. What characterizes that group? And what about feeling, considered as a special kind of awareness? One is aware of parts of the visual field, without "feeling" the visual "sensation." Feeling can be considered as that subgroup of awareness that entails a sense of pressure for action of some kind, but an action that requires information about an "external" world, information that must be learned and entails the whole organism's relation to that world. Feeling is a signal from an unconscious adjustive system to a different kind of adjustive system. The signal of feeling calls for action beyond the capability of the unconscious adjustive system, action that requires integrated information about a complex external environment – the utility of opening a window and how to go about it; the coordinated hunt for the flea set off by an itch; the search for any adequate action to escape further pain. Feeling and awareness mark the moment of an organism's encounter with an understood external world, which is understood in large part through learning and for humans, and in some partial analogous way for many other organisms, through cultural processes. We are now in a position to ask what is the relation of emotion to feeling in general; and what is the relation of culture to emotion.

I have made the assertion that the Tahitians do not recognize all the responses as "emotions" that would seem to be "emotion" from a cross-cultural point of view (although they do recognize the great majority). But what does it mean to recognize, or conceive of, a "feeling" as an "emotion"? The Tahitian language does not have any general term for "feeling" or "emotion," but the *class* of what I am calling "emotions" has some special features in Tahitian usage. Asked to describe such matters as anger, desire, fear, and so on, villagers say that their "place" is in "intestines," referring to those sensations in the abdomen that are part of the feeling response. These feelings can arise spontaneously in the "intestines," or they may be stirred up by some thought from the head, or by something that is seen by the eyes or heard by the ears. The feeling can lead to action directly, but this usually produces a bad result. It should first be thought over in the head, the seat of proper judgment, prior to taking action.

In ordinary speech Tahitians discard such differentiated description and say, "I am angry," "I am afraid." In contrast, they say of pain, "My tooth hurts" and so on, and of itching, "My leg is itching." The Sino-Tibetan–speaking Newars whom I studied in Nepal made similar verbal distinctions, as do we. Anger, desire, and fear involve, then, the "I," the "person," rather than a part of the person. But there are other "feelings" that also at first approach seem to involve the whole person, which Western thought rejects as "emotions." Thus, Tahitians, like us and like Newars, do say, "*I* am exhausted," "*I* am sick." When "sadness" is (mis)interpreted by Tahitians as "illness," the condition of the total "I" is still at issue.

In sickness, exhaustion, and so on, however, there is an emphasis on something wrong in the relation of *a person to his own body*, to his internal environment, to the physical support of the "I." But in an "emotion," say anger, there is an emphasis on something wrong in the relationship of *the person to his external physical and social context*, the world of actions, plans, and socially defined meanings. The difference between the non-emotional "My foot hurts me" and the emotional "I am angry with him because he stepped on my foot" involves in the second case a relationship with another. The emotions are feelings that are connected with the external relationships of the self, of "I." And this self in humans, and social animals, is intimately constructed out of group processes and interpersonal relationships.

So we may say, tentatively, that the class of feelings that Tahitians deal with as "emotions" (a) involves the whole "person" (a complex psychosocial creation) and (b) implies something about the relation of the person-as-a-whole to his or her environment, especially to the other persons (or personified elements) in that environment.

When an "emotional feeling" is dealt with as a "non-emotional feeling" it may be done either by ignoring the external relational cause (which, as I shall discuss, was "known" in some way during the "appraisal phase" of the emotion), as when loneliness is interpreted as sickness, or by denying that the whole person is involved and focusing on a part reaction – the hypochondriac's "My heart is acting peculiarly," which also blunts the relational information proposed by "I am afraid."

We may note here parenthetically another aspect of the idea of emotion as involving information about relationships of a certain sort, the very nexus of relationships, which in fact constitute the social person and his status. If, for the moment, we consider emotion not as an aspect of a person's understanding of the world around him but as a communication, and if we shift our attention to what is read by others in the community through the emotionally expressive behavior of someone whom they are observing, the question of the meaningful *relationship* of actor to social environment is still central. Expressed emotion, here, is a statement to others about an actor's relation to his ongoing social performance, to his socially constituted act. He is doing the cultural performance (playing chess, disciplining children, dealing with an interrupted plan) in a happy, angry, anxious, shame-ridden, and so on way. Even if he acts "without emotion," this is a message about his relationship to the act. One acts like a chief through cultural codes for leadership; but a proud, anxious, happy, depressed, hesitant, overeager, angry, or whatever chief is a metamessage about an actor's relationship to his socially coded behavior. (Of course, the role may call for some emotional expression in itself, but then there will still be messages concerning the relation of the actor to the conventional emotion.)

The idea of emotion as involving information about the relations of a person to his socially constituted world is of relevance for a set of feelings that are very common in Tahitian villagers and rare among adult Westerners. These are the emotions of the uncanny. Uncanny feelings are not localized in the abdomen but are felt in the head and on the skin. One feels the head swelling, the hair standing on end, and the flesh crawling. This occurs in situations of certain kinds where it is unclear whether the ordinary categories of orientation in the spaciotemporal world are operating – at twilight, in the bush outside the village, in the presence of phenomena that dissolve clear categorizations, for example, fires that glow without heat, people with peculiar faces. Bruner, Goodnow, and Austin (1956:12) have noted that "when an event cannot be . . . categorized and identified, we experience terror in the face of the uncanny. And indeed, 'the uncanny' is itself a category, even if only a residual one." But the Tahitian response is not terror. The uncanny sensation (or emotion) may turn into terror, but it is felt and interpreted as something different from fear. Not all difficulties in categorization lead to a sense of the uncanny. It seems to derive from difficulty in making those categorizations that help anchor us in "commonsense" reality – in familiar kinds of time, space, size, and causal and logical contexts. The uncanny is the emotion that signals the uncertain relationship of the self to such categories.

V

The emotional response has various elements and phases. Paul Ekman suggests (1977, 1980a, and in other works) that one has to consider (1) an *elicitor,* an "event which [is] appraised quickly as the occasion for one or another emotion"; (2) an *appraisal system,* "which determines when the affect program becomes operative" and which "selectively attends to those stimuli (external or internal) which are the occasion for activating the affect program"; and (3) an *affect program* "that directs emotional responses," some of which are modified and controlled through *display* rules, "the conventions, norms, and habits that develop regarding the management of emotional response." I wish to schematize the sequence somewhat differently for my present purposes as a sequence consisting of, in turn, (1) the initial appraisal of an eliciting situation (the two obviously form a logical unit), (2) the "emotional feeling" that enters into awareness as a result of the initial appraisal, and (3) the cognitive evaluation motivated by that feeling.

Izard (1980), responding to a question raised by Robert LeVine concerning the boundaries between the universal and the culture-specific in emotional experiences, claims that "the experiential component of emotion is a quality of consciousness or feeling, and at this level the emotion state is invariant across cultures." Things are probably not even this simple: There is no reason to think that some *dimensions* of the emotional feeling do not vary cross-culturally, their intensity perhaps, for we have some evidence that there may be variations in felt pain, at least among types of people, and such variations may perhaps also be characteristic of groups (e.g., Levy 1973:308–14). But the *qualitative* character of the emotional feeling probably has the same shape, the same initial stimulus characteristics. I will consider here the events preceding and following the emotional feeling, rather than the comparative quality of the feeling itself.

In the case of "sadness," a Tahitian may respond to the emotional feeling produced (in the viewpoint of an observer) by the loss of something he cared about in accordance with local cultural schemata as, say, the effect of spirits on his body. The emotional feeling has produced a problem for (secondary) cognitive evaluation (following Schacter and Marañon; see Mandler 1975), and in accordance with local cultural schemata, he interprets the emotion in (again from some transcultural viewpoint) a peculiar fashion. But, of course, in some sense the individual must "know" that he has undergone a loss. This, the result of an initial appraisal of an eliciting situation, is what generates the emotional feeling in the first place. That is, if we take emotions as involving responses of a "person" to a mostly social environment, the first phase of the generation of the emotional feeling requires some kind of first-order knowledge. Someone is frustrating me, hurting me, becoming detached from me, is sexually receptive, and so on. This is elementary knowledge about relationship and operates largely out of awareness. But it is this primary knowledge that in turn generates the emotional feeling, which then mobilizes in its turn a culturally structured system of understanding and response and a second-order knowledge (which is, or can be easily made, conscious). What is the relation to 'culture' of the first-order knowledge of relationship of the initial appraisal, on the one hand, and of the second-order knowledge of relationship involving the cognitive evaluation activated by the feeling signal, on the other?

We are told that in lower animals the initial appraisal at least is "sunk" into deep neurological structures. A "decorticate" cat, for example, is said to show its greatly augmented rage as goal-directed attacks on "appropriate environmental stimuli" (Grastyan 1974). Such data suggest, of course, that some aspects of knowledge about relationship are phylogenetically "learned" and in some fashion "prewired." There is in humans, in addition to the possibility of phylogenetically determined understandings, some kind of "cultural" influence on primary appraisal (the appraisal of the eliciting situation), but I will argue that this is significantly different (both in its structure and the way it is learned) from the influence of "culture" in secondary appraisal (the appraisal of the response to the eliciting situation).

I will in a later section return to the relation of 'culture' to the different phases of the emotional sequence. But let us here consider the differences between the kind of knowing that is involved prior to and after the emotional feeling or signal. There are at least two different ways in which the *learning* related to primary appraisal seems to differ from that related to secondary cognitive evaluation. First, much of the learning related to primary appraisal is relatively unshaped and random in respect to culture conceived as a control system, ideology, or system of knowledge. Culture so conceived acts as a series of filters, or hierarchic controls, which progressively (both in ontogenetic processes and in ongoing processes of behavioral control) modifies the knowledge resulting from these random processes in systematic and progressively more coherent ways. Second, insofar as the learning affecting primary appraisal is specifically shaped by local community forms, this specific learning has features that differ from the learning involved in secondary cognitive appraisal.

I will consider each point, briefly, in turn.

1. In thinking of learning as enculturation and socialization we tend to focus on those particular sequences of teaching and learning that prepare children for adult roles and orientations in the "culture." The

impulse, both among those influenced by psychoanalytic theory or some theory of pattern learning such as Bateson's, is to assert that the "basic" cultural forms were learned (or "internalized") very early in the development of a child's mind.

An alternative view was clearly stated by Ernest Schachtel in "On Memory and Childhood Amnesia." Some of the rich and diverse understandings of childhood experience, he wrote, are filtered out by a

> process [which] leaves the culturally unacceptable or unusable experiences and the memory thereof to starvation by the expedient of providing no linguistic, conceptual, and memory schemata for them and by channeling later experience into the experience schemata of the culture. As the person, in the process of education, gradually comes to live more and more exclusively within the framework of the culturally and conventionally provided experience schemata, there is less and less to remind him of the possibility of trans-schematic experience. (1949:47)

That is, in the relatively random experiences of children with others within a culture, a great variety of relational lessons are learned (including whatever may be necessary to complete prewired inherited "knowledge"). Later learning must operate to modify and control this primary knowledge.[5] The two phases may well be in some way related to the primary and secondary appraisals that precede and follow the signal of feeling.

As the members of the group conceive of the growing child as more and more of a "person," as more and more of a morally responsible actor, various sequential educational devices – the progressive learning of language, the correction of language to adult standards, the emphases on moral learning and responsibility, the sequences of educational rites of passage with their powerful symbolic transformations of orientation – serve to transform the first "rich and diverse" understandings in a culturally coherent direction. The "starved schemata" are left as a basis for creativity, dreams, humor, and transcultural understanding.

2. Insofar as the forms of a culture do *systematically* affect the early learning, which may modify the primary appraisal, this would seem to operate in large part by affecting the person's *reactivity* to the eliciting situation, his sensitivity to loss, frustration, and so on. Such learning, like "temperament," affects the reactive base, which the defining, evaluative, and programmatic schemas of culture must deal with during the secondary evaluation. The learning that affects the primary assessment phase probably involves the nature of experiencing rather than doctrines about experience. As a crude example, one would expect a child dependent on only one mothering, nurturant person to experience inevitable temporary separations from that person as a particularly dangerous loss in comparison with a child who had a number of substitute nurturant people at hand. The first child would presumably

react to later losses of loved ones differently from the second child. He would appraise eliciting situations more vigorously and extensively than the second. For him, the class of eliciting situations would be wider, and the import of a given one more serious than for the second. But in both, once the emotional feeling of sadness signaled the need for a secondary cognitive evaluation, the same learned cultural program would be used. Insofar as most people in a community shared similar shapings of experience there would be shared similarities in the nature of this reactivity in contrast to some other community.

The psychologist Howard Leventhal has differentiated similar components of knowing in relation to emotion. He categorizes what I have called the primary phase as involving perceptual memories or "schemata" and distinguishes them from "conceptual memories" involved with "social labels" and with discursive processes.

> The schematic and conceptual systems attach different types of cognitive processes to emotion. The schematic is in some sense the more primary and important; it integrates situational perceptions (*episodes*) with autonomic, subjective, expressive and instrumental responses in a concrete, patterned, image-like memory system. The conceptual system is more sequential and volitional in nature and corresponds more closely to social labelling processes. (1980:160; italics in original)

Furthermore, the processing of the conceptual system has to do with

> *the conclusions we draw about our feelings* – our guesses as to what internal events and actions make up emotion as well as the causes and consequences of emotion. Although these beliefs are based on information gleaned from sensory motor and schematic processing, there is no reason to assume that they accurately reflect the mechanisms, responses, eliciting conditions or consequences of emotional processing. (1980:181, italics mine)

If we are considering the standardized secondary labeling and explanatory systems of a cultural group, this means that *there is a sense in which these systems*, as I have claimed for Tahitian schemata about emotions of loss, *may in some transcultural sense be wrong*. These experientially shaped "schemata" (to use Leventhal's terminology) are related to Melford Spiro's idea (Chapter 12, this volume) about the "creation" of the emotions in "processes of social interaction, especially those occurring during early childhood." For Spiro, defining "culture" as "a cognitive system," this process of the "creation of emotion," which once created has various possible relations to "cultural norms," is "precultural."[6]

Once the intense and compelling feeling of emotion arises, with its components involving autonomic nervous system and central nervous system arousal, the processes of secondary evaluation, of cognition per se, begin. Here cultural systems and their private components and versions are centrally influential in naming, classifying, interpreting, directing. How this is done has been a central concern for psychologically oriented ethnography.

VI

I have proposed a sequence in which a primary knowing activates an "emotional feeling," which leads to the mobilization of a secondary kind of knowing (a process that may involve the collaboration of others after some initial response), and I have suggested that the two kinds of knowing differ in regard to the way they are learned and represented in individual minds. I am suggesting that the emotional feeling (more specifically than feeling in general) serves to *mobilize* culture (or, depending on one's basic definitions, a major dominant subsystem of culture), both as an internalized system of representations in response to the problem produced by the feeling and as the responses of others to the manifestations of that feeling. I will return to the implications of this for the theory of culture, but first I want to consider some further (and miscellaneous) implications of the analysis and of the field observations that motivated it.

KNOWING AND NOT KNOWING

In Tahiti, and presumably in other "simple" communities (the reason for the qualification will be noted in the next section), some domains (for Tahiti, anger, shame, and fear, for example) are *hypercognized;* others (for Tahiti, sadness and guilt) are *hypocognized.*[7] Both of these modes can be considered as ways of control, which are culturally standardized and functionally useful – they are ways among others of trying to ensure, as it were, that feelings of, say, hatred or of loss do not disrupt the group. But matters that are "controlled" by not being known and those that are "controlled" by being known in obsessive (and transforming) detail (a detail that also prescribes proper action) imply different kinds of process, with different psychological and social implications. Hypercognition involves a kind of shaping, simplifying, selecting, and standardizing, a familiar function of cultural symbols and forms. It involves a kind of making "ordinary" of private understandings. Hypocognition forces the (first order) understanding into some private mode. Hypocognition is related to such ideas as covert culture and tacit knowledge (Polanyi 1959; Sperber 1974) and to psychodynamic ideas of unconscious and preconscious processes. Questions as to how Tahitian hypocognized domains such as guilt or feelings of loss are represented in individual minds, how they operate in behavior, how, if at all, they are represented in disguised symbolic form, the relation of such covert processes to learning and social control, are, I think, empirical questions that can be studied by the methods of person-centered ethnography.

An examination of events entailing signs of Tahitian nonarticulated feelings of loss (similar general considerations apply to guilt, although there are important differences) indicate that hypocognition, and thus difficulty in representation to self and others, is associated with additional dynamic positive processes of various kinds directed against the generation and clear expression of the emotion. There are group forms and behaviors that serve to minimize the production of the feeling, to disguise it, and to rectify it once it is generated in nascent form. There are indications that the inchoate feelings of loss or guilt when stirred up are *particularly* distressing and immediately mobilize a variety of intrapsychic defenses and external corrective behaviors.

I am not, in regard to these powerful emotions, positing a simple Whorfian situation in which it is sufficient that the un-named cannot be thought. Un-naming is only part, albeit a critical part, of a complex redundant system of social and psychological forms and forces influencing certain behaviors that are systemically significant in the particular sociocultural system (see Levy 1978).[8]

The state of hypocognition and processes of dynamic repression have a systematic and amplifying relationship to each other. That is, if the vicissitudes of, say, "dependency feelings," including real or threatened loss, are disturbing to Tahitians, as I have tried to demonstrate at length in my ethnographic study that they are, their unarticulated, un-namable, and chaotic qualities when they become inadvertently stirred up make them even more disturbing.

COMPARATIVE WAYS OF CONTROLLING EMOTION

I have argued that culturally influenced cognitive evaluation, in responding to the awareness of feeling of a certain quality, acts as a system of control and integration affecting the projects, discharges, and internal readjustments consequent to that feeling and the associated arousal state. This cognitive control works best in what Goffman (1961) has called "total institutions," which include isolated, traditional, simple societies.

But there are other ways of dealing with emotion besides cognitively; much of psychoanalytic theory is involved with this. In a complex society and culture such as that of the Newars of Nepal, where there is, for example, compared with the Tahitian language, an enormous vocabulary (derived from Persian, Sanscrit, Nepali, and various Sino-Tibetan sources), there is a nuanced terminology for expressing and reflecting on almost any emotional possibility. In situations of such complexity, controls do not work primarily through culturally accepted elementary definitions of situations. Types of control systems have to be developed, involving special elaborations of moral controls, dramatic and compelling symbolic processes, and special kinds of internal controls. The question of the specific sociocultural variations in emotion-control methods, which may be related to other aspects of community structure, is still to be investigated.

THE IMPORTANCE OF THE FEELING ITSELF IN THE COGNITIVE EVALUATION

There are two issues here for which comparative data might be of interest. First is the relative weight given to eliciting situations versus the feeling itself in the secondary cognitive evaluation. When a Tahitian says "I knew there must have been a ghost nearby because I had gooseflesh," he is, apparently (with appropriate regard given to rhetoric), evaluating the situation primarily from the feeling. When he says "I knew that what I felt for her was love because she treated me so kindly," he is using the situation as his main reference for evaluation.

The first example brings us to a second question about the relation of feeling to a specific cognitive evaluation, the question of whether the feeling response has in itself a *special shape* that can be read for specific, differential information, that is, whether something more than a generalized arousal is involved. Uncanny emotion seems to have this specific form for Tahitians and is experientially differentiated from, say, abdominal feelings. I did not inquire as to whether my Tahitian informants felt other sensations beyond the abdominal ones, which helped them differentiate anger from, say, fear. One can guess that there were, for example, other feelings that helped them differentiate "desire" and its various subtypes. The question of differential emotional feeling and how it might enter into evaluation could well be investigated in cross-cultural studies.

THE LIMITS ON THE POSSIBILITIES OF CULTURAL DEFINITION

In comparative studies of color naming it seems that color categories in various cultures have the same "central reference"; that is, the colors we recognize as the purest, the ideal yellow, red, green, and so forth, are the same colors that are so named in other cultures, provided they have a name for the category at all. What differs are the boundaries within which the central term (e.g., yellow) applies: the point at which a greenish yellow becomes a yellowish green (Berlin & Kay 1969). Tahitian and Newar data suggest that in some similar fashion the central tendencies named by various emotional terms are probably universal but that the borders of the categories may differ. There are also, as in color naming, situations where two or more categories that are separated in one culture (although they seem in some sense closely related, or semantically "adjacent") are in another not differentiated.

That is, whatever the cultural peculiarities in the relations and associated meanings of Tahitian emotional terms, I had little trouble in recognizing, say, *ri'ari'a* as "fear," *riri* as "anger," *hina'aro* as "desire," *'oa'oa* as "happiness," *ha'ama* as "shame." That is, if an emotion was recognized and named at all, its "central tendency" seemed to be universally human.

However, the boundaries and condensations of categories in Tahiti differ from those in English. Thus, *ri'ari'a* (fear) also includes mild aversion to certain foods. The categories that we differentiate as "embarrassment" and "shame" are named as one category in Tahiti (and widely, perhaps universally, throughout Polynesia) and are also so grouped by the Newars. On the other hand, the subcategories of the various emotional domains are divided in different ways. The Tahitians, for example, distinguish verbally *ri'ari'a*, fear as a present experience ("I am afraid now because the dog is biting me"), from *mata'u*, anticipatory fear ("I fear that the dog might bite me"; "I am afraid of dogs").

THE RELATION OF EMOTIONS TO OTHER ASPECTS OF THE PERSON

This is the consideration of emotions in relation to a broader model of "personality" or "mind," and such relations vary from person to person and from group to group. These questions require the complex descriptions and models of psychologically oriented ethnology. I will here comment briefly on only one illustrative matter, the relation of feeling to action, of emotion to motivation among Tahitian villagers.

Tahitians seem to be comparatively dependent on the strength of emotion (including an inner sense of drive, energy, and enthusiasm) for the performance of a range of tasks. They are anxious and concerned when the inner sense of "enthusiasm" decreases. This seems to be related to the relative weakness of other motives for performance, for example, those related to "guilt." (Perhaps related to this is that Tahitian "depression," as seems to be the case for much of the non Judeo-Christian world, seems to be manifested by apathy and lack of initiative rather than by agitation and self-hatred. It seems to involve problems with the level of arousal, of feeling, rather than in the nature and force of conscience.)

THE EXPRESSION OF EMOTION

Although Tahitians and Newars, like members of all groups with shared traditions, have specific features in their style of emotional expression that can be related to other features of their personal organization and cultural system, I wish here to comment on expressive "universals." Aside from one or two temporarily confusing gestures, expressive behavior in both places was not difficult for me to understand.

Because of a traditional anthropological emphasis on cultural relativism and on the specific coding of communication within various groups, what is now perhaps most interesting about the expression of emotion are those universal features that Ekman (e.g., 1980b) and others have helped to document. Much of this seems to be species-specific, biologically rooted behavior, but I will suggest an additional dimension concerning the cross-cultural comprehensibility of expressive behavior.

Emotionally expressive behavior is both a "symptom" (or "index" in Peirce's terminology) and, with the possible addition of a transforming and purposeful component, a communication to observers.

These expressive/communicative signs include paralinguistic behaviors, which can be said to signal the relation of the speaker to his utterance in the same way that as I noted earlier, emotional behavior in general indicates to observers the relation of an individual to his culturally constituted act. Vocal elements indicate such features of the relation of the speaker to his utterance as irony, direct quotation, doubt, reference to the uncanny (the universal paralinguistics of the telling of ghost stories), and insincerity, as well as the more properly emotional relations – angry, anxious, seductive, depressed, enthusiastic, and so on.

It was thought that, aside from those paralinguistic signs of emotion universally produced by gross organismic influences on the production of speech, other information about the relation of the speaker to his utterance was culturally coded in the same arbitrary way that, for example, *vache* had come to stand for a French cow. In a pioneering study of paralinguistic behavior, *The First Five Minutes*, Pittenger, Hockett, and Danehy asserted that paralinguistic habits "show variation from culture to culture and from region to region. They are as much the product of experience as are one's language habits" (1960, p. 185). But, in fact, once a Westerner has painfully learned the arbitrarily coded semantics and syntax of a non-European language, he has (in my experience) little trouble understanding the relational aspects of the language, its paralinguistic forms. The reason for this is that such relational patterns are "analogically" coded rather than "digitally" coded. In Peirce's language they are "iconic," resembling in some features their referent, rather than "symbolic," that is, arbitrarily related to their referent by convention. Thus, for example, once one knows the standard intonation pattern of a declarative sentence in a particular language, one can recognize the analogical meaning of an *unresolved* intonation that indicates a question and the cautious articulation of the sentence that indicates doubt. It is possible that some of the universals in the expression of emotion in general, not only its vocal features, are "universal" in that they are analogically mediated (instead of by arbitrary code) and can be read by all humans, as well as by many other animals.

VII

CULTURE AND ITS ACQUISITION

I have presented an idealized schema in which (1) someone understands something about his relationship to something or someone else external to himself; followed by (2) an "emotional feeling"; which (3) acts as a signal to mobilize a culturally available program of another kind of understanding and action. The second kind of understanding belongs to the "person," whereas the knowing prior to the emotional feeling is often outside the person, the stuff of spirit possession, of intuition,[9] of mystical knowledge, of Homeric Greek *ate*.

According to Hugh Lloyd-Jones, *ate* to the Homeric Greeks was an "irrational" feeling, idea, or mental state, introduced from outside the person, often by Zeus. "*Ate* sent by Zeus, takes away the *phrenes* (mind, sense) of the person concerned; as a result his *thymos* (impulse, purpose) is rendered uncontrollable, his heart swels with *cholos* (bile, anger) and the knowledge of how to make a right decision which he possesses is rendered ineffective" (1971:23).

Where is culture (and its acquisition) in relation to such a schema? If we consider culture to be a system of control for producing integrated, adaptive, sane behavior, as the basis for "right decision," defined, say, as Freilich's (1980) "guidance system of logically interconnected rules for the production of proper behavior," then the emotional feeling in a sense activates (and sometimes overwhelms) the internalized components of "culture" in an individual, while the understanding prior to the feeling is outside the "person" and outside the "culture," albeit located somewhere in the variously constructed "human mind," or whatever it should be called, that cultures everywhere, as systems of knowledge, as ideologies, as guidance systems, have to deal with.

The cognitive response to an emotional feeling is clearly dependent upon "culture" by anyone's definition. How the rules, taxonomies, names, programs, strategies, ways of searching for and scanning "feedback" cues from others, which constitute the working out of the "affect program," operate and are acquired are general problems involved in the acquisition of any aspect of culture so conceived.[10]

But the understanding that generated the state of emotion that then, in turn, became labeled, understood, and dealt with as *ate* was, I have argued, both (1) a product of diffusely human structures involving some kind of general human understanding of relationship outside those granted by the culturally constitutive systems of knowledge and (2) a local product of regularities of group life which were prior to, and sometimes in opposition to, the definitions of the proper, communicable, sane, systematized "culture" whose function is to bring order out of chaos. This emotion-generating understanding is derived from special kinds of learning and teaching and has a different mental status – it is closer to intuition than to reason. Such understanding, and the meanings informing it, are more difficult for the Greeks, Tahitians, and us to grasp than are the more "rational" systems of the culture (the cognitive anthropologist's delight) and are everywhere of problematic status for the "person" and the "culture."

VIII

In a discussion of an earlier version of this chapter, in response to such phrases as "some kind of general understanding of relationship outside of culture," Clifford Geertz remarked that he did not think that "culture" in its general analytical form is usefully thought of as having an "inside" and an "outside." But it seems to me that the task of any developing cultural anthropologies is to give limits and structure to the anthropological intuition of "culture," to bound it clearly, and/or to designate clear and significant subaspects, structures, and processes within the overall concept. Much confusion ensues when "culture" is used in a sliding way, sometimes for coherent, shared, or interrelated cognitive systems, focusing, integrating, and simplifying the mental and behavioral life of a community (lucky enough to have one of Sapir's "Genuine Cultures") and sometimes for the total local system of historically derived regularities of which the first kind of culture is a subsystem. The nature, extent, and import of "culture" not only varies (both within the anthropological sample and, in contrast, generally left unexamined, between "anthropological places" and modern communities) but probably varies in ways that can be explained. This requires limits and discriminations in our concepts of culture and its subdivisions, and a limited concept can have an outside and an inside. Without such discriminations, a comparative study of "culture" is impossible. One is constrained to endless local exegeses, to atheoretical natural history.

Pace Leach, any close study of individuals in diverse premodern places indicates that *both* the reacting subject and the sociocultural environment are shaped beyond the wildest dreams of Social Anthropology and variously related in different local kinds of person/group transactions. To dissect a universal unproblematic actor out of these local systems may seem useful for a number of ideological and methodological reasons but is, unfortunately, empirically false.[11] The relation between individual mind and culture, between the "dancer and the dance," as Yeats put it, does in fact become Alice's croquet game. But it turns out that there is still a game; it is simply that the problems of analysis (let alone playing it) are much more intricate.

The actor who makes use of the public system of culture is locally shaped, but not in any simple, passive, symmetrical way, by the forms of the adult culture. To turn our attention one last time from Scylla to Charybdis, to seem to imply, as Geertz did in the quotation from *Negara*, that the *same* turn of mind informs both the cultural control system and the passions that respond to it, is to risk loosing the structure and tensions between the different components of "culture" and of "mind."

Notes

Portions of this chapter were presented at a conference on the emotions sponsored by Geissen University and the Werner-Reimers Foundation and have been published in *Social Science Information* 21, Nos. 4/5 (1982) and will be published as a chapter, "The Emotions in Comparative Perspective," in K. R. Scherer and P. Ekman, eds., *Approaches to Emotion* (Hillsdale, N.J.: Erlbaum).

1. Such statements about cultural variation were meant to imply something more than a cultural influence on superficial features. They were meant to imply that the expression of emotions and the arousing circumstances for emotion were radically and deeply constituted by local culture. Paul Ekman's work (e.g, 1980b) on extensive panhuman similarities in the expression of emotions and my present argument suggest limits of various kinds on the depth and power of this constitution by special and unique local forms.

2. All these statements echo the late eighteenth and early nineteenth century "counter-enlightenment" position on the primacy of emotion or feeling in knowing (see Berlin 1981).

3. In previous writings I erroneously used the terms "hypercognated" and "hypocognated."

4. This collaboration of others in the production of an acceptable normative response indicates, as do the details of the individual's response itself, that the static definitional controls of cultural ideologies must be reinforced dynamically in many cases. (For the struggles of readjustment, denial, and restitution, which the support of ideologies about personal loss entail, in Tahiti, see Levy 1973:288–306, and for the redundant and hierarchical controls on angry behavior, see Levy 1978.) I am concerned here with an individual's immediate emotional reaction and its implications for that individual's understanding of the event that produced the emotion. Subsequently, other people begin to react to the manifestations of the emotion in individual ways, which may augment and support the original private response. These responses are essential for understanding the full development of the sequence and its social shaping. They involve the additional problem of how others read and interpret the various kinds of symptoms and signs of the central actor's situation and expressed response. Their cognitive task is in some ways different from his.

5. This primary learning includes (1) what is learned from nonculturally ordered "random" experiences, (2) what is learned from the covert orderings of the culture, and (3) what is learned from attempts to deal with invariant and regular aspects of the physical and social world, their necessary structures, which leads to the universal cognitive orientations and skills, such as those that concerned Piaget.

6. See also Spiro (1980:97), where the issue is the panhuman aspects of "pre-cultural" social interaction, and Spiro (1967), where he considers culturally specific Burmese "pre-cultural" forms in relation to an explanation of the motivations for individuals' belief in the Burmese version of the supernatural.

7. As Silvan Tomkins has pointed out (personal communication), a distinction has to be made between culturally induced hypocognition and the cultural mislabeling of an emotion. Both the cultural nonrecognition of the relational causes of an emotional feeling and a set of substitute explanations, which may or may not be elaborated, are aspects of the same stance toward the emotion-generating situation, namely, denial.

8. Such system considerations are profoundly uncongenial to some cultural anthropologists, but to neglect these dynamic and systematic aspects of social, psychological, and cultural processes *where they exist as revealed in empirical analysis* is to fail to grasp the kinds of processes of coherence that are what give anthropology a legitimate scientific claim.

9. "Intuition" has an interesting Western history. In Milton's *Paradise Lost* intuitive reasoning is most characteristic of the thought of angels, discur-

sive reasoning most characteristic of men. Both kinds of reason, discursive and intuitive, were qualities of the soul: "The soul reason receives, and reason is her being, discursive or intuitive." But the intuitive was closer to the transcendent truth of God. As Alastair Fowler in his note on the relevant passage in *Paradise Lost* (Book V, lines 485–590) remarks: "The distinction between the *intuitive*, simple, undifferentiated operation of the contemplating intellect (*mens*) and the *discursive* or ratiocinative, piece-meal operation of the intellect working in conjunction with the reason (*ratio*) goes back ultimately to Plato. . . . It was customary to connect angels with intellect or intelligence only, and to say that they practiced only the first kind of reasoning" (1971:288).

10. I think it is useful not to talk of the "acquisition of culture" but rather of the "acquisition of protoculture" or some phrase, for what is acquired is something that only becomes "culture" in interaction with other people or with cultural objects. At the individual personal level we are dealing mostly with *part* formations. An individual's representations of aspects of the *whole* culture, his or her "objective" view of dyadic interactions, his or her view of himself or herself as a social object, a person, in that culture are only subsections of internalized "protoculture" in problematic and dynamic interaction with the internalized protocultural forms that he or she embodies and has learned. Furthermore, it is dubious to me that the protocultural forms, say, what two members of a dyad "know," which leads to a cultually acceptable interaction (and this is particularly true of intimate interactions), are "cognitive" in the same way as their "objective" view of how the interaction *should* be structured (their representation of the "culture"). The participants' "objective view" is only one (variable) control aspect of such a culturally regular interaction.

11. I may note summarily here that the Leach position about the fixed, universal, "genetically determined" (as a species, of course) human mind is a maximal version of the protean and slippery doctrine of "the psychic unity of mankind," anthropology's bulwark against racism and the apparent (and misconceived) warrant for the legitimacy of sociological and cultural explanations of exotic behaviors. Note Kroeber's statement that without the doctrine of psychic unity "we should have to consign most of history, anthropology and sociology to the scrap heap and begin over again with a [racial or tribal] psychosomatic genetic interpretation of man and his variety" (1948:573). That is, to talk about some local difference in the reactivity, the mind, the passions of the actor seems to Leach (1) to open the way for invidious racist statements about the essence of the native actor and (2) to produce methodological confusion by making problematic the nature of the actor, which sociological explanation presumes for its regularities. This is not to say that there is not, at some level and in some ways, a "psychic unity of mankind." The human similarities encompassing even the most exotic people is one of the most striking lessons of an anthropologist's experience. But the *nature* of this unity is an empirical question and not to be posited a priori as a methodological or ideological axiom.

References

Berlin, Brent, & Kay, Paul. 1969. *Basic Color Terms: Their Universality and Evolution.* Berkeley: University of California Press.

Berlin, Isaiah. 1981. *Against the Current: Essays in the History of Ideas*. Oxford: Oxford University Press.

Bruner, Jerome, Goodnow, Jacqueline, & Austin, George. 1956. *A Study of Thinking*. New York: Wiley.

Bruner, Jerome, Olver, Rose, & Greenfield, Patricia. 1966. *Studies in Cognitive Growth*. New York: Wiley.

D'Andrade, Roy. 1981. The cultural part of cognition. *Cognitive Science* 5:179–95.

Devereux, George 1979. Fantasy and symbol as dimension of reality. In R. H. Hook, ed., *Fantasy and Symbol*. New York: Academic Press.

DeVos, George, & Hippler, Arthur. 1969. Cultural psychology: comparative studies of human behavior. In Gardner Lindzey, ed., *The Handbook of Social Psychology*, 2nd ed. Reading, Mass.: Addison-Wesley.

Durkheim, Emile. 1915. *The Elementary Forms of the Religious Life*. London: Allen & Unwin.

Ekman, Paul. 1977. Biological and cultural contributions to body and facial movement. In John Blacking, ed., *The Anthropology of the Body*, ASA Monograph 15. London: Academic Press.

　1980a. Biological and cultural contributions to body and facial movement in the expression of emotion. In A. O. Rorty, ed., *Explaining Emotion*. Berkeley: University of California Press.

　1980b. *The Face of Man. Expressions of Universal Emotions in a New Guinea Village*. New York: Garland STPM Press.

Fowler, Alastair, ed. 1971. *Milton. Paradise Lost*, 2nd ed. London: Longman.

Freilich, Morris. 1980. *"Culture" is "proper" not "smart": a conceptualization which makes a difference*. Paper presented at the American Anthropological Association Annual Meeting, Washington, D.C

Geertz, Clifford. 1980. *Negara: The Theatre State in Nineteenth-Century Bali*. Princeton, N.J.: Princeton University Press.

Goffman, Erving. 1961. *Asylums*. Garden City, N.Y.: Doubleday (Anchor).

Grastyan, Endre. 1974. Emotion. In *Encyclopaedia Britannica*, 15th ed.

Hook, R. H. 1979. Phantasy [*sic*] and symbol: a psychoanalytic point of view. In R. H. Hook, ed., *Fantasy and Symbol*. New York: Academic Press.

Izard, Carroll E. 1980. *Emotions in personality and culture*. Unpublished discussion of a panel on Emotions in Personality and Culture, American Anthropological Association Annual Meeting, Washington, D.C.

Kapferer, Bruce. 1979. Emotion and feeling in Sinhalese healing rites. *Social Analysis*, No. 1 (February 1979):153–76.

Kluckhohn, Clyde. 1954. Culture and behavior. In Gardner Lindzey, ed., *Handbook of Social Psychology*. Reading, Mass.: Addison-Wesley.

Kroeber, Alfred H. 1948. *Anthropology*. New York: Harcourt, Brace.

Langer, Suzanne. 1967. *Mind: An Essay on Human Feeling*. Baltimore: Johns Hopkins University Press.

Leach, Edmund. 1981. A poetics of power (a review of Geertz's *Negara*). *New Republic* 184 (April 4, 1981):14.

Leventhal, Howard. 1980. Towards a comprehensive theory of emotion. In L. Berkowitz, ed., *Advances in Experimental Social Psychology*, vol. 13. New York: Academic Press.

LeVine, Robert I. 1973. *Culture, Behavior and Personality*. Chicago: Aldine.

Levy, Robert I. 1969. On getting angry in the Society Islands. In William Caudill and Tsung-Yi Lin, eds., *Research in Asia and the Pacific*. Honolulu: East-West Center Press.

1973. *Tahitians: Mind and Experience in the Society Islands*. Chicago: University of Chicago Press.

1978. Tahitian gentleness and redundant controls. In Ashley Montague, ed., *Learning Non-Aggression*. New York: Oxford University Press.

In preparation. *Mesocosm: Hinduism and the organization of a Newar city in Nepal.*

Lloyd-Jones, Hugh. 1971. *The Justice of Zeus*. Berkeley: University of California Press.

Lutz, Catherine. 1980 *Emotion, ethnopsychology, and parental goals on Ifaluk Atoll*. Unpublished paper, American Anthropological Association Annual Meeting, Washington, D.C.

1982. The domain of emotion words on Ifaluk. *American Ethnologist* 9:113–28.

Mandler, George. 1975. *Mind and Emotion*. New York: Wiley.

Pittenger, Robert E., Hockett, Charles, & Danehy, John. 1960. *The First Five Minutes*. Ithaca, N.Y.: Marineau.

Polanyi, Michael. 1959. *The Study of Man*. Chicago: University of Chicago Press.

Schachtel, Ernest. 1949. On memory and childhood amnesia. In Patrick Mullahy, ed., *A Study of Interpersonal Relations*. New York: Hermitage Press.

Sperber, Dan. 1974. *Rethinking Symbolism*. Cambridge: Cambridge University Press.

Spiro, Melford E. 1967. *Burmese Supernaturalism*. Englewood Cliffs, N.J.: Prentice-Hall.

1980. *Gender and Culture*. New York: Schocken Books.

Tomkins, Silvan S. 1981. The quest for primary motives: biography and autobiography of an idea. *Journal of Personality and Social Psychology* 14:306–29.

Turner, Victor. 1967. *The Forest of Symbols*. Ithaca, N.Y.: Cornell University Press.

Webster, Richard. 1981. Review. London *Observer*, February 1.

White, Geoffrey. 1981. *"Person" and "emotion" in A'ara ethnopsychology*. Paper prepared for the 10th Annual Meeting of the Association for Social Anthropology in Oceania.

9
Getting Angry
THE JAMESIAN THEORY OF EMOTION IN
ANTHROPOLOGY

Robert C. Solomon

> The Tahitians say that an angry man is like a bottle. When he
> gets filled up he will begin to spill over. (Tavana, quoted in Levy
> 1973:285)

The metaphor is so pervasive, it so dominates our thinking about our
feelings, that we find ourselves unable to experience our emotions without it. We find it in philosophy and medicine as well as in our poetry,
and we find it too in other cultures. Consequently, we believe what
the metaphor tells us instead of recognizing it as a metaphor, a cultural
artifact that systematically misleads us in our understanding of ourselves and, in anthropology, our understanding of other peoples.

The metaphor, captured succinctly in the Tahitian simile that an
angry man is like a bottle, is the *hydraulic metaphor*. It presents the
image of emotion as a force within us, filling up and spilling over.
Rendered as science, the same metaphor is made respectable in physiological garb. The medieval physicians theorized at length on the various "humours" that determined the emotions. And in this century,
the metaphor has been elegantly dressed in neurology and presented
as a scientific theory – indeed, the only theory that has thoroughly
dominated the subject over the past century. The theory is that an
emotion is an "inner experience," a "feeling" based on a physiological
disturbance of a (now) easily specifiable kind plus, perhaps, some outward manifestation and an interpretation according to which we identify this feeling as an emotion of a particular kind.

The theory received its classic formulation by William James (1884),
in "What Is an Emotion?" James answered his question with his theory: An emotion is the perception of a visceral disturbance brought
about by a traumatic perception, for example, seeing a bear leap out
in front of you or coming across a bucket filled with blood. The theory
(developed simultaneously by C. G. Lange in Europe) is now appropriately called the "Jamesian (James–Lange) theory of emotion." It
is, I shall argue, as misleading as it is pervasive.

Emotions in anthropology

> Emotions as biological events are the same the world over. (Lind-
> zey 1954; also see 1961)

The Jamesian theory has special appeal, and is particularly damaging, in anthropology. There is an obvious problem, given the nature of the theory. An emotion as an "inner feeling" is unobservable and inaccessible to the anthropologist, thus leaving any attempt at describing emotion in other peoples at the mercy of obviously anthropocentric "empathy." And yet, the theory (scientific or not) has been accepted as apparently useful for interpreting not only the emotional life of other peoples but also the language used by other peoples to describe their own emotions, thus suggesting a kind of double confirmation. The theory – that emotions, as feelings based upon physiological disturbances, can be understood in strictly biological terms – results in this familiar but fallacious consequence: Emotions can therefore be taken to be more or less universal human phenomena, the same in everyone, making allowances for certain minimal differences in physiology and, consequently, temperament. (In fact, I would argue that there is little reason to suppose that such differences or their emotional consequences are minimal, but that is not the thesis I wish to pursue here; see, e.g., Freedman 1974.)

Even if the emotions were essentially the same in all people, however, it is evident that the language and interpretation of emotions, as well as their causes, expressions, and vicissitudes, vary widely from culture to culture. The effects of epinephrine may be identical in angry people from Borough Hall in Brooklyn to the beaches of Bora Bora, but there are, nevertheless, differences in the emotional lives of various peoples, and this is where anthropology enters the picture.

The anthropological appeal of the Jamesian theory is obvious: It divides the phenomenon of emotion into two comprehensive components, a physiological feeling component, which can be presumed a priori (and falsely) to be more or less the same in all human beings, and a cultural component, which can be described by the anthropologist, using the same techniques of observation and interview that are appropriate for almost any other cultural phenomenon. Any mystery surrounding emotion is thus dispelled; the difficulty of "getting inside another person's head," without which one cannot understand another's feelings, is rendered unnecessary. Emotions are to be understood in the realm of physiology, not phenomenology, thus circumventing the hard problem of "empathy." The interpretation of emotions (including the basic interpretive act of naming and identifying one's emotion) is quite distinct from the emotion itself, thus leaving the emotion proper outside the realm of anthropology.

My argument turns on two related objections to the Jamesian theory. First, that the theory is not only incomplete but wholly mistaken. It trivializes, rather than captures, the nature of emotions.[1] Second, the distinction between an emotion and its interpretation is faulty and misleading in a variety of ways. The consequence of these objections is to insist that emotions themselves are the proper province of anthropology. My thesis is that emotions are to be construed as cultural acquisitions, determined by the circumstances and concepts of a partic- ular culture as well as, or rather much more than, by the functions of biology and, more specifically, neurology. There may be universal emotions, but this is a matter to be settled empirically, not by a priori pronouncement.

The variability of emotions

> Take aggression as an example. A distinction must be made be- tween the instrumental acts that are indices of aggression (e.g., hitting, insulting, nonco-operating) and the hypothetical "goal re- sponse" of the aggression motive (perceiving another person's re- actions to injury). It is the latter that one would expect to find transculturally. The aggressor's instrumental activities that serve to hurt someone else – and thus enable him to perceive reactions to injury in his victim – will differ from one culture to another. The form of an insult, for instance, depends on the values held by the insulted one. Or to take another example: automobile racing and football can be instrumental activities for competition only if the society has automobiles and knows how to play football. (Sears 1955)

The cultural specificity and variability of several dimensions of emotion are not in question. For instance, the various causes of emotion are clearly cultural in their specifics (whether or not there are also some causes of some emotions that might be argued to be universal or even "instinctual"). What makes a person angry depends upon those situ- ations or events that are considered offensive or frustrating. A New Yorker will become infuriated on standing in a queue the length of which would make a Muscovite grateful. The same action will inspire outrage in some societies and not others; consider, as examples, failing to shake hands, kissing on the lips, killing a dog, not returning a phone call. The same objects will provoke fear in one culture but not in others, for example, snakes, bewitchment, being audited by the IRS, not get- ting tenure, and being too rich or too thin. Causes of emotion vary from culture to culture; it does not follow that emotions do, or do not, vary as well.

The *names* of emotions clearly vary from culture to culture, along with most vocabulary entries and names for virtually everything else. But this obvious point hides a subtle and troublesome one; how do we know whether it is *only* the names (i.e., phonetic sequences) that vary, rather than their reference? The problem here is what W. V. O. Quine calls "radical intranslatability"; do the words "anger" in English and "*riri*" in Tahitian refer to "the same" emotion? How would we tell? Even if the causes are commensurable and the behavior seems to be similar, how do we gauge the similarity of the emotions? Names of emotions are clearly cultural artifacts, even "arbitrary" in the sense that it is now said as a matter of Paris-inspired cant that "all signs are arbitrary." But the identities of the phenomena that those names name are yet an open question, not obviously the same references for quaintly different vocabularies but clearly not entirely different either. We are, after all, identifying a shared reference to *something*.

A similar point can be made about the various *expressions* of emotion. Clearly some expressions, at least, differ from culture to culture as learned gestures and more or less "spontaneous" actions. Clenched fists are expressions of anger in one culture, not in another. Banging one's head on the wall is an expression of grief in one society, not in others. And the *verbal* expressions of emotion vary not only along with the language (of course) but also according to the familiar images and metaphors of the culture. (Not everyone would understand what we so easily and now clumsily refer to as "heartbroken.") There may well be emotional expressions that vary very little from culture to culture, particularly certain minimal facial expressions, as Paul Ekman (1975) has recently demonstrated. But that there are such universal expressions, if there are any, no more demonstrates the universality or "nature" of emotions than the wide variety of more complex expressions proves the variability of emotions. Again, this must at least start as an open question, for which the observation of emotional expressions may serve at most as a preliminary. Indeed, the more fundamental question – of what are these expressions expressive? – will have to wait for an account of the emotions themselves.

Finally, there is the series of metaphors to be found in almost every culture with any vocabulary of psychological self-description that are essentially explanations and diagnoses of emotions, rather than merely names for them. The Tahitian gentleman quoted at the start of this essay, for example, is expressing a theory, the hydraulic theory, which has long been dominant in discussions of emotion in our culture, too, in part because of (but also culminating in) Freud's "dynamic" and "economic" models of the psyche in terms of various "forces" within. Metaphors and theories of emotion are often related and even interchangeable. They also influence the experience of the emotions themselves. To believe that anger is a force building up pressure is to experience the physiological symptoms of anger as a force "inside," just as believing that "falling in love" is bound to have a certain irresponsible influence on one's loving.

It is a matter of no small interest that the same metaphors – the hydraulic metaphor in particular – can be found in societies of very different temperaments. But such metaphors are by no means universal. Catherine Lutz (1982) describes an emotional vocabulary among the Ifaluk that is relatively devoid of references to the hydraulic metaphor or the Jamesian theory,[2] and the prevalence of the metaphor by no means proves the Jamesian theory to be true. Nevertheless, the variability of emotion metaphors and theories can be counted among the various dimensions of variability of emotion, if, that is, it is true that beliefs about emotions influence or determine the nature of the emotions themselves. (On the Jamesian theory, it is hard to see how or why this should be so; on the alternative view I shall propose at the end of this essay, the mutual influence of beliefs and emotions should be quite transparent.).

Names of emotions do not yet entail metaphors or theories, but even so rudimentary a psychological activity as "naming one's feelings" already stakes out a network of distinctions and foci that are well on their way to extended metaphors and crude theories. The fact that one language has a dozen words for sexual affection and another has fifty words for hostility already anticipates the kinds of models that will be appropriate. A culture that emphasizes what David Hume called "the violent passions" will be ripe for the Jamesian theory, but a culture that rather stresses the "calm" emotions (an appreciation of beauty, lifelong friendship, a sense of beneficence and justice) will find the Jamesian theory and the hydraulic model that underlies it patently absurd. A culture that bothers to name an emotion pays at least some attention to it, and it is hard to find a culture with named emotions that does not also have theories about them, however primitive. In some cases, the theory might consist simply of the warning "anger is dangerous." In theory-enthusiastic cultures such as our own, the theories surrounding an emotion might more resemble the theology of the druids, thus prompting more or less perennial cries about emotional simplicity and "getting in touch with your feelings." But whether the theory at stake is the labyrinth of Jungian typologies or the homilies of Joyce Brothers, the beliefs people have *about* emotions vary considerably, and it remains to be seen just how this reflects – or doesn't reflect – the cross-cultural (and intracultural) variability of the emotions themselves.

(Not) getting angry: two examples

"My intestines were angry." (quoted in Levy, 1973:214)

Anger is an emotion that would seem to be universal and unlearned if any emotion is, however different its manifestations in various cultures. John Watson chose anger as one of his three "basic" emotions (fear and dependency were the other two). It is one of those emotions most evident even in infants, and Watson suggested that it is one of the building blocks for all other emotions. More recently, Robert Plutchik (1962) has developed an evolutionary model of emotions and emotional development in which anger, again, emerges as one of the (this time eight) basic building blocks of emotion. Anger is one of the most easily observable emotions; we might debate its nuances (outrage or indignation) and perhaps surmise its etiology (jealousy, frustration, or moral offense). The causes of anger might differ from culture to culture, and the expressions, at least the verbal expressions, might vary too. But it is too easy to assume that anger itself and its basic manifestations – the reddened face, visible irritability and what William James properly called "the tendency to vigorous action" – are much the same from the Philippines to the Lower East Side, from Bongo Bongo to the more boisterous committee meetings of the Social Science Research Council. Everyone gets angry – at least at some time and for some reason. Or so it would seem.

But let us consider two quite different accounts of anger, in two quite different societies. I want to discuss later in this chapter some of the methodological problems to which any such account is subject. But, as a first, superficial observation, let us make clear certain gross differences – or at least claims about certain gross differences – in two cultures: the Tahitian (Levy 1973) and the Utka (Utkuhikhalingmiut) Eskimos (Briggs 1970) in the Northwest Territories. In both cases, these people do not get angry. Some of this may be emphasis rather than substance, but that too constitutes a significant difference in emotional life. It might be argued, for instance, that Americans give far more importance to the emotions of anger and moral indignation than do the Russians or Japanese, for example, whether or not the emotions themselves are so significantly different. But having pointed out this difference in emphasis, have we not already indicated vast differences in temperament and emotional constitution as such? For both the Tahitians and the Utka, however, anger is as rare as it is feared.

The Tahitians, according to Levy, place an unusual amount of emphasis on anger. They talk about it and theorize about it extensively; it is "hypercognized," he tells us, in that "there are a large number of culturally provided schemata for interpreting and dealing with anger." (See Chapter 8, this volume.) Other emotions, sadness, for instance, are "hypocognized" and, Levy suggests, virtually unrecognized. Anger, however, is rare, no matter how much the object of concern. Does this mean, however, that it is indeed present but unaccounted for or, rather, that in circumstances in which *we* (for example) would most certainly have an emotion, they do not?

A partial answer to this crucial question can be couched in terms of the Tahitian theory of emotion, which is distinctively Jamesian. Emotions have a "place" in the body, the intestines, for example. Indeed, the language of emotion is often "it" rather than "I," although one must quickly add that this grammatical feature of the Tahitian language is not to be found only in the realm of emotions (Levy 1973:213) He quotes an informant:

> "In my youth, [it was] a powerful thing, very powerful, very powerful 'it' was [*sic*], when it came, and I tried to hold it down
>   there was something that was not right. That was the cause
> ot a lot of bad anger inside one . . . after a time . . . that thing,
> 'it' would go away." (ibid., p. 212)

Levy adds that "people will say 'my intestines were angry'" (ibid., p.213). This locution may seem slightly odd but certainly not unfamiliar; it indicates, however, a much deeper difference between our conception of anger and the Tahitian conception and, consequently and more important, a deep difference between Tahitian anger and our own.

Throughout the literature on Tahiti, Levy tells us, one message above all keeps repeating itself: "These are gentle people" and there are "extremely few reports of angry behavior." Morrison noted two centuries ago that the Tahitians are "slow to anger and soon appeased" (in Levy 1973:275). Levy quotes a contemporary policeman who talks of "the lack of a vengeful spirit" (ibid., p. 276), and though Levy reports some forty-seven terms referring to anger, he adds that the Tahitian concern with, and fear of, anger and its violent effects are "in the face of little experience of such anger" (ibid., p. 285). The pairing of so much attention and theorizing with so rare an emotion points to a curious relationship between the having of an emotion and the understanding of it, but it is clear from Levy's descriptions and reports that this relationship is *not* to be construed (as we might be likely to construe it in ourselves) as one of "suppression" or social "control" as such. It is the gentleness, the lack of anger itself that seems to be learned, not the inhibition or suppression of it. And part of this learning experience, ironically, is the acquisition of an enormous number of myths and metaphors about anger through which this rather rare emotion is explained – and feared.

In Jean Briggs's (1970) descriptions of the Utka Eskimos, they do not, as her title *Never in Anger* indicates, get angry, Not only do they not express anger; they do not "feel" angry, and, unlike the Tahitians, they do not talk about it. They do not get angry in circumstances that would surely incite us to outrage, and they do not get angry in other circumstances either. The Utka do not have a word or set of graded distinctions for anger, as we do and as the Tahitians do; indeed, the word with which they refer to angry behavior in foreigners and in children is also the word for "childish." There is no reason to suppose that, biologically, the Utka have any fewer or more impoverished epinephrine secretions than we do, and Dr. Briggs's descriptions show that, on occasion, they get just as "heated up" as we do. But they do not get angry, she assures us. They do feel annoyed, even hostile, and they can display raw violence, for example, in the beating of their dogs (in the name of "discipline," of course). But is this to be considered merely a nuance of terminology? Or something more significant?

There have been some severe objections to the observations and conclusions of this research, but the central claim remains intact, at least by way of a plausible hypothesis not yet refuted. Michelle Rosaldo (Chapter 5, this volume), for instance, has argued that Briggs confuses lack of anger with fear of anger, the sense – to be found in Tahitian society as well as in Filipino society and in our own – that anger is dangerous and can even destroy a society. But here again, we meet that suspicious and too-neat distinction between the essence of the emotion itself and talk *about* emotion, as if it can be assumed that the emotion remains more or less constant while our thoughts and feelings about the emotion alter its expression and its representation. But even if Briggs is wrong about the absence of anger as such, the context of that emotion and the peculiar absence of (what we would consider) the usual expressions and manifestations of it would have to be explained.

The problem of methodology

I see no reason to suppose that our wondering about the nature(s) of emotional states is any different, epistemologically, from our wondering about the nature of many seemingly natural kinds of phenomona. (Rey 1980)

What warrants an anthropologist's attributing emotions of a specific sort to persons in a very different society? We have already pointed out the obvious need to make allowances for differences in vocabulary and expression, differences in context and cause, differences in theories of emotion and etiology, as well as possible differences in etiology itself. But, assuming that an anthropologist with rapport can see through such differences, how can he or she refer with confidence to Jamesian feelings, themselves unseen and unseeable? A few years ago, in his *Rise of Anthropological Theory*, Marvin Harris expressed shock and professional outrage at the "horrifying confidence" of his colleague Margaret Mead in identifying the emotions of her Samoan subjects. Indeed, where should such confidence come from? Is there any justification for confidence in such matters at all?

Dr. Briggs, a *kapluna* (white foreigner) among Utka, is sensitive to such problems

Conscious of the pitfalls of misperception to which such a personal approach is subject, I shall try throughout to distinguish explicitly among the various kinds of data on which my statements are based and not to extrapolate from my own feelings to those of Utku without cautioning the reader that I am doing so. I hope, moreover, to present the material vividly enough so that the reader sharing to some extent my cultural background [middle-class, urban, Protestant New Englander], can also experience empathy and contrasts between his feelings and those of Utku. (1970:6).

But the key, despite the caution, is "empathy," and although Dr. Briggs succeeds in her "vivid" presentation, the problem remains: How is she (or are we) justified in understanding Utku feelings (or lack of feelings) on the basis of what she observes? How will she know, on the basis of their varied expressions, that the difference is one of emotion rather than merely expression? For example, she describes one of the dominant personalities of the group, Inuttiaq, in the following way:

Inuttiaq was, if I have read him correctly, an unusually intense person. He, too, kept strict control of his feelings, but in his case one was aware that something was being controlled. The effort of this control was caught in the flash of an eye, quickly subdued, in the careful length of a pause, or the painstaking neutrality of a reply. Occasionally, when he failed to stay within the acceptable bounds of expression, I learned from the disapproval of others what behavior constitutes a lapse and how disapproval is expressed. (1970:42)

Of the other Utku, she says, they "were so well controlled that my untutored eye could not detect their emotions" (p. 42). The problem should be evident. Here she is quite obviously talking about differences in the *expression of emotion*, not the emotion itself. To the contrary, she is openly recognizing the emotion beneath the controlled responses. This thesis, if it is all that is meant by "never in anger," is not enough to cast doubt on the universality of anger, nor does it seem to support the view that the Utku are emotionally different in any interesting way from ourselves. But how does the anthropologist read beyond the expressions to the emotion to suggest that something is being suppressed or to deny, as the stronger thesis would require, that the Utku do not get angry? How does one legitimately move from what is observed (the expression) to what cannot be observed (the emotion)? Can one do anything other than "extrapolate from [one's] own feelings to those of Utku" (p. 42), however cautiously?

Let me raise the problem, as philosophers are prone to do, to the level of an explicit paradox: The thesis or hypothesis under consideration is the alleged difference between Utku emotion and our own, particularly regarding emotions like anger. But insofar as the anthropologist assumes that she is capable of understanding the emotional expressions of her subjects, that is, understanding them as expressions of particular emotions, then she must assume from the outset precisely the hypothesis to be verified, namely, that different people have, and can mutually understand, essentially the same emotions. Insofar as empathy plays a role in these investigations, however cautiously, the paradox remains intact. But if the anthropologist gives up empathy as a tool, what can be left, other than a flat behavioral description of emotional expressions into which one is not allowed to "read" or "extrapolate" any emotions at all?

Jamesian "feelings"

Suppose an anthropologist, having had one too many lunches with a philosophical colleague, came to have the following doubts:

Observing some subjects in Bongo-Bongo (the only nonurban anthropological site easily accessible to most philosophers), he or she observed that certain people at certain times appeared to be scratching. Or at any rate, that would be the loose, dubious description. The tighter, more operational description would be that they made certain movements at certain times. A rather more suspicious description – of the sort that recalls Marvin Harris's (1968:410) utter horror in regard to Margaret Mead's confidence in identifying the inner states of others, would be that they are scratching an itch. The philosophical caution is the following: Given that all that one can observe is the overt behavior, how can one infer the nature of the "inner" states? In this case, presumptively, an itch. And for the anthropologist, though perhaps not for the philosopher, there are methodological restrictions of a troublesome kind: He or she cannot take at face value the descriptions or reports of the people themselves nor trust the words that are used to supposedly translate the name of one feeling to another.

There is no problem here, one might suppose, because itches and scratching, at least, are bound up together in a physiological package that is wired into the species, indeed, not only the species, and there seems no more room for serious (that is, extraphilosophical) doubt that a dog or a cat itches when it scratches than there is for the doubt that a foreign subject itches when he or she scratches. The experience, as well as the behavior, can be ascribed with confidence. To make matters slightly more complex, suppose that these certain people believe that itching is a sign of bewitchment, or, turning to the mythopathology of our own society, suppose a frequent sunbather believes, on the basis of continuous media reports, that itching is a certain sign of skin cancer. Can we continue to say with the same assurance that what he or she feels is the "same" feeling that we feel? One might suppose that, yes, the feeling – that is, the itch – is the same but that the *interpretation* is different. Perhaps, but how does one pry the interpretation from the feeling, at least in the occurrent view of the person who is feeling it? Suppose that because the neurological wiring and chemistry are the same (*if* they are the same, which is by no means a closed question), there is some feeling, the itch, that is common to the various cases and equally inferable in each case of scratching. If we compare the itch that I have, which is merely annoying, to the itch of the bewitched or the forewarned, it would still seem that we would want to say that the inference from their behavior – which would presumably involve much more than scratching – is a matter of interpretation with which it may be extremely difficult to empathize. And it is certainly no mere matter of biology and its sensational consequences.

Philosophers might push the argument one step further: Whatever the interpretation of the itch, one could argue, there remains the itch. But Wittgenstein long ago publicized his ill-formulated "private language argument," suggesting that the identification of such "inner" feelings could (logically) be based only upon overt behavior; the feeling itself, he told us, with poetic rather than philosophical insight, was "a wheel that played no part in the mechanism." One might then say that the interpretation is everything; it defines the itch even for the itcher-scratcher as well as for the observing anthropologist.

Emotions, quite obviously, have a physiological basis, though not always the violent visceral disturbance emphasized in the Jamesian theory. But emotions do have typical manifestations in our feelings, based on physiological occurrences. Are these sets of feelings, as James argued, the emotion? From the argument concerning so distinctive a feeling as an itch, it should be evident that the feelings present in emotion, which are not nearly so specific and are often very difficult to identify, cannot alone qualify as the emotion, whether or not one wants to argue that they are an essential ingredient in emotion.

An emotion is not a feeling (or a set of feelings) but an *interpretation*. Sometimes it is an interpretation of a feeling, but not usually so, and when it is, it is often so under the influence of the Jamesian theory. Thus Levy's Tahitians are Jamesian precisely in their insistence that it is their feelings that constitute the emotions they then interpret, as Levy himself is a Jamesian in his acquiescence to their distinction between the intestinal basis of anger and "cognitive" reflection of it. But the distinction between an emotion and its reflective interpretation is not so clear, precisely because an emotion is already a good deal of interpretation. Thus Levy cautiously limits much of his discussion of Tahitian anger to Tahitian conversations *about* anger, whereas Briggs, less cautiously, draws conclusions about her subjects' emotional life even while expressing doubts about the possibility of doing so. But both approaches display the deep problem raised by the Jamesian division between the emotion (as inner feeling) and the interpretations thereof: That the emotion itself is rendered unobservable and quite outside the province of the anthropologist perhaps leads also to the absurd, skeptical conclusions suggested by the Wittgensteinians. There is a way to escape such conclusions, but it involves a radical rethinking about the nature of emotion. It means that an emotion cannot be, in any interesting sense, a feeling. If the wheel so easily drops out of the mechanism, we might well conclude that it never played an essential role in the first place.

The cognitive theory of emotions: emotions as cultural artifacts

Not, only ideas, but emotions too, are cultural artifacts. (Geertz 1973:81)

. . . complete rubbish. (Leach 1981)

One need not challenge the obvious – that strong emotions such as rage, at least, include a predictable physiological reaction and its sensory consequences – to reject the Jamesian model in all its forms. An emotion is not primarily a physiological reaction *cum* sensations, with whatever embellishments and consequences. A strong emotion may well have as its predictable secondary effects the bodily responses that James identified as primary, but this is neither necessary nor always the case. It has long been argued (see, e.g., Cannon's 1927 reply to

James) that the same physiological reactions might be induced without any emotion whatever, that longer term emotions (e.g., long-standing anger) need not ever "explode" into a physiologically measurable response (though usually it does), and, more subtle but most important, that the physiological reaction itself is virtually never sufficient to distinguish one emotion from another, even in a gross way (anger versus jealousy or hatred but certainly not anger versus irritation or moral indignation). Anger is not just a physiological reaction *cum* sensation *plus* an interpretation, a cause and certain forms of behavior. It is *essentially* an interpretation, a view of its cause (more accurately, its "object") and (logically) consequent forms of behavior. By way of putting disagreement aside, one might yield the point that there is also, as a matter of causal uniformity, a physiological reaction and sensations, although the stronger thesis, which I will argue elsewhere, is that these are samplings from a faulty paradigm, the too exclusive focus on "urgent" emotions in emergency situations, which, quite naturally, involve bodily responses appropriate to such emergencies. But to be angry over a long period of time is certainly not to be any less angry, nor is it to be construed as a discontinuous sequence of angry reactions connected by a dispositional description. The anger *is* the interpretation plus the view of a cause (as well as the "object" of emotion) and consequent behavior. That anger also has biological backing and includes sensation is inessential to understanding the emotion, though no doubt significant in certain measurements, which only *contingently* correlate with the intensity of an emotion or its significance.

The thesis I am invoking here generally goes by the title "a cognitive theory of emotions." The strong version, which I support but am not arguing here, is that an understanding of the conceptual and learned appetitive functions of emotion is all that there is in identifying and distinguishing them from each other and from non-emotions; the weaker version, which is all that I am invoking here, is that an understanding of the conceptual and learned appetitive structures of emotion is sufficient for identifying them and distinguishing them from each other and from non-emotions. An emotion is a system of concepts, beliefs, attitudes, and desires, virtually all of which are context-bound, historically developed, and culture-specific (which is not to foreclose the probability that some emotions may be specific to *all* cultures). What we call an emotion is an important function of that part of our emotional life, and so is what we think of it and how we treat it. Here is the problem when the distinction between emotion and interpretation of (and talk about) emotion is too sharp: Both are interpretations, and the same concepts often enter into the structure of each. Being angry may be one thing; questioning the legitimacy of one's anger something else. But the crucial concepts (e.g., of legitimacy, blame, or responsibility) are just as much a part of the anger as they are a part of the questioning. If we had no concept of *righteous* anger, there would be no intelligibility, much less any point, to debating the legitimacy of anger, whether in this case or in general. Anger *is* a kind of interpretation, not of a feeling (which may or may not be co-present) but *of the world*. It is, one might say, not an "inner" phenomenon so much as a way of being-in-the-world, a relationship between oneself and one's situation.

Getting angry, for example, is not a matter of an inner experience – a feeling caused by a physiological disturbance that is, in turn, caused by a disturbing perception. There is, to be sure, an experience, and it may, but need not, be accompanied by certain characteristic physical sensations. But the experience of anger is an experience of interpreting the world in a certain way and is precisely summarized by Lewis Carroll in *Alice in Wonderland*, as a matter of fact:

I'll be judge, I'll be jury,
Said cunning old fury.

Anger, in other words, is essentially a *judgmental* emotion, a perception of an offense (as Aristotle argued in *Rhetoric*). It consists of a series of concepts and judgments that among other ingredients, involve the concept of *blame*. Getting angry is making an indictment (whether overtly or not). It involves concepts and evaluations that are clearly learned and, in their specifics, learned only in the context of a particular society with certain kinds of ethical views and theories. Again, this is not to deny that one might find anger (or some similar emotion) in every society, but the evidence seems to suggest that this is not the case. At any rate, also again, this should remain an open question for cross-cultural inquiry, not an a priori supposition based on the erroneous Jamesian theory of emotion.

The cognitive theory of emotions takes emotions to be composed (at least as their essential structure) of cognitions – concepts, perceptions, judgments, beliefs. But not only are (most of) these cognitions learned in a particular cultural context. They are themselves *public* phenomena, in the same sense that language and knowledge are public phenomena. One can mutter sentences to oneself in private, and one might well know what no one else does, but the shared concepts and cognitive structures that allow for mutual understanding also make possible the sentences and the knowledge in the first place. So too with emotions. Privacy may be a practical problem for the anthropologist, but it is not a logical problem. Feelings may be private in exactly the philosophically troublesome sense, but emotions are not. We might not understand a particular case of anger. ("Why are you angry about your winning a Jaguar in the lottery?") We might not understand the intensity of anger. ("Why kill him just because he looked at you oddly?") We might not understand the absence of anger. ("How could you let him do that to you, and not even care?") But these failings are in every case open to explanation, whether or not that explanation is acceptable or rational. What we do not find is a case of emotion, certain romantic pretensions aside, that is so different, so personal, so individual, that no one else could understand it or share it, if only the circumstances, the concepts, and the evaluations involved were known.

This becomes enormously complicated when the other person involved is from a different culture, with a language and a life we do not share. But the paradox, remember, was formulated not with just cross-cultural descriptions in mind but for *any* attempt to understand emotions in others, even one's husband or wife or best friend. Deflating the paradox, we now find the ascription and description of emotions in others on epistemologically firmer ground, problematic, perhaps, but not logically impossible. We want to know whether the word (Tahitian *riri*) is used in precisely the same contexts and with the same reference and significance as our own word (anger). But if there is no inaccessible private reference, then this problem is just part of the general translation problem in anthropology and no more difficult (but no easier either) than translating religious or domestic language whose references are attitudes and circumstances rather than concrete objects and actions. We have to be able to compare and contrast attitudes and circumstances, and this, in turn, already presupposes some familiarity with the language and views of the community. Our observation of behavior helps establish this familiarity, but, of course, informed observation already requires some sense of the proper interpretation of behavior, which presupposes some knowledge of the attitude and circumstances of the community, as well as some sense of the emotional life of the people. To understand an emotion, in other words, one must understand much more about a person or a people than their behavior in an isolated incident. It may be reasonable to suppose that a man who gnashes his teeth and shakes his fist – after he has been sideswiped by an ox – is angry. But that supposition is reasonable only insofar as we assume that he shares a substantial set of concepts with us; this is not always reasonable, and it is often incomplete.

Indeed, where emotions are in question, this is the essential point, for it has too long been presumed that emotions, unlike the more clearly cultural acquisitions of the community, have their own "inner" independent existence, based on biology and individual eccentricity, perhaps, but isolated from, and not to be understood in terms of, the rest of the culture, its language, and concepts. But what the cognitive theory of emotions implies and requires is that the concepts that make up virtually all emotions are essentially tied to the community and its conceptual apparatus. One cannot leap from the observation that we share *some* of the concepts constituting anger with another people to the conclusion that we share them *all*, that is, share the same emotion. One learns to identify the emotional life of a people along with learning everything else, including, not least, what they *say* about their own emotional life. But this is not a matter of taking their self-descriptions at face value (a suspicious business, in any case). It is rather understanding that what people say about their emotions and what they actually feel, though not precisely correlated (as Levy's Tahitians show so dramatically), are part of the same cultural, conceptual package.

It was Suzanne Langer, I believe, following the long tradition back to Rousseau and Hume, who suggested that the distinction of the human species was not so much reason as certain sorts of emotion and sentimentality. Thomas Hobbes, only partly in that tradition, pointed out that whereas animals might appreciate "damage," only humans had any sense of "injury." But this tangential wrinkle in the perennial dispute between reason and the passions can be settled – as all aspects of that dispute can be settled – by seeing that we are not here dealing with two dramatically different parts of the human soul but a single (not always integrated) system of concepts and attitudes, some of which enter into our calculations but most of which are built right into our immediate perception and conception of the world, seeing things, events, people, and actions as ugly or odious, offensive or enviable, lovable or admirable. But not only *what* these things, events, people, and actions may be, but the conceptions themselves, vary from culture to culture, community to community (whether or not from person to person within a community). The more obvious fact is that the causes, circumstances, and expressions, as well as the vocabulary of emotion, vary from place to place. The less obvious fact, in part because of the popularity of the Jamesian theory, is that emotions may vary from place to place as a matter of *kind*. The emotions may have a physiological-sensory base, but very little of anthropological interest follows from this. The fact (if it is a fact) of trans-species physiological similarity no more points to the uniformity of emotions than the universality of thirst points to uniformity in drinking habits from Dublin to Pago Pago. Emotions are conceptual constructions, and as go the concepts, so go the emotions as well.

Conclusion: emotions, concepts, and culture

The affective component of human information processing appears to be deeply imbedded in cultural representations . . . What advertising tries to do with problematic success, culture does with great effectiveness. (D'Andrade, Chapter 3, this volume)

My purpose in this limited essay has been to deflate (once more) a popular but pernicious theory of emotions, and with it, an old and vicious dichotomy between intellect and emotion. To develop the constructive thesis that emerges from this, it would be necessary to turn to a piece by piece investigation of the concepts that make up our various emotions and their complex permutations, side by side with more holistic investigations of a number of other societies, such as those offered us by Levy (1973) and Briggs (1970). The flat-footed question "Do these people get angry or not, and if so under what circumstances?" would be replaced by a broader inquiry into the overall evaluative-conceptual schemes of appraisal and self-identification that give structure to emotional life, including especially such concepts as blame and praise, status and responsibility, and all those other concepts that are so much a part of anthropological investigation but not, usually, a part of the analysis of emotions, except, perhaps, as an aspect of their causes or interpretations. But variation in emotional life is a very real part of cross-cultural differences and not only in the more obvious variations in circumstances and expression. Or at any rate, this should be an open question for investigation and not an a priori pronouncement based on an unacceptable philosophical theory. Indeed, Clifford Geertz has described anthropology as the desire to understand what it is to *be* a member of another culture. If emotions are ruled out of the investigation or simply assumed to be all alike, it is hard to imagine what content that desire might have or whether anthropology could give it any satisfaction at all.

Notes

This chapter was stimulated by the Social Science Research Council meeting in May 1981 on Concepts of Culture and Its Acquisition. Special thanks to Richard A. Shweder for his helpful criticism and encouragement. A portion of the "methodology" section has been adapted from my "Emotions and Anthropology" (*Inquiry* 21 [1978]:181–99), with the generous permission of the editors.

1. This has often been argued, and I shall not repeat the primary arguments here; see Solomon 1976, chap. 7; 1978.
2. It is worth noting, however, that the criterion used for distinguishing emotion words in Ifaluk was whether or not they were identified as "about our insides," despite the argument that "the Ifaluk see the emotions as evoked in, and inseparable from, social activity" rather than "internal feeling states" (Lutz 1982:114, 124).

References

Briggs, Jean L. 1970. *Never in Anger*. Cambridge, Mass.: Harvard University Press.

Cannon, W. B. 1927. The James-Lange theory of emotion. *American Journal of Psychology* 39:106–24.

Ekman, Paul. 1975. *Unmasking the Face*. Englewood Cliffs, N.J.: Prentice-Hall.

Freedman, D. G. 1974. *Human Infancy*. Hillsdale, N.J.: Erlbaum.

Geertz, Clifford. 1973. The growth of culture and the evolution of mind. In C. Geertz, *The Interpretation of Culture*. New York: Basic Books.

Harris, Marvin. 1968. *The Rise of Anthropological Theory*. New York: Crowell.

James, William. 1884. What is an emotion? *Mind* 9:188–205.

Langer, Suzanne. 1953. *Feeling and Form*. New York: Scribner.

Leach, Edmund. 1981. A poetics of power (a review of Geertz's *Negara*). *New Republic* 184 (April 4, 1981):14.

Levy, Robert I. 1973. *Tahitians*. University of Chicago Press.

Lindzey, Gardner. 1954. *Psychology*. Cleveland: Worth.
1961. *Projective Techniques and Cross-Cultural Research*. New York: Appleton-Century-Crofts.
Lutz, Catherine. 1982. The domain of emotion words in Ifaluk. *American Ethnologist* 9:113–28.
Mead, Margaret. 1958. Cultural determinants of character. In A. Roe & G. Simpsom, eds., *Culture and Behavior*. New Haven, Conn.: Yale University Press.
Plutchik, Robert. 1962. *The Emotions*. New York: Random House.
Rey, Georges. 1980. Functionalism and the emotions. In Amelie Rorty, ed., *Explaining Emotions*. Berkeley: University of California Press.
Sears, Robert R. 1955. Transcultural variables and conceptual equivalence. In Bert Kaplan, ed., *Studying Personality Cross-Culturally*. Evanston, Ill.: Row, Peterson.
Solomon, Robert C. 1976. *Passions*. New York: Doubleday.
1978. Emotions and anthropology. *Inquiry* 21:181–99.

PART III
Culture, language, and thought

10
The development of competence in culturally defined domains
A PRELIMINARY FRAMEWORK

Howard Gardner

Whether it be the niches assumed by individual members of a royal family or the more democratic choice among "butcher, baker and candlestick maker," every culture features a set of roles that must be filled by individuals in each generation and then passed on from one generation to the next. Some roles, such as those of a tribal chief or a singer of tales, are so specific that they are filled by only a single person or a handful of individuals: Others, such as a mother or a friend, are widely held positions, which can be assumed by a large proportion of the population. In addition to individually prescribed roles, each culture values certain competences that must be mastered by at least some members of each generation: One could cite the American preoccupation with technological expertise, the Japanese valuation of social finesse, the Balinese concern with artistic achievement. Some of the skills required for fulfilling these roles or mastering these competences contribute to survival in a direct sense, whereas others provide the less tangible, but equally important, sinew that allows a culture to function smoothly. Failure to acquire the relevant roles or skills severely limits the realization of the potential of an individual, a group, or the overall culture.

In this chapter I propose a framework for conceptualizing how various cultural competences might be transmitted from one generation to the next. In a manner of speaking, I attempt to bring to bear upon the agenda of culture (as formulated by Tylor and his successors) certain assumptions and tools of developmental psychology (as propounded by Piaget and his collaborators).

Given the centrality in social science of concepts of human development, the desirability of a theory of the acquisition of culture may seem self-evident; and, indeed, many scholars have perceived the relevance of this set of issues. Yet the amount of progress made on such issues as how an individual learns to be (or becomes) a king or a singer of tales, a mother or a friend, a skilled engineer, diplomat, or painter is distressingly scanty. Why we know so little about these issues is perhaps worth a moment's consideration.

Certainly, there has been considerable progress within the area of developmental psychology in explicating how individuals attain various cognitive and communicative skills. We have learned much about the acquisition of certain key facets of logical-rational thought, of language, and of other symbolic systems. But given the empirical, task-oriented nature of most developmental psychology, it has proved difficult for workers in this tradition to tackle the more pervasive, but more elusive, themes, topics, styles, and values that come to the fore in formulations of culture. Developmental psychologists lack a sense (and a method) of how to investigate the attainment of a competence (as in the political sphere) or a role (like that of a friend). At an extreme, there may be skepticism about whether such broad, vague, and inherently elusive aspects of culture are really a fit topic for scientific work.

From their perspective, anthropologists have no difficulty in affirming the reality of culture: In fact, the "super-organic" constitutes the keystone of their discipline. However, so pervasive is culture that there is resistance to the notion that it can ever have been absent from the life of the individual. Accordingly, there is a paradox in the notion of acquiring culture; for culture is as much (and as inviolate) a part of the child's surroundings as the air that he breathes or the talk that he hears. If one adds to this a suspicion of task-oriented investigations (with their risks of ethnocentrism) and a parallel resistance to the fragmentation, atomism, and reductionism all too often associated with empirical psychology, it becomes less mysterious why a program that investigates the acquisition of culture is considered risky by many in the anthropological camp.

To be sure, there have been many studies relevant to the acquisition of culture, from the camps of both developmental psychology and cultural anthropology: Much of the work done in the psychoanalytic and personality-and-culture schools may be thought of as contributions to a model of the acquisition of culture (Erikson 1963; Gorer 1948; Kardiner 1945; Kluckhohn & Murray 1953). It is worth noting, however, that most of this work is focused on the domains of personality and affect, that is, on the question of how individuals develop as single persons rather than on how they develop as productive and interacting members of their respective cultures. What has received much less attention are the processes by which individuals develop cognitive competences – those skills and modes of thinking requisite for assuming various roles in the technological and economic spheres of their society. In a way, this lack is not surprising, for, after all, an explicit concern with cognition has been only a recent trend in psychology and an even later arrival on the anthropological scene. Yet it is my own view (and hence, a burden of this essay) that many of the deepest insights about the acquisition of culture can only be attained if one examines the various cognitive skills that individuals accrue over a lifetime.

Devising a framework

To lay out a full-blown theory of the acquisition of culture is clearly beyond the ken of any contemporary researcher. Not only do we lack the empirical information about how these processes develop in various corners of the world, but we do not even possess an appropriate categorical scheme for confronting and analyzing the issues. Hence, the more modest, but still formidable, goal of the current exercise is to lay out a framework for thinking about the ingredients involved in acquiring competence in various cultural domains. Given the current state of knowledge in psychology and my own predilections this exercise will have an unmistakably cognitive bias. A second purpose of the chapter is to invoke certain findings, concepts, and insights from the field of developmental psychology that might eventually guide efforts to develop a field of study devoted to the acquisition of culture.

To make this project viable, it is necessary to make certain basic assumptions. The initial, if controversial, assumption is that culture need not be approached as a single, inviolate, and undifferentiable whole. Instead, it makes sense, at least for heuristic purposes, to divide culture into a number of discrete domains, each of which can be separately analyzed while still avoiding the fate of Humpty-Dumpty.

Delineation of domains involves judgments and flexibility. Domains can be relatively broad, for example, the cognitive versus the social domain, or far more specific, the domain of the algebraist, the nuclear physicist, or the flutist. The crucial point being urged is this: One may legitimately ferret out a particular area of accomplishment within a culture, describe the desired end state of a competent adult member of a culture, and then commence the exercise of defining various steps or stages en route to the attainment of an end state of competence. Such a "domain approach" assumes that, initially,the young organism within the society has but a nascent or imperfect competence within the domain, but that, given exposure to examples of cultural competence and perhaps explicit training as well, the young child has the potential of acquiring successively higher degrees of skills. I might note that this assumption now guides much work in the social sciences, including investigations by individuals who believe that the acquisition of various competences is largely a genetically determined process, such as Chomsky; those who believe that competence is basically a learned process, such as the behaviorists; and those who favor an intrinsically interactive approach, such as Piaget and most developmental psychologists (see Piatelli-Palmarini 1980). And indeed, one may adhere to these other quite divergent points of view and still join in an effort to describe the acquisition of cultural competences.

In addition to these assumptions about the existence and autonomy of different domains of competence, our effort to lay out a theory of cultural acquisition will require a consideration from four different perspectives or vantage points, which I'll reify for present purposes. The first two vantage points may be considered diametrically opposed to one another. At one extreme, there is the *culture* as a whole, with its domains, beliefs, and values, which have evolved over many years. This historical and geographical unit provides the agenda of what needs to be acquired by individuals within the culture. At the other extreme is the *individual*, equipped with his or her genetic inheritance, including various neurological and psychological mechanisms, which will ultimately permit the individual to achieve the competences that are essential or desirable within his or her culture.

A third vantage point explores the *symbol* systems within the culture, the inventions that have evolved over thousands of years – organized systems of meaning, such as forms of dance, dress, or address. The individual generally encounters symbol systems as they are captured in various organized productions (e.g., stories and rituals): The individual must become facile with such meaningful structures if he or she is to become a competent member of the culture. A final essential vantage point encompasses the various *loci* and *modes of transmission* of cultural competence: These are institutions devised and presided over by the culture wherein younger individuals are exposed to various models of cultural competence and given the opportunity, usually with some guidance, to attain such competence.

Of course, these various assumptions and vantage points entail simplifications, but not, I hope, of such magnitude as to render the entire analytic effort futile. Having introduced them, we can now proceed to consider in somewhat more detail the four principal aspects involved in the acquisition of culture.

Four aspects of the acquisition of culture

CULTURE

As a means of delineating the aspects of culture that need to be mastered by its members, I find it useful to consider three different realms that must necessarily be confronted in every corner of the world. It may be the case that these realms are not divided identically across the range of cultures and that domains are conceptualized differently within (and across) these realms, yet each culture must somehow come to terms with the existence and importance of each. The three realms are: (1) *the physical world*, the world of material natural objects and the elements as well as various forms of living matter; (2) *the world of man-made artifacts*, such as tools, works of art, and the less tangible world of words and ideas; (3) *the social world*, which includes other persons, those in the family, in one's community, and, increasingly, in the rest of the world as well.[1]

Every individual in every culture must acquire the skills needed to deal effectively with these three realms (Lockhart, Abrahams, & Osherson 1977; Nucci & Turiel 1978). Moreover, the individual must develop some ability to work in these worlds, both on an intuitive and practical level and at the level of explicit propositional knowledge. To invoke a distinction that has become widespread, the individual must acquire "know-how" as well as "know that" in each of these domains. Thus, early in life, individuals develop skills in dealing with the physical world so that they will not be harmed by natural causes and so that they can attain desired goals. These skills are later joined by propositional knowledge, which may be formalized in the area of physics or biology but also can exist, of course, in ritual, law, stories, and other less formal modes of discourse. Included in the latter area would be "folk knowledge" about the genesis, nature, and ultimate fate of the physical world. By the same token in the world of man-made objects and in the social world, the individual must also acquire practical skills as well as the more formal codes that prescribe how one is to behave and what one is to believe.

Of course, the differences across cultures in the way in which this cultural knowledge is encoded and negotiated constitutes a major issue for philosophers, anthropologists, and other social scientists. It scarcely needs saying that cultures differ vastly from one another in the way in which they define these three realms (and their constituent domains), in the gamut of more or less explicit forms of knowledge that have evolved, in the kind of knowledge that is captured in each realm, and, perhaps most important, in the values that they place upon each. For example, in Western culture we place a great deal of importance on explicit knowledge about the physical world, and indeed this knowledge is central to much of the educational system with its focus on the physical and natural sciences. More recently, of course, we have also emphasized explicit knowledge about the social world, and this has given rise, for good or ill, to the social sciences.

In many other corners of the world, explicit knowledge, particularly as it is captured in scientific form, is of much less importance; though, of course, there may be innumerable adages that capture less formal aspects of knowledge about the physical and social world. However, at the same time, in such cultures as Japan or India, knowledge about the social world and how one negotiates one's way within it is valued much more and harnesses far more energy than does knowledge about the physical world. Thus, it must be emphasized once again that the ways in which cultures divide the universe of cultural knowledge differ vastly. The constant is that every culture must have some way of dealing with these different domains and must attach some value, though it may be a shifting one, to implicit and explicit knowledge within each. An understanding of how one's culture divides the universe of knowledge and of the values placed on each of the individual domains represents an end state of cultural knowledge, which must ultimately be acquired by individuals growing up in any corner of the globe.

THE INDIVIDUAL

Situated at the opposite pole of our equation of cultural acquisition is the single biological organism, the human being, who, starting from a state of total ignorance about his or her particular culture, must within a decade or two acquire sufficient competence so that he or she can carry out productive work and interact effectively with other individuals to achieve valued ends. In one sense, the individual *is* his or her genetic inheritance: He or she can achieve nothing that lies beyond the potential of the species. In practice, however, this limitation need not be a major concern, for cultures have evolved in such a way as to reflect the capabilities and the limitations of the species. Ultimately, however, a fullblown theory of cultural acquisition must take into account what is known about human genetic heritage: the structure of the nervous system, the principles of brain development; the effects of early and later experiences on neurological and psychological maturing; and how these exercise a constraining (or, viewed differently, a liberating) role in the processes whereby the acquisition of culture takes place.

For present purposes, I propose to focus on the intellectual competences that human beings as a species seem to have the potential to acquire. The particular competences that I propose are controversial, and the full case for their existence and centrality has yet to be made.[2] For now, however, the precise identity of these cognitive potentials is less crucial than the claims that there exists a finite number of them and that a student of cultural acquisition needs to take each of them into account.

I contend that there exist at least seven separate computational or information-processing systems that human beings, as a species, have evolved over the millennia. Aspects of these computational systems can be located in other animals, though probably never in the precise forms or with the interconnections realized in human beings. These computational systems are best thought of as raw information-processing devices, neural mechanisms that are predisposed to take in certain forms of sensory information, either from the external world or from the viscera, to analyze and eventually to transform these "raw" forms of information in various ways. In most normal human beings, each of these computational devices operates with some fluency and fluidity, and by exploiting these individual computational systems, individuals can go on to acquire quite elaborate forms of knowledge. But computational mechanisms cannot work in a vacuum: They have evolved to expect organized sets of information from a culture, which they in turn analyze, organize, and synthesize (Geertz 1962). Individuals also differ from one another in the potential they have for elaborating each of these intelligences: It is a task of differential psychology to identify these differences and a task of education to deal with, exploit, or compensate for the differences.

It proves difficult to demonstrate the existence, and to unravel the operation, of each of these computational mechanisms in the normal functioning human being. One aspect of smooth and productive human functioning is the perpetual interaction of these competences. Therefore, a chief source of insight about their autonomous existence and their modes of processing comes from atypical populations: brain-damaged individuals in whom one or more forms of intelligence can be spared or destroyed in isolation; prodigies – individuals who show a precocious development in one or more competences; freaks or idiot savants – individuals with limited development in most intellectual competences but with an extreme or precocious development in one of these. Studies of specific mechanisms in animals, such as birdsong in sparrows or interpersonal rituals in chimpanzees, can also illuminate aspects of human intellectual competences (see Gardner, 1975, 1982).

With this sketchy introduction, let me list seven forms of information processing that appear to exist in human beings. It is necessary to furnish rough-and-ready labels in order to permit communication about their nature, but it should be stressed that we are actually dealing here with organismic *potentials:* They might well be marshaled in ways other than the current labels intimate.

1. *Linguistic competence*. Building upon the phonological and syntactic-analytic abilities subserved by certain regions of the left hemisphere of the brain, human beings have the potential to develop communication systems like the natural languages. In those cases where natural languages are not available in the environment, individuals may well develop *ersatz* communication systems, for example, the gestural systems contrived by deaf children, which nonetheless exhibit some of the syntactic, semantic, and distinctive-feature properties of natural language.

2. *Spatial competence*. Building upon the capacity of the nervous system to discern visual patterns, to transform them in various ways, and to calculate the depth element of visual displays, spatial intelligence forms the basis of such mature roles as architect, artist, engineer, and physicist. Spatial intelligence may develop to some extent in the absence of visual information, but achievement of full-blown competence in this sphere may well presuppose a functioning visual system.

3. *Logical-mathematical competence*. Built upon the human capacity to enumerate elements and to appreciate cause-and-effect relationships, the logical-mathematical capacity culminates in our society in the ability to carry out high-level mathematical and scientific work. Most of Piaget's descriptions pertain particularly to the development of logical-mathematical intelligence.

4. *Bodily kinesthetic competence*. Under discussion here is the capacity of human beings to carry out complex motor patterns and to harness these to the service of various utilitarian or aesthetic-expressive ends. Bodily kinesthetic intelligence is reflected in all manner of crafts, as well as in such roles as the athlete, the actor, the hunter, and the dancer.

5. *Musical competence*. Analogous in some respects to linguistic or numerical intelligence, the core of the musical faculty involves sensitivity to pitch and tonal relations as well as rhythmic structures. Whereas spatial intelligence may depend on visual processing, musical competence presupposes a functioning auditory system.

6. *Interpersonal competence.* Based initially on the child's interaction with his parents and various "significant others," social or interpersonal intelligence culminates in a sensitivity to the needs, desires, and fears of other individuals and capacity to collaborate with them and thus achieve one's goals in communal situations. This form of competence has been especially valued in certain non-Western societies, where cooperation, and even merging with others, are at a premium.

7. *Intrapersonal, or self, competence.* A form of knowledge especially valued in the West, knowledge of self consists of an individual's sensitivity to, and understanding of, his own needs, desires, anxieties, and the like. Quite possibly, it derives in the first instance from sensitivity to, and monitoring of, one's reactions to events and culminates in a mature "sense of self," "identity," or "executive function." Distinct from interpersonal intelligence, it is this form of knowledge that Rousseau sought so unsparingly and that Freud has so acutely described in his own writings. In a different garb, intrapersonal knowledge may also be the end state sought in certain Oriental religions.

Making the detailed case for the existence of these intelligences is, of course, a task for another occasion (see Gardner, 1983). At present a few clarifying remarks will have to suffice. First, although superficially similar to previous factor-analytic views of intelligence, this scheme purports to be quite different: Rather than deriving entirely from empirical correlations among test scores, it is based in the first instance on the putative existence of quasi-autonomous biological systems, which have their separate evolutionary course and which can be specified – and possibly localized – in the nervous system.

Indeed, this view of intelligence may serve as a critique of "general intelligence" approaches of the unitary (Spearman 1904) and the pluralistic sort, whether empirically derived (Thurstone & Thurstone 1941) or based in part on an a priori analysis (Guilford 1959). At the same time, this view doubles as a challenge to the Piagetian view of intelligence, where general operations are assumed to underlie work across disparate domains. In contradistinction to each of these approaches, it is claimed here that each intelligence has its own genesis and can evolve according to its own rules of processing. And, as part of this claim, I wish to call into question the notion that there exist general principles of psychology, such as learning, perception, attention, and memory, and generalized kinds of operations, such as transformations, which operate in identical fashion across different domains. Instead, a clear implication of this view is that there may be separate forms of perception, memory, and so on in each domain; whereas there may well be certain similarities across domains, there is no necessary link. For instance, musical memory may operate in a different fashion from, and have no intrinsic link to, a keen memory in the spatial, logical-mathematical, or interpersonal realms.[3]

Even if this view of intellectual competences has some validity and is supported by subsequent researches, it clearly neglects evidently important aspects of cognition and raises many enigmas. To mention just a few: It is by no means apparent how a belief in separate computational mechanisms could account for common sense, wisdom, metaphoric insights, synthesizing powers, or the g that customarily emerges in factor-analytic studies of tests of intellectual performance. The processes by which individuals recognize and deal with recurrent situations in daily life (how they devise, store, access, transform, and utilize "scripts" or "frames") have not been specified. Finally, it remains to be determined whether some general organizing "self" or "executive function" coordinates the intelligences and decides which should be selected or whether the implementation of particular intellectual competences or combinations of competences is better viewed as an automatic, unsupervised process.

Although I have chosen to describe seven forms of intellectual competence here, no magic inheres in the number or in the names. Clearly, each intelligence has subcomponents, and these may well be represented separately in neuroanatomical zones: We know, for example, that in the single sphere of linguistic intelligence phonological, syntactic, and semantic capacities can be affected in distinctive and nonoverlapping ways as a consequence of brain damage. By the same token, there are no doubt certain processes characteristic of one intelligence that can also be seen at work in other intelligences: Thus certain aspects of temporal processing are marshaled by both linguistic and musical intelligence, even as certain kinds of spatial intuition can be utilized by the spatial, the bodily kinesthetic, and the logical-mathematical forms of reasoning. The decision to nominate seven, rather than three or three hundred, intellectual competences is dictated by a trio of diverse considerations: (1) the belief that there exist discrete neurological systems subserving each, (2) the desire to describe competences of sufficient scope and flexibility that they correspond with broad skills that can be readily identified and deliberately exploited by a functioning community (language rather than phonological competence), and (3) the need for a set of categories sufficiently small to allow the analysis of particular ongoing activities and tasks but sufficiently comprehensive to cover most of the skills needed in a functioning culture.

It should be stressed that these intellectual proclivities do not ordinarily exist in pure form or function in isolation. Except in the case of certain "freaks," they are always absorbed and utilized with reference to meaning systems within the culture. Moreover, any role within a society will call upon a combination of intelligences, just as any intelligence can itself be put to a number of disparate purposes. As we have already seen, the spatial intelligence is exploited by individuals as diverse as an architect, a pilot, or an artist. By the same token, an individual (like a lawyer) may achieve competence through combinations of linguistic, logical-mathematical, and/or interpersonal skills, with a particular lawyer differing significantly from her or his brethren in terms of the particular intelligences that happen to be highlighted. Similarly, given cultures or subcultures may choose to highlight certain intelligences while minimizing or even negating certain other ones. (Both the labeling and the examples offered here necessarily exhibit a Western bias.) For example, logical-mathematical intelligence may be of crucial importance in our culture but of relatively little importance elsewhere, whereas musical or interpersonal intelligences may be valued much more in cultural settings other than our own.

SYMBOL SYSTEMS

The creations (or instrumentalities) whereby the culture's bodies of knowledge (Factor A) are transmitted to the individual with his intellectual competences (Factor B) are here termed *symbol systems*. These are sets of elements, sometimes physical (like pictures or texts), sometimes nonmaterial (like spoken words or unspoken thoughts), in which knowledge can be captured and transmitted from one individual to another. They are meaningful: That is, individual symbols, finished symbolic productions, and organized symbol systems can communicate particular referential and/or expressive meanings from one individual to another. And, indeed, because human beings are meaning-seeking and meaning-creating individuals, symbol systems are the *preferred* mechanisms for the development and cultivation of intelligences. Only in unusual or freakish individuals, such as autistic children, can one see an intelligence in its raw form, unmediated by systems of meaning (Rimland 1964; Selfe 1977).

How meanings are attached to behaviors and experiences is, of course, a pivotal and, as yet, poorly understood aspect of human psychology, one neglected by most information-processing approaches to cognition, which seem to pride themselves on their indifference to content. As a start, we can assume that the human infant is predisposed to be sensitive to, and to search for, meanings and that, as a result, meanings become attached to experiences from the earliest moments of life. Thus, individuals, objects, locations, and the like, no matter how arbitrary or inchoate they may seem to an alien observer, soon acquire significance for the young organism. These entities, accompanied by strong feelings of well-being, irritation, or terror, become consistently attached to rewards and punishments, predictable outcomes, specific products, and events and situations. Initially, such significances attach directly to the physical and social beings in the world. However, after the first year or two of life, the individual enters into negotiations not merely with physical or social objects but also, and increasingly, with sets of symbols and discourses of meaning with words, pictures, gestures, numbers, ritualistic activities, and other "mediators of significance"; and it is here that the differences across cultures become most manifest, increasingly profound, and sometimes irremediable.

With respect to each of the intelligences sketched here, one may nominate symbol systems and products that exist within our culture. For example, in the area of language, one has, of course, natural language, formal languages, and also various informal languages, which can be invented or transformed by individuals. The systems are realized and encountered in such products as stories, reports, formal messages, and daily conversations. In the area of spatial intelligence, one has the symbol systems of drawing and architecture; in number, various arithmetics; in kinesthetic and bodily intelligence, gestural communication and dance; in logic, the various symbol systems of the sciences. There are less particulate but equally pervasive symbol systems in the realm of personal (dream) and interpersonal (ritual) intelligence. It is the task of the culture to ensure that the beliefs, values, knowledge, and so on of greatest import can be suitably captured and expressed in the available symbol systems. It is the task of the individual, exploiting his intellectual competences, to master and then utilize these various symbol systems. It is the task of the analyst to examine cultural competences, including those as broad as successful friendship or skilled parenting, and to determine how these are captured, transmitted, and apprehended in symbol systems.

The question arises as to how these symbol systems map onto the two forms of knowledge that we distinguished in our discussion of cultural competence: the intuitive or direct "know-how" involved in dealing with the world of physical and social objects as opposed to explicit propositional knowledge, the "know that" which eventually emerges in various cultural domains. Tracing the connections between these forms of knowledge and the various symbol systems in the culture is a vexed issue, which cannot be dealt with here. As a preliminary suggestion, I propose that initial use of a symbol system is relatively intuitive and nonreflective, a species (at a higher level) of "know-how"; only with the codification of the symbol system and its use in a more reflective or "meta" way does one invade the realm of explicit propositional symbolic knowledge, the "know that," about a domain. For example, in the area of language or numbers the individual (like Molière's Monsieur Jourdain) first learns to use words or numbers as tools in an intuitive or nonreflective way. Later, the individual becomes capable of making statements about language or numbers that are much more explicit in form and involve "knowledge about" a domain. These statements may be in formats ranging from folk adages to mathematical proofs. Needless to add, cultures differ greatly in the extent to which they tolerate, or promote, such propositional knowledge about various intellectual domains; and individuals, too, differ in the extent to which they indulge in, and benefit from, such "metaknowledge."

MODES AND LOCI OF TRANSMISSION

Symbol systems represent the crystallized content or knowledge of a culture that the competent individual must master. However, the modes and the loci of transmission themselves constitute an area that requires separate attention. Our own review suggests the existence of several loci and modes of transmission, which cultures may variously exploit in order to transmit knowledge across generations. Although the following description focuses primarily on teaching, an analysis can be carried out equally well with respect to learning.

Turning first to loci of transmission, the processes whereby knowledge is passed on can take place at the home, around the home, within the community at large, or in specific institutions, ranging from schools to churches. The individuals involved may include parents, siblings, peers, other family members, and individuals designated specially by the community, including itinerant teachers, gurus, or master craftsmen. A final locus of transmission, which assumes special importance in the modern world, is a *medium of communication*, such as radio or television. In the latter case, vast amounts of information can be conveyed wherever a receiver exists without the intervention of any individual who is known personally to the student.

There is an equally wide range of methods whereby the learner acquires knowledge. Perhaps the simplest form is *sheer imitation* or *observation learning*, where the mature organism performs and the novice, either immediately or eventually, reproduces salient (though not always apt) features of that performance. This mode of transmission is basic: It exists as well in infrahuman primates and seems to be adopted spontaneously by young children the world over. In fact, for many types of learning, observation learning alone seems sufficient to produce a competent performance.

But simple observation is often supplemented by more focused forms of instruction. The instructor may issue verbal instructions, or where they are unlikely to be effective, paralinguistic cues, such as gestures or pantomime, may be preferred. Powerful positive or negative incentives may be provided. Considerable learning can also take place if proper materials are simply provided to the learner. There may be rules to follow or procedures to memorize. Should the individual learn how to read, he also has the option of instructing himself by studying works in which the acquisition of a skill or competence is described.

When information achieves a level of complexity where sheer demonstration, or learning a list of rules, is unlikely to lead to mastery, two new forms of information processing appear to evolve across cultures. One mode, here called the *master–apprentice relationship*, is used primarily to teach complex techniques, such as arts and crafts or meditation, to younger members of the culture. In a typical pattern, the young individual goes to live in the house of the master and initially serves simply as a helping hand with diverse aspects of the work, not least the drudgery. The formation of strong interpersonal and dependent bonds may be an intrinsic aspect of the first stages of this mode of mastery. Eventually, the novice is allowed to pass through a series of higher level steps, often called journeyman and master, and sometimes entailing a series of gradations that occupy a lifetime. How these steps are negotiated and what milestones must be passed is generally determined by the master.

Another form of transmission also suited to knowledge of greater complexity, and particularly associated with the invention of a literacy system, may be termed the *traditional* or *premodern school*. Frequently, the purpose of this school is to allow the individual to master a form of literacy, usually a written language, which preserves and transmits doctrine. Examples would include medieval church schools, the Hebrew cheder, the *gurukula* in India, and analogous schools in other parts of the world in which a scripture must be mastered.

In a system that shares certain features with the master–apprentice relationship, the young pupil initially forges a close tie with the master and also passes through a set of stages: These may begin with sheer memorization but eventually include the abilities to decode the language phonemically, to understand its meaning, to engage in critical discussion and interpretation of the text, to read secular writings as well, and perhaps even to contribute to the corpus of writings.

A final variety of transmission of knowledge is the *modern technological* or *secular school*. In contrast to the traditional school, there is no emphasis on religion here; the school is often age-graded, rather than ability-graded, and the individual studies an assortment of disciplines during abutting periods. Given textbooks and tests and a meritocratic mode of evaluation, there is little need for a close tie to the teacher: In fact, teachers can be replaced, and individuals can advance when they meet objective criteria. Emphasis is placed on critical analysis, on the abilities to summarize and to revise, rather than on sheer memorization (Cole & Scribner 1974; Greenfield & Bruner 1969). The context in which the knowledge will eventually be used is underplayed, and, indeed, there is a heightened emphasis on presenting materials that are abstract and far removed from the usual locus of practice. One assumption central to the secular school is that such "decontextualization" will ensure greater generalization and "transfer of learning" than can be expected from traditional modes of learning: At present, this assumption is a hope rather than an established fact.

The focus in developed societies on more sophisticated modes of transmission, such as modern technological schools, should not be interpreted as an effort to dismiss or undervalue more traditional modes. Observation learning continues to be effective for some purposes at every level and in every area of society. Also, even within the most modern forms of schooling – for example, graduate training in physics – such apparently elementary modes of transmission as imitation and the master–apprentice relationship are often important, though they are not frequently remarked upon (Polanyi 1958).

Summary

I have touched briefly upon four separate elements involved in the equation of cultural acquisition. To recapitulate, we begin with those forms of knowledge valued by the culture. These can exist in three realms – those of physical objects, social objects, and man-made objects. Cultures will differ in their emphasis upon intuitive knowledge within these realms (as opposed to explicit propositional knowledge about these realms). Arrayed at the opposite end of the equation is the individual, with his general biological proclivities toward learning, as well as the potential for intellectual competence in at least seven different realms, each of which may have a specific neurological underpinning.

The points of contact between the culture, with its valued forms of knowledge, and the individual, with his intellectual proclivities, are various symbol systems: the forms of crystallized knowledge within the culture to which the individual is exposed from his earliest years, which may be said to constitute the systems of meaning within that culture. Finally, one may also isolate several modes for the transmission of knowledge, ranging from simple observation to the most complex forms of technological and secularized schooling. The loci for these modes of transmission may also vary, running the gamut from direct interaction within the nuclear family to transmission over long distances by modern electronic equipment.

Implications and applications

Even if the present framework seems plausible, it provides at most a starting point for the investigation of the acquisition of culture. As already suggested, very little is known about these various components and about their interactions: A first and very important task is to examine specific cultures to determine whether, and to what extent, this particular framework has utility. Such work virtually demands close collaboration between anthropologists and developmental psychologists, who would have complementary gifts for such an inquiry.

As already noted, the present formulation is very heavily skewed toward the cognitive aspects of culture and toward those cultural skills important for the transmission of knowledge. Future work must take into much fuller account the roles of motivation, emotions, personality factors, and underlying values, all of which undoubtedly play an important role, if they do not entirely transmute the processes whereby culture is acquired. It may well also be necessary to develop instruments, such as new projective techniques, which will allow a nonobtrusive securing of information about what forms of knowledge are in fact valued, how they are codified within the culture, and what systems have been developed for these forms of transmission.

Whatever its theoretical utility, the practical usefulness of such a framework also merits brief comment. My own hope is that it may prove useful in analyzing the various educational interventions that have been introduced into disparate cultural settings. Typically, these programs, no matter how well motivated, are based on implicit assumptions about *what* knowledge is and *how* it should be transmitted. These assumptions may differ greatly in the minds of the planners of the program, the practitioners who are entrusted with implementing it, and those who are supposedly the beneficiaries.

Let me take as an example the recent efforts by the Ministry of Intelligence in Venezuela to raise the intelligence of the entire population of that country (Machado 1980; Skryzniarz 1981). This is not the place for a full-fledged critique of this ambitious program, which in any case is still in progress at the time of this writing. However, it seems evident that the planners of the program have adopted a monolithic view of intelligence, which is quite far removed from the perspective of this chapter and which also may be outmoded as far as contemporary cognitive science is concerned. Little attention has been paid to the indigenous knowledge systems that exist within the Venezuelan context, through which any new version of knowledge would presumably have to be transmitted. Perhaps more important, the project assumes a certain mode of transmission, that of technological secularized schooling, which may be at variance with forms that have been traditionally favored in Venezuela. None of these disparities necessarily predicts the failure of the Venezuelan project; nor, if it does fail, can we necessarily assume that the present analysis is telling. Nonetheless, it would seem that future efforts at intervention in knowledge transmission might well benefit from an analysis in terms of the four components introduced in this essay.

A related use for this framework is its application in those cases where a program has been judged ineffective. It may well be that recognition of a plurality of intelligences, symbol systems, and modes of transmission will allow a more precise determination of where problems may lie and suggest the use of prosthetics to circumvent them. This framework can serve a critical function, warning individuals away from various kinds of interventions that may turn out to be at odds with the most deeply held assumptions of a culture. And, finally, it may help to explain why certain interventions have proved successful in given settings.

In addition to its possible practical utility, this conceptualization of issues in the acquisition of culture may also be of scientific value. Nearly all of what is known about the development of human beings has been obtained from research carried out by Western investigators, almost always in Western settings. In truth, the developmental psychology of today *is* the story of the development of Western children. Only by studying human development in vastly different cultural contexts, where there are different value systems, alternative modes of transmission, and the like, do we have any hope of gaining a more universal and more valid human science. Indeed, if human sciences can validly exist at all, they can only do so when a relatively large and representative sample of the human population has been included.

To be sure, contemporary developmental psychology may help us as we undertake the search for a more universal discipline. To begin with, we can obtain some "working notions" of how children acquire specific skills and general competences. Even those at odds with the influential Piagetian position would likely agree that children should be thought of as hypothesis-generators, active problem-solvers, who are continually attempting to make sense of the objects, events, and symbol systems around them. Children will attempt to find or *make* order in any system or domain they encounter: They are able to over-look a fair amount of noise and, in any case, are much less likely to be crippled by it. In LeVine's terms (1981), children will assume that there is organization – not chaos – in their culture and will attempt to discern that organization. This assumption ought certainly to be em-braced – and tested – by workers in disparate cultural settings.

From studies conducted in the West, we can also introduce useful distinctions among domains of competence, in terms of the extent to which they are readily mastered by some or all normal youngsters and to the extent to which they are eventually available to normal adults within a culture. At one extreme we have the realm of natural language, which seems to be acquired without the need for explicit external in-terventions throughout the human world. Certain other competences are acquired with equal facility but only by a far smaller percentage of individuals within a culture. In our own culture, we can point to areas like music or mathematics where prodigies are not that rare (Feld-man 1980; Gardner 1982). Conversely, there are other areas that are acquired without undue difficulty by most individuals, like reading or visual-spatial competence, but pose surprisingly severe problems for a small proportion of the population. It is crucial to determine whether such domains, which engender "learning disabilities" within the Amer-ican context, give rise to an analogous bimodal distribution in cultures that have different reading systems or place a different value on visual-spatial intelligence.

Not all domains of knowledge are readily available to youngsters. Some, such as logical reasoning involving abstract propositions, may prove relatively difficult to master and relatively easy to forget, once the supporting contexts are no longer present (Wason & Johnson-Laird 1972). Other forms of knowledge, such as the ability to adjudicate among different value systems or sensitivity to the motivations behind individual utterances, are readily accessible to most adults but prove surprisingly opaque to preadolescents. Finally, moving away from the notion of cognition *sensu strictu*, there are predictable progressions in the area of moral development (Kohlberg 1969), social development (Selman 1980), and ego development (Loevinger 1976) that cry out for validation, or alteration, in the light of work in cultures with different end states of competence in these person-oriented domains. Attending to developmental psychology can provide plausible predictions or frameworks that can be critically examined in other cultural settings:

Indeed, the very definition or delineation of domains may be altered in the light of such inquiry.

From developmental psychology, one can also obtain models of how different aspects of the cultural equation may work. For example, the investigations of my collaborators at Harvard Project Zero suggest the existence of four principal stages in the mastery of symbol systems: (1) an initial mastery at two years of age of narrative or role-structuring formats, which permits the understanding of stories and play sequences; (2) the emerging ability around three years to capture in a visual-spatial form the topological similarities between a two- and three-dimensional object, as occurs in representational drawing; (3) the capacity at age four to appreciate simple numbers and numerical relations, which allows the capturing of precise correspondences rather than simple topological relationships; (4) the facility, around the age of five or six, to attain a new "second-order" level of symbolization, where one can invent various notations that themselves refer to earlier forms of symbolization; this final step smoothes the road to "knowledge about" as well as "knowledge that" (Shotwell, Wolf, & Gardner 1979; Wolf & Gardner 1982). Once again, the point of such a scheme is not to insist on its correctness but rather to invite examination, in the light of cross-cultural knowledge about symbol acquisition, and revision, consequent upon insights obtained from such an inquiry.

Having a theory of the acquisition of cultural competence seems a worthwhile scientific goal, and it is hoped that this chapter has provided some useful, if tentative, suggestions about how such a goal might be pursued. Paradoxically, however, it is only by a serious embarking on this research course that we can determine whether, in fact, the overall goal is tenable. That is, only by studying the acquisition of culture in a variety of settings will it ever become clear whether the parallels in approach and method across cultures lend themselves to systematization and simplification; or whether, on the contrary, the differences in construing the problem and in the actual transmission of knowledge are so profound as to render this an area more suited for humanistic speculation or literary re-creation rather than for the dogged collection of data. And only through such work can we determine whether a study of individual domains of knowledge, as I have proposed, can flow together and lead to increased understanding of the most pervasive motifs of a culture or whether such an inquiry instead proceeds like a group of radiating streams, each receding farther and farther from the central source.

Notes

Preparation of this chapter was made possible by a grant to the Harvard Graduate School of Education from the Bernard Van Leer Foundation of the Hague. I am grateful to all my colleagues on that project for many discussions on these topics; no longer can I determine where their ideas end and my own begin.

The empirical research described in this essay was supported by grants from the Spencer Foundation, the Carnegie Corporation, the National Institute of Neurological Diseases, Communication Disorders and Stroke (NS 11408), and the Veterans Administration.

1. This scheme has some parallels to, but is by no means identical with, the theory of "three worlds" put forth by the British philosopher Karl Popper (1972).
2. Such an inquiry, which includes an examination of the neurobiological bases of intellectual competence, is being pursued at the Harvard Van Leer Project on Human Potential. See Gardner (1983).
3. This point of view has certain parallels with the "modularity hypothesis" about cognition, which is currently being developed by Jerry Fodor (1983) and others at MIT. An analysis of the distinctions between the two approaches should eventually be undertaken.

References

Cole, M., & Scribner, S. 1974. *Culture and Thought: A Psychological Introduction*. New York: Wiley.

Erikson, E. 1963. *Childhood and Society*, 2nd ed. New York: Norton.

Feldman, D. 1980. *Beyond Universals in Cognitive Development*. Norwood, N.J.: Ablex.

Fodor, J. 1983. *The Modularity of Mind*. Cambridge Mass.: Bradford Books, 1983.

Gardner, H. 1975. *The Shattered Mind*. New York: Knopf.

1982. *Art, Mind, and Brain*. New York: Basic Books.

1983. *Frames of Mind: The Theory of Multiple Intelligences*. New York: Basic Books.

Geertz, C. 1962. The growth of culture and the evolution of mind. In J. M. Scher, ed., *Theories of the Mind*. New York: Free Press.

Gorer, Geoffrey. 1948. *The American People, a Study in National Character*. New York: Norton.

Greenfield, P. M., & Bruner, J. S. 1969. Culture and cognitive growth (revised version). In D. A. Goslin, ed., *Handbook of Socialization Theory and Research*. Chicago: Rand McNally.

Guilford, J. P. 1959. Three faces of intellect. *American Psychologist* 14:469–79.

Kardiner, Abram. 1945. *The Psychological Frontiers of Society*. New York: Columbia University Press.

Kluckhohn, Clyde and Henry A. Murray. 1953. *Personality in Nature, Society, and Culture*, 2nd ed. New York: Knopf.

Kohlberg, L. 1969. Stage and sequence: the cognitive-developmental approach to socialization. In D. A. Goslin, ed., *Handbook of Socialization Theory and Research*. Chicago: Rand McNally.

LeVine, R. 1981. Remarks at the SSRC conference on Concepts of Culture and Its Acquisition, New York.

Lockhart, K. L., Abrahams, B., & Osherson, D. N. 1977. Children's understanding of uniformity in the environment. *Child Development* 48:1521–31.

Loevinger, Jane. 1976. *Ego Development: Conceptions and Theories*. San Francisco: Jossey-Bass.

Machado, L. A. 1980. *The Right to Be Intelligent*. New York: Pergamon Press.

Nucci, L. P., & Turiel, E. 1978, Social interactions and the development of social concepts in preschool children. *Child Development* 49:400–7.

Piatelli-Palmarini, M., ed. 1980. *Language and Learning: The Debate Between Jean Piaget and Noam Chomsky*. Cambridge, Mass.: Harvard University Press.

Polanyi, Michael. 1958. *Personal Knowledge: Towards a Post-critical Philosophy*. Chicago: University of Chicago Press.

Popper, K. 1972. *Objective Knowledge: An Evolutionary Approach*. Oxford: Clarendon Press.

Rimland, B. 1964. *Infantile Autism*. New York: Appleton-Century-Crofts.

Selfe, L. 1977. *Nadia*. London: Academic Press.

Selman, R. 1980. *The Growth of Interpersonal Understanding*. New York: Academic Press.

Shotwell, J., Wolf, D., & Gardner, H. 1979. Styles of achievement in early symbolization. In M. Foster & S. Brandes, eds., *Symbols as Sense*. New York: Academic Press.

Skryzniarz, W. S. 1981. *A review of projects to develop intelligence in Venezuela: developmental, philosphical, policy, and cultural perspectives on intellectual potential*. Unpublished manuscript.

Spearman, C. 1904. General intelligence objectively determined and measured. *American Journal of Psychology* 15:840–8.

Thurstone, L. L., & Thurstone, T. G. 1941. *Factorial Studies of Intelligence*, Psychometric Monographs, no. 2. Chicago: University of Chicago Press.

Wason, Peter C., & Johnson-Laird, P. N. 1972. *Psychology of Reasoning: Structure and Content*. Cambridge, Mass.: Harvard University Press.

Wolf, D. P., & Gardner, H. 1982. On the structure of early symbolization. In R. Schiefelbusch & D. Bricker, eds., *Early Language: Acquisition and Intervention*. Baltimore: University Park Press.

11
Language acquisition and socialization
THREE DEVELOPMENTAL STORIES AND THEIR
IMPLICATIONS

Elinor Ochs & Bambi B. Schieffelin

This chapter addresses the relationship between communication and culture from the perspective of the *acquisition of* language and socialization *through language*. Heretofore the processes of language acquisition and socialization have been considered as two separate domains. Processes of language acquisition are usually seen as relatively unaffected by cultural factors such as social organization and local belief systems. These factors have been largely treated as "context," something that is *separable* from language and its acquisition. A similar attitude has prevailed in anthropological studies of socialization. The language used both *by* children and *to* children in social interactions has rarely been a source of information on socialization. As a consequence, we know little about the role that language plays in the acquisition and transmission of sociocultural knowledge. Neither the forms, the functions, nor the message content of language have been documented and examined for the ways in which they *organize* and *are organized by* culture.

Our own backgrounds in cultural anthropology and language development have led us to a more integrated perspective. Having carried out research on language in several societies (Malagasy, Bolivian, white-middle-class American, Kaluli [Papua New Guinea], and Western Samoan), focusing on the language of children and their caregivers in three of them (white middle-class American, Kaluli, Western Samoan), we have seen that the primary concern of caregivers is to ensure that their children are able to display and understand behaviors appropriate to social situations. A major means by which this is accomplished is through language. Therefore, we must examine the language of caregivers primarily for its socializing functions, rather than for only its strict grammatical input function. Further, we must examine the prelinguistic and linguistic behaviors of children to determine the ways they are continually and selectively affected by values and beliefs held by those members of society who interact with them. What a child says, and how he or she says it, will be influenced by local cultural processes in addition to biological and social processes that have universal scope. The perspective we adopt is expressed in the following two claims:

1. The process of acquiring language is deeply affected by the process of becoming a competent member of a society.
2. The process of becoming a competent member of society is realized to a large extent through language, by acquiring knowledge of its functions, social distribution, and interpretations in and across socially defined situations, i.e., through exchanges of language in particular social situations.

In this chapter, we will support these claims through a comparison of social development as it relates to the communicative development of children in three societies: Anglo-American white middle class, Kaluli, and Samoan. We will present specific theoretical arguments and methodological procedures for an ethnographic approach to the development of language. Our focus at this point cannot be comprehensive, and therefore we will address developmental research that has its interests and roots in language development rather than anthropological studies of socialization. For current socialization literature, the reader is recommended to see Briggs 1970; Gallimore, Boggs, & Jordon 1974; Geertz 1959; Hamilton 1981; Harkness & Super 1980; Korbin 1978; Leiderman, Tulkin, & Rosenfeld 1977; LeVine 1980; Levy 1973; Mead & MacGregor 1951; Mead & Wolfenstein 1955; Montagu 1978; Munroe & Munroe 1975; Richards 1974; Wagner & Stevenson 1982; Weisner & Gallimore 1977; Whiting 1963; Whiting & Whiting 1975; Williams 1969; and Wills 1977.

Approaches to communicative development

Whereas interest in language structure and use has been a timeless concern, the child as a language user is a relatively recent focus of scholarly interest. This interest has been located primarily in the fields of linguistics and psychology, with the wedding of the two in the establishment of developmental psycholinguistics as a legitimate academic specialization. The concern here has been the relation of language to thought, both in terms of conceptual categories and in terms of cognitive processes (such as perception, memory, recall). The child has become one source for establishing just what that relation is. More specifically, the language of the child has been examined in terms of the following issues:

1. The relation between the relative complexity of conceptual categories and the linguistic structures produced and understood by young language-learning children at different developmental stages (Bloom 1970, 1973; Bowerman 1977, 1981; Brown 1973; Clark 1974; Clark & Clark 1977; Greenfield & Smith 1976; Karmiloff-Smith 1979; MacNamara 1972; Nelson 1974; Schlessinger 1974; Sinclair 1971; Slobin 1979).
2. Processes and strategies underlying the child's construction of grammar (Bates 1976; Berko 1958; Bloom, Hood, & Lightbown 1974; Bloom, Lightbown, & Hood 1975; Bowerman 1977; Brown & Bellugi

1964; Brown, Cazden, & Bellugi 1969; Dore 1975; Ervin-Tripp 1964; Lieven 1980; MacWhinney 1975; Miller 1982; Scollon 1976; Shatz 1978; Slobin 1973).

3. The extent to which these processes and strategies are language universal or particular (Berman in press; Bowerman 1973; Brown 1973; Clancy in press; Clark in press; Johnston & Slobin 1979; MacWhinney & Bates 1978; Ochs 1982b, in press; Slobin 1981, in press; Asku & Slobin in press).

4. The extent to which these processes and strategies support the existence of a language faculty (Chomsky 1959, 1968, 1977; Fodor, Bever, & Garrett 1974; Goldin-Meadow 1977; McNeill 1970; Newport 1981; Newport, Gleitman, & Gleitman 1977; Piattelli-Palmarini 1980; Shatz 1981; Wanner & Gleitman 1982).

5. The nature of the prerequisites for language development (Bates et al. in press; Bloom 1973; Bruner 1975, 1977; Bullowa 1979; Carter 1978; de Lemos 1981; Gleason & Weintraub 1978; Golinkoff 1983; Greenfield & Smith 1976; Harding & Golinkoff 1979; Lock 1978, 1981; Sachs 1977; Shatz in press; Slobin 1973; Snow 1979; Snow & Ferguson 1977; Vygotsky 1962; Werner & Kaplan 1963).

6. Perceptual and conceptual factors that inhibit or facilitate language development (Andersen, Dunlea, & Kekelis 1982; Bever 1970; Greenfield & Smith 1976; Huttenlocher 1974; Menyuk & Menn 1979; Piaget 1955/1926; Slobin 1981; Sugarman 1984; Wanner & Gleitman 1982).

Underlying all these issues is the question of the *source* of language, in terms of not only what capacities reside within the child but the relative contributions of biology (nature) and the *social* world (nurture) to the development of language. The relation between nature and nurture has been a central theme around which theoretical positions have been oriented. B. F. Skinner's (1957) contention that the child brings relatively little to the task of learning language and that it is through responses to specific adult stimuli that language competence is attained provided a formulation that was subsequently challenged and countered by Chomsky's (1959) alternative position. This position, which has been termed nativist, innatist, rationalist (see Piattelli-Palmarini 1980), postulates that the adult verbal environment is an inadequate source for the child to inductively learn language. Rather, the rules and principles for constructing grammar have as their major source a genetically determined language faculty:

Linguistics, then, may be regarded as that part of human psychology that is concerned with the nature, function, and origin of a particular "mental organ." We may take UG (Universal Grammar) to be a theory of the language faculty, a common human attribute, genetically determined, one component of the human mind. Through interaction with the environment, this faculty of mind becomes articulated and refined, emerging in the mature

person as a system of knowledge of language. (Chomsky
1977:164)

It needs to be emphasized that an innatist approach does not eliminate
the adult world as a source of linguistic knowledge; rather, it assigns
a different role (vis-à-vis the behaviorist approach) to that world in the
child's attainment of linguistic competence: The adult language presents the relevant information that allows the child to select from the
Universal Grammar those grammatical principles specific to the particular language that the child will acquire.

One of the principal objections that could be raised is that although
"the linguist's grammar is a theory of this [the child's] attained competence" (Chomsky 1977:163), there is no account of *how* this linguistic
competence is attained. The theory does not relate the linguist's gram-
mar(s) to processes of acquiring grammatical knowledge. Several psy-
cholinguists, who have examined children's developing grammars in
terms of their underlying organizing principles, have argued for similarities between these principles and those exhibited by other cognitive
achievements (Bates et al. 1979; Bever 1970).

A second objection to the innatist approach has concerned its characterization of adult speech as "degenerate," fragmented, and often
ill formed (McNeill 1966; Miller & Chomsky 1963). This characterization, for which there was no empirical basis, provoked a series of
observational studies (including tape-recorded documentation) of the
ways in which caregivers speak to their young language-acquiring children (Drach 1969; Phillips 1973; Sachs, Brown, & Salerno 1976; Snow
1972). Briefly, these studies indicated not only that adults use well-
formed speech with high frequency but that they modify their speech
to children in systematic ways as well. These systematic modifications,
categorized as a particular speech register called baby-talk register
(Ferguson 1977), include the increased (relative to other registers) use
of high pitch, exaggerated and slowed intonation, a baby-talk lexicon
(Garnica 1977; Sachs 1977; Snow 1972, 1977b) diminuitives, redupli-
cated words, simple sentences (Newport 1976), shorter sentences, in-
terrogatives (Corsaro 1979), vocatives, talk about the "here-and-now,"
play and politeness routines – peek-a-boo, hi–good-bye, say "thank
you" (Andersen 1977; Gleason & Weintraub 1978), cooperative expression of propositions, repetition, and expansion of one's own and the
child's utterances. Many of these features are associated with the
expression of positive affect, such as high pitch and diminutives. However, the greatest emphasis in the literature has been placed on these
features as evidence that caregivers *simplify* their speech in addressing
young children (e.g., slowing down, exaggerating intonation, simplifying sentence structure and length of utterance). The scope of the
effects on grammatical development has been debated in a number of
studies. Several studies have supported Chomsky's position by demonstrating that caregiver speech facilitates the acquisition of only lan-

guage-specific features but not those features widely (universally) shared across languages (Feldman, Goldin-Meadow, & Gleitman 1978; Newport, Gleitman, & Gleitman 1977). Other studies, which do not restrict the role of caregiver speech to facilitating only language-specific grammatical features (Snow 1977b, 1979), report that caregivers appear to adjust their speech to a child's cognitive and linguistic capacity (Cross 1977). And as children become more competent, caregivers use fewer features of the baby-talk register. Whereas certain researchers have emphasized the direct facilitating role of caregiver speech in the acquisition of language (van der Geest 1977), others have linked the speech behavior of caregivers to the caregiver's desire to communicate with the child (Brown 1977; Snow 1977a, 1977b, 1979). In this perspective, caregivers simplify their own speech in order to make themselves understood when speaking to young children. Similarly, caregivers employ several verbal strategies to understand what the child is trying to communicate. For example, the caregiver attends to what the child is doing, where the child is looking, and the child's behavior to determine the child's communicative intentions (Foster 1981; Golinkoff 1983; Keenan, Ochs, & Schieffelin 1976). Further, caregivers often request clarification by repeating or paraphrasing the child's utterance with a questioning intonation, as in Example 1 (Bloom 1973:170):

Example 1*

Mother	Allison (16 mos 3 wks)
(A picks up a jar, trying to open it)	more wídə/ə wídə/
	ə wídə/ ə wídə/
(A holding jar out to M)	up/ Mama/ Mama/
	Mama ma ə wídə/
	Mama Mama ə wídə/
What, darling?	
	Mama wídə/ Mama/
	Mama wídə/ Mama
	Mama wídə/
What do you want Mommy to do?	
	—/ ə wídə ə wídə/
(A gives jar to M)	
	—/here/
(A tries to turn top on jar in M's hand)	
	Mama/Mama/ə wídət/
Open it up?	
	up/
Open it? OK.	
(M opens it)	

In other cases, the caregiver facilitates communication by jointly expressing with the child a proposition. Typically, a caregiver asks a

* Examples 1–5 follow transcription conventions in Bloom and Lahey 1978.

question to which the child supplies the missing information (often already known to the caregiver), as in Example 2 (Bloom 1973:153):

Example 2

Mother	*Allison*
What's Mommy have (*M* holding cookies)	
(*A* reaching for cookie)	
	cookie/
Cookie! OK. Here's a cookie for you	
(*A* takes cookie; reaching with other	
hand toward others in bag)	
	more/
There's more in here. We'll have it	
in a little while.	
(*A* picking up bag of cookies)	
	bag/

These studies indicate that caregivers make extensive accommodations to the child, assuming the perspective of the child in the course of engaging him or her in conversational dialogue. Concurrent research on interaction between caregivers and prelinguistic infants supports this conclusion (Bruner 1977; Bullowa 1979; Lock 1978; Newson 1977; 1978; Schaffer 1977; Shotter 1978). Detailed observation of white middle-class mother–infant dyads (English, Scottish, American, Australian, Dutch) indicates that these mothers attempt to engage their very young infants (starting at birth) in "conversational exchanges." These so-called protoconversations (Bullowa 1979) are constructed in several ways. A protoconversation may take place when one party responds to some facial expression, action, and/or vocalization of the other. This response may be nonverbal, as when a gesture of the infant is "echoed" by his or her mother.

> As a rule, prespeech with gesture is watched and replied to by exclamations of pleasure or surprise like "Oh, my my!", "Good heavens!", "Oh, what a big smile!", "Ha! That's a big one!" (meaning a story), questioning replies like, "Are you telling me a story?", "Oh really?", or even agreement by nodding "Yes" or saying "I'm sure you're right". . . . A mother evidently perceives her baby to be a person like herself. Mothers interpret baby behavior as not only intended to be communicative, but as verbal and meaningful. (Trevarthen 1979a:339)

On the other hand, mother and infant may respond to one another through verbal means, as, for example, when a mother expresses agreement, disagreement, or surprise following an infant behavior. Social interactions may be sustained over several exchanges by the mother assuming both speaker roles. She may construct an exchange by responding on behalf of the infant to her own utterance, or she may verbally interpret the infant's interpretation. A combination of several strategies is illustrated in Example 3 (Snow 1977a:12).

Example 3

Mother	*Ann* (3 mos)
	(smiles)
Oh what a nice little smile!	
Yes, isn't that nice?	
There.	
There's a nice little smile.	(burps)
What a nice wind as well!	
Yes, that's better, isn't it?	
Yes.	
Yes.	(vocalizes)
Yes!	
There's a nice noise.	

These descriptions capture the behavior of white middle-class caregivers and, in turn, can be read for what caregivers believe to be the capabilities and predispositions of the infant. Caregivers evidently see their infants as sociable and as capable of intentionality, particularly with respect to the intentional expression of emotional and physical states. Some researchers have concluded that the mother, in interpreting an infant's behaviors, provides meanings for those behaviors that the infant will ultimately adopt (Lock 1981; Ryan 1974; Shotter 1978) and thus emphasize the active role of the mother in socializing the infant to her set of interpretations. Other approaches emphasize the effect of the infant on the caregiver (Lewis & Rosenblum 1974), particularly with respect to the innate mechanisms for organized, purposeful action that the infant brings to interaction (Trevarthen 1979b).

These studies of caregivers' speech to young children have all attended to what the child is learning from these interactions with the mother (or caregiver). There has been a general movement away from the search for *direct* causal links between the ways in which caregivers speak to their children and the emergence of grammar. Instead, caregivers' speech has been examined for its more general communicative functions, that is, how meanings are negotiated, how activities are organized and accomplished, and how routines and games become established. Placed within this broader communicative perspective, language development is viewed as one of several achievements accomplished through verbal exchanges between the caregiver and the child.

The ethnographic approach

ETHNOGRAPHIC ORIENTATION

To most middle-class Western readers, the descriptions of verbal and nonverbal behaviors of middle-class caregivers with their children seem very familiar, desirable, and even natural. These descriptions capture in rich detail what goes on, to a greater or lesser extent, in many middle-class households. The characteristics of caregiver speech (baby-talk register) and comportment that have been specified are highly valued by members of white middle-class society, including researchers, readers, and subjects of study. They are associated with good mothering and can be spontaneously produced with little effort or reflections. As demonstrated by Shatz and Gelman (1973), Sachs and Devin (1976), and Andersen and Johnson (1973), children as young as 4 years of age often speak and act in these ways when addressing small children.

From our research experience in other societies as well as our acquaintance with some of the cross-cultural studies of language socialization (Blount 1972; Bowerman 1981; Clancy in press; Eisenberg 1982; Fischer 1970; Hamilton 1981; Harkness 1975; Harkness & Super 1977; Heath 1983; Miller 1982; Philips 1983; Schieffelin & Eisenberg in press; Scollon & Scollon 1981; Stross 1972; Ward 1971; Watson-Gegeo & Gegeo 1982; Wills 1977) the general patterns of white middle-class caregiving that have been described in the psychological literature are characteristic neither of all societies nor of all social groups (e.g., all social classes within one society). We would like the reader, therefore, to reconsider the descriptions of caregiving in the psychological literature as ethnographic descriptions.

By ethnographic, we mean descriptions that take into account the perspective of members of a social group, including beliefs and values that underlie and organize their activities and utterances. Ethnographers rely heavily on observations and on formal and informal elicitation of members' reflections and interpretations as a basis for analysis (Geertz 1973). Typically, the ethnographer is not a member of the group under study. Further, in presenting an ethnographic account, the researcher faces the problem of communicating world views or sets of values that may be unfamiliar and strange to the reader. Ideally, such statements provide for the reader a set of organizing principles that give coherence and an analytic focus to the behaviors described.

Psychologists who have carried out research on the verbal and non-verbal behavior of caregivers and their children draw on both methods. However, unlike most ethnographers, the psychological researcher *is* a member of the social group under observation. (In some cases, the researcher's own children are the subjects of study.) Further, unlike the ethnographer, the psychologist addresses a readership familiar with the social scenes portrayed.

That the researcher, reader, and subjects of study tend to have in common a white middle-class literate background has had several consequences. For example, by and large, the psychologist has not been faced with the problem of cultural translation, as has the anthropologist. There has been a tacit assumption that readers can provide the larger cultural framework for making sense out of the behaviors documented, and, consequently, the cultural nature of the behaviors and principles presented have not been explicit. From our perspective, language and culture as bodies of knowledge, structures of understanding, conceptions of the world, and collective representations are extrinsic to any individual and contain more information than any individual could know or learn. Culture encompasses variations in knowledge between individuals, but such variation, although crucial to what an individual may know and to the social dynamic between individuals, does not have its locus within the individual. Our position is that culture is not something that can be considered separately from the accounts of caregiver–child interaction; rather, it is what organizes and gives meaning to that interaction. This is an important point, as it affects the definition and interpretation of the behaviors of caregivers and children. How caregivers and children speak and act toward one another is linked to cultural patterns that extend and have consequences beyond the specific interactions observed. For example, how caregivers speak to their children may be linked to other institutional adaptations to young children. These adaptations, in turn, may be linked to how members of a given society view children more generally (their "nature," their social status and expected comportment) and to how members think children develop.

We are suggesting here that the sharing of assumptions between researcher, reader, and subjects of study is a mixed blessing. In fact, this sharing represents a paradox of familiarity. We are able to apply without effort the cultural framework for interpreting the behavior of caregivers and young children in our own social group; indeed, as members of a white middle-class society, we are socialized to do this very work, that is, interpret behaviors, attribute motives, and so on. Paradoxically, however, in spite of this ease of effort, we can not easily isolate and make explicit these cultural principles. As Goffman's work on American society has illustrated, the articulation of norms, beliefs, and values is often possible only when faced with violations, that is, with gaffes, breaches, misfirings, and the like (Goffman 1963, 1967; Much & Shweder 1978).

Another way to see the cultural principles at work in our own society is to examine the ways in which *other* societies are organized in terms of social interaction and of the society at large. In carrying out such research, the ethnographer offers a point of contrast and comparison with our own everyday activities. Such comparative material can lead us to reinterpret behaviors as cultural that we have assumed to be natural. From the anthropological perspective, every society will have its own cultural constructs of what is natural and what is not. For example, every society has its own theory of procreation. Certain Australian Aboriginal societies believe that a number of different factors contribute to conception. Von Sturmer (1980) writes that among the Kugu-Nganychara (West Cape York Peninsula, Australia) the spirit of the child may first enter the man through an animal that he has killed and consumed. The spirit passes from the man to the woman through sexual intercourse, but several sexual acts are necessary to build the child (see also Hamilton 1981; Montagu 1937). Even within a single society there may be different beliefs concerning when life begins and ends, as the recent debates in the United States and Europe concerning abortion and mercy killing indicate. The issue of what is nature and what is nurtured (cultural) extends to patterns of caregiving and child development. Every society has (implicitly or explicitly) given notions concerning the capacities and temperament of children at different points in their development (see, e.g., Dentan 1978; Ninio 1979; Snow, de Blauw, & van Roosmalen 1979), and the expectations and responses of caregivers are directly related to these notions.

THREE DEVELOPMENTAL STORIES

At this point, using an ethnographic perspective, we will recast selected behaviors of white middle-class caregivers and young children as pieces of one "developmental story." The white middle-class developmental story that we are constructing is based on various descriptions available and focuses on those patterns of interaction (both verbal and nonverbal) that have been emphasized in the literature. This story will be compared with two other developmental stories from societies that are strikingly different: Kaluli (Papua New Guinea) and Western Samoan.

A major goal in presenting and comparing these developmental stories is to demonstrate that communicative interactions between caregivers and young children are culturally constructed. In our comparisons, we will focus on three facets of communicative interaction: (1) the social organization of the verbal environment of very young children, (2) the extent to which children are expected to adapt to situations or that situations are adapted to the child, (3) the negotiation of meaning by caregiver and child. We first present a general sketch of each social group and then discuss in more detail the consequences of the differences and similarities in communicative patterns in these social groups.

These developmental stories are not timeless but rather are linked in complex ways to particular historical contexts. Both the ways in which caregivers behave toward young children and the popular and scientific accounts of these ways may differ at different moments in time. The stories that we present represent ideas currently held in the three social groups.

The three stories show that there is more than one way of becoming social and using language in early childhood. All normal children will become members of their own social group, but the process of becoming social, including becoming a language user, is culturally constructed. In relation to this process of construction, every society has its own developmental stories that are rooted in social organization, beliefs, and values. These stories may be explicitly codified and/or tacitly assumed by members.

An Anglo-American white middle-class developmental story. The middle class in Britain and the United States includes a broad range of lower middle-, middle middle-, and upper middle-class white-collar and professional workers and their families.[1] The literature on communicative development has been largely based on middle middle- and upper middle-class households. These households tend to consist of a single nuclear family with one, two, or three children. The primary caregiver almost without exception is the child's natural or adopted mother. Researchers have focused on communicative situations in which one child interacts with his or her mother. The generalizations proposed by these researchers concerning mother–child communication could be an artifact of this methodological focus. However, it could be argued that the attention to two-party encounters between a mother and her child reflects the most frequent type of communicative interaction to which most young middle-class children are exposed. Participation in two-party as opposed to multiparty interactions is a product of many considerations, including the physical setting of households, where interior and exterior walls bound and limit access to social interaction.

Soon after an infant is born, many mothers hold their infants in such a way that they are face-to-face and gaze at them. Mothers have been observed to address their infants, vocalize to them, ask questions, and greet them. In other words, from birth on, the infant is treated as a *social being* and as an *addressee* in social interaction. The infant's vocalizations and physical movements and states are often interpreted as meaningful and are responded to verbally by the mother or other caregiver. In this way, protoconversations are established and sustained along a dyadic, turn-taking model. Throughout this period and the subsequent language-acquiring years, caregivers treat very young children as communicative partners. One very important procedure in facilitating these social exchanges is the mother's (or other caregiver's) taking the perspective of the child. This perspective is evidenced in her own speech through the many simplifying and affective features of the baby-talk register that have been described and through the various strategies employed to identify what the young child may be expressing.

Such perspective taking is part of a much wider set of accommodations by adults to young children. These accommodations are manifested in several domains. For example, there are widespread material accommodations to infancy and childhood in the form of cultural artifacts designed for this stage of life, for example, baby clothes, baby food, miniaturization of furniture, and toys. Special behavioral accommodations are coordinated with the infant's perceived needs and capacities, for example, putting the baby in a quiet place to facilitate and ensure proper sleep; "baby-proofing" a house as a child becomes increasingly mobile, yet not aware of, or able to control, the consequences of his or her own behavior. In general, the pattern appears to be one of prevention and intervention, in which situations are adapted or modified to the child rather than the reverse. Further, the child is a focus of attention, in that the child's actions and verbalizations are often the starting point of social interaction with more mature persons.

Although such developmental achievements as crawling, walking, and first words are awaited by caregivers, the accommodations have the effect of keeping the child dependent on, and separate from, the adult community for a considerable period of time. The child, protected from those experiences considered harmful (e.g., playing with knives, climbing stairs), is thus denied knowledge, and his or her competence in such contexts is delayed.

The accommodations of white middle-class caregivers to young children can be examined for other values and tendencies. Particularly among the American middle class, these accommodations reflect a discomfort with the competence differential between adult and child. The competence gap is reduced by two strategies. One is for the adult to simplify her/his speech to match more closely what the adult considers to be the verbal competence of the young child. Let us call this strategy the self-lowering strategy, following Irvine's (1974) analysis of inter-caste demeanor. A second strategy is for the caregiver to richly interpret (Brown 1973) what the young child is expressing. Here the adult acts *as if* the child were more competent than his behavior more strictly would indicate. Let us call this strategy the child-raising (no pun intended!) strategy. Other behaviors conform to this strategy, such as when an adult cooperates in a task with a child but treats that task as an accomplishment of the child.

For example, in eliciting a story from a child, a caregiver often cooperates with the child in the telling of the story. This cooperation typically takes the form of posing questions to the child, such as "Where did you go?" "What did you see?" and so on, to which the adult knows the answer. The child is seen as telling the story even though she or he is simply supplying the information the adult has preselected and organized (Greenfield & Smith 1976; Ochs, Schieffelin & Platt 1979; Schieffelin & Eisenberg 1984). Bruner's (1978) description of scaffolding, in which a caregiver constructs a tower or other play object, allowing the young child to place the last block, is also a good example of this tendency. Here the tower may be seen by the caregiver and others as the child's own work. Similarly, in later life, caregivers playing games with their children let them win, acting as if the child can match or more than match the competence of the adult.

The masking of incompetence applies not only in white middle-class relations with young children but also in relations with mentally, and to some extent to physically, handicapped persons as well. As the work of Edgerton (1967) and the recent film *Best Boy* indicate, mentally retarded persons are often restricted to protected environments (family households, sheltered workshops or special homes) in which trained staff or family members make vast accommodations to their special needs and capacities.

A final aspect of this white middle-class developmental story concerns the willingness of many caregivers to interpret unintelligible or partially intelligible utterances of young children (cf. Ochs 1982c), for example, the caregiver offers a paraphrase (or "expansion"; Brown & Bellugi 1964; Cazden 1965), using a question intonation. This behavior of caregivers has continuity with their earlier attributions of intentionality to the ambiguous utterances of the infant. For both the prelinguistic and language-using child, the caregiver provides an explicitly verbal interpretation. This interpretation or paraphrase is potentially available to the young child to affirm, disconfirm, or modify.

Through exposure to, and participation in, these clarification exchanges, the young child is socialized into several cultural patterns. The first of these recognizes and defines an utterance or vocalization that may not be immediately understood. Second, the child is presented with the procedures for dealing with ambiguity. Through the successive offerings of possible interpretations, the child learns that more than one understanding of a given utterance or vocalization may be possible. The child is also learning who can make these interpretations and the extent to which they may be open to modification. Finally, the child is learning how to settle upon a possible interpretation and how to show disagreement or agreement. This entire process socializes the child into culturally specific modes of organizing knowledge, thought, and language.[2]

A Kaluli developmental story. A small (population approximately 1,200), nonliterate egalitarian society (Schieffelin 1976), the Kaluli people live in the tropical rain forest on the Great Papuan Plateau in the southern highlands of Papua New Guinea.[3] Most Kaluli are monolingual, speaking a non-Austronesian verb final ergative language. They maintain large gardens and hunt and fish. Traditionally, the sixty to ninety individuals that comprise a village lived in one large longhouse without internal walls. Currently, although the longhouse is maintained, many families live in smaller dwellings that provide accommodations for two or more extended families. It is not unusual for at least a dozen individuals of different ages to be living together in one house consisting essentially of one semipartitioned room.

Men and women use extensive networks of obligation and reciprocity in the organization of work and sociable interaction. Everyday life is overtly focused around verbal interaction. Kaluli think of, and use, talk as a means of control, manipulation, expression, assertion, and appeal. Talk gets you what you want, need, or feel you are owed. Talk is a primary indicator of social competence and a primary means of socializing. Learning how to talk and become independent is a major goal of socialization.

For the purpose of comparison and for understanding something of the cultural basis for the ways in which Kaluli act and speak to their children, it is important first to describe selected aspects of a Kaluli developmental story that I have constructed from various ethnographic data. Kaluli describe their babies as helpless, "soft" (*taiyo*), and "having no understanding" (*asugo andoma*). They take care of them, they say, because they "feel sorry for them." Mothers, the primary caregivers, are attentive to their infants and physically responsive to them. Whenever an infant cries, it is offered the breast. However, while nursing her infant, a mother may also be involved in other activities, such as food preparation, or she may be engaged in conversation with individuals in the household. Mothers never leave their infants alone and only rarely with other caregivers. When not holding their infants, mothers carry them in netted bags suspended from their heads. When the mother is gardening, gathering wood, or just sitting with others, the baby sleeps in the netted bag next to the mother's body.

Kaluli mothers, given their belief that infants "have no understanding," never treat their infants as partners (speaker/addressee) in dyadic communicative interactions. Although they greet their infants by name and use expressive vocalizations, they rarely address other utterances to them. Furthermore, a mother and infant do not gaze into each other's eyes, an interactional pattern that is consistent with adult patterns of not gazing when vocalizing in interaction with one another. Rather than facing their babies and speaking to them, Kaluli mothers tend to face their babies outward so that they can see, and be seen by, other members of the social group. Older children greet and address the infant, and the mother responds in a high-pitched nasalized voice "for" the baby while moving the baby up and down. Triadic exchanges such as that in Example 4 are typical (Golinkoff 1983).

Example 4

Mother is holding her infant son Bage (3 mo). Abi (35 mo) is holding a stick on his shoulder in a manner similar to that in which one would carry a heavy patrol box (the box would be hung on a pole placed across the shoulders of the two men).

Mother	*Abi*
(A to baby)	Bage/ do you see my box here?/
	Bage/ ni bokisi we badaya?/
	Do you see it?/
	olibadaya?/
(high nasal voice talking as if she is the baby, moving the baby who is facing Abi):	
My brother, I'll take half, my brother.	
nao, hɛbɔ ni diɛni, nao.	
(holding stick out)	mother give him half/
	nɔ hɛbɔ emɔ dimina/ mother,
	my brother here/here take half/
	nao we/we hɛbɔ dima/
(in a high nasal voice as baby):	
My brother, what half do I take?	
nao, hɛbɔ diɛni hɛh?	

What about it? my brother, put it on the
shoulder!
Wangaya? nao, kɛlɛnɔ wɛla diɛfoma!

(to Abi in her usual voice):
Put it on the shoulder.
kɛlɛnɔ wɛla diɛfɔndo.

(Abi rests stick on baby's shoulder)
There, carefully put it on.
ko dinafa diɛfoma. (stick accidently
pokes baby) Feel sorry, stop.
Heyɔ, kadɛfoma.

When a mother takes the speaking role of an infant she uses language
that is well formed and appropriate for an older child. Only the na-
salization and high-pitch mark it as "the infant's." When speaking as
the infant to older children, mothers speak assertively, that is, they
never whine or beg on behalf of the infant. Thus, in taking this role
the mother does for the infant what the infant cannot do for itself, that
is, appear to act in a controlled and competent manner, using language.
These kinds of interactions continue until a baby is between 4 and 6
months of age.

Several points are important here. First, these triadic exchanges are
carried out primarily for the benefit of the older child and help create
a relationship between the two children. Second, the mother's utterances in these exchanges are not based on, nor do they originate with,
anything that the infant has initiated – either vocally or gesturally.
Recall the Kaluli claim that infants have no understanding. How could
someone with "no understanding" initiate appropriate interactional
sequences?

However, there is an even more important and enduring cultural
construct that helps make sense out of the mother's behaviors in this
situation and in many others as well. Kaluli say that "one cannot know
what another thinks or feels." Although Kaluli obviously interpret and
assess one another's available behaviors and internal states, these interpretations are not culturally acceptable as topics of talk. Individuals
often talk about their own feelings (I'm afraid, I'm happy, etc.). However, there is a cultural dispreference for talking about or making claims
about what another might think, what another might feel, or what another is about to do, especially if there is no external evidence. As we
shall see, these culturally constructed behaviors have several important
consequences for the ways in which Kaluli caregivers verbally interact
with their children and are related to other pervasive patterns of language use, which will be discussed later.

As infants become older (6–12 months), they are usually held in the
arms or carried on the shoulders of the mother or an older sibling. They
are present in all ongoing household activities, as well as subsistence
activities that take place outside the village in the bush. During this
time period, babies are addressed by adults to a limited extent. They

are greeted by a variety of names (proper names, kin terms, affective and relationship terms) and receive a limited set of both negative and positive imperatives. In addition, when they do something they are told not to do, such as reach for something that is not theirs to take, they will often receive such rhetorical questions such as "who are you?!" (meaning "not someone to do that") or "is it yours?!"(meaning "it is not yours") to control their actions by shaming them (*sasidiab*). It should be stressed that the language addressed to the preverbal child consists largely of "one-liners" that call for no verbal response but for either an action or termination of an action. Other than these utterances, very little talk is directed to the young child by the adult caregiver.

This pattern of adults treating infants as noncommunicative partners continues even when babies begin babbling. Although Kaluli recognize babbling (*dabedan*), they call it noncommunicative and do not relate it to the speech that eventually emerges. Adults and older children occasionally repeat vocalizations back to the young child (age 12–16 months), reshaping them into the names of persons in the household or into kin terms, but they do not say that the baby is saying the name nor do they wait for, or expect, the child to repeat those vocalizations in an altered form. In addition, vocalizations are not generally treated as communicative and given verbal expression except in the following situation. When a toddler shrieks in protest of the assaults of an older child, mothers say "I'm unwilling" (using a quotative particle), referring to the toddler's shriek. These are the only circumstances in which mothers treat vocalizations as communicative and provide verbal expression for them. In no other circumstances did the adults in the four families in the study provide a verbally expressed interpretation of a vocalization of a preverbal child. Thus, throughout the preverbal period very little language is directed to the child, except for imperatives, rhetorical questions, and greetings. A child who by Kaluli terms has not yet begun to speak is not expected to respond either verbally or vocally. As a result, during the first 18 months or so very little sustained dyadic verbal exchange takes place between adult and infant. The infant is only minimally treated as an addressee and is not treated as a communicative partner in dyadic exchanges. Thus, the conversational model that has been described for many white middle-class caregivers and their preverbal children has no application in this case. Furthermore, if one defines language input as language directed to the child then it is reasonable to say that for Kaluli children who have not yet begun to speak there is very little. However, this does not mean that Kaluli children grow up in an impoverished verbal environment and do not learn how to speak. Quite the opposite is true. The verbal environment of the infant is rich and varied, and from the very beginning the infant is surrounded by adults and older children who spend a great deal of time talking to one another. Furthermore, as the infant develops and begins to crawl and engage in play activities and other independent actions, these actions are frequently referred to, described, and commented upon by members of the household, especially older children, to each other. Thus the ongoing activities of the preverbal child are an important topic of talk among members of the household, and this talk about the here-and-now of the infant is available to the infant, though it is not talk addressed to the infant. For example, in referring to the infant's actions, siblings and adults use the infant's name or kin term. They say, "Look at Seligiwo! He's walking." Thus the child may learn from these contexts to attend the verbal environment in which he or she lives.

Every society has its own ideology about language, including when it begins and how children acquire it. The Kaluli are no exception. Kaluli claim that language begins at the time when the child uses two critical words, "mother" (*no*) and "breast" (*bo*). The child may be using other single words, but until these two words are used, the beginning of language is not recognized. Once a child has used these words, a whole set of interrelated behaviors is set into motion. Once a child has begun to use language, he or she then must be "shown how to speak" (Schieffelin 1979). Kaluli show their children language in the form of a teaching strategy, which involves providing a model for what the child is to say followed by the word *ɛlɛma*, an imperative meaning "say like that." Mothers use this method of direct instruction to teach the social uses of assertive language (teasing, shaming, requesting, challenging, reporting). However, object labeling is never part of an *ɛlɛma* sequence, nor does the mother ever use *ɛlɛma* to instruct the child to beg or appeal for food or objects. Begging, the Kaluli say, is natural for children. They know how to do it. In contrast, a child must be taught to be assertive through the use of particular linguistic expressions and verbal sequences.

A typical sequence using *ɛlɛma* is triadic, involving the mother, child (20–36 months), and other participants, as in Example 5 (Schieffelin 1979).

Example 5

Mother, daughter Binalia (5 yrs), cousin Mama (3 1/2 yrs), and son Wanu (27 mos) are at home, dividing up some cooked vegetables. Binalia has been begging for some, but her mother thinks that she has had her share.

M → W →» B:*
Whose is it?! say like that.
Abɛnowo?! ɛlɛma.

> whose is it?!/
> abɛnowo?!/

Is it yours?! say like that.
Gɛnowo?! ɛlɛma.

> is it yours?!/
> gɛnowo?!/

Who are you?! say like that.
ge oba?! ɛlɛma.

who are you?!/
ge oba?!/

Mama → W →> B:
Did you pick?! say like that.
gi suwo?! ɛlema.

did you pick?!/
gi suwo?!/

M → W →> B:
My grandmother picked! say like that.
ni nuwɛ suke! ɛlema.

My grandmother picked!/
ni nuwɛ suke!/

Mama → W →> B:
This my g'mother picked! say like that
we ni nuwɛ suke! ɛlema.

This my g'mother picked!/
we ni nuwɛ suke!/

*→ = speaker → addressee
→> = addressee → intended addressee

In this situation, as in many others, the mother does not modify her language to fit the linguistic ability of the young child. Instead, her language is shaped so as to be appropriate (in terms of form and content) for the child's intended addressee. Consistent with the way she interacts with her infant, what a mother instructs her young child to say usually does not have its origins in any verbal or nonverbal behaviors of the child but in what the mother thinks should be said. The mother pushes the child into ongoing interactions that the child may or may not be interested in and will at times spend a good deal of energy in trying to get the child verbally involved. This is part of the Kaluli pattern of fitting (or pushing) the child into the situation rather than changing the situation to meet the interests or abilities of the child. Thus mothers take a directive role with their young children, teaching them what to say so that they may become participants in the social group.

In addition to instructing their children by telling them what to say in often extensive interactional sequences, Kaluli mothers pay attention to the form of their children's utterances. Kaluli correct the phonological, morphological, or lexical form of an utterance or its pragmatic or semantic meaning. Because the goals of language acquisition include the development of a competent and independent child who uses mature language, Kaluli use no baby-talk lexicon, for they said (when I asked about it) that to do so would result in a child sounding babyish, which was clearly undesirable and counterproductive. The entire process of a child's development, of which language acquisition plays a very important role, is thought of as a hardening process and culminates in the child's use of "hard words" (Feld & Schieffelin 1982).

The cultural dispreference for saying what another might be thinking or feeling has important consequences for the organization of dyadic exchanges between caregiver and child. For one, it affects the ways in which meaning is negotiated during an exchange. For the Kaluli, the responsibility for clear expression is with the speaker, and child speakers are not exempt from this. Rather than offering possible interpretations or guessing at the meaning of what a child is saying, caregivers make extensive use of clarification requests such as "huh?" and "what?" in an attempt to elicit clearer expression from the child. Children are held to what they say and mothers will remind them that they in fact have asked for food or an object if they don't act appropriately on receiving it. Because the responsibility of expression lies with the speaker, children are also instructed with ɛlɛma to request clarification (using similar forms) from others when they do not understand what someone is saying to them.

Another important consequence of not saying what another thinks is the absence of adult expansions of child utterances. Kaluli caregivers put words into the mouths of their children, but these words originate from the caregiver. However, caregivers do not elaborate or expand utterances initiated by the child. Nor do they jointly build propositions across utterances and speakers except in the context of sequences with ɛlɛma in which they are constructing the talk for the child.

All these patterns of early language use, such as the lack of expansions and the verbal attribution of an internal state to an individual are consistent with important cultural conventions of adult language usage. The Kaluli avoid gossip and often indicate the source of information they report. They make extensive use of direct quoted speech in a language that does not allow indirect quotation. They use a range of evidential markers in their speech to indicate the source of speakers' information, for example, whether something was said, seen, heard or gathered from other kinds of evidence. These patterns are also found in a child's early speech and, as such, affect the organization and acquisition of conversational exchanges in this face-to-face egalitarian society.

A Samoan developmental story. In American and Western Samoa, an archipelago in the southwest Pacific, Samoan, a verb-initial Polynesian language, is spoken.[4] The following developmental story draws primarily on direct observations of life in a large, traditional village on the island of Upolu in Western Samoa; however, it incorporates as well analyses by Mead (1927), Kernan (1969), and Shore (1982) of social life, language use, and childhood on other islands (the Manu'a islands and Savai'i).

As has been described by numerous scholars, Samoan society is highly stratified. Individuals are ranked in terms of whether or not they have a title, and if so, whether it is an orator or a chiefly title – bestowed on persons by an extended family unit (*aiga potopoto*) – and within each status, particular titles are reckoned with respect to one another.

Social stratification characterizes relationships between untitled persons as well, with the assessment of relative rank in terms of generation and age. Most relevant to the Samoan developmental story to be told here is that caregiving is also socially stratified. The young child is cared for by a range of untitled persons, typically the child's older siblings, the mother, and unmarried siblings of the child's mother. Where more than one of these are present, the older is considered to be the higher ranking caregiver and the younger the lower ranking caregiver (Ochs 1982c). As will be discussed in the course of this story, ranking affects how caregiving tasks are carried out and how verbal interactions are organized.

From birth until the age of 5 or 6 months, an infant is referred to as *pepemeamea* (baby thing thing). During this period, the infant stays close to his or her mother, who is assisted by other women and children in child-care tasks. During this period, the infant spends the periods of rest and sleep near, but somewhat separated from, others, on a large pillow enclosed by a mosquito net suspended from a beam or rope. Waking moments are spent in the arms of the mother, occasionally the father, but most often on the hips or laps of other children, who deliver the infant to his or her mother for feeding and in general are responsible for satisfying and comforting the child.

In these early months, the infant is talked *about* by others, particularly in regard to his or her physiological states and needs. Language addressed *to* the young infant tends to be in the form of songs or rhythmic vocalizations in a soft, high pitch. Infants at this stage are not treated as conversational partners. Their gestures and vocalizations are interpreted for what they indicate about the physiological state of the child. If verbally expressed, however, these interpretations are directed in general not to the infant but to some other more mature member of the household (older child), typically in the form of a directive.

As an infant becomes more mature and mobile, he or she is referred to as simply *pepe* (baby). When the infant begins to crawl, his or her immediate social and verbal environment changes. Although the infant continues to be carried by an older sibling, he or she is also expected to come to the mother or other mature family members on his or her own. Spontaneous language is directed to the infant to a much greater extent. The child, for example, is told to "come" to the caregiver.

To understand the verbal environment of the infant at this stage, it is necessary to consider Samoan concepts of childhood and children. Once a child is able to locomote himself or herself and even somewhat before, he or she is frequently described as cheeky, mischievous, and willful. Very frequently, the infant is negatively sanctioned for his actions. An infant who sucks eagerly, vigorously, or frequently at the breast may be teasingly shamed by other family members. Approaching a guest or touching objects of value provokes negative directives first and mock threats second. The tone of voice shifts dramatically from that used with younger infants. The pitch drops to the level used in casual interactions with adult addressees and voice quality becomes loud and sharp. It is to be noted here that caregiver speech is largely talk directed *at* the infant and typically caregivers do not engage in "conversations" *with* infants over several exchanges. Further, the language used by caregivers is not lexically or syntactically simplified.

The image of the small child as highly assertive continues for several years and is reflected in what is reported to be the first word of Samoan children: *tae* (shit), a curse word used to reject, retaliate, or show displeasure at the action of another. The child's earliest use of language, then, is seen as explicitly defiant and angry. Although caregivers admonish the verbal and nonverbal expression of these qualities, the qualities are in fact deeply valued and considered necessary and desirable in particular social circumstances.

As noted earlier, Samoan children are exposed to, and participate in, a highly stratified society. Children usually grow up in a family compound composed of several households and headed by one or more titled persons. Titled persons conduct themselves in a particular manner in public, namely, to move slowly or be stationary, and they tend to disassociate themselves from the activities of lower status persons in their immediate environment. In a less dramatic fashion, this demeanor characterizes high ranking caregivers in a household as well, who tend to leave the more active tasks, such as bathing, changing, and carrying an infant to younger persons (Ochs 1982c).

The social stratification of caregiving has its reflexes in the verbal environment of the young child. Throughout the day, higher ranking caregivers (e.g., the mother) direct lower ranking persons to carry, put to sleep, soothe, feed, bathe, and clothe a child. Typically, a lower ranking caregiver waits for such a directive rather than initiate such activities spontaneously. When a small child begins to speak, he or she learns to make his or her needs known to the higher ranking caregiver. The child learns not to necessarily expect a direct response. Rather, the child's appeal usually generates a conversational sequence such as the following:

Child appeals to high-ranking caregiver	(A → B)
High ranking caregiver directs lower ranking caregiver	(B → C)
Lower ranking caregiver responds to child	(C → A)

These verbal interactions differ from the ABAB dyadic interactions described for white middle-class caregivers and children. Whereas a white middle-class child is often alone with a caregiver, a Samoan child is not. Traditional Samoan houses have no internal or external walls, and typically conversations involve several persons inside and outside the house. For the Samoan child, then, multiparty conversations are the norm, and participation is organized along hierarchical lines.

The importance of status and rank is expressed in other uses of language as well. Very small children are encouraged to produce certain speech acts that they will be expected to produce later as younger (i.e., low ranking) members of the household. One of these speech acts is reporting of news to older family members. The reporting of news by lower status persons complements the detachment associated with relatively high status. High status persons ideally (or officially) receive information through reports rather than through their own direct involvement in the affairs of others. Of course, this ideal is not always realized. Nonetheless, children from the one-word stage on will be explicitly instructed to notice others and to provide information to others as Example 6 illustrates.

Example 6

Pesio, her peer group including Maselino 3 yrs 4 mos, and Maselino's mother, Iuliana, are in the house. They see Alesana (member of research project) in front of the trade store across the street. Iuliana directs the children to notice Alesana.

Pesio (2 yrs 3 mos)	*Others*
	Iuliana: Va'ai Alesana.
	Look (at) Alesana!
ā?/	
Huh?	
	Iuliana: Alesana
	Maselino: Alesaga/
ai Alesaga/	
Look (at) Alesana	
	Iuliana: Vala'au Alesana
	Call (to) Alesana.
((very high, loud))	
SAGA?/	((high, soft))
Alesana!	Iuliana: Mālō.
	(Greeting)
((loud))	
ALŌ!	
(Greeting)	
	Iuliana: (Fai) o Elegoa lea.
	(Say) prt. Elenoa here.
	(say "Elenoa [is]
	here.")
Sego lea/	
Elenoa here	
(Elenoa [is] here.)	

The character of these instructions is similar to that of the triadic exchanges described in the Kaluli developmental story. A young child is to repeat an utterance offered by a caregiver to a third party. As in the Kaluli triadic exchanges, the utterance is designed primarily for the third party. For example, the high, soft voice quality used by Iuliana expresses deference in greeting Alesana, the third party. Caregivers use such exchanges to teach children a wide range of skills and knowledge. In fact, the task of repeating what the caregiver has said is *itself* an object of knowledge, preparing the child for his or her eventual role as messenger. Children at the age of 3 are expected to deliver *verbatim* messages on behalf of more mature members of the family.

The cumulative orientation is one in which even very young children are oriented toward others. In contrast to the white middle-class tendencies to accommodate situations to the child, the Samoans encourage the child to meet the needs of the situation, that is, to notice others, listen to them, and adapt one's own speech to their particular status and needs.

The pervasiveness of social stratification is felt in another, quite fundamental aspect of language, that of ascertaining the meaning of an utterance. Procedures for clarification are sensitive to the relative rank of conversational participants in the following manner. If a high status person produces a partially or wholly unintelligible utterance, the burden of clarification tends to rest with the hearer. It is not inappropriate for high status persons to produce such utterances from time to time. In the case of orators in particular, there is an expectation that certain terms and expressions will be obscure to certain members of their audiences. On the other hand, if a low status person's speech is unclear, the burden of clarification tends to be placed more on the speaker.

The latter situation applies to most situations in which young children produce ambiguous or unclear utterances. Both adult and child caregivers tend not to try to determine the message content of such utterances by, for example, repeating or expanding such an utterance with a query intonation. In fact, unintelligible utterances of young children will sometimes be considered as not Samoan but another language, usually Chinese, or not language at all but the sounds of an animal. A caregiver may choose to initiate clarification by asking "What?" or "Huh?" but it is up to the child to make his or her speech intelligible to the addressee.

Whereas the Samoans place the burden of clarification on the child, white middle-class caregivers assist the child in clarifying and expressing ideas. As noted in the white middle-class developmental story, such assistance is associated with good mothering. The good mother is one who responds to her child's incompetence by making greater efforts than normal to clarify his or her intentions. To this end, a mother tries to put herself in the child's place (take the perspective of the child). In Samoa good mothering or good caregiving is almost the reverse: A young child is encouraged to develop an ability to take the perspective of higher ranking persons in order to assist them and facilitate their well-being. The ability to do so is part of showing *fa'aaloalo* (respect), a most necessary demeanor in social life.

We can not leave our Samoan story without touching on another dimension of intelligibility and understanding in caregiver–child interactions. In particular, we need to turn our attention to Samoan attitudes toward motivation and intentionality (cf. Ochs 1982c). In philosophy, social science, and literary criticism, a great deal of ink has been spilled over the relation between act and intention behind an act. The pursuit and ascertaining of intentions is highly valued in many societies, where acts are objects of interpretation and motives are treated as explanations. In traditional Samoan society, with exceptions such as teasing and bluffing, actions are not treated as open to interpretation. They are treated for the most part as having one assignable meaning. An individual may not always know what that meaning is, as in the case of an oratorical passage; in these cases, one accepts that there is one meaning that he may or may not eventually come to know. For the most part as well, there is not a concern with levels of intentions and motives underlying the performance of some particular act.

Responses of Samoan caregivers to unintelligible utterances and acts of young children need to be understood in this light. Caregivers tend not to guess, hypothesize, or otherwise interpret such utterances and acts, in part because these procedures are not generally engaged in, at least explicitly, in daily social interactions within a village. As in encounters with others, a caregiver generally treats a small child's utterances as either clear or not clear, and in the latter case prefers to wait until the meaning becomes known to the caregiver rather than initiate an interpretation.

When young Samoan children participate in such interactions, they come to know how "meaning" is treated in their society. They learn what to consider as meaningful (e.g., clear utterances and actions) procedures for assigning meaning to utterances and actions, and procedures for handling unintelligible and partially intelligible utterances and actions. In this way, through language use, Samoan children are socialized into culturally preferred ways of processing information. Such contexts of experience reveal the interface of language, culture, and thought.

IMPLICATIONS OF DEVELOPMENTAL STORIES: THREE PROPOSALS

Interactional design reexamined. We propose that infants and caregivers do not interact with one another according to one particular "biologically designed choreography" (Stern 1977). There are many choreographies within and across societies, and cultural as well as biological systems contribute to their design, frequency, and significance. The biological predispositions constraining and shaping the social behavior of infants and caregivers must be broader than thus far conceived in that the use of eye gaze, vocalization, and body alignment are orchestrated differently in the social groups we have observed. As noted earlier, for example, Kaluli mothers do not engage in sustained gazing at, or elicit and maintain direct eye contact with, their infants as such behavior is dispreferred and associated with witchcraft.

Another argument in support of a broader notion of a biological predisposition to be social concerns the variation observed in the participant structure of social interactions. The literature on white middle-class child development has been oriented, quite legitimately, toward the two-party relationship between infant and caregiver, typically infant and mother. The legitimacy of this focus rests on the fact that this relationship is primary for infants within this social group. Further, most communicative interactions are dyadic in the adult community. Although the mother is an important figure in both Kaluli and Samoan developmental stories, the interactions in which infants are participants are typically triadic or multiparty. As noted, Kaluli mothers organize triadic interactions in which infants and young children are oriented away from their mothers and toward a third party. For Samoans, the absence of internal and external walls, coupled with the expectation that others will attend to, and eventually participate in, conversation, makes multiparty interaction far more common. Infants are socialized to participate in such interactions in ways appropriate to the status and rank of the participants.

This is not to say that Kaluli and Samoan caregivers and children do not engage in dyadic exchanges. Rather, the point is that such exchanges are not accorded the same significance as in white middle-class society. In white middle-class households that have been studied, the process of becoming social takes place predominantly through dyadic interactions, and social competence itself is measured in terms of the young child's capacity to participate in such interactions. In Kaluli and Samoan households, the process of becoming social takes place through participation in dyadic, triadic, and multiparty social interactions, with the latter two more common than the dyad.

From an early age, Samoan and Kaluli children must learn how to participate in interactions involving a number of individuals. To do this minimally requires attending to more than one individual's words and actions and knowing the norms for when and how to enter interactions, taking into account the social identities of at least three participants. Further, the sequencing of turns in triadic and multiparty interactions has a far wider range of possibilities vis-à-vis dyadic exchanges and thus requires considerable knowledge and skill. Whereas dyadic exchanges can only be ABABA . . . , triadic or multiparty exchanges can be sequenced in a variety of ways, subject to such social constraints as speech content and the status of speaker (as discussed in the Samoan developmental story). For both the Kaluli and the Samoan child, triadic and multiparty interactions constitute their earliest social experiences and reflect the ways in which members of these societies routinely communicate with one another.

Caregiver register reexamined. A second major proposal based on these three developmental stories is that the simplifying features of white middle-class speech are not necessary input for the acquisition of language by young children. The word "input" itself implies a directionality toward the child as information processor. The data base for the child's construction of language is assumed to be language directed *to* the child. It is tied to a model of communication that is dyadic, with participation limited to the roles of speaker and addressee. If we were to apply this strict notion of input (language addressed to the child) to the Kaluli and Samoan experiences, we would be left with a highly restricted corpus from which the child is expected to construct language. As we have emphasized in these developmental stories, the very young child is less often spoken to than spoken about. Nonetheless, both Kaluli and Samoan children become fluent speakers within the range of normal developmental variation.

Given that the features of caregivers' speech cannot be accounted for primarily in terms of their language-facilitating function, that is, as input, we might ask what can account for the special ways in which caregivers speak to their children. We suggest that the particular features of the caregiver register are best understood as an expression of a basic sociological phenomenon. Every social relationship is associated with a set of behaviors, verbal and nonverbal, that set off that relationship from other relationships. Additionally, these behaviors indicate to others that a particular social relationship is being actualized. From this point of view, the "special" features of caregiver speech are not special at all, in the sense that verbal modifications do occur wherever social relationships are called into play. This phenomenon has been overlooked in part because in describing the language of caregivers to children it is usually contrasted with a generalized notion of the ways in which adults talk to everyone else. The most extreme example of this is found in interviews with adults in which they are asked to describe special ways of talking to babies (Ferguson 1977). A less extreme example is found in the procedure of comparing caregiver speech to children with caregiver speech to the researcher/outsider (Newport, Gleitman, & Gleitman 1977). In the latter case, only one adult-adult relationship is used as a basis of comparison, and this relationship is typically formal and socially distant.

The social nature of caregiver speech has been discussed with respect to its status as a type of speech register. Nonetheless, the language-simplifying features have been emphasized more than any other aspect of the register. The dimension of simplification is significant with respect to the white middle-class caregiver registers documented; however, the notion of simplification has been taken as synonymous with the caregiver register itself. More to the point of this discussion is the apparent tendency to see simplification as a universal, if not natural, process. Ferguson's insightful parallel between caregiver speech and foreigner talk (1977) has been taken to mean that more competent speakers everywhere spontaneously accommodate their speech to less competent interactional partners, directly influencing language change in contact situations (pidgins in particular) as well as in acquisition of a foreign language. Ferguson's own discussion of "simplified registers" does not carry with it this conclusion, however. Further, the stories told here of Kaluli and Samoan caregiver speech and comportment indicate that simplification is culturally organized in terms of when, how, and extent. In both stories, caregivers do not speak in a dramatically more simplified manner to very young children. They do not do so for different cultural reasons: The Kaluli do not simplify because such speech is felt to inhibit the development of competent speech, the Samoans because such accommodations are dispreferred when the addressee is of lower rank than the speaker.

The cultural nature of simplification is evidenced very clearly when we compare Samoan speech to young children with Samoan speech to foreigners (*palagi*). As discussed by Duranti (1981), "foreigner talk" *is* simplified in many ways, in contrast to "baby talk." To understand this, we need only return to the social principle of relative rank. Foreigners typically (and historically) are persons to whom respect is appropriate – strangers or guests of relatively high status. The appropriate comportment toward such persons is one of accommodation to their needs, communicative needs being basic. The Samoan example is an important one, because we can use it to understand social groups for whom speaking to foreigners is like speaking to children. That is, we can at least know where to *start* the process of understanding this speech phenomenon; to see the phenomenon as expressive of cultural beliefs and values. Just as there are cultural explanations for why and how Samoans speak differently to young children and foreigners, so there are cultural explanations for why and how white middle-class adults modify their speech in similar ways to these two types of addressees. These explanations go far beyond the attitudes discussed in the white middle-class story. Our task here is not to provide an adequate cultural account but rather to encourage more detailed research along these lines. An understanding of caregiver or baby-talk register in a particular society will never be achieved without a more serious consideration of the sociological nature of register.

What caregivers do with words. In this section we build on the prior two proposals and suggest that:

1. A functional account of the speech of both caregiver and child must incorporate information concerning cultural knowledge and expectations;
2. Generalizations concerning the relations between the behavior and the goals of caregivers and young children should not presuppose the presence or equivalent significance of particular goals across social groups.

In each of these developmental stories we saw that caregivers and children interacted with one another in culturally patterned ways. Our overriding theme has been that caregiver speech behavior must be seen as part of caregiving and socialization more generally. What caregivers say and how they interact with young children are motivated in part by concerns and beliefs held by many members of the local community.

As noted earlier, these concerns and beliefs may not be conscious in all cases. Certain beliefs, such as the Kaluli notions of the child as "soft" and socialization as "hardening" the child, are explicit. Others, such as the white middle-class notions of the infant and small child as social and capable of acting intentionally (expressing intentions), are not explicitly formulated.

To understand what any particular verbal behavior is accomplishing, we need to adopt ethnographic procedures, namely, to relate particular behaviors to those performed in other situations. What a caregiver is doing in speaking to a child is obviously related to what she or he does and/or others do in other recurrent situations. We have suggested, for example, that the accommodations that middle-class (particularly American) caregivers make in speaking to young children are linked patterned ways of responding to incompetence in general (e.g., handicapped persons, retardates). Members of this social group appear to adapt situations to meet the special demands of less competent persons to a far greater extent than in other societies, for example, Samoan society. We have also suggested that the heavy use of expansions by middle-class caregivers to query or confirm what a child is expressing is linked to culturally preferred procedures for achieving understanding, for example, the recognition of ambiguity, the formulation and verification of hypotheses (interpretations, guesses). In participating in interactions in which expansions are used in this way, the child learns the concepts of ambiguity, interpretation, and verification, and the procedures associated with them.

A common method in child language research has been to infer function or goal from behavior. The pitfalls of this procedure are numerous, and social scientists are acutely aware of how difficult it is to establish structure–function relations. One aspect of this dilemma is that one cannot infer function on the basis of a structure in isolation. Structures get their functional meaning through their relation to contexts in which they appear. The "same" structure may have different functions in different circumstances. This is true within a society, but our reason for mentioning it here is that it is true also across societies and languages. Although caregivers in two different societies may expand their children's utterances, it would not necessarily follow that the caregivers shared the same beliefs and values. It is possible that their behavior is motivated by quite different cultural processes. Similarly, the absence of a particular behavior, such as the absence of expansions among caregivers, may be motivated quite differently across societies. Both the Kaluli and the Samoan caregivers do not appear to rely on expansions, but the reasons expansions are dispreferred differ. The Samoans do not do so in part because of their dispreference for guessing and in part because of their expectation that the burden of intelligibility rests with the child (as lower status party) rather than with more mature members of the society. Kaluli do not use expansions to resay or guess.

what a child may be expressing because they say that "one cannot know what someone else thinks," regardless of age or social status.

Our final point concerning the structure–function relation is that the syntax of our claims about language acquisition must be altered to recognize variation across societies. The bulk of research on communicative development has presupposed or asserted the universality of one or another function, for example, the input function, the communicative function, and the illustrated verbal and nonverbal behaviors that follow from, or reflect, that function. Our three stories suggest that generalizations must be context-restricted. Thus, for example, rather than assuming or asserting that caregivers desire to communicate with an infant, the generalization should be expressed: "Where caregivers desire communication with an infant, then . . ." or "If it is the case that caregivers desire communication with an infant then . . ."

A typology of socialization and caregiver speech patterns

At this point, with the discussion nearing its conclusion, we have decided to stick our necks out a bit further and suggest that the two orientations to children discussed in the developmental stories – adapting situations to the child and adapting the child to situations – distinguish more than the three societies discussed in this chapter. We believe that these two orientations of mature members toward children can be used to create a typology of socialization patterns. For example, societies in which children are expected to adapt to situations may include not only Kaluli and Samoan but also white and black working-class Anglo-Americans (Heath 1983; Miller 1982; Ward 1971).

The typology of course requires a more refined application of these orienting features. We would expect these orientations to shift as children develop; for example, a society may adapt situations to meet the needs of a very small infant, but as the infant matures, the expectation may shift to one in which the child should adapt to situations. Indeed, we could predict such a pattern for most, if not all, societies. The distinction between societies would be in terms of *when* this shift takes place and in terms of the *intensity* of the orientation at any point in developmental time.

Having stuck our necks out this far, we will go a little further and propose that these two orientations will have systematic reflexes in the organization of communication between caregivers and young children across societies: We predict, for example, that a society that adapts or fits situations to the needs (perceived needs) of young children will use a register to children that includes a number of simplifying features, for example, shorter utterances, with a restricted lexicon, that refer to here-and-now. Such an orientation is also compatible with a tendency for caregivers to assist the child's expression of intentions through expansions, clarification requests, cooperative proposition building and the like. These often involve the caregiver's taking the perspective

Table 11.1. *Two orientations toward children and their corresponding caregiver speech patterns*

Adapt situation to child	Adapt child to situation
Simplified register features baby-talk lexicon	Modeling of (unsimplified) utterances for child to repeat to third party (wide range of speech act, not simplified)
Negotiation of meaning via expansion and paraphrase	
Cooperative proposition building between caregiver and child	Child directed to notice others
Utterances that respond to child-initiated verbal or nonverbal act	Topics arise from range of situational circumstances to which caregiver wishes child to respond
Typical communicative situation: two-party	Typical communicative situation: multiparty

of a small child and correlate highly with allowing a small child to initiate new topics (evidencing child-centered orientation).

On the other hand, societies in which children are expected to meet the needs of the situation at hand will communicate differently with infants and small children. In these societies, children usually participate in multiparty situations. Caregivers will socialize children through language to notice others and perform appropriate (not necessarily polite) speech acts toward others. This socialization will often take the form of modeling, where the caregiver says what the child should say and directs the child to repeat. Typically, the child is directed to say something to someone other than the caregiver who has modeled the original utterance. From the Kaluli and Samoan cases, we would predict that the utterances to be repeated would cover a wide range of speech acts (teasing, insulting, greeting, information requesting, begging, reporting of news, shaming, accusations, and the like). In these interactions, as in other communicative contexts with children, the caregivers do not simplify their speech but rather shape their speech to meet situational contingencies (Table 11.1).

A model of language acquisition through socialization (the ethnographic approach)

CULTURAL ORGANIZATION OF INTENTIONALITY

Like many scholars of child language, we believe that the acquisition of language is keyed to accomplishing particular goals (Bates et al. 1979; Greenfield & Smith 1976; Halliday 1975; Lock 1978; Shotter 1978; Vygotsky 1962). As Bates and her colleagues (1979) as well as Carter (1978) and Lock (1981) have pointed out, small children perform communicative acts such as drawing attention to an object and requesting and offering before conventional morphemes are produced. They have acquired knowledge of particular social acts before they have acquired language in even the most rudimentary form. When language emerges, it is put to use in these and other social contexts. As Bates and her colleagues suggest, the use of language here is analogous to other behaviors of the child at this point of development; the child is using a new means to achieve old goals.

Although not taking a stand as to whether or not language is like other behaviors, we support the notion that language is acquired in a social world and that many aspects of the social world have been absorbed by the child by the time language emerges. This is not to say that functional considerations determine grammatical structure but rather that ends motivate means and provide an orienting principle for producing and understanding language over developmental time. Norman (1975), as well as Hood, McDermott, and Cole (1978), suggests that purpose/function is a mnemonic device for learning generally.

Much of the literature on early development has carefully documented the child's capacity to react and act intentionally (Harding & Golinkoff 1979). The nature and organization of communicative interaction is seen as integrally bound to this capacity. Our contribution to this literature is to spell out the social and cultural systems in which intentions participate. The capacity to express intentions is human but which intentions can be expressed by whom, when, and how is subject to local expectations concerning the social behavior of members. With respect to the acquisition of competence in language use, this means that societies may very well differ in their expectations of what children can and should communicate (Hymes 1967). They may also differ in their expectations concerning the capacity of young children to understand intentions (or particular intentions). With respect to the particular relationship between a child and his or her caregivers, these generalizations can be represented as follows:

Social expectations and language acquisition

Expectations	*Influence*	Participation in social situations	How & which intentions are expressed by child	Structure of child language
			Influences	*Influence*
			How & which intentions are expressed by caregiver	Structure of caregiver language

Let us consider examples that illustrate these statements. As noted in the Samoan development story, Samoans have a commonly shared expectation that a child's first word will be *tae* (shit) and that its communicative intention will be to curse and confront (corresponding to the adult for '*ai tae* (eat shit). Whereas a range of early consonant-vowel combinations of the child are treated as expressing *tae* and communicative, other phonetic strings are not treated as language. The Kaluli consider that the child has begun to use language when he or she says "mother" and "breast." Like the Samoans, the Kaluli do not treat other words produced before these two words appear as part of "language," that is, as having a purpose.

Another example of how social expectations influence language acquisition comes from the recent work by Platt (1980) on Samoan children's acquisition of the deictic verbs "come," "go," "give," "take." The use of these verbs over developmental time is constrained by social norms concerning the movement of persons and objects. As noted in the Samoan story, higher ranking persons are expected to be relatively inactive in the company of lower ranking (e.g., younger) persons. As a consequence, younger children who are directed to "come" and who evidence comprehension of this act, tend not to perform the same act themselves. Children are socially constrained not to direct the more mature persons around them to move in their direction. On the other hand, small children are encouraged to demand and give out goods (particularly food). At the same developmental point at which the children are *not* using "come," they *are* using "give" quite frequently. This case is interesting because it indicates that a semantically more complex form ("give" – movement of object and person toward deictic center) may appear in the speech of a child earlier than a less complex form ("come" – movement of person toward deictic center) because of the social norms surrounding its use (Platt 1980).

Although these examples have focused on children's speech, we also consider caregiver speech to be constrained by local expectations and the values and beliefs that underlie them. The reader is invited to draw on the body of this chapter for examples of these relationships, for example, the relation between caregivers who adapt to young children and use of a simplified register. Indeed, the major focus of our developmental stories has been to indicate precisely the role of sociocultural processes in constructing communication between caregiver and child.

SOCIOCULTURAL KNOWLEDGE AND CODE KNOWLEDGE

In this section we will build on our argument that children's language is constructed in socially appropriate and culturally meaningful ways. Our point will be that the process of acquiring language must be understood as the process of integrating code knowledge with sociocultural knowledge.

Sociocultural knowledge is generative in much the same way that knowledge about grammar is generative. Just as children are able to produce and understand utterances that they have never heard before, so they are able to participate in social situations that don't exactly match their previous experiences. In the case of social situations in which language is used, children are able to apply both grammatical and sociocultural principles in producing and comprehending novel behavior. Both sets of principles can be acquired out of conscious awareness.

Sociocultural → code
knowledge   ← knowledge

(with vertical axis label "Developmental time")

In the case of infants and young children acquiring their first language(s), sociocultural knowledge is acquired hand-in-hand with the knowledge of code properties of a language. Acquisition of a foreign or second language by older children and adults may not necessarily follow this model. In classroom foreign-language learning, for example, a knowledge of code properties typically precedes knowledge of the cultural norms of code use. Even where the second language is acquired in the context of living in a foreign culture, the cultural knowledge necessary for appropriate social interaction may lag behind or never develop, as illustrated by Gumperz (1977) for Indian speakers in Great Britain.

Another point to be mentioned at this time is that the sociocultural principles being acquired are not necessarily shared by all native speakers of a language. As noted in the introduction, there are variations in knowledge between individuals and between groups of individuals. In certain cases, for example, children who are members of a nondominant group, growing up may necessitate acquiring different cultural frameworks for participating in situations. American Indian and Australian Aboriginal children find themselves participating in interactions in which the language is familiar but the interactional procedures and participant structures differ from earlier experiences (Philips 1983). These cases of growing up monolingually but biculturally are similar to the circumstances of second-language learners who enter a cultural milieu that differs from that of first socialization experiences.

ON THE UNEVENNESS OF LANGUAGE DEVELOPMENT

The picture we have built up suggests that there is quite a complex system of norms and expectations that the young language acquirer must attend to, and does attend to, in the process of growing up to be a competent speaker-hearer. We have talked about this system as affecting structure and content of children's utterances at different points in developmental time. One product of all this is that children come to use and hear particular structures in certain contexts but not in others.

In other words, children acquire forms in a subset of contexts that has been given "priority" by members.

Priority contexts are those in which children are encouraged to participate. For example, Kaluli and Samoan children use affect pronouns, for example, "poor-me," initially in begging, an activity they are encouraged to engage in. The use of affect pronouns in other speech acts is a later development. Similarly, many white middle-class children use their first nominal forms in the act of labeling, an activity much encouraged by caregivers in this social group. Labeling is not an activity in which Kaluli and Samoan caregivers and children engage in. Each social group will have its preferences, and these, in turn, will guide the child's acquisition of language.

ON LACK OF MATCH BETWEEN CHILD AND CAREGIVER SPEECH

Those who pursue the argument concerning how children acquire language often turn to correlational comparisons between children's and caregivers' speech strategies. Lack of match is taken as support for some input-independent strategy of the child and as evidence that some natural process is at work. We suggest that this line of reasoning has flaws.

If the reader has accepted the argument that societies have ideas about how children can and should participate in social situations and that these ideas differ in many respects from those concerning how more mature persons can and should behave, then the reader might further accept the conclusion that children may speak and act differently from others because they have learned to do so. Why should we equate input exclusively with imitation, that is, with a match in behavior? Of course there are commonalities between child and adult behavior, but that does not imply that difference is not learned. In examining the speech of young children, we should not necessarily expect their speech and the functions to which it is put to match exactly those of caregivers. Children are neither expected nor encouraged to do many of the things that older persons do, and, conversely, older persons are neither expected nor encouraged to do many of the things that small children do. Indeed, unless they are framed as "play," attempts to cross these social boundaries meet with laughter, ridicule, or other forms of negative sanctioning.

A NOTE ON THE ROLE OF BIOLOGY

Lest the reader think we advocate a model in which language and cognition are the exclusive product of culture, we note here that sociocultural systems are to be considered as *one* force influencing language acquisition. Biological predispositions, of course, have a hand in this process as well. The model we have presented should be considered as a subset of a more general acquisition model that includes both influences.

Social expectations		Language over
	Influence	developmental
Biological predispositions		time

Conclusions

This is a chapter with a number of points but one message: That the process of acquiring language and the process of acquiring sociocultural knowledge are intimately tied. In pursuing this generalization, we have formulated the following proposals:

1. The specific features of caregiver speech behavior that have been described as simplified register are neither universal nor necessary for language to be acquired. White middle-class children, Kaluli children, and Samoan children all become speakers of their languages within the normal range of development and yet their caregivers use language quite differently in their presence.
2. Caregivers' speech behavior expresses and reflects values and beliefs held by members of a social group. In this sense, caregivers' speech is part of a larger set of behaviors that are culturally organized.
3. The use of simplified registers by caregivers in certain societies may be part of a more general orientation in which situations are adapted to young children's perceived needs. In other societies, the orientation may be the reverse, that is, children at a very early age are expected to adapt to requirements of situations. In such societies, caregivers direct children to notice and respond to other's actions. They tend not to simplify their speech and frequently model appropriate utterances for the child to repeat to a third party in a situation.
4. Not only caregivers' but children's language as well is influenced by social expectations. Children's strategies for encoding and decoding information, for negotiating meaning, and for handling errors are socially organized in terms of who does the work, when, and how. Further, every society orchestrates the ways in which children participate in particular situations, and this, in turn, affects the form, the function, and the content of children's utterances. Certain features of the grammar may be acquired quite early, in part because their use is encouraged and given high priority. In this sense, the process of language acquisition is part of the larger process of socialization, that is, acquiring social competence.

Although biological factors play a role in language acquisition, sociocultural factors have a hand in this process as well. It is not a trivial fact that small children develop in the context of organized societies. Cultural conditions for communication organize even the earliest interactions between infants and others. Through participation as audience, addressee, and/or "speaker," the infant develops a range of skills, intuitions, and knowledge enabling him or her to communicate in culturally preferred ways. The development of these faculties is an integral part of becoming a competent speaker.

CODA

This chapter should be in no way interpreted as proposing a view in which socialization determines a fixed pattern of behavior. We advocate a view that considers human beings to be flexible and able to adapt to change, both social and linguistic, for example, through contact and social mobility. The ways in which individuals change is a product of complex interactions between established cultural procedures and intuitions and those the individual is currently acquiring. From our perspective, socialization is a continuous and open-ended process that spans the entire life of an individual.

Notes

This chapter was written while the authors were research fellows at the Research School of Pacific Studies, the Australian National University. We would like to thank Roger Keesing and the Working Group in Language and Its Cultural Context. Ochs's research was supported by the National Science Foundation and the Australian National University. Schieffelin's research was supported by the National Science Foundation and the Wenner-Gren Foundation for Anthropological Research. We thank these institutions for their support.

1. This story is based on the numerous accounts of caregiver–child communication and interaction that have appeared in both popular and scientific journals. Our generalizations regarding language use are based on detailed reports in the developmental psycholinguistic literature, which are cited throughout. In addition, we have drawn on our own experiences and intuitions as mothers and members of this social group. We invite those with differing perceptions to comment on our interpretations.

2. We would like to thank Courtney Cazden for bringing the following quotation to our attention: "It seems to us that a mother in expanding speech may be teaching more than grammar; she may be teaching something like a world-view" (Brown & Bellugi 1964).

3. This analysis is based on the data collected in the course of ethnographic and linguistic fieldwork among the Kaluli in the Southern Highlands Province between 1975 and 1977. During this time, E. L. Schieffelin, a cultural anthropologist, and S. Feld, an ethnomusicologist, were also conducting ethnographic research. This study of the development of communicative competence among the Kaluli focused on four children who were approximately 24 months old at the start of the study. However, an additional twelve children were included in the study (siblings and cousins in residence), ranging in age from birth to 10 years. The spontaneous conversations of these children and their families were tape-recorded for one year at monthly intervals with each monthly sample lasting from 3 to 4 hours. Detailed contextual notes accompanied the taping, and these annotated transcripts, along with interviews and observations, form the data base. A

total of 83 hours of audio-tape were collected and transcribed in the village. Analyses of Kaluli child acquisition data are reported in Schieffelin 1981, in press-a, and in press-b.

4. The data on which this analysis is based were collected from July 1978 to July 1979 in a traditional village in Western Samoa. The village, Falefa, is located on the island of Upolu, approximately 18 miles from the capital, Apia. The fieldwork was conducted by Alessandro Duranti, Martha Platt, and Elinor Ochs. Our data collection consisted of two major projects. The first, carried out by Ochs and Platt, was a longitudinal documentation, through audio- and videotape, of young children's acquisition of Samoan. This was accomplished by focusing on six children from six different households, from 19 to 35 months of age at the onset of the study. These children were observed and taped every five weeks, approximately three hours each period. Samoan children live in compounds composed of several households. Typically, numerous siblings and peers are present and interact with a young child. We were able to record the speech of seventeen other children under the age of 6, who were part of the children's early social environment. A total of 128 hours of audio and 20 hours of video recording were collected. The audio material is supplemented by handwritten notes detailing contextual features of the interactions recorded. All the audio material has been transcribed in the village by a family member or family acquaintance and checked by a researcher. Approximately 18,000 pages of transcript form the child language data base. Analyses of Samoan child language are reported in Ochs 1982a, 1982b, and in press.

References

Aksu, A., & Slobin, D. I. In press. Acquisition of Turkish. In D. I. Slobin, ed., *The Crosslinguistic Study of Language Acquisition*. Hillsdale, N.J.: Erlbaum.

Andersen, E. 1977. *Learning to speak with style*. Unpublished doctoral dissertation, Stanford University.

Andersen, E. S., Dunlea, A., & Kekelis, L. 1982. *Blind children's language: resolving some differences*. Paper presented at the Stanford Child Language Research Forum, Stanford, Calif.

Andersen, E. S., & Johnson, C. E. 1973. Modifications in the speech of an eight-year-old to younger children. *Stanford Occasional Papers in Linguistics*, No. 3:149–60.

Bates, E. 1976. *Language and Context: the Acquisition of Pragmatics*. New York: Academic Press.

Bates, E., Beeghly-Smith, M., Bretherton, I., & McNew, S. In press. Social bases of language development: a reassessment. In H. W. Reese & L. P. Lipsitt, eds., *Advances in Child Development and Behavior*, vol. 16. New York: Academic Press.

Bates, E., Benigni, L., Bretherton, I., Camaioni, L., & Volterra, V. 1979. *The Emergence of Symbols*. New York: Academic Press.

Berko, J. 1958. The child's learning of English morphology. *Word* 14:150–77.

Berman, R. In press. Acquisition of Hebrew. In D. I. Slobin, ed., *The Crosslinguistic Study of Language Acquisition*. Hillsdale, N.J.: Erlbaum.

Bever, T. 1970. The cognitive basis for linguistic structure. In J. R. Hayes, ed., *Cognition and the Development of Language*. New York: Wiley.

Bloom, L. 1970. *Language Development: Form and Function in Emerging Grammars.* Cambridge, Mass.: MIT Press.

1973. *One Word at a Time.* The Hague: Mouton.

Bloom, L., Hood, L., & Lightbown, P. 1974. Imitation in language development: if, when, and why? *Cognitive Psychology* 6:380–420.

Bloom, L., & Lahey, M. 1978. *Language Development and Language Disorders.* New York: Wiley.

Bloom, L., Lightbown, P., & Hood, L. 1975. Structure and variation in child language. *Monographs of the Society for Research in Child Development* 40(2, serial no. 160).

Blount, B. 1972. Aspects of socialization among the Luo of Kenya. *Language in Society* 1:235–48.

Bowerman, M. 1973. *Early Syntactic Development: A Cross-linguistic Study with Special Reference to Finnish.* Cambridge: Cambridge University Press.

1977. Semantic and syntactic development: A review of what, when and how in language acquisition. In R. Schiefelbusch, ed., *Bases of Language Intervention.* Baltimore: University Park Press.

1981. Language development. In H. Triandis & A. Heron, eds., *Handbook of Cross-cultural Psychology,* vol. 4. Boston: Allyn & Bacon.

Briggs, J. L. 1970. *Never in Anger: Portrait of an Eskimo Family.* Cambridge, Mass.: Harvard University Press.

Brown, R. 1973. *A First Language: The Early Stages,* Cambridge, Mass.: Harvard University Press.

1977. Introduction. In C. Snow & C. Ferguson, eds., *Talking to Children: Language Input and Acquisition.* Cambridge: Cambridge University Press.

Brown, R., & Bellugi, U. 1964. Three processes in the child's acquisition of syntax. *Harvard Educational Review* 34:133–51.

Brown, R., Cazden C., & Bellugi, U. 1969. The child's grammar from I to III. In J. P. Hill, ed., *Minnesota Symposium on Child Psychology,* vol. 2. Minneapolis: University of Minnesota Press.

Bruner, J. S. 1975. The ontogenesis of speech acts. *Journal of Child Language* 2:1–19.

1977. Early social interaction and language acquisition. In H. R. Schaffer, ed., *Studies in Mother-Infant Interaction.* London: Academic Press.

1978. The role of dialogue in language acquisition. In A. Sinclair, R. J. Jarvella, & W. J. M. Levelt, eds., *The Child's Conception of Language.* New York: Springer-Verlag.

Bullowa, M. 1979. Introduction: prelinguistic communication: a field for scientific research. In M. Bullowa, ed., *Before Speech: The Beginnings of Interpersonal Communication.* Cambridge: Cambridge University Press.

Carter, A. L. 1978. From sensori-motor vocalizations to words. In A. Lock, ed., *Action, Gesture and Symbol: The Emergence of Language.* London: Academic Press.

Cazden, C. 1965. *Environmental assistance to the child's acquisition of grammar.* Unpublished doctoral dissertation, Harvard University.

Chomsky, N. 1959. Review of *Verbal Behavior* by B. F. Skinner. *Language* 35:26–58.

1965. *Aspects of the Theory of Syntax.* Cambridge, Mass.: MIT Press.

1968. *Language and Mind.* New York: Harcourt Brace Jovanovich.

1975. *Reflections on Language*. Glasgow: Fontana/Collins.

1977. *Essays on Form and Interpretation*. New York: North Holland.

Clancy, P. In press. Acquisition of Japanese. In D. I. Slobin, ed., *The Crosslinguistic Study of Language Acquisition*. Hillsdale, N.J.: Erlbaum.

Clark, E. V. 1974. Some aspects of the conceptual basis for first language acquisition. In R. L. Schiefelbusch & L. Lloyd, eds., *Language Perspectives: Acquisition, Retardation and Intervention*. Baltimore: University Park Press.

In press. Acquisition of Romance, with special reference to French. In D. I. Slobin, ed., *The Crosslinguistic Study of Language Acquisition*. Hillsdale, N.J.: Erlbaum.

Clark, H. H., & Clark, E. V. 1977. *Psychology and Language*. New York: Harcourt Brace Jovanovich.

Corsaro, W. 1979. Sociolinguistic patterns in adult-child inter-action. In E. Ochs & B. B. Schieffelin, eds., *Developmental Pragmatics*. New York: Academic Press.

Cross, T. 1977. Mothers' speech adjustments: the contributions of selected child listener variables. In C. Snow & C. Ferguson, eds., *Talking to Children: Language Input and Acquisition*. Cambridge: Cambridge University Press.

de Lemos, C. 1981. Interactional processes in the child's construction of language. In W. Deutsch, ed., *The Child's Construction of Language*. London: Academic Press.

Dentan, R. K. 1978. Notes on childhood in a nonviolent context: the Semai case. In A. Montagu, ed., *Learning Non-aggression: The Experience of Nonliterate Societies*. Oxford: Oxford University Press.

Dore, J. 1975. Holophrases, speech acts and language universals. *Journal of Child Language* 2:21–40.

Drach, K. 1969. *The language of the parent*. Working paper 14, Language Behavior Research Laboratory, University of California, Berkeley.

Duranti, A. 1981. *The Samoan Fono: A Sociolinguistic Study*. Pacific Linguistic Series B, vol. 80. Canberra: Australian National University.

Edgerton, R. 1967. *The Cloak of Competence: Stigma in the Lives of the Mentally Retarded*. Berkeley: University of California Press.

Eisenberg, A. 1982. *Language acquisition in cultural perspective: talk in three Mexicano homes*. Unpublished doctoral dissertation, University of California, Berkeley.

Ervin-Tripp, S. 1964. Imitation and structural change in children's language. In E. Lenneberg, ed., *New Directions in the Study of Language*. Cambridge, Mass.: MIT Press.

Feld, S., & Schieffelin, B. B. 1982. Hard words: A functional basis for Kaluli discourse. In D. Tannen, ed., *Analyzing Discourse: Talk and Text*. Washington, D.C.: Georgetown University Press.

Feldman, H., Goldin-Meadow, S., & Gleitman, L. 1978. Beyond Herodotus: the creation of language by linguistically deprived deaf children. In A. Lock, ed., *Action, Gesture and Symbol*. London: Academic Press.

Ferguson, C. 1977. Baby talk as a simplified register. In C. Snow & C. Ferguson, eds., *Talking to Children: Language Input and Acquisition*. Cambridge: Cambridge University Press.

Fischer, J. 1970. Linguistic socialization: Japan and the United States. In R. Hill & R. Konig, eds., *Families in East and West*. The Hague: Mouton.

Fodor, J., Bever, T., & Garrett, M. 1974. *The Psychology of Language*. New York: McGraw-Hill.

Foster, S. 1981. The emergence of topic type in children under 2,6: a chicken and egg problem. *Papers and Reports in Child Language Development*, No. 20. Stanford, Calif.: Stanford University Press.

Gallimore, R., Boggs, J., & Jordan, C. 1974. *Culture, Behavior and Education: a Study of Hawaiian Americans*. Beverly Hills, Calif.: Sage.

Garnica, O. 1977. Some prosodic and para-linguistic features of speech to young children. In C. Snow & C. Ferguson, eds., *Talking to Children: Language Input and Acquisition*. Cambridge: Cambridge University Press.

Geertz, C. 1973. *The Interpretation of Cultures*. New York: Basic Books.

Geertz, H. 1959. The vocabulary of emotion: a study of Javanese socialization processes. *Psychiatry* 22:225–37.

Gleason, J. B., & Weintraub, S. 1978. Input language and the acquisition of communicative competence. In K. Nelson, ed., *Children's Language*, vol. 1. New York: Gardner Press.

Goffman, E. 1963. *Behavior in Public Places*. New York: Free Press.

1967. *Interaction Ritual: Essays on Face to Face Behavior*. Garden City, N.Y.: Doubleday (Anchor Books).

Goldin-Meadow, S. 1977. Structure in a manual language system developed without a language model: language without a helping hand. In H. Whitaker & H. A. Whitaker, eds., *Studies in Neurolinguistics*, vol. 4. New York: Academic Press.

Golinkoff, R., ed. 1983. *The Transition from Prelinguistic to Linguistic Communication*. Hillsdale, N.J.: Erlbaum.

Goody, E. 1978. Towards a theory of questions. In E. Goody, ed., *Questions and Politeness*. Cambridge: Cambridge University Press.

Greenfield, P. 1979. Informativeness, presupposition and semantic choice in single-word utterances. In E. Ochs & B. B. Schieffelin, eds., *Developmental Pragmatics*, New York: Academic Press.

Greenfield, P. M., & Smith, J. H. 1976. *The Structure of Communication in Early Language Development*. New York: Academic Press.

Gumperz, J. 1977. The conversational analysis of interethnic communication. In E. L. Ross, ed., *Interethnic Communication. Proceedings of the Southern Anthropological Society*. Athens: University of Georgia Press.

Halliday, M. A. K. 1975. *Learning How to Mean: Explorations in the Development of Language*, London: Arnold.

Hamilton, A. 1981. *Nature and Nurture: Aboriginal Childrearing in North-Central Arnhem Land*. Canberra, Australia: Institute of Aboriginal Studies.

Harding, C., & Golinkoff, R. M. 1979. The origins of intentional vocalizations in prelinguistic infants. *Child Development* 50:33–40.

Harkness, S. 1975. Cultural variation in mother's language. In W. von Raffler-Engel, ed., *Child Language – 1975, Word* 27:495–8.

Harkness, S., & Super, C. 1977. Why African children are so hard to test. In L. L. Adler, ed., *Issues in Cross Cultural Research: Annals of the New York Academy of Scences* 285:326–331.

eds. 1980. *Anthropological Perspectives on Child Development*. New Directions for Child Development, no. 8. San Francisco: Jossey-Bass.

Heath, S. B. 1983. *Ways with Words: Language, Life and Work in Communities and Classroom*. Cambridge: Cambridge University Press.

Hood, L., McDermott, R., & Cole, M. 1978. *Ecological niche-picking* (Working Paper 14). Unpublished manuscript, Rockefeller University, Laboratory of Comparative Human Cognition, New York.

Huttenlocher, J. 1974. The origins of language comprehension. In R. L. Solso, ed., *Theories of Cognitive Psychology*. Hillsdale, N.J.: Erlbaum.

Hymes, D. 1967. Models of the interaction of language and social setting. *Journal of Social Issues* 23(2):8–28.

    1974. *Foundations in Sociolinguistics: An Ethnographic Approach*. Philadelphia: University of Pennsylvania Press.

Irvine, J. 1974. Strategies of status manipulation in the Wolof greeting. In R. Bauman & J. Sherzer, eds., *Explorations in the Ethnography of Speaking*. Cambridge: Cambridge University Press.

Johnston, J. R., & Slobin, D. I. 1979. The development of locative expressions in English, Italian Serbo-Croatian and Turkish. *Journal of Child Language* 6:529–45.

Karmiloff-Smith, A. 1979. *A Functional Approach to Child Language*. Cambridge: Cambridge University Press.

Keenan, E., Ochs E., & Schieffelin, B. B. 1976. Topic as a discourse notion: a study of topic in the conversations of children and adults. In C. Li, ed., *Subject and Topic*. New York: Academic Press.

Kernan, K. T. 1969. *The acquisition of language by Samoan children*. Unpublished doctoral dissertation, University of California, Berkeley.

Korbin, J. 1978. *Caretaking Patterns in a Rural Hawaiian Community*. Unpublished doctoral dissertation, University of California, Los Angeles.

Leiderman, P. H., Tulkin, S. R., & Rosenfeld, A., eds. 1977. *Culture and Infancy*. New York: Academic Press.

LeVine, R. 1980. Anthropology and child development. *Anthropological Perspectives on Child Development*. New Directions for Child Development, no. 8. San Francisco: Jossey-Bass.

Levy, R. 1973. *The Tahitians*, Chicago: University of Chicago Press.

Lewis, M., & Rosenblum, L. A., eds. 1974. *The Effect of the Infant on its Caregiver*. New York: Wiley.

Lieven, E. 1980. Different routes to multiple-word combinations? *Papers and Reports in Child Language Development*, no. 19, Stanford University, Stanford, Calif.

Lock, A. 1981. *The Guided Reinvention of Language*, London: Academic Press.

    1978. *Action, Gesture and Symbol*, London: Academic Press.

MacNamara, J. 1972. The cognitive basis of language learning in infants. *Psychological Review* 79:1–13.

McNeill, D. 1966. The creation of language by children. In J. Lyons & R. J. Wales, eds., *Psycholinguistic Papers*. Edinburgh: Edinburgh University Press.

    1970. *The Acquisition of Language*. Harper & Row.

MacWhinney, B. 1975. Rules, rote and analogy in morphological formation by Hungarian children. *Journal of Child Language* 2:65–77.

MacWhinney, B., & Bates, E. 1978. Sentential devices for conveying givenness and newness: a cross-cultural developmental study. *Journal of Verbal Learning and Verbal Behavior* 17:539–58.

Mead, M. 1927. *Coming of Age in Samoa*. New York: Blue Ribbon Books.

    1975. *Growing Up in New Guinea*. New York: Morrow. Originally published, 1935.

Mead, M., & MacGregor, F. 1951. *Growth and Culture*. New York: Putnam.

Mead, M., & Wolfenstein, M. 1955. *Childhood in Contemporary Cultures*. Chicago: University of Chicago Press.

Menyuk, P. & Menn, L. 1979. Early strategies for the perception and production of words and sounds. In P. Fletcher & M. Garman, eds., *Language Acquisition*. Cambridge: Cambridge University Press.

Miller, G., & Chomsky, N. 1963. Finitary models of language users. In R. Bush, E. Galanter, & R. Luce, eds., *Handbook of Mathematical Psychology*, vol. 2. New York: Wiley.

Miller, P. 1982. *Amy, Wendy and Beth: Learning Language in South Baltimore*. Austin: University of Texas Press.

Montagu, A. 1937. *Coming into Being Among the Australian Aborigines: A Study of the Procreation Beliefs of the Native Tribes of Australia*. London: Routledge.

ed. 1978. *Learning Non-aggression: The Experience of Nonliterate Societies*. Oxford: Oxford University Press.

Much, N., & Shweder R. 1978. Speaking of rules: the analysis of culture in breach. In W. Damon, ed., *Moral Development*. New Directions for Child Development, no. 2. San Francisco: Jossey-Bass.

Munroe, R. L., & Munroe R. N. 1975. *Cross Cultural Human Development*. Monterey, Calif.: Brooks/Cole.

Nelson, K. 1974. Concept, word and sentence: interrelations in acquisition and development. *Psychological Review* 81:267–85.

Newport, E. L. 1976. Motherese: The speech of mothers to young children. In N. J. Castellan, D. B. Pisoni, & G. R. Potts, eds., *Cognitive Theory*, vol. 2. Hillsdale, N.J.: Erlbaum.

1981. Constraints on structure: evidence from American sign language and language learning. In W. A. Collins, ed., *Minnesota Symposium on Child Psychology*, vol. 14. Hillsdale, N.J.: Erlbaum.

Newport, E. L., Gleitman, H., & Gleitman, L. R. 1977. Mother, I'd rather do it myself: some effects and non-effects of maternal speech style. In C. Snow & C. Ferguson, eds., *Talking to Children: Language Input and Acquisition*. Cambridge: Cambridge University Press.

Newson J. 1977. An intersubjective approach to the systematic description of mother-infant interaction. In H. R. Schaffer, ed., *Studies in Mother-Infant Interaction*. London: Academic Press.

1978. Dialogue and development. In A. Lock, ed., *Action, Gesture and Symbol*. London: Academic Press.

Ninio, A. 1979. The naive theory of the infant and other maternal attitudes in two subgroups in Israel. *Child Development* 50:976–80.

Norman, D. A. 1975. Cognitive organization and learning. In P. M. A. Rabbitt & S. Dornic, eds., *Attention and Performance V*. New York: Academic Press.

Ochs, E. 1982a. *Affect in Samoan child language*. Paper presented to the Stanford Child Language Research Forum, Stanford, Calif.

1982b. Ergativity and word order in Samoan child language: a sociolinguistic study. *Language* 58:646–71.

1982c. Talking to children in Western Samoa. *Language in Society* 11:77–104.

In press. Variation and error: a sociolinguistic study of language acquisition in Samoa. In D. I. Slobin, ed., *The Crosslinguistic Study of Language Acquisition*. Hillsdale, N.J.: Erlbaum.

Ochs, E., Schieffelin, B. B., & Platt, M. 1979. Propositions across utterances and speaker. In E. Ochs & B. B. Schieffelin, eds., *Developmental Pragmatics*. New York: Academic Press.

Philips, S. 1983. *The Invisible Culture*. New York: Longman.

Phillips, J. 1973. Syntax and vocabulary of mothers' speech to young children: age and sex comparisons. *Child Development* 44:182–5.

Piaget, J. 1955. *The Language and Thought of the Child*. London: Routledge & Kegan Paul. Originally published, 1926.

Piattelli-Palmarini, M., ed. 1980. *Language and Learning: The Debate Between Jean Piaget and Noam Chomsky*. Cambridge, Mass.: Harvard University Press.

Platt, M. 1980. The acquisition of "come," "give," and "bring" by Samoan children. *Papers and Reports in Child Language Development*, no. 19. Stanford, Calif.: Stanford University.

Richards, M. P. M., ed. 1974. *The Integration of a Child into a Social World*. Cambridge: Cambridge University Press.

Ryan, J. 1974. Early language development: towards a communicational analysis. In M. P. M. Richards, ed., *The Integration of a Child into a Social World*. Cambridge: Cambridge University Press.

Sachs, J. 1977. Adaptive significance of input to infants. In C. Snow & C. Ferguson, eds., *Talking to Children: Language Input and Acquisition*. Cambridge: Cambridge University Press.

Sachs, J., Brown, R., & Salerno, R. 1976. Adults speech to children. In W. von Raffler Engel & Y. Lebrun, eds., *Baby Talk and Infant Speech*. Lisse: Riddler Press.

Sachs, J., & Devin, J. 1976. Young children's use of age-appropriate speech styles. *Journal of Child Language* 3:81–98.

Schaffer, H. R., ed. 1977. *Studies in Mother-Infant Interaction*. London: Academic Press.

Schieffelin, B. B. 1979. Getting it together: an ethnographic approach to the study of the development of communicative competence. In E. Ochs & B. B. Schieffelin, eds., *Developmental Pragmatics*. New York: Academic Press.

   1981. A developmental study of pragmatic appropriateness of word order and case marking in Kaluli. In W. Deutsch, ed., *The Child's Construction of Language*. London: Academic Press.

   In press-a. Acquisition of Kaluli. In D. I. Slobin, ed., *The Crosslinguistic Study of Language Acquisition*. Hillsdale, N.J.: Erlbaum.

   In press-b. *How Kaluli Children Learn What to Say, What to Do and How to Feel*. Cambridge: Cambridge University Press.

Schieffelin, B. B., & Eisenberg, A. 1984. Cultural variation in children's conversations. In R. L. Schiefelbusch & J. Pickar, eds., *Communicative Competence: Acquisition and Intervention*. Baltimore: University Park Press.

Schieffelin, E. L. 1976. *The Sorrow of the Lonely and the Burning of the Dancers*. New York: St. Martin's Press.

Schlesinger, I. M. 1974. Relational concepts underlying language. In R. Schiefelbusch & L. Lloyd, eds., *Language Perspectives – Acquisition, Retardation and Intervention*. Baltimore: University Park Press.

Scollon, R. 1976. *Conversations with a One Year Old*. Honolulu: University Press of Hawaii.

Scollon, R. & Scollon, S. 1981. The literate two-year old: the fictionalization of self. Abstracting themes: a Chipewyan two-year-old. *Narrative, Literacy and Face in Interethnic Communication*. vol. 7 of R. O. Freedle, ed., *Advances in Discourse Processes*. Norwood, N.J.: Ablex.

Shatz, M. 1978. The relationship between cognitive processes and the development of communication skills. In C. B. Keasey, ed., *Nebraska Symposium on Motivation*, vol. 25. Lincoln: University of Nebraska Press.

1981. Learning the rules of the game: four views of the relation between social interaction and syntax acquisition. In W. Deutch, ed., *The Child's Construction of Language*. London: Academic Press.

In press. Communication. In J. Flavell & E. Markman, eds., *Cognitive Development*, P. Mussen, gen. ed., *Carmichael's Manual of Child Psychology*, 4th ed. New York: Wiley.

Shatz, M., & Gelman, R. 1973. The development of communication skills: modifications in the speech of young children as a function of listener. *Monographs of the Society for Research in Child Development*, 152 (38, serial no. 5).

Shore, B. 1982. *Sala' Ilua: A Samoan Mystery*. New York: Columbia University Press.

Shotter, J. 1978. The cultural context of communication studies: theoretical and methodological issues. In A. Lock, ed., *Action, Gesture and Symbol*. London: Academic Press.

Sinclair, H. 1971. Sensorimotor action patterns as a condition for the acquisition of syntax. In R. Huxley & E. Ingram, eds., *Language Acquisition: Models and Methods*. New York: Academic Press.

Skinner, B. F. 1957. *Verbal Behavior*. New York: Appleton-Century-Crofts.

Slobin, D. I. 1973. Cognitive prerequisites for grammar. In C. Ferguson & D. I. Slobin, eds., *Studies in Child Language Development*. New York: Holt, Rinehart and Winston.

1979. *Psycholinguistics*, 2nd ed. Glenview, Ill.: Scott Foresman.

1981. The origin of grammatical encoding of events. In W. Deutsch, ed., *The Child's Construction of Language*. London: Academic Press.

1982. Universal and particular in the acquisition of language. In E. Wanner, & L. R. Gleitman, eds., *Language Acquisition: The State of the Art*. Cambridge: Cambridge University Press.

ed. 1967. *A Field Manual for Cross-cultural Study of the Acquisition of Communicative Competence*. Language Behavior Research Laboratory, University of California, Berkeley.

ed. In press. *The Crosslinguistic Study of Language Acquisition*. Hillsdale, N.J.: Erlbaum.

Snow, C. 1972. Mothers' speech to children learning language. *Child Development* 43:549–65.

1977a. The development of conversation between mothers and babies. *Journal of Child Language* 4:1–22.

1977b. Mothers' speech research: from input to inter-action. In C. Snow & C. Ferguson, eds., *Talking to Children: Language Input and Acquisition*. Cambridge: Cambridge University Press.

1979. Conversations with children. In P. Fletcher & M. Garman, eds., *Language Acquisition*. Cambridge: Cambridge University Press.

Snow, C., de Blauw, A., & van Roosmalen, G. 1979. Talking and playing with babies: the role of ideologies of child-rearing. In M. Bullowa, ed., *Before*

Speech: The Beginnings of Interpersonal Communication. Cambridge: Cambridge University Press.

Snow, C., & Ferguson, C., eds. 1977. *Talking to Children: Language Input and Acquisition.* Cambridge: Cambridge University Press.

Stern, D. 1977. *The First Relationship: Infant and Mother.* Cambridge, Mass.: Harvard University Press.

Stross, B. 1972. Verbal processes in Tzeltal speech socialization. *Anthropological Linguistics* 14:1.

Sugarman, S. 1984. The development of preverbal communication: its contribution and limits in promoting the development of language. In R. L. Schiefelbusch & J. Pickar, eds., *Communicative Competence: Acquisition and Intervention.* Baltimore: University Park Press.

Trevarthen, C. 1979a. Communication and cooperation in early infancy: a description of primary intersubjectivity. In M. Bullowa, ed., *Before Speech: The Beginnings of Interpersonal Communication.* Cambridge: Cambridge University Press.

1979b. Instincts for human understanding and for cultural cooperation: their development in infancy. In M. von Cranach, K. Foppa, W. Lepenies, & D. Ploog, eds., *Human Ethology: Claims and Limits of a New Discipline.* Cambridge: Cambridge University Press.

van der Geest, T. 1977. Some interactional aspects of language acquisition. In C. Snow & C. Ferguson, eds., *Talking to Children: Language Input and Acquisition.* Cambridge: Cambridge University Press.

von Sturmer, D. E. 1980. *Rights in nurturing.* Unpublished master's thesis, Australian National University, Canberra.

Vygotsky, L. S. 1962. *Thought and Language.* Cambridge, Mass.: MIT Press.

Wagner, D., & Stevenson, H. W., eds. 1982. *Cultural Perspectives on Child Development.* San Francisco: Freeman.

Wanner E., & Gleitman, L. R., eds. 1982. *Language Acquisition: The State of the Art.* Cambridge: Cambridge University Press.

Ward, M. 1971. *Them Children: A Study in Language Learning.* New York: Holt, Rinehart and Winston.

Watson-Gegeo, K., & Gegeo, D. 1982. *Calling out and repeating: two key routines in Kwara'ae children's language acquisition.* Paper presented at the American Anthropological Association meetings, Washington, D.C.

Weisner, T. S., & Gallimore, R. 1977. My brother's keeper: child and sibling caretaking. *Current Anthropology* 18(2):169–90.

Werner, H., & Kaplan, B. 1963. *Symbol Formation.* New York: Wiley.

Whiting, B., ed. 1963. *Six Cultures: Studies of Child Rearing.* New York: Wiley.

Whiting, B., & Whiting J. 1975. *Children of Six Cultures.* Cambridge, Mass.: Harvard University Press.

Williams, T. R. 1969. *A Borneo Childhood: Enculturation in Dusun Society.* New York: Holt, Rinehart and Winston.

Wills, D. 1977. *Culture's cradle: social structural and interactional aspects of Senegalese socialization.* Unpublished doctoral dissertation, University of Texas, Austin.

PART IV
Commentary

12

Some reflections on cultural determinism and relativism with special reference to emotion and reason

Melford E. Spiro

A conception of culture

As I see it, "culture" designates a cognitive system, that is, a set of "propositions," both descriptive (e.g., "the planet earth sits on the back of a turtle") and normative (e.g., "it is wrong to kill"), about nature, man, and society that are more or less embedded in interlocking higher-order networks and configurations. Cultural and noncultural propositions differ in two important dimensions. First, cultural propositions are *traditional*, that is, they are developed in the historical experience of social groups, and as a social heritage, they are acquired by social actors through various processes of social transmission (enculturation) rather than constructed by them from their private experience. Second, cultural propositions are encoded in *collective*, rather than private, signs (indices and icons, to employ Peirce's distinctions, as well as symbols). Hence, they exist and (in the first instance) are discoverable by anthropologists in the collective representations of social groups without their having to probe for them in the private representations of social actors (though, as I shall soon argue, many of them are also found there, albeit in a different form). This is not to say that cultural statements, rules, values, norms, and the like are always stated in propositional form, for clearly they are not, but that they are susceptible of statement in that form.

This restricted conception of culture has important implications for what "culture" does not designate. First, although by this conception, culture is obviously an important – though only one – determinant of behavior, culture as such does not consist of behavior. Moreover, although culture – to broaden this implication – includes propositions referring to social structure, social organization, social behavior, and the like, culture as such does not consist of them. It might be added that because the latter have noncultural (situational, ecological, economic, political, biological, emotional, etc.) as well as cultural (ideational) determinants, the cultural propositions comprising the emic models of social structure, social organization, and the like cannot in themselves provide a reliable basis for predicting their content or their shape. For the same reason, cultural models cannot be reliably deduced from the observation of social behavior alone.

Second, although by this conception "culture" designates a cognitive system, it is not the only – though it is clearly the most important – source of the cognitions and schemata held by social actors. The other source, of course, consists of their own experience. Thus, on the basis of their social experience, a group of actors may come to construct a conception of their social universe as hostile and threatening even though such a conception is not transmitted to them by intentional enculturative processes and may even be inconsistent with cultural propositions that convey the very opposite message. Although conceptions of this type – beliefs or cognitive orientations constructed by social actors as an unintended consequence of social experience – have important effects on the social behavior, social structure, and world view of social groups, they are not, by our definition, "cultural." Usually, but not always, unconscious, they are not encoded in collective signs, and they are (therefore) not transmitted by means of intentional enculturative processes. (They are discovered by the anthropologist as an inference from clinically oriented interviews, dreams, projective tests, and culturally constituted projective systems such as myths, folklore, and the like.)

Third, although many cultural propositions have emotional antecedents, and although others have emotional consequences – they arouse emotional responses in social actors – and although some even prescribe the proper conditions for the expression of emotions, culture as such – a cognitive system encoded in collective representations – does not consist of emotions.

The exclusion of emotion from this conception of culture is not based on the view – which, it might be thought, I hold either from ignorance or foolishness – that emotions occur without thought or thought without emotions. Even if I held such a misguided view (which I do not), it would hardly be germaine to the present issue because – although I have defined "culture" as a cognitive system – culture does not consist of thought (thinking) any more than it consists of emotion (feeling). As thinking and feeling are properties of persons, and as culture – neither by this definition nor by any other that I am aware of – does not consist of persons – though society does – it is hard to see how either could be part of culture.

Although not a part of culture, thinking and feeling are often determined by culture. That is, we most often think by means of the concepts comprising cultural propositions, and our emotions are often aroused by them; in short, many of our thoughts and emotions are (what might be termed) "culturally constituted." But just because thoughts and emotions are culturally constituted, it is logically impermissible to conclude that culture, as such, consists of emotion or thought any more than it can be concluded that culture consists of behavior or social structure, although they too are culturally constituted (cultural propositions serve to motivate behavior and to provide a model for special structure). The conflation of culture and culturally constituted phenomena is based on a confusion of logical types, of cause with effect, structure with function, producer with product. (It is that very confusion that invalidates my earlier attempt [Spiro 1950] to understand the relationship between mind and culture by arguing – as I now see it – fallaciously that "culture" and "personality" are synonymous.)

If, then, the exclusion of emotion from this conception of culture is not based on the misguided view that feeling is isolated from thinking, neither is it based on the view that while emotions (because they are "located" in the mind) are private events, thoughts (because culture is "located" in collective representations) are public. In fact, I reject that view, not because I believe that emotions are public – although their expression is – but because I believe that thoughts are also private. Hence, as culture is a public system, thoughts no less than emotions are, by definition, excluded from "culture."

Culture is public because it consists of propositions that are encoded in collective representations, or public signs, usually, but not always, symbols. It is precisely for that reason that anyone – and not only a native – can learn the culture of any social group. Since, then, the "meanings" of those signs consist of the concepts they designate and represent, cultural propositions are public because – as Saussure (1966) has shown – their meanings are "located," as it were, in the signs themselves: the signs, to employ his terms, function simultaneously as both signified (concept) and signifier (sign vehicle). When, however, cultural propositions are learned by social actors, they become personal thoughts that, like emotions, are private; they are now "located" in the mind.

However, because these private thoughts are derived from, though they may be less than isomorphic with, cultural propositions, they are (to employ a term introduced earlier) culturally constituted. Nevertheless, inasmuch as they are "located" in the (private) mental representations of social actors, rather than in the (public) collective representations of their group, to conclude that culture consists of these culturally constituted thoughts is to commit the logical fallacies mentioned earlier.

Finally, this conception of culture does not imply that the meanings of the symbols and other signs – both "discursive" and "presentational" – in which cultural propositions are represented are only conscious, nor (in the latter case) only denotative. This conception of culture recognizes that cultural symbols have unconscious and connotative meanings, as well – the meanings that are expressed in metaphor, metonymy, and other tropes. Moreover, as it is in these meanings that most of the emotional action of symbols is found, it is in respect to them that the interaction between culture and emotion is most pronounced. As these meanings, however, do not constitute the (conventional) meanings of symbols but are rather the meanings that social actors, consciously or unconsciously, intend for them to have, they are "located" not in the symbols themselves but in the minds of social actors. Hence, if we distinguish between the meanings *of* cultural symbols and the meanings that they have *for* social actors, the range of meanings that a culture has *for* social actors is much broader than the range of meanings *of* (conventional) cultural symbols.

Because of this difference in range, although anyone, not only the natives, can learn a culture, the meanings that it has for the natives may be very different from those that it has for non-natives. In learning a foreign culture a non-native may acquire as firm a grasp of the meanings *of* the culture as a native, but not having been socialized in the group, he or she has not had those social experiences that, alone, serve to invest the culture with those surplus meanings, that it has *for* the native.

That is why, too, we must distinguish between learning a culture and becoming enculturated. To learn a culture is to acquire its propositions; to become enculturated is, in addition, to "internalize" them as personal beliefs, that is, as propositions that are thought to be true, proper, or right. This is especially the case for those propositions that Shweder (Chapter 1, this volume) calls "cultural frames," propositions that can be neither proved nor disproved. Thus, for example, a non-Buddhist scholar of Buddhism may have studied its textual doctrines and may know their meanings in much greater detail than a Buddhist. Nevertheless, the scholar is rarely converted to Buddhism – its textual doctrines do not become personal beliefs – because, not having been socialized in a Buddhist society, its textual doctrines do not have for him the connotative meanings, nor do they arouse in him the emotional responses, that alone serve to transform cultural frames into culturally constituted beliefs. I shall return to this thesis later.

That is also why, even for the natives themselves, many cultural frames are, or become, what might be called "cultural clichés" – propositions to which actors may give nominal assent but which are not "internalized" by them as personal beliefs. Although this may occur for many reasons, the most important, in my view, is that these particular propositions do not have, or have lost, emotional importance for them.

Finally, that is why the anthropologist who is interested in the meanings that a culture has *for* the social actors must investigate the personality of the actors with the same diligence that he investigates their cultural symbol systems. For, in addition to the fact that, as D'Andrade has observed (Chapter 3, this volume), there is considerable slippage in the transformation of cultural propositions into (culturally constituted) beliefs, the surplus meanings of cultural symbols are "located" in the minds of the actors.

The aims of this chapter

Given the cognitive and public conception of culture sketched in the preceding section, the primary questions I wish to address in this chapter are the questions of cultural determinism and relativism. The reason for addressing these traditional questions in particular is that they form the core issues of the essays I was asked to discuss at the SSRC conference – the essays by Shweder and Rosaldo (Chapters 1 and 5, respectively, this volume) – and the excellence of those essays, together with the ensuing discussion of them, served to focus in sharp relief those dimensions of cultural determinism and relativism from which I dissent. In my view the essays and discussion alike attribute much more social and psychological power to particular cultures than I believe is justified; and from the variability among cultures, they draw relativistic conclusions that are more radical than I believe is warranted.

Almost all anthropologists, I take it, would agree that descriptive cultural propositions related to scientific (or ethnoscientific) domains can be judged to be true or false by normal canons of scientific evidence. Hence, what is at issue here is that subset of cultural propositions, both descriptive and normative, that Shweder calls "cultural frames." Cultural frames, of course, constitute a large – perhaps the largest – proportion of all the propositions comprising any culture.

That cultural systems display a wide range of variability in their cultural frames is of course an empirical generalization that anthropology has documented both richly and abundantly. However, that no comparative judgments can be made, as some relativists claim, concerning these frames is, in my view, a non sequitur. For if, as I believe, the processes that characterize the working of the human mind are the same everywhere – even though human cultures are different – then there are certain psychological criteria by which such judgments can be made. For example, judgments concerning the rationality of cultural frames can be made according to the criterion of "reality testing": that is by the degree to which they rest on a failure to distinguish fantasy from reality. Again, judgments concerning their utility can be made according to the criterion of functional consequences, that is by the degree to which they lead to emotional disturbance and to disruptive social relationships rather than the reverse, and so on. These and other criteria will be examined in detail.

The validity of these criteria, of course, rests on the assumption that, as mentioned earlier, the human mind works (or has the capacity to work) the same everywhere so that, in respect to my examples, their validity presumes that all humans have the capacity to distinguish fantasy from reality, to prefer pleasurable to painful feelings, to welcome nonconflictual over conflictual relationships, and so forth.

Having mentioned two psychological criteria for comparing the relative merits of different cultures, I am not suggesting that culture can be "reduced" to psychology. Far from it. For to say (as I have) that the propositions comprising culture are "traditional" propositions is to say that culture is quintessentially a historical product. Hence, any adequate account of culture is necessarily a historical account. Nevertheless, once a cultural proposition is acquired as a personal belief by social actors, its acquisition is a psychological event, and that event requires a "psychological" explanation. This can perhaps be best understood by reference to the concept of the cognitive salience of cultural propositions.

Somewhat schematically, and in ascending order of importance, those propositions that, following Shweder, we are calling "cultural frames" may be said to comprise a hierarchy of cognitive salience consisting of the following five levels.

1. As a result of normal enculturative processes, social actors *learn about* the propositions; they acquire an "acquaintance" with them, as Bertrand Russell would say.
2. In addition to learning about the propositions, the actors also *understand* their traditional meanings as they are interpreted, for example, in authoritative texts or by recognized specialists.
3. Understanding their traditional meanings, the actors "internalize" the propositions – they hold them to be true, correct, or right. It is only then that they are acquired as personal beliefs. The transformation of a cultural proposition into a culturally constituted belief does not in itself, however, indicate that it importantly affects the manner in which the actors conduct their lives, which leads to the fourth level.
4. As culturally constituted beliefs, cultural propositions inform the behavioral environment of social actors, serving to structure their perceptual worlds and, hence, to *guide* their actions.
5. At this level, culturally constituted beliefs serve not only to guide but to *instigate* action, that is, they possess emotional and motivational, as well as cognitive, salience. Thus, for example, one who acquires the religious doctrine of infant damnation as a personal belief at this level of cognitive salience not only incorporates it as part of his (theological) belief system but also internalizes it as part of his motivational system: It arouses strong affect (anxiety), which, in turn, motivates him to action (the baptism of his children) whose purpose is to save them from damnation. (For a detailed explication of the consequences of this hierarchy, see Spiro 1982.)

A cultural frame that is acquired as a personal belief at the highest three levels of cognitive salience has a legitimacy and a moral and emotional urgency that are absent from other cultural frames. Thus, as was noted earlier, although the existence of such a frame as part of the cultural heritage of the group requires a historical explanation, its internalization as a personal belief requires a "psychological" explanation. This can perhaps be clarified by our previous example of the Augustinian doctrine of infant damnation.

The doctrine of infant damnation, a cultural proposition that is part of the theological system of certain Christian denominations, must be explained, in the first instance, by the history of Christian theology.

The moment, however, that some Christian actor says, "By God, it's true!" it is internalized as a personal belief, and its internalization requires a psychological explanation. For why this actor (or any other) should believe that a just God would condemn little children to damnation must now be explained by reference not to the history of Christian doctrine (which the believer is probably ignorant of anyway) but to the cognitive orientations, perceptual sets, and motivational dispositions that led him to assent to its truth.

Again, in saying that the transformation of a cultural frame into a personal belief entails an explanatory shift from a historical to a psychological perspective, I am not saying that this represents a shift from a group to an individual level of explanation. For the psychological characteristics of social actors must also be explained by reference to a group phenomenon – not, however, by reference to culture but, rather, at least in my view, to society, a distinction that (for me at any rate) is crucial. If "culture" refers to traditional propositions about nature, man, and society, then "society," as I am using that term, refers to traditional forms of social relations, in which "social" refers to a range extending from a dyad to a nation-state.

Cultural acquisition begins in childhood, and children acquire culture from persons who are their "significant others," that is, persons – usually parents or parent surrogates – with whom they have a powerful emotional involvement, both positive and negative. Hence, their mental representations of these parenting figures not only persist; they often constitute as well a template for their perception of other superordinate beings, both human and divine. It is the mental representation that a child forms of a particular type of parenting figure that explains (in part) how an otherwise benevolent Christian might come to believe that a just God can send unbaptized infants to hell. For in their modes of socialization and enculturation, not only do parents intentionally transmit the meanings or messages *of* cultural propositions to their children, but they also unintentionally transmit another set of messages to them: messages about the kinds of persons they (the parents) are, the conditions under which they offer and withhold love, and punishment, and the like. It is from these latter messages, acquired by (as Bateson calls it) deutero-learning, that children form their parental representations. If the particular concept of God that is implicit in the doctrine of infant damnation is consistent with the child's parental representation, then, when he later learns that doctrine, it makes "psychological" sense to him and that is one reason he might internalize it as a personal belief.

That cultural frames make emic, or intracultural, sense does not imply, however, that they are immune from valid transcultural, or etic, judgment (as Shweder argues), let alone that they are the primary, if not the exclusive, determinants of what social actors think and feel or how they behave (as Rosaldo argues). Before examining these arguments, however, I wish to emphasize that where I disagree with them, my disagreement is with the two dominant themes of contemporary culture theory that they represent and not with Rosaldo's and Shweder's able formulations of these themes. Indeed, because their formulations are clearer and more cogent than any I previously encountered, I was able to more clearly discern my own disagreement with these two themes – the themes (as I shall call them) of *particularistic* cultural determinism and *normative* cultural relativism.

Particularistic cultural determinism

"Culture patterns," Rosaldo wrote in an earlier draft of her chapter, "provide a template for *all* human action, growth, and understanding" (my italics), and again, "culture does not dictate simply *what* we think but how we feel about and live our lives" (italics in original).[1] Such comprehensive claims, no doubt, gratify our anthropological egos, for as the main keepers of the flame of culture, we thereby assure ourselves that we travel the royal road to human understanding. Gratifying as it is, we must nevertheless ask to what extent such claims are true. Is there nothing in biology or in social relations, for example, that might also affect our action, growth, and understanding? And is there nothing in imagination and fantasy that might also affect the way we feel about and live our lives? In short, to advert to the first question, are our "action, growth, and understanding" never influenced by our transcultural biologically acquired drives and socially acquired selves or are they only influenced by culture patterns? Moreover, to advert to the second question, do our egos never transcend the constraints of all three determinants – the biological, the social, and the cultural alike – and thereby achieve some degree of autonomy, if only in fantasy and imagination?

Now because, as Rosaldo claims, culture dictates what we think and feel, *we* (following the dictates of *our* culture) "think of hidden or forgotten affects as disturbing energies repressed [and] see in violent actions the expression of a history of frustrations buried in a fertile but unconscious mind," but the Ilongots (following the dictates of *their* culture) think and see nothing of the kind.

Although I am not convinced that, except for some few Freudian theorists, most of *us* do not think and see things as the Ilongot do, the relevant issue is not whether we, but not they, entertain the former theory about the relationship between affects, frustration, and violence, but whether that theory – let us call it the "Western" theory – can account both for their behavior and ours. For if it can, then much of *their* behavior and *ours*, alike, must be explained not by the "dictates" of our respective (and different) culture patterns but rather, as the "Western" theory claims, by the transcultural characteristics of the human mind. Let us briefly examine that claim by examining the paradigmatic case that Rosaldo cites from her fieldwork among the Ilongot.

In that case, a man who was ostensibly offended by the carelessness of his "brother" in making some plans got drunk and fought with him. That his aggression was not caused (as the Western theory would claim) by some "repressed" resentment, which finally surfaced when he was drunk, is proved, Rosaldo says, by the absence of "symptoms" of resentment in his subsequent sober behavior. Hence, she argues, that these "brothers" (and the Ilongots in general) were and are successful in "keeping 'anger' from disrupting bonds of kin suggests that in important ways their feelings and the ways their feelings work must differ from our own" (Chapter 5, this volume).

Although that is one possible conclusion, it is not the only one. In the first place, so far as the working of "our own" feelings is concerned, the Ilongot case can surely be duplicated in spades in our own society. The documentary evidence – from history, biography, sociology, psychoanalysis, and, of course, fiction, let alone the evidence from our personal observations of kin relations (if not of others, then of our own) – is too abundant to require comment. Indeed, it is the very abundance of that evidence that led, in the first instance, to the development of the theory of repression and to the study of the various defense mechanisms by which, according to the "Western" theory, repressed emotions and motives find disguised expression.

In the second place, to return to the Ilongot case, it is not at all clear from the available data that the brothers in fact did not "repress" their anger for each other or that the frustration-induced anger in their relationship is in fact not expressed in violent action – not, to be sure, against each other, but in culturally approved violence against enemies. In the absence of the relevant psychological data for testing this hypothesis, I am not claiming that this in fact is what *does* occur, but in the absence of the relevant data it cannot be concluded that it does *not* occur. At the same time there are hints in Rosaldo's description that suggest that it *might* occur.

The Ilongots, Rosaldo informs us, "think of 'anger' as a thing that, if expressed, will necessarily destroy social relations . . . [they] respond to conflict with immediate fear of violent death; they say they must forget things lest expression make men kill . . . [therefore] disputing persons either separate or fight – and the expression of violent feelings is seen as always dangerous" (ibid.).

Now I would submit that a psychocultural context in which it is believed that the expression of anger destroys social relations and that any conflict arouses fear of homicide is a context, par excellence, in which the "repression" of anger and the "denial" of conflict, most especially in kin relations, are most expected, as the Ilongots themselves explicitly recognize. For what else can the injunction to "forget things lest expression make men kill" possibly *mean* if it does not mean, "Since anger (my own and alter's) is so powerful that once aroused it leads to murder, in order to avoid such a consequence (either for me or for alter), it is crucial that I (and he) 'deny' those frustrating events that arouse our anger.''

Now what there is about Ilongot social relations that arouses anger of such intensity or what there is about the lack of controls in Ilongot personality that transforms anger into homicidal impulses, we do not know. However, that the one or the other (or both) should lead to '''forgetting anger' in those contexts [kinship] where a show of violence has no place'' (ibid.) is now not only understandable but also predictable by the ''Western'' theory. Is there any other way that a kin-based, face-to-face society, whose members have those personality characteristics, might possibly survive? In short, rather than confuting the view of the ''Western'' theory that the human mind, including its affective dimension, works the same everywhere, the Ilongot case in fact supports it. More particularly, it supports its claim that profoundly disturbing affects and events are dealt with, *inter alia*, by repression and denial regardless of cultural differences and the ''dictates'' of culture patterns.

But what about the other claim of the ''Western'' theory, the claim that ''violent actions [are] the expression of a history of frustrations buried in a fertile but unconscious mind.'' That claim is especially confuted, Rosaldo argues, by the fact that, in the case of the two brawling Ilongot ''brothers,'' no ''symptoms'' of any antagonism were evident in the antagonist once he became sober. But given the psychocultural context that has just been described, the ''Western'' theory would not expect such ''symptoms'' to be evident in the relationship between the ''brothers.'' Rather, it would predict precisely what Rosaldo describes, *namely*, that the Ilongot would be ''quite capable of 'forgetting anger' in those contexts where a show of violence has no place,'' the fraternal relationship being, par excellence, one of those contexts.

That theory would also predict, however, that their ''forgetting anger'' in their relationship with each other does not mean that the anger of the ''brothers'' had disappeared. Rather, it would predict that having ''repressed'' the anger that is aroused in the ''history of frustrations'' with each other, they would express it in symbolic disguise in other ''contexts where a show of violence has [its] place.''

Given that prediction, however, I do not know enough about the Ilongots to describe or even to guess at the various symbolic forms by which, or the various contexts in which, repressed anger between siblings (or anyone else) might be expressed. However, because the Ilongots have a long tradition of headhunting and because few actions are as violent as hacking off a man's head (which is what Ilongot headhunters do), I would suggest that the headhunting expedition is perhaps the most important symbolic form by which – just as ''enemy'' territory is a most important context in which – repressed anger toward their fellows (including siblings) is both displaced and gratified. This suggestion, of course, can only be verified by a symbolic investigation of

Ilongot headhunting to determine whether the headhunter's victim is an unconscious symbolic representation of his frustrating fellows. Although the data for that kind of analysis are not available, this suggestion is consistent with the following characteristics of Ilongot headhunting, described in R. Rosaldo's *Ilongot Headhunting*.

Item 1. Although headhunting expeditions are usually instigated by insults or wrongs, some of them (at least from our point of view) are trivial in the extreme. Moreover, they are sometimes undertaken without any recognizable motive at all as, for example, when the prospective victim is in a "vulnerable" state and happens to fall victim to "youths with characteristic relentless zeal to take heads as they grow into manhood" (Rosaldo 1980:63).

Item 2. Even when ostensibly instigated by some insult, retaliation is seldom directed to the offender or even his family; rather, it will "encompass a wider target of population, including men and women and adults and children, all equal in their shared liability as victims" (ibid.).

Item 3. One of the characteristics of the relentlessly zealous headhunting youths is their emotional volatility, "their moods and passions [being] subject to dramatic ups and downs; and many youths describe themselves in song and story alike as weeping in their fierce, as yet frustrated, desire to 'arrive' and take a head" (ibid., p. 139).

Item 4. The source of their fierce desire "is above all envy of their peers and elders, those men who . . . have taken a head and thus won the coveted right to wear [the insignia of a headhunter]" (ibid., p. 140).

Item 5. "The point in Ilongot headhunting . . . [is] not to capture a trophy, but to 'throw away' a body part, which by a principle of sympathetic magic represents the cathartic throwing away of certain burdens of life – the grudge an insult has created, or the grief over the death in the family, or the increasing 'weight' of remaining a novice when one's peers have left that status" (ibid.).

Item 6. "Taking a head is a symbolic process designed less to acquire anything . . . than to remove something. What is ritually removed, Ilongots say, is the weight that grows on one's life like vines on a tree. Once cleansed [by taking a head] the men are said to become 'light' in weight, 'quick' of step, and 'red' in complexion. . . . In other words, the raiders regress through this ritual process to a culturally idealized phase of life" (ibid.).

Item 7. After hacking off the victim's head, the men (in one reported case, presumably not atypical, that was taped by Rosaldo) "vented their pent-up anger on the cadaver and chopped it up until 'it had no body and you couldn't see its bones,' until 'it was like ashes'" (ibid., p. 162).

Item 8. Following the decapitation, the men fled, pausing "now and again to shout and to sing the song of celebration" (ibid., p. 162).

Item 9. Before stopping for the night, they collected some fern leaves and tucked them into their armbands "in order to modify and preserve the smell of their victim" (ibid., p. 163).

Item 10. Upon their return to the village, both men and women joined in the song of celebration and dancing and singing throughout the night while their "hearts lengthened with joy" (ibid., p. 163).

Although these characteristics of Ilongot headhunting speak for themselves as implicit support of the prediction of the "Western" theory, still it might be well perhaps to indicate explicitly why I believe they support my suggestion that the Ilongot handling of anger is entirely consistent with the "Western" theory of emotions. Because the victims of headhunting are clearly not the instigators of the hunters' anger (Items 1 and 2), the violence that the Ilongot display in hacking off the head of an 'enemy' and in their treatment of the cadaver (Item 7) expresses anger that is clearly displaced from somewhere else. That that anger, whatever its instigation, is repressed and consequently (in an almost classical hydraulic model of the emotions) presses for discharge is equally clear (Items 1 and 3). That their anger is instigated in the first instance by frustrations within the group, frustrations related (among other things) to envy and status rivalry, is also clear (Item 4), and I would guess that their envy and, therefore, their repressed anger have a long history, beginning with sibling rivalry in early childhood. That this might be so is suggested by the Ilongot metaphor according to which men carry a "weight" in them, the removal of which is the motive for, and is achieved after, a successful headhunting raid (Item 6). The latter has the cathartic effect of removing that burden (Item 5), so that the headhunter "regresses" to that "idealized phase of life" (pre-sibling rivalry?) prior to the imposition of that weight (Item 6). That that "weight" represents their "pent-up" (repressed?) anger is shown both by the savoring of their victim's memory even after their hacking him to bits (Item 9) and especially by the exaltation (a manic state?) that they both feel and express following the violence displayed in the raid (Items 8 and 10).

To sum up this discussion, I would suggest that it is not the case, insofar as anger is concerned at least, that "in important ways [Ilongot] feelings and the ways their feelings work must differ from our own" (Rosaldo, Chapter 5, this volume). To be sure, their anger seems to be much more intense than ours, and its expression is much more violent, but, these quantitative dimensions aside, their anger and ours seem to work in similar ways. They, like we, get angry when frustrated, and they, like we, usually repress their anger in culturally inappropriate contexts only to express it symbolically in culturally appropriate ones. This indicates, I would suggest, that human feelings and the ways in which they work are determined not so much by the characteristics of particularistic culture patterns but by the transcultural characteristics of a generic human mind.

That those characteristics are in turn determined in large measure, however, by the transcultural characteristics of a set of universal culture patterns is of course – for me at least – axiomatic. But that kind of *generic* cultural determinism – one that rests on certain assumptions about the universality of human biological and social characteristics (which we cannot go into here) and their symbolic expressions and cultural transformations – is very different from the *particularistic* cultural determinism proposed by cultural determinists of the relativistic school.

Briefly put, particularistic cultural determinism views the process of enculturation as a process by which a neonate learns to become a completely enculturated Iatmul, Ifaluk, Ifugao, and the like – a process, according to that view, by which each of the three learns to become radically different from the others. Although in one sense that thesis is also held by generic cultural determinism, the latter views enculturation as first and foremost a process of *humanization*, a process, that is, in which the neonate, by becoming an Iatmul, Ifaluk, or Ifugao, is also transformed from a mammal into a human being.

This is not to deny, on the one hand, that having become enculturated the human being is no longer a mammal – much of this chapter argues that the contrary is the case. Nor is it to deny, on the other hand, that an Iatmul human being is different in important respects from an Ifaluk human being – human beings do come in different cultural shapes and forms. Rather, it is to affirm (to advert to the second point) that insofar as it is culture that makes us human and insofar as an enculturated Iatmul, Ifaluk, and Ifugao are equally human, the deep structure similarities in their cultures (and in all other cultures) comprise a set of universal culture patterns, which, in interaction with a common biological heritage and common features of social interaction, creates a generic human mind. It is to affirm, in short, that despite the surface structure differences in their cultures – and perhaps in their deep structures too – the minds of the Iatmul, the Ifaluk, and the Ifugao (and everyone else) work in accordance with the same principles ("the psychic unity of mankind"). Starting from different premises and concerned with different intellectual problems, Chomsky and Lévi-Strauss, of course, among others, have most notably propounded the psychic unity thesis in our time.

So far as the emotions are concerned, the perspective and strategy of generic cultural determinism is very different from that of particularistic determinism. Whereas the former type leads to a search for a set of universal principles that, insofar as they are derived from the transcultural characteristics of the human mind, underlie the manifest cultural differences in the display of emotions, the latter type views such a search as futile. Perhaps so. But if the preceding analysis of Ilongot anger is valid, it may not be so futile after all.

Normative cultural relativism

Because, according to the theory of particularistic cultural determinism, emotions and the self (and almost everything else) are determined by culture, and because particular cultures are markedly different, it follows, according to what might be termed "descriptive cultural relativism," that emotions and the self (and almost everything else) vary as a function of the variability in cultures. To what extent those cultural variations are themselves susceptible of judgments concerning their relative worth is a question that descriptive cultural relativism does not address, and Rosaldo does not address it in Chapter 5.

Shweder, on the other hand, addresses that very question, for his essay (Chapter 1, this volume) is a defense of what might be termed "normative cultural relativism," the second strand in the classical theory of cultural relativism. Because, according to this strand, there are no transcultural standards by which the variable propositions of particular cultures can be validly evaluated, there is no way by which their relative worth can be judged. (A similar distinction between these two kinds of relativism is made by Swartz and Jordan 1976:70–2.)

Shweder, however, both broadens and narrows this claim. He narrows it by restricting it to a subset of cultural propositions, which he calls "cultural frames." He broadens it to include explanation as well as evaluation. That is, he also claims (for reasons to be elucidated later) that there are no transcultural theories by which cultural frames can be validly explained.

"Cultural frames," as I have already indicated, consist of that subset of cultural propositions that are susceptible of neither confirmation nor disconfirmation. They can be neither confirmed nor disconfirmed according to Shweder, because they are (1) *arbitrary*, being grounded in neither logic nor experience, and (2) being arbitrary, they are neither rational nor irrational but *nonrational*. These characteristics of cultural frames have two implications so far as their explanation and evaluation are concerned. As for the former, cultural frames "fall beyond the sweep of logical and scientific evaluation," so that the most the anthropologist can hope to do is "document" the differences among the cultural frames of different cultures and explicate the "internal rules of coherence" of those comprising the same culture. As for evaluation, "there are no standards worthy of universal respect dictating what to think or how to act," so that alternative frames are neither "better" nor "worse" but only "different." In short, the "whole thrust [of this position] is to defend the co-equality of fundamentally different 'frames' of understanding" (ibid.).

Finally, the cultural frames of different cultures are not only "fundamentally different," but they are "irreconcilable" (ibid.); and because there are no "deep structures" underlying their surface content, "the more we attend to surface content, the less common is the culture of man" (ibid.). Since, therefore, cultural frames do not reflect but rather construct reality, there is no single reality – none at least that can ever be known; there are only "diverse realities."

Although there is much in this argument with which I agree, I believe that it is both over- and understated. Specifically, I believe, on the one hand, that cultural propositions are less arbitrary and, on the other, that they are more irrational than normative cultural relativism claims. That being the case, I believe that cultures are susceptible of a greater degree of explanation and comparative evaluation than a relativistic view allows. I shall begin with the degree of arbitrariness of cultural propositions.

In my view cultural relativism overstates the arbitrariness of cultural propositions because, despite their undoubted variability, their range is not all *that* variable. For any cultural domain, and for any sample of cultures, the diversity of cultural propositions is much smaller than the number of cultures comprising the sample; and the diversity becomes smaller yet when we observe that even at the level of surface content – let alone at the level of deep structure, which Shweder rejects – the diversity can be radically reduced to, and yet adequately described by, a small number of types.

Although cultural propositions (including cultural systems of classification) may be arbitrary, they are not all *that* arbitrary. Shweder is correct, of course, when he says that "logically, any classification is possible." But he himself adduces an important constraint when he observes that any actual classification is a function of "some special purpose of man." Given this relationship between "purpose" and classification (and even omitting unconscious purposes), the fact that in our kinship system parents' brothers and parents' sisters' husbands are classified as "uncle" does not, as Shweder claims, make such a classification of these kin types "arbitrary." Indeed, in discovering their classificatory principles, Kroeber (1909) and others have been able to elucidate the logic not only of the putatively nonrational and arbitrary classification of these kin types but also of the entire classificatory systems in which they are embedded. Moreover, by demonstrating systematic relationships between kinship systems and a small set of ecological, political, economic, and other determinants, Murdock (1949) and others have been able to causally *explain* the distribution of these types.

To be sure, were we to discover a system in which not only parents' sisters' husbands, but parents' brothers' wives, or brothers' sons' wives, as well, were also classified with parents' brothers, that would certainly count as "arbitrary." But there is no need to reach for such extreme counterfactual examples to make my simpleminded point that, inasmuch as the range of cultural variability is not unconstrained, many cultural classifications are only apparently nonrational.

That still leaves, of course, a large number of cultural propositions that are unquestionably nonrational: They are grounded in neither logic nor evidence. That they are, therefore, arbitrary (thereby eluding the net of causal explanation) is perhaps true of some of them. To claim, however, that it is true of all of them is to overlook another possible determinant of cultural propositions.

Although, beginning with its title and persisting as a pervasive theme of the chapter, Shweder argues that "there's a lot more in the mind than reason and evidence," including "culture, the arbitrary, the symbolic, the expressive, the semiotic," he does not mention the emotional part of that "more," nor does he explicitly attend to emotions in his discussion. If, however, we attend to that emotional part, then, although many cultural propositions may not be determined by logic or evidence, it may nevertheless not be the case that they are arbitrary, for they may be determined by emotion. In that case, they do not – in principle at least – elude the net of scientific explanation, if by "explanation" is meant the discovery of systematic relationships or regularities between cultural propositions and noncultural conditions that might account for cross-cultural variation.

Even if relativists were to concede that some cultural propositions might be grounded in emotional needs, they might counter that they are nevertheless arbitrary precisely because there seems to be no systematic or predictable relationship between such propositions and their putative emotional determinants. Food taboos and witchcraft propositions, to take but two examples, are often claimed to have emotional determinants, and yet there is no obvious reason why this should be the case, nor are there any predictable emotions to which they are attached.

This riposte is well founded if we attend exclusively to the public and conscious meanings *of* cultural propositions. If, however, we also attend to the cognitive meanings that they have *for* social actors – especially their unconscious meanings – it is often the case that their emotional determinants can be discovered, for (like the emotional determinants of dreams) they are most frequently related to the unconscious meanings that they have for social actors.

That conclusion rests on two assumptions. First, in some cases, at least, the conscious meanings of cultural propositions (like the manifest content of dreams) are "surface structure" meanings, and their unconscious meanings (like the latent content of dreams) are "deep structure" meanings. Second, the latter meanings are unconscious because conscious awareness of them (like the conscious awareness of the latent content of dreams) arouses anxiety, shame, guilt, and the like. On these assumptions the emotional determinants of cultural propositions can only be discovered by investigating their possible deep structure meanings. Until such investigations are undertaken in regard, say, to food taboos, witchcraft propositions, and others, we cannot assume a priori that they are arbitrary even when they appear to be in respect to their conscious meanings.

This thesis also applies to seemingly arbitrary and inexplicable classifications. Classes whose members appear to share no distinctive features may nevertheless be shown to be logically classified when their unconsciously perceived similarities are discovered. In that case it is usually found that class membership is based on the same logical principles by which tropes are constituted, particularly the type of trope referred to as synechdoche. For example, one of the reasons that, in his "maternal transference," a psychoanalytic patient classified his therapist with his mother is that (as he saw it) the vital "nourishment" that the therapist gave him in the form of words was an unconscious symbolic representation of the nourishment that, as a child, he had received from his mother in the form of milk. The use of unconscious distinctive features as the basis for seemingly bizarre classifications applies not only to private but to cultural classification as well.

By attending to the relationship between emotion and culture, we may discover not only that many cultural propositions (because they are not arbitrary) are susceptible of scientific explanation but also that alternative cultural frames are susceptible of being judged as "better" or "worse." That is because cultural propositions may have not only emotional antecedents, as in the case of the previous example, but emotional consequences as well. If those consequences are ignored, then, viewed "in terms of comparative adequacy," it might indeed be the case, to take Shweder's example, that the only judgment that can be made as between those who empathize with starving Armenians and those who take the heads of their neighbors is that they are "obviously different." Many of the headhunters that I have read about – and the one that I knew – do not, however, share that view, not because they necessarily share the Western cultural frame that to give life is better than to take it but because in headhunting societies the hunter is also the hunted, a prospect which leaves him in a state – actual or potential – of terror.

Now some relativists might retort that the emotional consequences of nonrational ideas and actions cannot constitute a measure of "comparative adequacy," because inasmuch as the assessment of emotions, like the assessment of reality, is culturally relative, headhunters, unlike Americans, may prefer to live in terror. Such a retort, however, would constitute an empirical disagreement, which, presumably, could be resolved by collection of the relevant data.

By not attending more explicity to the relationship between emotion and culture, Shweder, in my view, not only *overstates* the arbitrariness of culture but he also *understates* its irrationality. For Shweder, the "irrational" is confined to errors in thinking or thought (the verb). But inasmuch as cultural propositions are *traditional* ideas or thoughts (the noun), they are acquired by social actors from the cultural heritage of their group, not as a product of their own thought (the verb). Since they therefore elude Shweder's criterion for assessing "irrationality," by an unintended sleight of hand many cultural propositions become "nonrational" – neither rational nor irrational. To the degree, however, that the internalization of cultural propositions is motivated by the wish to satisfy emotional needs, many of those that are internalized at the highest three levels of cognitive salience mentioned previously are arguably "irrational" rather than "nonrational." I am referring to the subset of emotionally motivated propositions that are *emotionally driven* and are therefore obsessional and "magical." To better understand this contention, let us briefly describe the characteristics of "obsessional" and "magical" thoughts, beginning with the former.

An obsessional idea or thought is an all-consuming thought, that, typically, is driven by a powerful emotional need to prevent an unconscious thought, which it has replaced, from entering consciousness because the latter arouses an uncontrollable, forbidden, or painful emotion, such as lust, hatred, or guilt, respectively. In short, an obsessional thought is a defense against powerful and potentially overwhelming anxiety. The reason for calling thoughts of this type, whether privately or culturally constituted, "irrational" is that they are impervious to reason or evidence. Even when confronted with logical inconsistencies in holding them, or with disconfirmatory evidence in respect to them, those who hold such thoughts resist any change – lest the anxiety they are defending against erupt into consciousness. Held in thrall by these thoughts, they cannot let them go. Although clinical psychiatry is a storehouse of thoughts (including cultural propositions) of this type, let us illustrate them by an example taken from the storehouse of ethnography.

Consider, for example, the widely prevalent cultural proposition that various forms of misfortune are caused by witchcraft. As a proposition – but not necessarily as an internalized belief – this appears to be a good example of a cultural frame. Indeed, when found in prescientific societies, one might go so far as to call it a "rational" proposition even though, from a modern scientific perspective, it is false. In the former societies, such a proposition is validly deduced from a culturally constituted world view; it is inductively supported by a great deal of empirical evidence; it is compatible with whatever reliable scientific knowledge is available in those societies; and it is consistent with all the other cultural propositions of those societies. In short, it is a proposition that in prescientific societies does not rest on fallacious inductive or deductive reasoning, does not violate the law of contradiction, and – given their scientific knowledge – is not empirically absurd.

Whether rational or nonrational, however, if the social actors, driven by imperious emotional needs, develop an obsessional concern with witchcraft – as happened, for example, in sixteenth- and seventeenth-century Europe and seventeenth-century New England – their witchcraft propositions can be said to be not nonrational, let alone rational, but irrational. Having become obsessive, they are no longer just another of those many cultural propositions that social actors are taught and to which they give assent. Rather, being emotionally driven, the actors are not free – regardless of evidence, logic, or reason – to let them go.

The same may be true not only of relatively dramatic cultural propositions like those concerning witchcraft but also of seemingly trivial ones like those concerning food preferences. One need only observe, for example, the obsessional concern of some few orthodox Muslims, Jews, or Hindus with their respective food taboos to realize that some food preferences, at least, can hardly be characterized as merely non-rational. That they are rather irrational is evidenced by the acute anxiety the actors suffer even by the prospect, let alone the act, of violating them.

That in neither of these cases, clearly, is there anything in the (conscious) meanings *of* these propositions that would explain – or permit us to predict – why they should be emotionally driven, and hence obsessive, suggests that the explanation lies in the (unconscious) meanings that they have *for* the social actors. To uncover those meanings, of course, requires a separate investigation of each of these frames, case by case, in their ethnographic context.

Emotionally driven cultural frames are sometimes not only obsessional but also magical, and all the more irrational. A "magical" thought, as I am using it here, is based on an impairment in "reality testing," that is, the ability to distinguish mental events that occur in the inner world (the mind) from physical events that occur in the external world. By this definition, if a cultural proposition asserts that heaven is populated by seven gods, each possessing seven heads, it is not based on any impairment in reality testing. Nor could it properly be said to rest on such an impairment even if, driven by powerful emotional needs, the social actors have a fantasy of such a heaven. If, however, they were to construe such a fantasy – an image in their minds – as a perception of such a heaven, then inasmuch as the fantasy had become a hallucination, the proposition is now based on impaired reality testing, and is "irrational."

In short, to say that a "magical" thought is based on an impairment of reality testing is to say that it is a thought in which inner reality is mistaken for outer reality, impulses stemming from the internal world are mistaken for stimuli coming from the external world, a mental representation of an object or event is mistaken for the object or event that it represents, and so on. If, then, because they are emotionally driven, cultural propositions are based on an impairment in reality testing, they are clearly irrational as they are based on the most primitive form of empirical error. (For a similar view of the relationship between culture and the irrational, see Devereux 1980:chap. 1.)

For an actual, rather than a hypothetical, example of the relationship between cultural frames and magical thinking, let us turn once again to witchcraft. From the cultural frame that misfortune is caused by witches, not only do social actors acquire a belief in the existence of such a class of malevolent human beings, but they also form composite mental representations of them, which (more or less) correspond to the collective representation of witches. Their mental representations of witches can be called a fantasy – a culturally constituted fantasy – and so long as they are just that, they reflect no impairment of reality testing. If, however, driven by emotional conflicts, an actor comes to believe that some specific person, X, is a witch and that X is bewitching him, his belief *is* characterized by magical thinking because the fantasy is now mistaken for reality.

Take, for example, the ailing Burmese villager, Mr. G, who told me that he was being attacked by a witch, whose spirit or soul has possessed him, and that the witch was in fact his wife. This belief, in my view, was based on a complex set of obsessional and magical thoughts. Enraged by his wife's repeated and flagrant adulteries, but unable to cope with his rage, Mr. G projected it onto his wife, thereby constructing a mental representation of her as malevolent and punitive. Identifying this mental representation of his wife with his composite mental representation of witches, he thereby perceived his wife to be a witch. That is, he modified his mental representation of his wife to correspond to that of a witch, although she is not one.

But if that is not irrational enough, consider then that his belief that his wife, now a witch, possessed him was based on an even more serious impairment in reality testing. For his sensation of his body having been invaded by her could only be based on his reification of his mental representation of the witch, and then mistaking it for the witch herself. As a reification, her mental representation was no longer experienced by him as an image that he "located" in his mind; rather, he experienced it as his wife herself (more accurately, as her spirit or soul), which he now "located" in his body.

Although witchcraft beliefs, as such, may be nonrational, if – because emotionally driven – they are based on, or eventuate in, an impairment of reality testing, they are clearly irrational. Relativism rejects this view on the grounds, it will be recalled, that inasmuch as culture constructs reality, there is no other reality that can be used to judge them. Hence, there is no criterion "worthy of universal respect" by which such beliefs and other beliefs that are logically consistent with them can be judged on a scale of rationality. And that is where the issue is joined. Although Mr. G's belief that he was possessed by a witch is entirely consistent with the cultural frame of Burmese witchcraft, and although his fellow villagers, therefore, fully shared his belief that he was possessed, in my view his belief was no less irrational than if it had been inconsistent with it. For in both cases such a belief is based on an hallucination – on a confusion of fantasy with reality – as those terms have been defined here.

In sum, in ignoring – either from principle or from neglect – the emotional motivation for the internalization of cultural propositions, normative cultural relativism underestimates the degree of irrationality in cultural propositions by construing many of them as nonrational – as cultural frames – when (as I have attempted to demonstrate) they are more properly construed as irrational. Hence, by the two criteria that I suggested for the assessment of irrationality – there may be others – we may conclude this section by drawing the following – anti-relativistic – conclusions. (1) The alternative cultural propositions comprising different cultural systems can be compared on a scale of rationality. (2) On such a scale, many cultural propositions are cultural frames – nonrational – and are therefore merely "different" from each other. (3) Many cultural propositions that are seemingly nonrational, and are so viewed by cultural relativists, can be assessed by this scale as irrational, and they may therefore be judged as either "better" or "worse" than their cross-cultural alternatives. (4) If total cultural systems differ in the extent to which they comprise irrational propositions, by such a scale cultural systems can be similarly judged to be "better" or "worse."

Concluding remarks

I should like to conclude with some personal observations. Thus far I have examined particularistic cultural determinism and normative cultural relativism in theoretical terms alone. But theories also have consequences, and these theories have some (largely unintended) consequences, which – given my values – I consider unfortunate. Because values, whether personally constructed or culturally constituted, may be frames, it would be a conceit to claim that the values on which this judgment is based are grounded in logic or evidence or that they are free of emotional determinants. Because the contrary is very likely the case, I refer to these remarks as "personal observations."

Shweder, entirely correctly in my view, places (normative) cultural relativism in the "romantic" movement, a movement that tends to place a high value on the nonrational. Hence, (normative) cultural relativism not only defends the "coequality of fundamentally different 'frames' of understanding" but, consistent with its intellectual heritage, also celebrates them precisely because they are nonrational. Shweder puts this view forthrightly: "Don't knock the mystical, the transcendental, or the arbitrary," he exhorts us even though the "arbitrary" in his discussion ranges, on the one hand, from differences between one kin type classification and another to the difference between taking heads and feeding starving Armenians, on the other.

Now, by this time it should be abundantly clear that I fully agree with Shweder's twin contentions that "there's something more to thinking than reason and evidence" and that reason is in short supply. But it is precisely because reason is in short supply, and because (in my view) its alternatives are not only the nonrational and the logically fallacious irrational but also the emotionally driven irrational, that I believe that it is reason and those aspects of culture that are based on it that should be celebrated. To be concrete, it is not only because the emotionally driven irrational leads to witchcraft accusations, food taboos, and head hunting, but because it also leads to the destruction of scholarly papers and scientific laboratories – and I am referring not only to the Arabian armies that sacked Alexandria in 640 but also to the university students who sacked Columbia, Cornell, and Wisconsin in the 1960s – that I am dubious about celebrating the mystical, the transcendental, and the arbitrary. In short, it is because reason is in short supply that I prefer – as Freud once put it in expressing the goal of psychoanalytic therapy – "where id was, there ego shall be."

By the same token, it is because the emotionally driven irrational has no limits or – to be more cautious – because its limiting case is Auschwitz that I believe that there *are* standards "worthy of universal respect" by which cultural frames can be evaluated. That is the case, of course, only if it can be agreed that those standards – to advert to Freud's metaphors for the different parts of the mind – are the standards not of the "id" but of the self-reflective "ego." Assuming agreement on that, then, inasmuch as the preference for headhunting over the feeding of starving Armenians is based on the standards of the former, while the contrary preference is based on those of the latter, the latter preference can then be judged to be superior to the former.

To be sure, not all social actors have self-reflective egos. But on the assumption that self-reflection is a characteristic at least of philosophers and saints, and that all societies, including – as Radin has observed – primitive societies, have their philosophers (and probable saints too), the preference for feeding starving Armenians over the taking of heads is based on a standard that, I would argue, is universal in that it is found in at least the reflective members of all societies.

If, however, it turned out that in some headhunting societies – the Ilongot, for example – even the philosophers judged headhunting to be preferable to feeding, say, the starving Ifugao, I would then argue that the contrary judgment of the Buddha and Christ, of Isaiah and Laotzu, of Socrates and Gandhi is worthy of greater respect. For, I would contend, the Ilongot philosophers are unable because of emotional constraints to apply the standards of their self-reflective ego to this question.

Given my values, particularistic cultural determinism and normative cultural relativism have a second consequence that I consider to be unfortunate. As these theories have come increasingly to dominate anthropological thought, the vision of anthropology as the "study of man" has been gradually eroded and replaced by the vision of anthropology as the "study of men."

The latter vision, which represents a departure from an attempt to discover cross-cultural regularities and to formulate theories that might explain them, challenges the status of anthropology as a "science" (as I characterized that term earlier) because it views each culture (so far at least as its cultural frames are concerned) as a kind of Leibnitzian cultural monad. The diversity of cultures, from the perspective of this new vision, represents a very Babel of voices, each expressing a set of arbitrary ideas encoded in a set of arbitrary symbols. The noncommensurability of cultural frames renders them incomprehensible to each other and recalcitrant to scientific explanation, and their power – like that of God's voice at Creation – is sufficient to construct reality itself.

The result of this vision is well known. Although anthropology has made much progress in the meticulous recording and reporting of the ideas and institutions of particular cultures, it has made little progress in relating its findings to the development of a theory of culture. The latter enterprise, we are now increasingly told, is precluded in principle by the proclaimed incommensurability of cultures. Thus, we can't have a cross-cultural theory of incest taboos, for example, because "incest" has different meanings in different cultures; we can't have a cross-cultural theory of religion, because "religion" means very different things in different cultures and so on.

That view, in my opinion, is unfortunate, and has the potentiality for becoming even more unfortunate. For as the premises of this new vision gain currency, it might then be contended – as indeed some have already contended – that one or more of the following conclusions may be derived from those premises. (1) Anthropologists cannot adequately describe, let alone explain, any culture different from their own. (2) For any culture to be adequately described and understood, it must be investigated by an anthropologist who himself has been enculturated in it. (3) For the latter to adequately convey the ideas and institutions of that culture, they must be reported in the native language, for there is no adequate way of rendering the conceptual system of one culture by the concepts of another – not even those of (anthropological) science, which is just another culture-bound (Western) conceptual system. All science is ethnoscience.

Such a scenario may be the *reductio ad absurdum* of the new vision of culture rather than its logical entailment. Nevertheless, we have seen it enacted (sometimes with the encouragement of anthropologists) in another form is some American universities. Thus, there are some few programs in ethnic and women's studies that claim that only ethnics are qualified to teach the former and women the latter. Given the new vision of culture, why should the same logic not apply to the teaching of Confucian philosophy, the Old Testament, or the French Revolution?

However, even if the former scenario is only the *reductio* of the new vision of culture, insofar as it is a potential consequence of that vision, I would hope that the present ascendancy of particularistic cultural determinism and normative cultural relativism might be subjected to continuous and searching scrutiny.

Notes

Although we continue to disagree on some key issues, this chapter has importantly benefited from the suggestions and comments of Roy D'Andrade, Richard Shweder, Marc Swartz, and Donald Tuzin.
1. In its published version, this quotation has been modified to read, "Culture makes a difference that concerns not simply *what* we think but how we feel about and live our lives." Since this modified version is one that every

anthropologist, not only a cultural determinist, would unqualifiedly assent to, I have used the earlier version as representing the view of particularistic cultural determinism, even though Rosaldo herself apparently no longer subscribed to it.

References

Devereux, George. 1980. *Basic Problems of Ethnopsychiatry*. Chicago: University of Chicago Press.

Kroeber, A. L., 1909. Classificatory systems of relationship. *Journal of the Royal Anthropological Institute* 39:77–85.

Murdock, George Peter. 1949. *Social Structure*. New York: Macmillan.

Rosaldo, Renato. 1980. *Ilongot Headhunting*. Stanford Calif.: Stanford University Press.

Saussure, Ferdinand de. 1966. *Course in General Linguistics*. New York: McGraw-Hill.

Spiro, Melford E. 1950. Culture and personality: the natural history of a false dichotomy. *Psychiatry* 13:9–204.

　　1970. *Buddhism and Society: A Great Tradition and Its Burmese Vicissitudes*. New York: Harper & Row.

　　1982. Collective representations and mental representations in religious symbol systems. In Jacques Maquet, ed. *On Symbols in Cultural Anthropology: Essays in Honor of Harry Hoijer*. Malibu, Calif.: Udena.

Swartz, Marc J., and Jordan, David K. 1976. *Anthropology: Perspective on Humanity*. New York: Wiley.

Contributors and conference participants

Wanni Anderson
School of Education
Harvard University

*Edmund J. Bourne
Catholic Community Services
San Diego, California

Jerome S. Bruner
Department of Psychology
New School for Social Research

Robbins Burling
Department of Anthropology
University of Michigan

*Roy G. D'Andrade
Department of Anthropology
University of California, San
Diego

Michael M. J. Fischer
Department of Anthropology
Rice University

*Howard Gardner
School of Education
Harvard University

*Clifford Geertz
Institute for Advanced Study

Jürgen Habermas
Max Planck Institute

Martin L. Hoffman
Department of Psychology
University of Michigan

Paul Kay
Department of Anthropology
University of California, Berkeley

*Robert A. LeVine
School of Education
Harvard University

*Robert I. Levy
Department of Anthropology
University of California, San
Diego

John A. Lucy
Committee on Human Development
University of Chicago

*Elinor Ochs
Department of Linguistics
University of Southern California

Peter B. Read
Social Science Research Council

*Michelle Z. Rosaldo
Department of Anthropology
Stanford University

*Bambi B. Schieffelin
School of Education
University of Pennsylvania

David M. Schneider
Department of Anthropology
University of Chicago

*Richard A. Shweder
Committee on Human Development
University of Chicago

Michael Silverstein
Department of Anthropology
University of Chicago

Catherine Snow
School of Education
Harvard University

*Robert C. Solomon
Department of Philosophy
University of Texas at Austin

*Melford E. Spiro
Department of Anthropology
University of California, San Diego

Elliot Turiel
Department of Education
University of California, Berkeley

*Zeno Vendler
Department of Philosophy
University of California, San Diego

* Contributor to this volume.

Name index

Abelson, R., 102–3
Abrahams, B., 260
Agar, M., 33
Aksu, A., 278
Anderson, E. S., 278, 279, 283
Anscombe, G. E. M., 92
Aristotle, 250
Aronson, E., 106
Austen J., 213
Austin, J. L., 42, 94, 162, 202, 222

Bailey, F. G., 111
Baillargeon, R., 50, 51
Baker, E., 51
Bates, E., 277, 278, 279, 305–6
Bateson, G., 104, 225, 329
Bayes, 31, 162
Bellugi, U., 277–8, 311
Bem D., 151
Benedict, R., 19, 28, 40, 41, 67, 149,
    152, 153, 154, 164
Bentham, J., 93
Berko, J., 277
Berlin, B., 33–4, 59, 153, 160, 162,
    229
Berlin, I., 234
Berman, R., 278
Bever, T. G., 50, 51, 278, 279
Black, M., 39
Bloom, L., 277, 278, 280–1
Bloomfield, L., 88
Blount, B., 283
Boggs, J., 277
Borges, J. L., 43
Bostwick, G. L., 194
Bourne, E. J., 21, 23, 36, 41, 46
Bowerman, M., 277, 278, 283
Brainerd, C. L., 50
Breedlove, D. E., 33, 34
Briggs, J., 154, 243–6, 252, 277

Brown, C. H., 34, 277, 278, 279,
    280, 288
Brown, R., 311
Bruner, J., 4, 37, 60, 88, 166, 169,
    179, 219, 222, 269, 278, 281, 287
Bullock, M., 50
Bullowa, M., 278, 281
Burton, M., 108, 184

Campbell, J., 154
Cannon, W. B., 248–9
Carlsmith, J. M., 106
Carroll, L., 250
Carter, A. L., 278, 305–6
Casson, R. W., 89
Castanada, C., 94
Castillo Vales, V., 36
Cazden, C., 278, 288, 311
Child, I., 60
Chodorow, N., 151
Chomsky, N., 7, 27, 59, 88, 206,
    259, 278–9, 335
Cicourel, A., 95–6, 105
Clancy, P., 278, 283
Clark, E. V., 277, 278
Clark, H. H., 277
Clausen, J., 5
Coffey, H. S., 185
Cohen, L. J., 37
Cole, M., 37, 50, 59, 60, 113, 269,
    306
Collier, J., 154
Collingwood, R. J., 40, 165
Condorcet, 27
Conklin, H., 160
Converse, P. E., 56
Corsaro, W., 279
Crapanzano, V., 152
Cross, T., 280

D'Andrade, D., 60
D'Andrade, R. G., 2, 7, 8, 11–12,
    16, 20–1, 23, 33–6, 39, 45, 51–
    2, 60, 73, 99, 100, 101, 108, 113,
    115, 151, 188, 192, 217–18, 252,
    326, 345
Danehy, J., 231
Darwin, C., 81
Davis, N., 152
Davitz, J., 152
de Blauw, A., 285
de Lemos, C., 278
Dentan, R. K., 285
Derrida, J., 152
Devereux, G., 218, 341
Devin, J., 283
DeVos, G., 214
Diderot, D., 27
Dieterlan, G., 152
Dilthey, W., 134
Dodds, E., 153
Doi, T., 153
Donato, E., 152
Dore, J., 278
Douglas, M., 151
Drach, K., 279
Driver, H. E., 73
Dumont, L., 40, 41, 168, 185, 190,
    191, 192
Dunlea, A., 278
Duranti, A., 302
Durkheim, E., 140, 193, 215

Edgerton, R., 287
Egan, M., 99
Einhorn, H., 37
Eisenberg, A., 283, 287
Eisenstadt, 52
Ekman, P., 152, 223, 230, 233, 234,
    241
Eliade, M., 59
Elias, N., 46
Ellsworth, P. C., 106
Erikson, E., 151, 258
Ervin-Tripp, S., 278
Evans-Pritchard, E. E., 40–1, 161

Fairbairn, W., 151
Feld, S., 294, 311
Feldman, D., 272
Feldman, H., 280

Fenton, W., 106
Ferguson, C., 278, 279, 301
Festinger, L., 151
Feyerabend, P., 28, 163
Findley, J. D., 171
Fischer, J., 283
Flavell, E. R., 50–1
Flavell, J. H., 4, 50–1
Flexer, B. K., 50
Fodor, J., 274, 278
Fortes, M., 145, 153, 193
Fortune, R. F., 10
Foster, S., 280
Foucault, M., 41, 43–7, 138, 152
Fowler, A., 235
Frake, C. O., 33, 171
Frazer, J. G., 27, 30, 31, 33, 35, 36,
    39, 49, 59, 163
Freedman, D. G., 239
Freilich, M., 232
Freud, S., 73, 75, 80, 139, 142, 241,
    264, 344
Friedman, M., 192, 194
Friedman, R., 192, 194
Friedrich, P., 94
Frye, N., 10

Gallie, W. B., 6
Gallimore, R., 277
Gardner, H., 22, 23, 263, 264, 272,
    273, 274
Garnica, O., 279
Garrett, M., 278
Geertz, C., 1, 2, 6–10, 12–16, 18–
    21, 23, 28, 41, 45, 69, 73, 78,
    88, 90, 101, 115, 116, 140, 151–
    4, 161, 167, 168, 216–17, 232,
    233, 248, 253, 262, 283
Geertz, H., 69, 152, 154, 277
Gegeo, D., 283
Gelman, R., 50, 51, 283
Geoghegan, W., 89
Gerber, E., 108
Gerety, T., 194
Gleason, J. B., 278, 279
Gleitman, H., 278, 280, 301
Gleitman, L. R., 278, 280, 301
Glick, J., 192–3
Goebbels, J., 209–10
Goethe, J. von, 28

Goffman, E., 104, 151, 153, 194, 228, 284
Goldberg, S., 50
Goldin-Meadow, S., 278, 280
Golinkoff, R., 278, 280, 289-90, 306
Goodenough, W., 7, 88, 89
Goodman, N., 40, 41, 43-6, 48, 165
Goodnow, J., 222
Goody, J., 169, 179
Gorer, G., 59, 258
Grastyan, E., 224
Greenberg, J. H., 34
Greenfield, P. M., 37, 166, 169, 179, 219, 269, 277, 278, 287, 305
Greenstone, J. D., 60
Grice, P., 152
Guilford, J. P., 264
Gumperz, J., 152, 308

Hall, W., 88
Halliday, M. A. K., 305
Hallowell, A. I., 11, 13, 14, 145, 153
Hamilton, A., 277, 283, 285
Harding, C., 278, 306
Harkness, S., 277, 283
Harris, M., 154, 245, 247
Hart, H. L. A., 161
Hartshorne, H., 192
Hartup, W. W., 4
Hayes, J. R., 50
Heath, S. B., 283, 304
Hempel, C. G., 165
Higgins, E. T., 4, 55
Hippler, A., 214
Hirsch, E. D., 2
Hobbes, T., 27, 31, 252
Hochschild, A., 151, 153
Hockett, C., 231
Hofstadter, D., 101-2
Holland, D., 105
Hood, L., 277, 306
Horton, R., 36, 59, 166, 170, 193
Hume, D., 28, 242
Hutchins, E., 33
Huttenlocher, J., 278
Hymes, D., 152, 306

Inhelder, R., 49
Irvine, J., 287
Izard, C. E., 2, 13, 14, 217, 223

Jackson, J., 153
James, W., 238, 242-3, 248-9
Jenkins, H. M., 56
Jesperson, O., 170, 171
Johnson, M., 99, 188, 195, 278, 283
Johnson-Laird, P. N., 36-7, 50, 195, 272
Jordan, D. K., 109, 116, 277, 336

Kahneman, D., 36, 59, 60
Kakar, S., 194
Kant, E., 213
Kapferer, B., 215-16
Kaplan, B., 166, 278
Kardiner, A., 152, 258
Kareev, 52
Karmiloff-Smith, A., 277
Kay, P., 17-20, 27, 33-4, 59, 153, 160, 162, 229
Keats, J., 134-5
Keeler, W., 154
Keenan, E., 280
Keesing, R. M., 110-11, 311
Kekelis, L., 278
Kenny, D., 112
Kernan, K. T., 294
Kirk, L., 108
Kline, M., 218
Kluckhohn, C., 214, 258
Kohlberg, L., 31-2, 162, 169, 272
Kohut, H., 124, 151
Korbin, J., 277
Kracke, W. H., 113
Kroeber, A. L., 171, 235, 337
Kuhn, T., 28, 40, 48, 76

Lakoff, G., 99, 188, 199
Lange, C. G., 238
Langer, S., 9, 217, 218, 252
Lantz, D., 35-6
Leach, E., 216-17, 235, 248
Leary, T., 185
Leibnitz, G. von, 28
Leiderman, P. H., 277
Lempers, J. D., 50
Leventhal, H., 226
LeVine, B. B., 71
Levine, D., 60
LeVine, R. A., 2, 5-6, 13-16, 20-1, 23, 71, 151, 214-15, 223, 272, 277

LeVine, S., 83
Levi-Strauss, C., 27, 33, 59, 60, 75,
    88, 151, 160, 215, 335
Levy, R. A., 19, 22, 23, 101, 116,
    151, 152, 153, 166, 169–70, 219,
    223, 234, 243–4, 248, 252, 277
Levy-Bruhl, L., 28, 30, 38–9, 59
Lewis, M., 282
Lieven, E., 278
Lightbown, P., 277
Lindzey, G., 238
Lloyd-Jones, H., 232
Lock, A., 278, 281, 282, 305–6
Lockhart, K. L., 260
Loevinger, J., 272
Lorr, M., 185
Lovejoy, A. O., 27, 28
Lucy, J. A., 33, 36
Luria, A., 166, 169, 179, 180, 192
Lutz, C., 153, 216, 241, 253
Lynd, H., 153
Lyon, D., 36
Lyons, J., 42

MacAloon, J. J., 104
McDaniel, C. K., 34
McDermott, R., 306
McFeat, T., 106
MacGregor, J. F., 277
Machado, L. A., 271
MacIntyre, A., 41
Mackie, J. L., 31
McNair, D. M., 185
MacNamara, J., 51, 277
McNeill, D., 278, 279
MacWhinney, B., 278
Malinowski, B., 59, 60, 72, 123–5,
    134
Mandler, G., 152, 223
Marañon, G., 223
March, J. G., 37, 38
Marriott, M., 190
Marsella, A., 195
Mauss, M., 145, 153, 193
May, M. A., 192
May, W. H., 36, 99
Mayer, Philip, 71
Mead, G. H., 145, 153
Mead, M., 55, 152, 245, 247, 277,
    294
Mehan, H., 40

Mehler, J., 50, 51
Melden, A. I., 207
Menn, L., 278
Menyuk, P., 278
Metzger, D., 105, 109
Mill, J. S., 31, 33, 50, 70, 162, 163
Miller, G. A., 7, 279
Miller, J .G., 44
Miller, P., 278, 283, 304
Milton, J., 234
Miron, M. S., 36, 99
Mischel, W., 151, 192
Montagu, A., 277, 285
Morgan, L. H., 171
Morley, L., 36
Morrison, 244
Much, N. C., 31, 49, 50, 51, 53, 57,
    85, 94, 284
Munroe, R. L., 277
Munroe, R. N., 277
Murdock, G. P., 73, 74
Murray, H. A., 258
Myers, G., 152
Myers, W., 50

Nadel, S. F., 115
Nagel, T., 212
Nelson, E. L., 277
Nerlove, S., 34, 160–1
Newcomb, T. M., 192
Newport, E. L., 278, 279, 280, 291
Newson, J., 281
Newton, I., 162
Ninio, A., 285
Nisbett, R. E., 36, 59, 192
Norman, D. A., 306
Nucci, L., 31, 50, 51, 260

Obeyesekere, G., 152
Ochs, E., 22–3, 51, 57, 84, 278, 280,
    287, 288, 294, 296, 298, 312
Olivier, D. C., 184
Olson, C. L., 51
Olver, R. R., 37, 219
Ortner, S., 151, 152
Osgood, C. E., 36, 99, 160
Osherson, D. N., 260

Pareto, V., 165
Parsons, J. E., 55
Parsons, T., 46

Paul, R., 152
Peirce, C., 46, 230, 231
Pepper, S. C., 188
Perelman, C., 41, 163
Perlmutter, M., 50
Perry, J., 152, 153
Philips, S., 283, 308
Phillips, D. C., 172, 189, 279
Piaget, J., 27, 29, 31, 49–57, 60, 85,
    88, 162, 166, 234, 259, 278
Piattelli-Palmarini, M., 259, 278
Piers, G., 154
Pittenger, R., 231
Pitt-Rivers, J., 154
Plato, 235
Platt, M., 287, 307
Plutchik, R., 242
Polanyi, M., 227, 269
Pool, D., 50
Popper, K., 274
Praharaj, G. C., 183–4
Price-Williams, D. R., 167

Quine, W. V. O., 40, 200, 240
Quinn, N., 90, 97

Radcliffe-Brown, A. R., 75
Raven, P. H., 33, 34
Rawls, J., 31, 95, 162
Read, K. E., 167, 168
Read, P. B., 23
Reddy, M., 99
Rey, G., 245
Richards, M. P. M., 277
Ricoeur, P., 139, 140, 142
Rimland, B., 266
Robarchek, C., 154
Roberge, J. J., 50
Roberts, J. M., 108, 109
Roheim, G., 13
Romney, A. K., 34, 45, 108, 160–1
Rorty, R., 165
Rosaldo, M. Z., 21, 23, 41, 138, 152,
    154, 217, 244, 327, 329–34, 336,
    346
Rosaldo, R., 151, 152, 333
Rosch, E., 43
Rose, E., 106
Rosenblum, L. A., 282
Rosenfeld, A., 277
Ross, L., 4, 36, 59

Rousseau, J. J., 264
Ruble, D. N., 4
Rumelhart, D. E., 104
Russell, B., 328
Ryan, J., 282
Ryle, G., 73

Sachs, J., 278, 279
Sahlins, M., 28, 45, 46, 47
Salerno, R., 279
Sapir, E., 195
Saussure, F. de, 88, 325
Schachtel, E., 225
Schachter, S., 152, 223
Schaefer, R., 151
Schaffer, H. R., 281
Schank, R., 102–3
Scherer, R., 233
Schieffelin, B., 22–3, 51, 57, 84,
    152, 280, 283, 287, 292–4
Schieffelin, E., 153, 311
Schiller, J. C. F. von, 28
Schleiermacher, F. E. D., 28
Schlessinger, I. M., 277
Schneider, D. M., 28, 41, 45, 57, 60,
    88, 92, 93, 94, 101, 115, 116,
    151, 152
Schutz, A., 40
Schwartz, T., 2, 4, 10, 13, 14, 56
Scollon, R., 278, 283
Scollon, S., 283
Scribner, S., 37, 59, 60, 269
Searle, J. R., 42–3, 90–4, 152, 165
Sears, R. R., 240
Selby, H. A., 190
Selfe, L., 266
Selman, R., 272
Sewell, W., 152
Shatz, M., 51, 278, 283
Shore, B., 294
Shotter, J., 281, 282, 305
Shotwell, J., 273
Shweder, R. A., 2, 4, 6, 8–10, 12,
    13–16, 20, 21, 23, 31, 32, 34–6,
    41, 44, 46, 48–51, 53, 57, 85,
    94, 101, 116, 151, 180, 183, 184,
    188, 192, 217, 253, 284, 326–30,
    336–9, 343, 345
Siegler, R. S., 50
Silverstein, M., 2, 153
Simmel, A., 194

Simon, H. A., 50, 59
Sinclair, H., 277
Singer, J., 152
Singer, M., 154
Skinner, B. F., 278
Skryzniarz, W. S., 271
Slack, M., 151
Slobin, D. I., 277, 278
Slovic, P., 36
Smith, M. B., 152
Smith, M. W., 195, 277, 278, 287, 305
Snow, C., 278, 279, 280, 282, 285
Snyder, M., 151
Socrates, 27
Solomon, R. C., 22, 23, 152, 253
Spearman, C., 264
Sperber, D., 227
Spinoza, B., 27
Spiro, M. E., 2, 6, 10, 11, 14, 16, 23, 57–8, 60, 97–9, 114, 116, 152, 215, 226, 234, 325, 328
Spitzer, L., 134–5
Stefflre, V., 35–6, 45, 165
Stephens, W., 73
Stern, D., 299
Stevenson, H. W., 277
Strathern, A., 154
Stross, B., 283
Sugarman, S., 278
Super, C. M., 170, 277, 283
Suppes, P., 114–15
Swartz, M. J., 109, 116, 336, 345
Sweetser, D. A., 73

Tambiah, S. J., 39
Thurstone, L. L., 264
Thurstone, T. G., 264
Tomkins, S., 215, 234
Trabasso, T., 51
Trevarthen, C., 281
Trilling, L., 168, 194
Tulkin, S. R., 277
Turiel, E., 31, 49, 50, 51, 85, 116, 260
Turner, T., 152

Turner, V. W., 45, 77, 81, 85, 139–40, 151, 216
Tuzin, D., 345
Tversky, A., 36, 59, 60
Tyler, S. A., 33
Tylor, E. B., 27, 30, 31, 33, 35, 36, 39, 49, 59, 73, 76, 257

van der Geest, T., 280
van Roosmalen, G., 285
Vendler, Z., 21–3, 94, 203
Voltaire, 27, 31
Vonnegut, K., 166
von Sturmer, D. E., 284–5
Vygotsky, L. S., 278, 305

Wagner, D., 277
Wallace, A. F. C., 88
Wanner, E., 278
Ward, M., 283, 304
Ward, W. C., 56
Wason, P. C., 36, 50, 195, 272
Watanabe, S., 43, 44
Watson, J., 123, 242
Watson-Gegeo, K., 283
Webster, R., 215
Weintraub, S., 278, 279
Weisner, T. S., 277
Werner, H., 166, 278
White, G. M., 36, 108, 185, 195, 216
Whiting, B., 59, 60, 112, 277
Whiting, J. W. M., 60, 152, 277
Whorf, B. L., 2, 28, 44, 59, 60
Williams, B., 152
Williams, G., 105, 109, 277
Wills, D., 277, 283
Wilson, M. H., 79
Winnicott, D. W., 151
Wittgenstein, L., 27, 28, 40, 161, 212, 247
Wolf, D., 273
Wolfenstein, M., 277
Wood, H., 40

Young, F., 112

Zajonc, R., 152

Subject index

"absolute given," 165
accommodation, 51
acts, instrumental, 46
affect, 99, 138, 140–1, 143
"affective reaction system," 36
affective recall thesis, 100
affect program, 223
aggression, 240
American Kinship: A Cultural Account, 45
analysis, formal semantic, 77
analytic a posteriori and a priori statements, 40
anger, 150, 249–51
  and Ilongot, 144–5, 149, 150, 331–2, 334
  in Tahiti, 218–19, 238, 240, 243–4
  and Utka Eskimos, 243–5
anthropology, 105, 253
  cognitive, 27–60
  developmentalist enlightened cognitive, 31–3
  enlightened cognitive, 27–8, 30–8, 45, 57–60
  romantic cognitive, 28–9, 38–60
  symbolic, 45
  universalist enlightened cognitive, 31–3
a posteriori statements, 40
appraisal system, 223
a priori statements, 40
arbitrariness, principle of, 28, 39–40, 44, 164, 337
assertives, 42–3
assimilation, 51
ate, 231–2
autonomy, 194
awareness, 22, 220–1
Azande, 29, 30, 41, 161

Bali
  birth-order names in, 129–30
  individualism in, 41, 167
  kinship in, 69
  self–concept in, 12–13
  and theory of passions, 216–17
behavior, emotionally expressive, 230–1
behaviorism, 88
body as metaphor, 189–92
brideservice groups, 150
bridewealth groups, 150

caregiver, 276, 282, 284, 285
caregiver register, 301
caregiver speech
  of Kaluli, 288–94, 299, 300, 302–4
  of Samoans, 294–300, 302–4
  of white middle class, 279–83, 286–8, 300
caste hierarchy, 185–6
centrists, cultural, 81
child, 49–57, 78, 84–6, 225, 287
cholos, 232
classification, stimulus, 36
"closed intellectual predicament," 36
cognition, 226–7
color lexicon, 33–4
color-naming studies, 229
commissives, 42
communication, transmission metaphor of, 99
communicative acts, 42
competence
  cognitive, 258
  intellectual, 22, 263–7
complexes, functional, 192
concept, 325
concreteness, differential, 170

confusionism, 158
constraints, interpersonal, 55–6
contents, 21
context, 109
  priority, 309
contextualization rule, 164
cultural determinism
  generic, 334–5
  particularistic, 330, 335, 340
cultural relativism, 57, 158, 159,
  164–6, 188–93
  descriptive, 336
  normative, 162–3, 330, 335–6,
  342–4
culture
  acquisition of, 84–6, 258–60, 329
  as code, 45
  cognitive paradigm of, 89
  collective property of, 68–72
  as constituted, 93
  defined before 1957, 7
  defined by D'Andrade, 20
  defined by Freilich, 232
  defined by Geertz, 1, 7
  defined by Keesing, 111
  defined by LeVine, 20, 67
  defined by Rosaldo, 140
  defined by Schneider, 115
  defined by Spiro, 226, 323–5
  domains of, 8, 82, 259
  and emotion, 214–17, 324–5
  frames of, 326–8, 336
  interpretative concept of, 137–8
  and knowledge, 89–115
  meaning in, 20, 96–8
  models of, 140
  multiplexity of, 76–80
  organized nature of, 72–6
  propositions about, 323–5, 327–8,
  337–9
  rationale of, 79–80
  and symbols, 1–2, 5, 325–6
  variability of, 80–4
  views about, 115–16
"Culture and Behavior," 214
Culture and Practical Reason, 45

data attenuation rule, 159–62
declarations, 42, 43
deficits, cognitive, 169–70
definitions, 114–15

deixis, 153 n19
deutero-learning, 329
Diary in the Strict Sense of the
  Word, A, 123–4
dimensions, universal, 160
directives, 42
discourse, reflective, 81
dissonance, cognitive, 138
Double Helix, The, 123
dyadic exchange, 282, 286, 293–4,
  300

egocentrism, 49, 190, 193
embeddedness, cultural, 169–70
embodiment, 141
emic, 82, 124, 323, 329
emotion, 141–5
  appraisal system and, 223
  basic, 242
  cognitive theory of, 250
  as communication, 222–3, 230
  and culture, 214–17, 324–5
  defined by James, 238
  defined by Levy, 214
  defined by Solomon, 238–40, 248,
  249
  elicitor of, 223
  expressing, 241
  and feeling, 248
  functioning of, 22
  hypercognized, 22, 219, 227–43
  hypocognized, 22, 219–20, 227–8,
  243
  Jamesian theory of, 238–9
  judgmental, 250
  and knowing, 218–33
  naming of, 240–2
  Tahitian theory of, 221–3, 243–4
empathy, 208–9
enculturation, 323, 326, 335, 345
episodes, 226
ethnography, 84, 283
ethnopsychology, 216
ethnoscience, 33–8, 345
etic, 82, 124, 329
evidence, 30
evolutionism, 158–60, 162–4, 169–70
"experience-distant" concepts, 124–
  5
"experience-near" concepts, 124–5
experimentation, 106–8

expressives, 42, 45–6
extended case-study method, 77

facts, brute, 92, 139
feeling, 220, 248
First Five Minutes, The, 231
Forest of Symbols, The, 45
frames, 40, 47–8, 104–5
frame switching, 40–1, 54–5
free association, 3
Freud and Philosophy, 139

Gahuku-Gama, 29, 167–9
galaxies, 93
games, 91
Gödel, Escher, Bach, 101
"Growth of Culture and the
    Evolution of the Mind, The,"
    101
guilt, 148–9, 219, 227–8
Gusii, 71–5, 82–3

Harvard Project Zero, 273
Hausa, 74
hermeneutic circle, 134
higher-order generality rule, 159–62
holism, 172, 189, 190, 191, 193
Hopi, 10, 11
hydraulic metaphor, 238, 241
hypercognized emotion, 22, 219,
    227, 243
hypocognized emotion, 22, 219–20,
    227–8, 243

icons, 46
ideational product, 188–9
idiot savants, 263
Ifaluk, 241
Ilongot
    and anger, 144–5, 149, 150, 331–
        2, 334
    and discourse, 142–3
    and headhunting, 332–3
    and "heart," 145–6, 149
    self-concept among, 145–7
    and shame, 148–9
Ilongot Headhunting, 333
imagination, 201
imitation, 268
indexes, 46

infant damnation, doctrine of, 8,
    328–9
"innocent eye," 165
input, 300–1
"institutional facts," 92
intentionality, 306
interaction, communicative, 285
interpretation, 141, 247–9
intranslatability, radical, 240
irrational, 37, 339–40, 342–3
isomorphism, 102

Javanese, 148
J-curve of conformity behavior, 70
justice, 161–2

Kaluli, 288–94
kin-avoidance, 73–6
knowledge
    acquisition of, 268–9
    and culture, 89–115
    forms of, 22, 203–5, 260, 267, 273
    propositional, 261
    realms of, 22, 260, 270
    sociocultural, 307–8
Kugu-Nganychara, 284–5

labeling, 309
language, 276–9
    natural, 272
learning
    observational, 268–9
    other-dependent, 51–2
lek, 130, 142
lexicalization, 33–4
linguistics, 278
logic, 5
logical equidistance among objects,
    44

Macbeth, 10–11
Manus, 10, 55
marriage, 90–1
material flow, 110–12
MDSCALE, 184
meaning, 1–8, 20–1, 325–6
    and affect, 99
    assigning, 101–3, 299
    as attached to experience, 266
    consensus of, 68–9

meaning (*cont.*)
  constructive function of, 96, 100, 116
  in cultural symbols, 85–6
  deep structure of, 32, 338
  directive function of, 96–8, 100, 116
  evocative function of, 96, 100, 116
  as public fact, 140
  representational function of, 96–7, 100, 101, 116
  surface structure of, 338
  systems of, 1–2, 104, 109–13
memory, 35–6
  conceptual, 226
metaknowledge, 267
metaphor, 36
  body as, 189–92
morality, 31–2, 85
mourning rites, 215
myth, 10, 12

Ndembu, 29, 77
Negara: The Theater State in Nineteenth-Century Bali, 216–17
Never in Anger, 244
nonrational, 39–49, 52–4, 165, 336, 339
"normal science," 76
norms, 93, 94, 115–16
Nyakyusa, 79

Ojibwa, 11
"On Memory and Childhood Amnesia," 225
Oriya, 172–88, 191

paradigms, 40, 165
  cognitive, 88
Patterns of Culture, 67
person, concept of, 126–34
personality, 113–14, 138, 142
phenomenologists, cultural, 80–1
phonemics, 124
phonetics, 124
phrenes, 232
presentism, 163–4
presuppositions
  absolute, 40
  constitutive, 40, 165

"primitive mind," 30, 36–7, 39
privacy, 194
private language argument, 8, 247
process, intellectual, 188–9
procreation theories, 284–5
prodigies, 262–3
progress, 163
propositions
  descriptive, 323, 327
  normative, 323
protoconversation, 281, 286
psycholinguistics, developmental, 277
Pueblo, 9

rain dance, 9–11
rational, 38
rationalization, 80
reality, 78
  testing, 327, 341
reason, 30
reductionists, cultural, 80–1
register, simplified, 279–80, 283, 286, 310
representations
  collective, 56
  internal, 88
research
  cross-cultural, 15
  heuristics, 3–4
Rise of Anthropological Theory, 245
ritual, 215–16
rule
  constitutive, 91–6, 111
  contextualization, 164
  data attenuation, 159–62
  display, 223
  higher-order generality, 159–62
  regulatory, 93–4

salience, hierarchy of cognitive, 328
Samoa
  intentionality in, 298–9
  language acquisition in, 294–9
  stratification in, 294–8
schemata, 104, 226
science, aim of, 200
self-concept, 12–13, 145–50, 191–2
self-engagement, 143
self-lowering strategy, 287
self-reflection, 344

self-representation, 14, 17
sentiment, 165
shame, 148–9, 219, 291
significance, mediators of, 266
sign vehicle, 325
social exchange network, 111
social facts, 140
socialization, 23, 97–8, 194, 276–7, 301–8
social organization, 47, 109, 110, 111, 257
social thinking, 166
society, 329
sociocentrism, 190, 191, 193
sociocultural system, 110–11
speech acts, declarative, 165
statements, 40
structure, 32
    conceptual, 115–16
    deep, 32, 338
    surface, 338
success, 95, 96, 98
symbolization, 218
symbols, 1, 45–6, 103–5, 139–40, 231, 325–6
    embedded, 101
    marked, 101
    ritual, 77, 85, 216
    systems of, 135, 260, 266–7, 270, 273
synesthesia, 36
synthetic a posteriori and a priori statements, 40
system
    appraisal, 223
    computational, 262–4
systematic distortion hypothesis, 35

taboos, food, 340–1

Tahiti
    anger in, 218–19, 221, 238, 240, 243–4
    contextual embeddedness in, 169–70
    guilt in, 219, 227–8
    loss in, 223–4, 227
    shame in, 219
    and theory of emotion, 221–2, 243–4
    uncanny in, 222–3, 229
thinking
    abstract, 169–71, 179–80, 185
    animistic, 55
    magical, 339–42
    obsessional, 339–40
    preoperational, 49, 50, 54
thymos, 232
time, 17–18
transmission
    loci of, 260, 267–8
    as metaphor of communication, 99
    modes of, 260, 267–9
triadic exchange, 289–90, 297, 300

uncanny, 222–3, 229
understanding, 21–2, 102, 202–12
universal grammar, 278–9
universalism, 158–62, 170–2
Utka Eskimos, 243–6
utterances, performance, 165

value, categorical judgments of, 165

witchcraft, 71–3, 340–2
"word magic," 34–5

Yir-Yiront, 29

Zapotec, 190–1